STILL
Following

Donald Coulter

Cover design, interior design and composition: Words to World Publishing

First published, 2023

Published by: Chewing the Cud Publications

ISBN (pbk):   978-1-78798-959-7
ISBN (hbk):   978-1-78798-960-3
ISBN (epub):   978-1-78798-961-0

27 26 25 24 23   10 9 8 7 6 5 4 3

ACKNOWLEDGEMENTS

I want to thank Mrs Margaret Rodgers for spending many hours reading over the manuscript making necessary spelling, punctuation and grammar corrections.

I further want to express my thanks to Matthew Craig of Words to Word Publishing who designed the cover and prepared the manuscript for publication

Donald Coulter

FOREWORD

They left everything and followed him.

Luke 5:11

During the COVID period I was led to write and publish a daily devotional called 'Still Walking'. Since then the Lord has put on my heart to continue bringing together more daily devotional thoughts. The title of this devotional is 'Still Following'.

At Christmas after my conversion on the 9th October 1978 the devil was trying his best to pull me back into the world. On the 31st December of that year I attended a 'Watch Night' service in Enniskillen Independent Methodist Church. At that meeting one of the members requested that we sing 'I have decided to follow Jesus'. That night I completely 'decided to follow Jesus, no turning back, no turning back':

I have decided to follow Jesus;
I have decided to follow Jesus;
I have decided to follow Jesus;
no turning back, no turning back.

Though none go with me, I still will follow;
though none go with me, I still will follow;
though none go with me, I still will follow;
no turning back, no turning back.

The world behind me, the cross before me;
the world behind me, the cross before me,
the world behind me, the cross before me;
no turning back, no turning back.

(attributed to: Simon Marak)

Since then with God's help and the power of God the Holy Spirit I have followed the Lord Jesus. He is my Lord, Saviour, Shepherd and Friend. While I have failed Him, He has never failed me. And He won't. Over the years I have been blessed by sitting under the ministry, preaching and teaching of godly Pastors and Ministers on a weekly basis and also periodically listened to various Bible teachers, missionaries, evangelists and expositors at special meetings and conferences. I gleaned and noted many points from their messages. In addition to this I have recorded points that helped me spiritually from various sermons I listened to, books, magazines, paper clippings that I read and the list goes on, that have been a blessing to me as I have followed Jesus. I have drawn notes, points, extracts and quotes from these sources as I wrote these devotions. In a number of cases it has been impossible to reference these sources.

It is my prayer that the thoughts throughout this devotional will bless, challenge, feed, encourage and inspire those who read it and bring glory to the one I follow, the Lord Jesus Christ.

Donald Coulter

1ST JANUARY

GOD WILL TAKE CARE OF YOU

The eyes of the LORD your God are always upon it,
from the beginning of the year to the end of the year.

Deuteronomy 11:12

The gates of the old year are closed. Through the past twelve months God has guided by ways that we could not always see, over unknown roads, some rough, some smooth. However He remained faithful throughout. Now we are beginning our pilgrim journey down the months of a new year.

What better way to commence this year than with the promise God gave the children of Israel before they entered the Promised Land: 'a land that the Lord your God cares for. The eyes of the Lord your God are always upon it, from the beginning of the year to the end of the year'.

The Lord committed to watching over their land and over them as well.

As Christians, each year is a land to be possessed. A year that may have many unknowns. But we are assured from God's Word that He is concerned for each of His children from the beginning of the year to the end of the year.

So let us go into this New Year trusting God with His promise that: 'The eyes of the LORD your God are always upon it, from the beginning of the year to the end of the year'.

God will take care of you, be not afraid;
He is your safeguard through sunshine and shade;
Tenderly watching and keeping His own,
He will not leave you to wander alone.

(Fanny Crosby)

God will take care of you,
Through ev'ry day, o'er all the way;
He will take care of you,
God will take care of you.

(Civilla D. Martin)

2ND JANUARY

GOD KNOWS

For I, the LORD your God, hold your right hand; it is I
who say to you, Fear not, I am the one who helps you.

Isaiah 41:13

Queen Elizabeth (the Queen mother) brought to her husband's attention a little known poem written by Minnie Louise Haskins, entitled 'God knows'. As a result, King George VI quoted it in his 1939 Christmas broadcast that first December of the Second World War. The words were a source of inspiration and comfort to Queen Elizabeth II, particularly after World War II. The words of the poem are inscribed at the entrance to the George VI memorial chapel in St George's Chapel, Windsor, and in a window at the Queen's Chapel of the Savoy. The poem was read at the funeral of Elizabeth, the Queen Mother in 2002. The following are the words of the poem:

And I said to the man who stood
at the gate of the year:
'Give me a light that I may tread
safely into the unknown.'

And he replied:
'Go out into the darkness and
put your hand into the Hand of God.
That shall be to you better than light
and safer than a known way.'

So I went forth, and finding the Hand
of God, trod gladly into the night.
And He led me towards the hills and
the breaking of day in the lone East.

So heart be still:
What need our little life
Our human life to know,
If God hath comprehension?
In all the dizzy strife
Of things both high and low,
God hideth His intention.

God knows. His will is best.
The stretch of years
Which wind ahead, so dim
To our imperfect vision,
Are clear to God. Our fears
Are premature; In Him,
All time hath full provision.

Then rest: until
God moves to lift the veil
From our impatient eyes,
When, as the sweeter features
Of Life's stern face we hail,
Fair beyond all surmise
God's thought around His creatures
Our mind shall fill.

(Minnie Louise Haskins)

As we face another New Year with all its unknowns, we have one great 'known'—that the Lord Jesus Christ the 'King of Kings' knows when we need His help. He undertakes to hold our 'right hand', saying . . . 'Fear not; I am the one who helps you'.

Let us too, with our hand in His, 'tread gladly' into another year.

3RD JANUARY

JESUS, SAVIOUR, PILOT ME

*On that day, when evening had come, He said
to them, Let us go across to the other side.*

Mark 4:35

They came to the other side of the sea.

Mark 5:1

Charles and Lettie Cowman were founders of the Oriental Missionary Society in 1901. Lettie would go on to write the well-known devotional called 'Streams in the Desert'. I had the privilege of serving with OMS (Then renamed One Mission Society) between 2007 and 2022.

The following is an extract of an article Mrs Cowman wrote in an early publication of OMS:

'It is the prevailing custom to take an inventory at the close of the year. There is a proverb in the business world that the man who takes no inventories finally becomes bankrupt. At the New Year the Lord's children also take spiritual inventories and humbly seek to put their lives in alignment with the will of God. We open our hearts for our own inspection. We ask the Holy Spirit to probe to the bottom and ferret out every secret thing, that we may look at ourselves stripped of every disguise. The result of this spiritual inventory may be discouraging, but let no one give over to everlasting bankruptcy. Confess the great need to our Great Advocate; believe His promise for immediate and instantaneous cleansing... Begin the New Year with a page clean and white. . . . Now we are ready to start out on our three hundred and sixty five day voyage. We have no fear of what we might encounter, as our Great Captain is in command of the vessel'.

It is wonderful to be able to start a New Year with a clean sheet as we set out with Jesus on 'Life's tempestuous sea', knowing that He will safely guide us through the calms and storms of another year.

Jesus, Saviour, pilot me,
Over life's tempestuous sea:
Unknown waves before me roll,
Hiding rocks and treach'rous shoal;
Chart and compass come from Thee–
Jesus, Savior, pilot me!

(Edward Hopper)

4TH JANUARY

HOLD TO GOD'S UNCHANGING HAND!

For I the LORD do not change; therefore you,
O children of Jacob, are not consumed.

Malachi 3:6

While I was reflecting early one morning, at the time of writing this, on the many changes taking place in my life the Lord lead my thoughts to the fact that He is a God who changes not. At a personal level I had retired at sixty five after working for forty seven years, the past fifteen years of those had been in missions work. I was now entering a new era of ministry and service. Lorraine and I decided to downsize our home at this juncture of our life and moved house. On the date of my birthday a major conflict erupted in Europe between Russia and the Ukraine, Russia being the aggressor. This affected the cost of living dramatically increasing the price of fuel and grain which had a major impact on inflation. At a national level our Prime Minister was forced to resign and a new prime minister was put in place. Two days later our Queen died and we had a new King - King Charles the third. In many ways these changes were unsettling. However in the midst of thinking on these things the Lord beautifully reminded me through His Word in Malachi 3:16 that as His child He was a constant in my life and changes not. The words of the following two lovely hymns were also brought to my attention:

Time is filled with swift transition—
Naught of earth unmoved can stand—
Build your hopes on things eternal,
Hold to God's unchanging hand.

Hold to God's unchanging hand!
Hold to God's unchanging hand!

Build your hopes on things eternal,
Hold to God's unchanging hand.

Trust in Him who will not leave you,
Whatsoever years may bring,
If by earthly friends forsaken,
Still more closely to Him cling.

When your journey is completed,
If to God you have been true,
Fair and bright the home in glory,
Your enraptured soul will view.

(Jennie Wilson)

Scenes of the world are shifting,
Friends are in time forgot;
But tho' the mountains crumble—
He changes not.

He changes not! He changes not!
Love Him who faileth never—He changes not.

Winter gives place to springtime,
Winds blow both cold and hot;
Only our God is stable—He changes not.

Daily we grieve and wonder,
Over man's changing lot;
Only our God remaineth—He changes not.

How could we live each moment,
If ever we forgot
The loving God above us—Who changeth not.

(Kathleen R. Wheeler)

As we move into a New Year let us remember that we go into it with an unchanging God. Therefore let us hold tightly to His unchanging hand.

5TH JANUARY

GREAT IS THY FAITHFULNESS

The steadfast love of the Lord never ceases; his mercies never come to an end; they are new every morning; great is your faithfulness.

Lamentations 3:22–23

Thomas Chisholm, author of the well-known hymn: Great is Thy Faithfulness: by all accounts led a fairly ordinary life. He did not write this hymn during a period of intense grief or after encountering God in a profound way. Instead, he found truth in the words he encountered in Lamentations 3:22–23.

However Jeremiah when he wrote these lovely verses inspired by the Holy Spirit was living in a period of terrible circumstances. The people to whom he prophesied did not listen, and he was disregarded and isolated because of what God called him to do. He also lamented the consequences of their faithlessness. God allowed them to be conquered by the Babylonians, resulting in their entire world being laid to waste. But in the midst of that utter devastation, Jeremiah still offers them hope on the horizon: they are not completely destroyed because of the LORD's compassion and faithfulness. Things will be better in the future.

Whether we enter this first month of a new year where everything is fairly good and normal in our lives, or whether we are going through a difficult time we can be assured that 'The steadfast love of the Lord never ceases; his mercies never come to an end; they are new every morning; great is your faithfulness'. No matter what our circumstances, God never changes and will be faithful to us, sustaining us in his compassion and faithfulness each and every day.

Let us reflect today on the words of this great hymn 'Great is Thy faithfulness' as we consider God's faithfulness in His unending mercies and love:

Great is thy faithfulness, O God my Father,
there is no shadow of turning with thee.
Thou changest not, thy compassions, they fail not;
as thou hast been, thou forever wilt be.

Great is thy faithfulness! Great is thy faithfulness! Morning by morning new mercies I see;
all I have needed thy hand hath provided. Great is thy faithfulness, Lord, unto me!

Summer and winter and springtime and harvest,
sun, moon, and stars in their courses above
join with all nature in manifold witness
to thy great faithfulness, mercy, and love.

Pardon for sin and a peace that endureth,
thine own dear presence to cheer and to guide,
strength for today and bright hope for tomorrow,
blessings all mine, with ten thousand beside!

(Thomas O. Chisholm)

6TH JANUARY

THE LOST AGONY

*For what does it profit a man to gain the
whole world and forfeit his soul?*

Mark 8:36

George Whitefield cried, 'Give me souls, or take my soul ... There is a passion for souls, a depth of burden for men, a care for the flock of God that beggars words and sighs and tears'.

Surely this is the need of the hour in every generation but particularly for ours. Have we really a passion for souls. Let us sincerely ask God to restore to us a desire to see the lost won for Christ. Oh that we would seek God to give us a real burden to pray for our family, our loved ones, our neighbours, our friends, our workmates, our associates and our town and nation. And then really seek Him in prayer how best we can go about reaching the lost for Him.

I had the privilege of meeting Dr Wesley Duewel (A past President of the Mission agency I served with for 15 years) on a number of occasions before his home call at the age of ninety nine. The following an extract he wrote about soul-winning in 1957 the year I was born: 'The history of mighty revival is the history of the mighty power of God and the tireless prayer and effort of God's people. Over the salvation of many a soul could be written 'purchased by blood, tears, and sweat'. Christ's blood, Christ's tears, and Christ's physical labour and agony were supplemented by prayers, tears, and agony of one of His soul-hungry disciples who made up that which was necessary on man's part that souls might be won. Man's effort can never in itself save a soul, but God has chosen to work through man. How many souls will never be saved until you really take their salvation seriously and give yourself unreservedly in real effort to win them? Souls are purchased by blood, tears, soul agony, and sweat'.

Give me a passion for souls, dear Lord,
A passion to save the lost;
O that Thy love were by all adored,
And welcomed at any cost.

Jesus, I long, I long to be winning
Men who are lost, and constantly sinning;
O may this hour be one of beginning
The story of pardon to tell.

Herbert G. Tovey

7TH JANUARY

DAY BY DAY

This is the day that the Lord has made;
let us rejoice and be glad in it.

Psalm 118:24

I first met Bruce and Mabel Callendar in 2008 when I was undergoing missionary training at the OMS headquarters in Indiana USA. Bruce and Mabel served as missionaries in both Ecuador and Mozambique for many years. Mabel originally came from N. Ireland and Bruce from the USA. I was greatly blessed at that time as they shared their testimony and missionary experiences at the training event. Recently I read their most recent prayer letter. In it they shared how music and the singing of hymns and spiritual songs had been an important part of OMS training and Church planting. This does not surprise me. We read in Psalm 96:1–4: 'Oh sing to the Lord a new song; sing to the Lord, all the earth! Sing to the Lord, bless his name; tell of his salvation from day to day. Declare his glory among the nations, his marvellous works among all the peoples! For great is the Lord, and greatly to be praised; he is to be feared above all gods'.

In their prayer letter Bruce recalls being blessed by the singing of the hymn 'Day by Day' in Spanish by one of his missionary colleagues at a Lord's Day service in Guayaquil, Ecuador. I was constrained to look the hymn up and reflect on its words. I too was blessed. The hymn was written originally in Swedish by Carolina Sandell and translated into English by A. L. Skoog. I want to share the hymn with you today. I trust you will know God's blessing and help day by day throughout another year:

Day by day and with each passing moment,
Strength I find to meet my trials here;
Trusting in my Father's wise bestowment,
I've no cause for worry or for fear.
He whose heart is kind beyond all measure
Gives unto each day what he deems best–
Lovingly, its part of pain and pleasure,
Mingling toil with peace and rest.

Ev'ry day the Lord himself is near me,
With a special mercy for each hour;
All my cares he gladly bears and cheers me,
He whose name is Counsellor and Pow'r.
The protection of his child and treasure
Is a charge that on himself he laid:
As your days, your strength
shall be in measure–
This the pledge to me he made.

Help me then in ev'ry tribulation
So to trust your promises, O Lord,
That I lose not faith's sweet consolation
Offered me within your holy Word.
Help me, Lord, when, toil
and trouble meeting,
E'er to take, as from a father's hand,
One by one, the days, the moments fleeting,
Till I reach the promised land.

8TH JANUARY

ABUNDANCE OF ANTS

Go to the ant, O sluggard; consider her ways, and be wise.

Proverbs 6:6

While on holiday in Portugal I read the following extracts from an article about 'Ants' in the Portuguese edition of the Daily Mail: "They are tiny creatures who play a giant role in the life of the planet. Now the number of ants on Earth has been calculated at a mind-blowing 20 quadrillion – or two and a half million for every human being" Now that's a lot of ants: 20,000,000,000,000,000.

This figure was calculated by researchers at the University of Wurzburg in Germany. This made me realise that the wise King Solomon inspired by the Holy Spirit knew what he was doing when he suggested that we should consider the ant. Everyone on Earth knows something about the ant. Therefore it is ideal as an object lesson.

'The article went on to say: Ants help plants and animals to thrive by dispersing seeds, aerating soil—and acting as prey for predators'.

One commentator on this verse said: 'It is interesting that man, with all his influence and sophistication, is sent by the Lord to an institute led by an ant'.

The following are some takeaway thoughts about the ant for us to consider today:

THE PRIORITY THE ANT AWAKES: consider her ways, walk with the ant and learn from her.

THE PURPOSE THE ANT ASCRIBES: The writer of Proverbs is telling the sluggard to consider the purpose of the ant and be wise. In other words observe qualities that belong to the ant and do likewise. What are some of these qualities? They work wisely, harmoniously, fearlessly, in unity and in colonies. Ants are little, not lazy. As believers we should be good workers wherever God has placed us. We should also be good workers for the Kingdom.

Let us labour for the Master
From the dawn till setting sun,
Let us talk of all His wondrous love and care;
Then when all of life is over,
And our work on earth is done,
And the roll is called up yonder,
I'll be there.

(James M. Black)

THE PRODUCTIVITY THE ANT ASSUMES: They are all volunteers, they live in an ant colony. We belong to the colony of Heaven. We are citizens of Heaven. As followers of Jesus we all need to pull our weight and use our gifts for Him as productive Christians.

9TH JANUARY

CHOMPERS BECOME CARRIERS

*The ants are a people not strong, yet they
provide their food in the summer.*

Proverbs 30:25

I cut an interesting article entitled 'How ants look after their old' out of a daily paper a number of years ago (I didn't reference the date or which paper). The following are some extracts from the article:

'Ants deservedly have a reputation for strength and teamwork. Now scientists have discovered one of the keys to their success is the ability to organise workers according to age. A study of leaf-cutter ants in Central America has shown that the younger and more vigorous members of the colony are given the toughest job of cutting through the leaves they harvest because their sharp young teeth do the job so efficiently. But as they get older their teeth become worn and blunt. However, rather than being retired, the ageing ants are given a new role more suited to their physical abilities. The former chompers become carriers, transporting the leaves back to the colony where they are harvested for food. Like humans, these insects recognise that older members of the group can still make a worthwhile contribution to society. The findings of the researchers from the University of Oregon and the Oregon State University support previous research showing the survival of a leaf-cutter colony depends on its efficiency'.

Solomon had recorded the efficiency and productivity of ants many thousands of years earlier in the book of Proverbs.

In Proverbs 6:6–8 we read: 'Go to the ant, O sluggard; consider her ways, and be wise. Without having any chief, officer, or ruler, she prepares her bread in summer and gathers her food in harvest'.

One Bible teacher describes the ants as Creative creatures, Tiny teachers and Powerful preachers, while another describes them as a sermon on six legs: So what can we learn for God's glory and our good from the ant:

- Ants are little but not lazy. It may seem that our sphere of service is little but that is not a reason for being lazy. Solomon in the book of Ecclesiastes writes: 'Whatever your hand finds to do, do it with your might' Ecclesiastes 9:10
- The ants are known for teamwork, for working in partnership, so should each member of the Church local and global. They work in unity, love, harmony towards a common goal. So should we.
- They don't display ageism. There is a role for all. They labour according to their own ability.
- They make provision for this life and preparation for the future.

I trust we all can learn some spiritual application from the ant for our individual life today.

10TH JANUARY

MOONS AGO

*Cast your bread upon the waters, for you
will find it after many days.*

Ecclesiastes 11:1

Thirty seven years after speaking to the youth of the local church of which I was youth leader at that time I was sent the following Messenger message from one of the then young people:

'Hi Donald. Hope you are well. Just thinking about something you spoke about moons ago - the need to grow, glow, and go'. Paul went to Bible College sometime after this and has now been in full-time Christian service for many years.

This just reminded me of Ecclesiastes 11:1, and was an encouragement to me as I trust it will also help you to keep on sharing God's Word and then leave the results to Him.

The following are some commentary notes I have noted in my Bible beside this verse:

THE REQUIREMENT: 'Cast your bread'. The bread (Seed) is the Word of God.

'But he answered, it is written, Man shall not live by bread alone, but by every word that comes from the mouth of God.' Matthew 4:4.

'For as the rain and the snow come down from heaven and do not return there but water the earth, making it bring forth and sprout, giving seed to the sower and bread to the eater, so shall my word be that goes out from my mouth; it shall not return to me empty, but it shall accomplish that which I purpose, and shall succeed in the thing for which I sent it. Isaiah 55:10–11

'Upon the waters'. The waters are multitudes of people. 'The waters that you saw, where the prostitute is seated, are peoples and multitudes and nations and languages' Revelation 17:15

THE RETURN: 'You will find it after many days'. The sureness of the return: 'You will find it'. The season of the return: 'After many days'.

'Cast thy bread upon the waters,'
Ye who have abundant store;
It may float on many a billow,
It may strand on many a shore;
You may think it lost forever,
But, as sure as God is true,
In this life, or in the other,
It will yet return to you.

(John J. Hood)

11TH JANUARY

BUT GROW

*But grow in the grace and knowledge of our Lord
and Savior Jesus Christ. To him be the glory both
now and to the day of eternity. Amen.*

2 Peter 3:18

In yesterday's devotion I shared about a young man who sent me a message about something I spoke about thirty seven years earlier at the 'youth Fellowship' at the Church where I was youth leader. He said 'I've just written this, inspired by your talk about the need to grow, glow, and go': 'Faith is organic. It's all about growth. Soil, water, light. Before you go you need to glow. Before you glow you need to grow. He's helping you grow so that you glow and go in His mighty power'.

A growing Christian is a maturing Christian because spiritual maturity is becoming more like Jesus.

So how do we grow as Christians?

- We need to be born again of the Spirit of God. We must be saved.
- You must be first planted in grace before you grow in grace, being saved by grace, we are to grow in grace.
- Growth takes place over time. There is no instant maturity; we experience growth through time spent with Jesus Christ. 'But grow in the grace and knowledge of our Lord and Savior Jesus Christ'. 2 Peter 3:18
- Growth requires nourishment; we have to feed on the Word of God. 'Like new born infants, long for the pure spiritual milk, that by it you may grow up into salvation' 1 Peter 2:2

Herman A. Hoyt commenting on 2 Peter 3:17–18 said: 'Peter desires to see on the part of believers a definite progression towards perfection, this perfection to be fully realised at the Second Coming of Christ'. He goes on to say that to achieve this the solution is: 'the progressive transformation of the believer into the likeness of Christ. There must be spiritual growth in order to achieve this final goal. That is what Peter means by the words BUT GROW. In these two words contrast, continuity, and capacity related to growth, are definitely contained. There is the element of Contrast in the word BUT. In the former verse there was the danger of being led away with the error of the wicked. The solution to this contrast is to grow in the grace and knowledge of our Lord and Saviour Jesus Christ. There is an element of continuity in the word GROW. Being in the present tense, the word means continue growing'. Hoyt goes on to say: 'An additional idea is in this verb, namely that of capacity, which means that growing is a process in which there is increase in spiritual stature'.

The end result of our growth is to glorify God.

I close with a thought from Sinclair Ferguson: 'Spiritual growth depends on two things: first a willingness to live according to the Word of God; second, a willingness to take whatever consequences emerge as a result'.

12TH JANUARY

GLOW

You are the light of the world. A city set on a hill cannot be hidden. Nor do people light a lamp and put it under a basket, but on a stand, and it gives light to all in the house. In the same way, let your light shine before others, so that they may see your good works and give glory to your Father who is in heaven.

Matthew 5:14-16

We are not saved by good works: 'For by grace you have been saved through faith. And this is not your own doing; it is the gift of God, not a result of works, so that no one may boast'. Ephesians 2:8-9. However verse 10 of Ephesians 2 goes on to say: 'For we are his workmanship, created in Christ Jesus for good works, which God prepared beforehand, that we should walk in them'.

So as born again followers of Jesus we are to glow in our communities through our good works. This will result in bringing glory to God. The answer to question 1 of the Westminster Shorter Catechism points out that Man's chief end is to glorify God, and to enjoy him forever.

Back in the 1980 two well-known Northern Ireland gospel singers Speedy Moore and Victor Hutchinson regularly sang in the church I attended. Their theme song went as follows:

This little light of mine, I'm gonna let it
Let it shine all the time, let
it shine, all the time

Hide it under a bushel, no!
I'm gonna let it shine
Let it shine all the time, let
it shine, all the time.

Don't let Satan (blow) it out,
I'm gonna let it shine
Let it shine all the time, let
it shine, all the time.

Shine around the neighbourhood,
I'm gonna let it shine
Let it shine all the time, let
it shine, all the time.

Speedy was a correspondence with one of the local newspapers. However he had a problem with alcohol which led him to being an alcoholic. God graciously saved him and delivered him from his addiction. From that time on Speedy truly glowed for Jesus until He took him home.

Dr Stuart Briscoe commenting on these verses said: 'what did Jesus mean when He said: You are the light of the world? I think He meant we are the continuation, clarification, and coordination of His ministry'.

Stuart goes on to point out the:

- METHOD OF SHINING: works!
- THE MEANS OF SHINING: light a lamp on the stand – where everyone can see.
- THE MOTIVATION OF SHINING: Our works are to glorify our Father in heaven. That's why we are lights in the world!

'That you may be blameless and innocent, children of God without blemish in the midst of a crooked and twisted generation, among whom you shine as lights in the world' Philippians 2:15

Let us continually be growing, glowing and going Christians.

13TH JANUARY

GO

*And he said to them, Go into all the world and
proclaim the gospel to the whole creation.*

Mark 16:15

Several major things happened to me on both my birthdays while writing this devotional. At my natural birthday on the 24th February I retired at my 65th birthday, was appointed as a deacon in my local church and the Russian/Ukraine war commenced. On my spiritual birthday on the 9th October my 44th birthday (Which on this occasion fell on a Sunday) I had COVID and therefore housebound. In the morning I listened to Dr Jack Graham preach on TBN from Romans 9 about having a passionate burden for the lost. In the remainder of the day I read from a book called 'Measure Your Life -17 ways to evaluate your life from God's perspective' written by Dr Wesley Duewel, whom I had the pleasure of meeting and praying with on a number of occasions.

One of the 17 measurements he suggests is: 'measure your life by its world dimension'. Jack's sermon and Wesley's book really challenged me afresh about the real necessity of not only growing and glowing as a Christian but going. Of course there are several ways we can go. We can go through physically going, praying, paying, encouraging and sending or a combination of these but one way or other reaching the world with the gospel is an essential part of our following Jesus as our Lord and Master.

The following is an extract from Dr Duewel's book: 'World missions is not a minor activity of a few chosen people of Christ's church. It is a priority assignment to the whole church. Christ emphasized our going to the world more than our coming to church'.

He went on to say: 'First, He emphasized the absolute necessity of His followers being clothed (Luke 24:48), empowered (Luke 24:48; Acts 1:8), and filled with His Spirit so they could be and do all that Jesus desired of them as His representatives. The task He committed to them was too great for them without divine equipping. Second, He emphasized the absolute priority of reaching the whole world with the salvation He had just provided on the cross. Their witness and assignment had a worldwide dimension. They were to reach all nations (Matt 28:19, Luke 24:47), all the world (Mark 16:15), to the very ends of the earth (Acts 1:8). Those two priorities are Jesus' priorities until He comes again. Our mandate is agelong. Our commission is unchanging'.

Is this our priority today or do we need to do some readjusting?

All the world, all the world!
Nothing less will do.
All the world, all the world!
Share God's heart anew!
God's great task has but begun;
Millions must be sought and won.
Reach your love to everyone
In the whole wide world

(Wesley Duewel)

14TH JANUARY

THERE IS NO LOVE LIKE THE LOVE OF JESUS

Jesus wept. So the Jews said, See how he loved him!

John 11:35–36

As you read through John's Gospel you will pick up on many themes. Not least of these is the theme of God's love. The following is a summary of comments made by the late W.H. Griffith Thomas of ways He loved Martha, Mary and Lazarus:

- PERSONAL LOVE: It was concentrated on each of the three. Love is always and necessarily personal, whether it is love of pity or pleasure, love for the disobedient or obedient. The realisation of Christ's pitying love brings the sinner to repentance, while the consciousness of personal love brings joy and peace to the believer.
- PERFECT LOVE: Christ's love was always unselfish, self-denying, and self-sacrificing: 'Greater love has no one than this, that someone lay down his life for his friends'. John 15:13
- PARTICULAR LOVE: Christ loved Lazarus and yet allowed him to die. His love could see far ahead and knew death would result in greater blessing to all. He loved Martha in an entirely different way. He knew that she was a strong woman. He therefore could speak to her in a direct fashion knowing she could handle it. His love for Mary was quite different. He knew she was overwhelmed by grief and therefore brought words of comfort.
- PERPETUAL LOVE: Here and elsewhere it is clearly seen that Christ loves for all time.

His love is:

- PERSEVERING: Now before the Feast of the Passover, when Jesus knew that his hour had come to depart out of this world to the Father, having loved his own who were in the world, he loved them to the end. John 13:1.
- POWERFUL: 'No, in all these things we are more than conquerors through him who loved us' Rom 8:37.
- PERMANENT: 'Who shall separate us from the love of Christ? Shall tribulation, or distress, or persecution, or famine, or nakedness, or danger, or sword? Rom 8:35.
- PRACTICAL: As in all other passages Jesus' love is calm and balanced. Christ's love was passionate as well as reverent.

It is for us to:

- RECEIVE THIS LOVE: 'So we have come to know and to believe the love that God has for us. God is love, and whoever abides in love abides in God, and God abides in him'. 1 John 4:16.
- RESPOND TO THIS LOVE: 'We love because he first loved us'. 1 John 4:19.
- REFLECT THIS LOVE: 'And walk in love, as Christ loved us and gave himself up for us, a fragrant offering and sacrifice to God'. Eph 5:2.

There is no love like the love of Jesus,
Never to fade or fall,
Till into the fold of the peace of God
He has gathered us all.

Jesus' love! Precious love!
Boundless and pure and free!
Oh, turn to that love, weary, wand'ring soul!
Jesus pleadeth with thee.

(William E. Littlewood)

15TH JANUARY

MY FRIEND?

*Go home to your friends and tell them how much the Lord
has done for you, and how he has had mercy on you.*

Mark 5:19

As followers of Jesus we are to tell others about Him. We are to warn our friends, our loved ones and those next door of their great need of a Saviour. We are to warn them of impending eternal danger and loss. The following is a poem I have in my possession for many years which challenges me to the core every time I read it:

*My friend, I stand in the judgement
And feel you are to blame somehow.
On earth, I walked and talked with you day by day
And never did you point the way.*

*You knew the Lord in truth and glory,
But never did you tell the story.
My knowledge then was very dim;
You could have led me safe to Him.*

*Though we lived together on the earth.
You never told me of the second birth.
And now I stand this day condemned.
Because you failed to mention Him.*

*You taught me things, that's true;
I called you 'friend' and trusted you.
But I now learn that it's too late,
You could have kept me from this fate.*

*We walked by day and talked by night,
And yet you showed me not the light.
You let me live and love and die;
You knew I'd never live on high.*

*Yes, I called you 'friend' in life,
And trusted you through joy and strife.
And yet on coming to the end.
I cannot now call you 'My Friend'*

(Author Unknown)

I trust that you like me will be challenged enough today so that we will be moved to share to all He has placed in the sphere of our influence the gospel message in truth and in love.

The psalmist could say:

'Come and hear, all you who fear God, and I will tell what he has done for my soul'. Psalm 66:16

'My mouth will tell of your righteous acts, of your deeds of salvation all the day, for their number is past my knowledge. With the mighty deeds of the Lord God I will come; I will remind them of your righteousness, yours alone'. Psalm 71:15–16

*Tell what the Lord has done for you,
Speak just a word, speak just a word;
Stand for the right, be brave and true,
Speak just a word for Jesus.
Speak just a word, speak just a word,
Gladly His love proclaim;
Tell what the Lord has done for you,
Speak just a word for Jesus.*

(E. C. Avis)

16TH JANUARY

HIS PLANS FOR ME

For I know the plans I have for you, declares the Lord, plans for welfare and not for evil, to give you a future and a hope.

Jeremiah 29:11

I was told by an experienced Church Planter in the Republic of Ireland that this is one of the misquoted verses in the Bible.

Therefore it is important to put the verse in its context. This promise and encouraging words were written to the many Jews who were taken into captivity in Babylon. Jeremiah wrote an encouraging letter to those taken into captivity as recorded in Jeremiah 29:1–14. In his letter he outlined that this captivity would last seventy years (v 10). He encouraged them to settle down in this difficult situation. They were to re-establish normality in their new situation as directed and defined by the Lord (v 1–7). In their new situation they were to reject any unrealistic dreams (v 8–9). And in all of this they were to remember that God is in control and He has plans for His people.

We as Christians can be encouraged from this as we face difficulties, situations, trials and pressures realising that God is in control and has plans for our lives even though we don't fully understand all that is happening at this moment:

What though the path be steep and rough,
It is God's plan for me;
His grace will always prove enough –
It is His plan for me.
When all things seem to go amiss,
And shattered every dream of bliss,
My soul, be thou content with this:

It is His plan for me.
I thought my own way was best;
Twas not His plan for me.
I longed for ease and quiet rest;
Twas not His plan for me.
Storms swept across a sunny sky,
And troubles looked like mountains high,
No refuge or relief seem nigh –
It was His plan for me.

He sought to wean my wayward heart,
This was His plan for me,
To draw me from a world apart –
This was His plan for me.
To know Him more, To seek His face,
To prove His all sufficient grace
To meet my need in every case;
This was His plan for me.

I am not always quick to learn
What He has planned for me;
At times, alas, I fain would turn
From what He plans for me;
As if He did not know the best,
For He can make all sorrow blest,
And keep the heart in perfect rest.
This is His plan for me.

Then teach me Lord from day to day
To love Thy plan for me;
Looking to Thee to choose my way,
So Thou shalt plan for me.
And when my journey here is o'er,
I'll praise and own for evermore –
Thy plan was BEST for me.

17TH JANUARY

JESUS ALONE IS THE GIVER

*And this is the testimony, that God gave us
eternal life, and this life is in his Son.*

1 John 5:11

'God gave us eternal life'—What a wonderful truth to ponder upon today. Just think of it: 'eternal' and 'life'. These two words include everything for the spiritual life now and hereafter:

REMISSION OF SIN:

'To him all the prophets bear witness that everyone who believes in him receives forgiveness of sins through his name' Acts 10:43

RECEPTION INTO GOD'S FAVOUR:

'But now in Christ Jesus you who once were far off have been brought near by the blood of Christ' Ephesians 2:13.

'But to all who did receive him, who believed in his name, he gave the right to become children of God' John 1:12.

RENEWAL IN THE SPIRIT:

'He saved us, not because of works done by us in righteousness, but according to his own mercy, by the washing of regeneration and renewal of the Holy Spirit' Titus 3:5

REUNION HEREAFTER:

'For the Lord himself will descend from heaven with a cry of command, with the voice of an archangel, and with the sound of the trumpet of God. And the dead in Christ will rise first. Then we who are alive, who are left, will be caught up together with them in the clouds to meet the Lord in the air, and so we will always be with the Lord' 1 Thessalonians 4:16–17

The means of this eternal life is: 'in his Son'. Only in Christ is this gift possible: 'And there is salvation in no one else, for there is no other name under heaven given among men by which we must be saved' Acts 4:12.

Life! life! eternal life!
Jesus alone is the Giver:
Life! life! abundant life!
Glory to Jesus forever!

(William Leslie)

Eternal life refers only to Christians and to them alone. Therefore there is limitation of this gift. It is only to those who are willing to receive, those who accept through faith the new and divine life.

Come believing! come believing!
Come to Jesus! look and live!
Come believing! come believing!
Come to Jesus! look and live!

(D. W. Whittle)

'Everyone who believes that Jesus is the Christ has been born of God, and everyone who loves the Father loves whoever has been born of him' 1 John 5:1

18TH JANUARY

ENOCH WALKED WITH GOD

It was also about these that Enoch, the seventh from Adam, prophesied, saying, Behold, the Lord comes with ten thousands of his holy ones, to execute judgment on all and to convict all the ungodly of all their deeds of ungodliness that they have committed in such an ungodly way, and of all the harsh things that ungodly sinners have spoken against him.

Jude 14–15

Everyone has favourite Bible characters for various and different reasons. Over the years I have studied many Bible characters. Some have books named after them. Some have chapters written about them. However amongst my favourite Old Testament Bible characters is that of Enoch. There are just three short portions of Scripture which record the life of Enoch: Genesis 5:18–24; Hebrews 11:5; and Jude 14–15. However there is much we can learn from these verses about this man of God which are helpful to us to day. Enoch lived in a sinful age. John Phillips described the age he lived in as follows: socially it was an age of permissiveness; scientifically it was an age of progressiveness; and spiritually it was an age of presumptuousness. It sounds like an age very similar to today. Yet in the midst of such an age Enoch had an encounter with God at age 65 resulting in a changed life and a commencement of a 300 year period of walking with God. Enoch ended up being a man of faith who had a testimony that he pleased God.

The following is a hymn about Enoch's life and testimony written by a Baptist Pastor called Benjamin Beddome who pastored a church at Bourton-on-the-Water for fifty years in the 1700s. It summarises Enoch's life succinctly and has many helpful guidelines for us as believers living in this present age:

Enoch walked with God,
His patron and his friend
Sacred the path in which he trod,
And happier still his end.

While others went astray,
Or vile companions chose
His soul maintained the heavenly way
In spite of all his foes.

The cause of truth he owned
In that degenerate age
And God the Lord with honour crowned,
His lengthened pilgrimage.

The scoffing of men he bore,
But God his way approved;
The unbelieving world no more
Shall scorn the man he loved.

Borne on an angel's wing,
He mounts above the skies;
Exempt from death's envenomed sting
Behold him joyful rise.

Upheld by power supreme,
There's nought but I could do
Could boldly enter Jordan's stream
And pass in triumph too.

I trust that it will be said of us that we walked with God, that we maintained the heavenly way, that our walk with God will be approved of God, and that one day whether through death or the Lord's return we too will pass in triumph into God's presence.

19TH JANUARY

JESUS CHRIST'S LAST COMMAND: GO

Zebulun is a people who risked their lives to the death; Naphtali, too, on the heights of the field.

Judges 5:18

I had the privilege of serving the Lord with a mission agency from 2007 to 2022. One of the joys was to cast the vision for missions -whether in person, prayer or purse or indeed a combination or all of these. Over the years I have collected various bites of literature on various missionaries and mission ambassadors that are helpful in casting the vision in advancing the missionary cause. One such was C. T. Studd the founder of WEC. The following are some quotes and poems written by him that I trust will help to encourage us to fulfil our role which God has called us to in mission:

'If Jesus Christ be God and died for me, then no sacrifice can be too great for me to make for Him'

'Some wish to live within the sound of Church or Chapel bell, I want to run a rescue shop within a yard of Hell' C.T.Studd then quotes our verse for today Judges 5:18, followed by the following challenging poem:

O for a thousand men to do
My Saviour's last command,
To take the Gospel of our God
To every heathen land.

We want a few of the dare-devil crew
Who never know when they're beat,
But will fire away all night and day
And flatly refuse to retreat.

Not statesmanlike men of subtle craft
Can chase or charm away evil,
But men whose shot is pointed hot,
And who'll fire it at the Devil.

Don't come for a mere experiment
Just for a year or two,
But come as to war with a lion's roar
To see the campaign through

You won't regret that it cost you a lot,
When you get to the other side,
But oh, the shame if you earn the name
'A miser he lived and died!'

With what joyful feet you shall run up
The street,
That leads to the throne of God,
If you've given your ALL FOR CHRIST
And walked
The road that the Martyrs trod.

Studd then writes: 'I think Paul was no fool, he was ever seeking to suffer more when he needn't have bothered, because he realised in his own soul that even down here suffering brought instant joy to his soul from God which obliterated the pain'.

Quite challenging. Let us keep on keeping on being obedient to our Lord and Saviour's last command—GO.

20TH JANUARY

LEARNING FROM NOAH.

These three men, Noah, Daniel, and Job.

Ezekiel 14:14

Many years ago I was asked to start a 'Men's Fellowship' in the Church I attended at that time. In the course of that first year we looked at character studies of various men in the Bible. We started our first three character studies based on Ezekiel 14:14: 'these three men, Noah, Daniel, and Job'.

The actual context of this verse was pointing out that if these three men were living at this time in Israel's history they could not deliver it, due to its spiritual state. Yet they themselves would be delivered as individuals. That said, these men are used as examples of righteous lives. One of the themes of our men's fellowship at that time was 'Men of God and Godly Men'.

So what can we learn from these three men: Noah, Daniel and Job that will help us in our walk with God today?:

Let's start with Noah:

NOAH'S FAVOUR WITH GOD: 'But Noah found favour in the eyes of the Lord' Genesis 6:8. Noah found grace or favour with God. Before we find favour with God we must see ourselves as sinners in need of a Saviour. No doubt Noah learned this from his grandfather Enoch. Grace is unmerited favour. Enoch was saved at 65 years of age at the time his son Methuselah was born. We can rejoice as believers in Jesus that we are saved by grace and have experienced His unmerited favour and because of this we are saved for time and eternity. In many cases we can also praise God for a godly heritage.

NOAH FEARED GOD: 'By faith Noah, being warned by God concerning events as yet unseen, in reverent fear constructed an ark for the saving of his household. By this he condemned the world and became an heir of the righteousness that comes by faith'. Hebrews 11:7. In a world of godlessness we too as followers of Jesus have a 'reverent fear' of God. And we also want our households saved. 'By faith Noah, being warned by God concerning events as yet unseen, in reverent fear constructed an ark for the saving of his household. By this he condemned the world and became an heir of the righteousness that comes by faith'. 2 Peter 2:4–5

NOAH HAD HIS FAITH IN GOD: 'By faith Noah'. Hebrews 11:7. Noah was a man of faith. Without faith we cannot please God. By faith Noah . . . constructed an ark for the saving of his household. The ark is a type of Christ. It is in Christ we have our safety for all eternity.

'On Calvary's Hill an Ark has been built,
Costing the blood of God's Son
With its door opened wide,
There is safety inside,
Anybody who will may get in'

(Unknown)

Let us praise God for His unmerited FAVOUR, live by FAITH with reverential FEAR.

21ST JANUARY

DARE TO HAVE A PURPOSE FIRM

*Even if Noah, Daniel, and Job were in it, they would
deliver but their own lives by their righteousness.*

Ezekiel 14:20

In Ezekiel 14 Noah, Daniel and Job are grouped together as an illustration of righteous lives.

Ellicott in his Commentary writes: 'These three are selected, doubtless, not only as examples of eminent holiness themselves, but as men who had been allowed to be the means of saving others'.

Yesterday we considered Noah, today we will consider Daniel and hopefully learn lessons from him on how we can be godly men and women in an ungodly world.

Daniel was a well-known Jewish Prophet fourth of the so-called Major Prophets. Jesus himself described him as Daniel the Prophet: 'So when you see the abomination of desolation spoken of by the prophet Daniel'. Matt 24:15.

Many things could be said about Daniel but we will just consider one: Daniel was a man of purpose. This leads us to ask the question are we people of purpose in this our generation. We read in Daniel 1:8: 'But Daniel purposed in his heart that he would not defile himself with the portion of the king's meat, nor with the wine which he drank: therefore he requested of the prince of the eunuchs that he might not defile himself' (KJV). To have a purpose means to have a deliberate intention. The word implies a decided resolution. Daniel purposed in his heart. It all began in the heart. The heart of the matter is the matter of the heart. We read in Romans 10:9–10: 'because, if you confess with your mouth that Jesus is Lord and believe in your heart that God raised him from the dead, you will be saved. For with the heart one believes and is justified, and with the mouth one confesses and is saved'.

Daniel purposed in his heart that he would obey God's law given to God's people Israel, this was to be his lifelong testimony. It led to a life of: Self-control: Daniel 1:8; 10:3; Courage: Daniel 5:22–23; Constant integrity: Daniel 6:4; Unceasing prayer life: Daniel 2:17–18, 6:16; Humility: Daniel 10:17; and Wisdom: Daniel 7:9,15; 10:5–6.

It is no wonder we were taught as children to sing:

Standing by a purpose true,
Heeding God's command,
Honour them, the faithful few!
All hail to Daniel's band!

Dare to be a Daniel,
Dare to stand alone!
Dare to have a purpose firm!
Dare to make it known.

Many mighty men are lost
Daring not to stand,
Who for God had been a host
By joining Daniel's band.

Many giants, great and tall,
Stalking through the land,
Headlong to the earth would fall,
If met by Daniel's band.

Hold the Gospel banner high!
On to vict'ry grand!
Satan and his hosts defy,
And shout for Daniel's band.

(Philip Paul Bliss)

22ND JANUARY

MY SERVANT JOB

Even if these three men were in it, . . .
they alone would be delivered.

Ezekiel 14:16

The three men referred to in Ezekiel 14:16 are Noah, Daniel and Job. Ezekiel 14: 14 and 20 features three individuals whom God had delivered: Noah's family owed their deliverance to him Gen 6: 6–9 and 7:1; Daniel's companions were similarly delivered (Dan 2: 12, 17, 49), and Job's three friends were delivered because of Job's intercession on their behalf (Job 42:7–9).

We learn from scripture that: Noah was perfect or righteous (Gen 6: 9), Daniel was greatly loved (Dan 10:11), and Job, unequalled in the earth (Job 1:8). Over the past two days we looked at Noah and Daniel.

Today we are going to consider Job and apply what we learn to our walk with God. Job is described by God as: 'my servant Job'. Job 1:8' 42:8.

One of the things we learn from the book of Job is that we don't always have to understand. God did not give Job all the answers to why he suffered so much. We learn from Job's life that: 'God often digs wells of joy with the spade of sorrow' and to quote Charles H Spurgeon: 'We cannot always trace God's hand but we can always trust God's heart' . This reminds me of the words of the chorus of the following hymn written by Ira Stanphil:

Many things about tomorrow,
I don't seem to understand;
But I know who holds tomorrow,
And I know who holds my hand.
So what did Job do in his time of trial?

HE WORSHIPPED THE PERSON OF GOD: 'Then Job arose and tore his robe and shaved his head and fell on the ground and worshipped. And he said, Naked I came from my mother's womb, and naked shall I return. The Lord gave, and the Lord has taken away; blessed be the name of the Lord'. Job 1:20–22

HE WALKED IN THE PATHS OF GOD: 'My foot has held fast to his steps; I have kept his way and have not turned aside'. Job 23:11.

HE WAITED ON THE PURPOSES OF GOD: 'Behold, I go forward, but he is not there, and backward, but I do not perceive him; on the left hand when he is working, I do not behold him; he turns to the right hand, but I do not see him. But he knows the way that I take; when he has tried me, I shall come out as gold'. Job 23:8–10

I trust you were blessed, encouraged and challenged as we considered some aspects of the life of Noah, Daniel and Job over these past three days. These were recognised as being godly men and men of God.

23RD JANUARY

ONE THING I DO KNOW

He answered, whether he is a sinner I do not know. One thing I do know, that though I was blind, now I see.

John 9:25

Some years ago I did an interesting study on the 'One Things' of the Bible. Over the next few days we will consider some of these. I trust they will be a blessing and benefit to you as you meditate upon them.

The first one I want to look at concerns 'One Thing I do know': The Assurance of Salvation.

The man that was blind from birth as recorded in John chapter 9 was hounded by the religious leaders of his day asking him various questions about Jesus and how He had healed him. The man said that there were things he didn't know about Jesus, but this he did know that he once was blind but now he could see. So it is with everyone whom the Lord saves. We can truly say once I was blind spiritually but now I see. Our salvation is a know 'so' salvation. On thinking of this I immediately thought about the following song:

I wandered so aimless life filled with sin
I wouldn't let my dear saviour in
Then Jesus came like a stranger in the night
Praise the Lord I saw the light.

I saw the light I saw the light
No more darkness no more night
Now I'm so happy no sorrow in sight
Praise the Lord I saw the light.

Just like a blind man I wandered along
Worries and fears I claimed for my own
Then like the blind man that God gave back his sight
Praise the Lord I saw the light.

I was a fool to wander and stray
Straight is the gate and narrow the way
Now I have traded the wrong for the right
Praise the Lord I saw the light.

(Hank Williams)

As believers we can testify to one thing we know: That at one time we were blinded by the god of this world –Satan 2 Corinthians 4:4. But then the glorious gospel shone on our darkened hearts and minds. We responded to the gospel by repentance towards God for our sins and put our faith in our Lord Jesus Christ alone for salvation. We were transformed by the power of the Gospel, made a new creation in Christ and now we can see.

'But I am not ashamed, for I know whom I have believed, and I am convinced that he is able to guard until that day what has been entrusted to me'. 2 Timothy 1:12

'I write these things to you who believe in the name of the Son of God, that you may know that you have eternal life' 1 John 5:13

24TH JANUARY

UNLESS YOU WEAR THE SHOES HE WEARS

Brothers, if anyone is caught in any transgression, you who are spiritual should restore him in a spirit of gentleness. Keep watch on yourself, lest you too be tempted. Bear one anothers burdens, and so fulfil the law of Christ.

Galatians 6:1–2

I once read an article on discipleship which I have often thought about. It suggests that there are four areas that we can be involved in as disciple makers. The first three were based on Matthew 28 v. 18–20: And Jesus came and said to them, all authority in heaven and on earth has been given to me. Go therefore and make disciples of all nations, baptizing them in the name of the Father and of the Son and of the Holy Spirit, teaching them to observe all that I have commanded you. And behold, I am with you always, to the end of the age.'

- MAKE DISCIPLES: Go therefore and make disciples of all nations
- MARK DISCIPLES: baptizing them in the name of the Father and of the Son and of the Holy Spirit
- MATURE DISCIPLES: teaching them to observe all that I have commanded you

But the writer went on to say we also have to:

MEND DISCIPLES from time to time. I have on my weekly prayer schedule the privilege of praying for Irish Baptist missionaries in Peru, Ireland, Spain and France each Tuesday. On their

webpage they quote Matthew 28:18–20. I have written beside this on my printed copy: Make, Mark, Mature and Mend Disciples. It is my prayer that the various missionary workers mentioned will be involved in some or all of these aspects of making disciples in their area of service.

But the area on my heart for today is mending disciples. Along the way some dear brother or sister may need mending. Perhaps God is calling you to reach out to someone in need of mending today. This reminded me of the following little poem:

Don't find fault with the man who limps
Or stumbles along the road-
Unless you wear the shoes he wears
And bend beneath his load.

Perhaps there are nails in the shoes he wears,
Which are hidden from your view.
The burden he bears, if placed on your back,
Might make you stumble, too!

(Unknown)

'Therefore, confess your sins to one another and pray for one another, that you may be healed. The prayer of a righteous person has great power as it is working' James 5:16

25TH JANUARY

JESUS, THOU EVERLASTING KING

The Lord is king forever and ever.

Psalm 10:16

Queen Elizabeth 11 was born on the 21st April 1926. . Elizabeth succeeded to the throne in 1952 at the age of 25, following the death of her father, King George VI, as the monarch of the United Kingdom and 15 Commonwealth realms. On 6 February 2022, Elizabeth 11 became the first British monarch to reign for 70 years. Elizabeth 11 died on 8 September 2022, at the age of 96 years and 140 days, after reigning for 70 years and 214 days. She reigned the longest time of any British monarch and the longest verified reign of any female monarch in history.

Up to the date of her death she reigned as Queen for all of my life (over 65 years). For me as a citizen of the UK she brought constancy, consistency and a sense of security. I felt honoured to be one of her subjects. I was deeply moved and saddened at her passing.

That said, I became a citizen of Heaven on the 9th October 1978 under the reign of the Lord Jesus Christ. Scripture teaches that He is 'King forever' Psalm 10:16; 'and of His reign there will be no end' and of his kingdom there will be no end. This brings great and eternal constancy and consistency to the life of every born again child of God. The following are the words of the verses of two hymns that take up this glorious theme:

Sing we the king who is coming to reign,
Glory to Jesus, the Lamb that was slain.
Life and salvation His empire shall bring,
Joy to the nations when Jesus is king.

(Charles S. Horne)

Jesus, Thou everlasting king,
Accept the tribute which we bring;
Accept the well-deserved renown,
And wear our praises as Thy crown.

(Isaac Watts)

Charles Rolls writing on this topic said: 'Do we realise there is a King at the centre of this great universe, who in His mystic being and majestic bearing knows and loves and cares, and who is constantly ministering munificent blessings for our present well-being and future welfare?' He goes on to say: 'None but Christ could ever claim to seven Kingships, But He is King of the Jews, King of Israel, King of righteousness, King of the ages, King of saints, King of Heaven, King of glory, and over and above all, King of Kings'.

Majesty, worship His Majesty: Unto Jesus be all glory, honour, and praise.
Majesty, kingdom authority, Flow from His throne unto His own, His anthems raise.
So exalt, lift up on high the name of Jesus. Magnify, come glorify Christ Jesus, the King.
Majesty, worship HIs Majesty, Jesus who died, now glorified, King of all Kings.

(Jack Hayford)

26TH JANUARY

THE WESLEYAN COVENANT PRAYER

Pray without ceasing.

1 Thessalonians 5:17

All scripture is given by inspiration of God.

2 Timothy 3:16

I had the privilege of being part of an outreach team at the 2019 Fleadh Cheoil in Drogheda. The team has kept in touch through a whatsapp group which is now known as the 'Drogheda Fleadh Outreach'. Since then various team members post messages, prayer requests, words of encouragement and challenging quotes. One of the team at the beginning of a New Year posted the following insightful Charles Spurgeon quote: 'when asked: What is more important: prayer or reading the Bible? I ask, what is more important: breathing in or breathing out?' Another way of saying that both are equally important. When we pray we talk to God. When we read His Word He talks to us.

When I had just completed reading this message I read an article circulated by email from another ministry I have an association with. The devotion read: 'Has God spoken to you through Scripture and prayer?' The article then went on to speak about The Wesleyan Covenant Prayer which was adapted from a Puritan tradition. The Wesleyan Covenant Prayer was adapted by John Wesley, the co-founder of Methodism (along with his brother, Charles). Wesley says that the prayer was first used in a covenant renewal service held on Monday, August 11, 1755, in London, with 1800 people present. Since then, the Wesleyan Covenant Prayer has often been used in Methodist services around the world on the first Sunday of the year.

The following are the words of the prayer:

I am no longer my own, but thine.
Put me to what thou wilt, rank
me with whom thou wilt.
Put me to doing, put me to suffering.
Let me be employed for thee
or laid aside for thee,
exalted for thee or brought low for thee.
Let me be full, let me be empty.
Let me have all things, let me have nothing.
I freely and heartily yield all things
to thy pleasure and disposal.
And now, O glorious and blessed God,
Father, Son and Holy Spirit,
thou art mine, and I am thine.
So be it.
And the covenant which I have made on earth,
let it be ratified in heaven.
Amen

Let this be a year of complete surrender to God through prayer and reading His Word.

27TH JANUARY

COUNT YOUR MANY BLESSINGS

*Blessed be the Lord, who daily bears us
up; God is our salvation. Selah.*

Psalm 68:19 ESV

*Blessed be the Lord, who daily loadeth us with
benefits, even the God of our salvation. Selah.*

Psalm 68:19 KJV

Psalm 68:19 has been described as a picture of a loaded wagon. The wagon is ours and God has loaded us with benefits. God is continually loading us each and every day of our lives with blessing.

The word 'loaded' here depicts heaping in excess. Everyday God is supplying to you and me His blessings in excess, more than you and I can handle. He just doesn't give enough to survive, but He supplies in excess because that is His way of doing things.

To us that are saved we praise Him each day for His saving and keeping power, we praise Him for every temporal and spiritual blessing He bestows.

Psalm 103 was my mother's favourite Psalm. In verse 2 we are encouraged not to forget the benefits God bestows upon us: 'Bless the Lord, O my soul, and forget not all his benefits.'

The Psalmist goes on to outline some of these benefits:

- He forgives all our sins
- He heals all our diseases
- He redeems our lives from destruction
- He crowns us with loving-kindness and tender mercies
- He satisfies us with good things
- He renews our youth (makes us feel young and strong again)
- He does not treat (or punish) us as our sins deserve

Jeremiah writing in Lamentations 3:22–23 reminds us: 'The steadfast love of the Lord never ceases; His mercies never come to an end; they are new every morning; great is your faithfulness'.

*Great is thy faithfulness, O God my father,
Morning by morning new mercies I see;
All I have needed thy hand hath provided,
Great is thy faithfulness, Lord unto me.*

(Thomas O. Chisholm)

*Count your blessings, name them one by one;
Count your blessings, see what God hath done;
Count your blessings, name them one by one;
Count your many blessings, see
what God hath done.*

(Johnson Oatman)

What a tremendous word of praise should be lifted heavenward on a daily basis for His blessings and His benefits on our lives.

28TH JANUARY

I HAVE A PRECIOUS BOOK

More to be desired are they than gold, even much fine gold.

Psalm 19:10

Various N Ireland newspapers carried the story of an upcoming sale of a 1615 Geneva Bible at an Auction House in Belfast. A spokesman at the Auction House described it as follows: 'Our first sale of the year includes some absolutely superb pieces of antique furniture, really quality fine art, rarely seen on sale in Ireland. One of the highlights of the show is a bible dated 1615 which travelled from Devon with Elizabeth Pole to what is now Massachusetts. Because of the historic importance of the bible, we are expecting considerable interest not just from the UK but from the USA.

The Geneva Bible has been described as one of the most historically significant translations of the bible. It was the first mechanically printed, mass-produced bible available to the public and pre-dates the King James Bible by 50 years. Copies of it were carried by the Pilgrims on the Mayflower to the New World.

The particular edition being sold by this Auction House was owned by Ms Pole, who travelled with her brother on the Speedwell to the Plymouth Colony in 1633 and founded the town of Taunton, Massachusetts. She is believed to be the first woman to establish a town in North America.

The Elizabeth Pole Bible was printed in 1615 by Robert Barker, printer to Elizabeth I and James I. The bible was presented to Sir William Pole, by the then Archbishop of Canterbury in recognition of his services to the Church and the poor of Devon. Sir William gave it to his son William and daughter Elizabeth on their journey to the New World, and upon Elizabeth's death the bible was returned to her family in Devon.

It remained in the possession of the Pole-Carew family until the mid-20th century when it was sold to a collector from Northern Ireland. Other items on sale from the same collection are two paintings by the renowned Victorian artist Thomas Sidney Cooper.

It was expected that the Bible would fetch between £5,000-£10,000. On the day it sold for £20,000.

On reading up on the various articles published in the press about this Bible, the Lord brought into my mind the words of the following children's hymn:

I Have A Precious Book, It's
The Word Of God.
It's The Only Book That God Has Given.
As I Read, God Speaks To Me,
I See Christ And Calvary.
The Wonderful Word Of God.
Forever It Will Stand As The Ages Roll,
It's The Living And Eternal Word.
It's My Guiding Light Each Day,
And Without It I Would Stray;
The Wonderful Word Of God.
Dear Lord May I Each Day
Read Thy Precious Word.
May I Love It And Obey It Too.
May I Grow To Be Like Thee.
May My Friends See Christ In Me.
In Jesus' Name, Amen.

(Unknown)

29TH JANUARY

HOW PRECIOUS IS THE BOOK DIVINE

Your word is a lamp to my feet and a light to my path.

Psalm 119:105

A special edition 1615 Geneva Bible was sold at an Auction business in Belfast. One local paper in an article described its sale as follows: 'A rare copy of the Bible has sold for £20,000 at an auction in Belfast. The Geneva Bible, which is believed to date back to 1615, attracted a lot of interest. The auctioneer said that bidding at the auction started at £6,000 before swiftly reaching five figures and finishing with the winning bid of £20,000 on Tuesday afternoon (10th January 2023). Later the BBC News revealed that a retired Free Presbyterian Minister Rev David McIlveen was one of a group who bought the 1615 Bible. Mr McIlveen told the BBC that he: 'saw it as a vision in terms of reaching out to schoolchildren and also to libraries as well. Something like this - I would pray - could reactivate that interest in the scriptures. I see it not only as an artefact but as a message that is so relevant for this generation'.

Over the years I have had the privilege of purchasing significant quantities of copies of the Bible as low as £1 each to distribute to folk who requested them. No matter the monetary cost of one copy of the Bible it is still the most precious book one can have in their possession. Why? The psalmist David said: 'Your word is a lamp to my feet and a light to my path' Psalm 119:105. The Apostle Paul said: 'All Scripture is breathed out by God and profitable for teaching, for reproof, for correction, and for training in righteousness, that the man of God may be complete, equipped for every good work' 2 Timothy 3:16–17. It is eternal. The Bible is the only

ancient text that is eternally relevant. Can I encourage you to make reading Scripture a daily habit.

How precious is the Book Divine,
By inspiration giv'n!
Bright as a lamp its doctrines shine
To guide our souls to heav'n,
To guide our souls to heav'n.

Its light, descending from above
Our gloomy world to cheer,
Displays a Savior's boundless love
And brings His glories near,
And brings His glories near.

It shows to us our wand'ring ways
And where his feet have trod,
And brings to view the matchless grace
Of a forgiving God,
Of a forgiving God.

O'er all the straight and narrow way
Its radiant beams are cast;
A light whose never weary ray
Grows brightest at the last,
Grows brightest at the last.

It sweetly cheers our drooping hearts
In this dark vale of tears,
Life, light, and joy it still imparts
And quells our rising fears,
And quells our rising fears.

This lamp through all the tedious night
Of life shall guide our way
Till we behold the clearer light
Of an eternal day,
Of an eternal day.

(John Fawcett :1782)

30TH JANUARY

O HOW HE LOVES YOU AND ME

Now Jesus loved Martha and her sister and Lazarus.

John 11:5

As you read John 11 you observe various ways Jesus demonstrated His love to Lazarus, Martha, and Mary. Jesus' love was displayed differently to all three:

TO LAZARUS HE WAS THE MIGHTY LORD: 'When he had said these things, he cried out with a loud voice, Lazarus, come out. The man who had died came out, his hands and feet bound with linen strips, and his face wrapped with a cloth. Jesus said to them, Unbind him, and let him go' v. 43–44.

TO MARTHA HE WAS THE ETERNAL LIFE: 'Jesus said to her, I am the resurrection and the life. Whoever believes in me, though he die, yet shall he live, and everyone who lives and believes in me shall never die. Do you believe this? She said to him, Yes, Lord; I believe that you are the Christ, the Son of God, who is coming into the world' 25–27.

TO MARY HE WAS THE INCARNATE LOVE: 'Now when Mary came to where Jesus was and saw him, she fell at his feet, saying to him, Lord, if you had been here, my brother would not have died. When Jesus saw her weeping, and the Jews who had come with her also weeping, he was deeply moved in his spirit and greatly troubled. And he said, where have you laid him? They said to him, Lord, come and see. Jesus wept. So the Jews said, See how he loved him!' 32–36.

Jesus demonstrated His love to the whole family. However He showed His love to each individual in a way that was most appropriate and meaningful to each individual member. Today God loves your family and He also loves you as an individual member of it. Jesus loves the family of God. In fact He loves us so much He died on the cross on our behalf. And yet He loves each member of His Church individually:

O, How He Loves You And Me,
O, How He Loves You And Me.
He Gave His Life,
What More Could He Give?

Oh How He Loves You,
Oh How He Loves Me,
Oh How He Loves
You And Me.

Jesus To Calvary Did Go,
His Love For Mankind To Show;
What He Did There
Brought Hope From Despair

Oh How He Loves You,
Oh How He Loves Me,
Oh How He Loves
You And Me.

31ST JANUARY

I'VE FOUND A FRIEND, OH, SUCH A FRIEND!

*A man of many companions may come to ruin, but
there is a friend who sticks closer than a brother.*

Proverbs 18:24

The following are extracts from an interesting article I read in the Daily Mail written by Xantha Leatham about turning an acquaintance into a good friend: 'We all have friends we've known for many years, and some we have known for a few weeks. But how long does it take before an acquaintance becomes a real buddy. Around 34 hours is the answer, according to experts. A study of more than 2,000 individuals has revealed we require 2,040 minutes of commitment to make the change. The results were analysed by Oxford University Professor Robin Dunbar. . . . The analysis revealed that the ultimate formula for friendship involves 11 interactions, each lasting three hours and four minutes, over a period of five and a half months. . . . Professor Dunbar said: 'Friendships are the single most important factor influencing our psychological and our physical health and wellbeing".

Jesus is the best friend we can have. On reading the article it reminded me of a little verse in Job which says: 'Acquaint now thyself with him, and be at peace: thereby good shall come unto thee' Job 22:21 (KJV). When we repent from our sins and we put our faith and trust Him' alone for salvation He becomes our forever friend. This led me to think on the lovely words of the following hymn which clearly illustrates just what a wonderful friend Jesus is:

I've found a Friend, oh, such a Friend!
He loved me ere I knew Him;
He drew me with the cords of love,
And thus He bound me to Him.
And round my heart still closely twine
Those ties which naught can sever,
For I am His, and He is mine,
Forever and forever.

I've found a Friend, oh, such a Friend!
He bled, He died to save me;
And not alone the gift of life,
But His own self He gave me.
Naught that I have my own I call,
I hold it for the Giver;
My heart, my strength, my life, my all,
Are His, and His forever.

I've found a Friend, oh, such a Friend!
So kind, and true, and tender,
So wise a Counsellor and Guide,
So mighty a Defender!
From Him who loves me now so well,
What power my soul can sever?
Shall life or death, or earth or hell?
No? I am His forever.

(James G. Small)

1ST FEBRUARY

THERES NOT A FRIEND LIKE THE LOWLY JESUS

Greater love has no one than this, that someone lay down his life for his friends. You are my friends if you do what I command you.

John 15:13–14

Yesterday I shared some extracts that I had read in one of the daily newspapers about friendship. The following are further extracts from the article which I trust helps you consider how we need friends and should have friends and also recognising how wonderful a friend we have in Jesus: The research: 'also revealed that each person supposedly has five close shoulders to cry on friends—with being there for each other during hard times ranking as the most important quality in a best friend.... This study shows how two thirds of us have a best friend who provides those moments of emotional support and advice when we need it most. This makes finding friends and maintaining friendships all the more important.'

After reading the article I scribbled the title of the following hymn below it:

There's not a friend like the lowly Jesus–
No, not one! no, not one!
None else could heal all our soul's diseases–
No, not one! no, not one!

Jesus knows all about our struggles,
He will guide till the day is done;
There's not a friend like the lowly Jesus–
No, not one! no, not one!

No friend like Him is so high and holy–
No, not one! no, not one!
And yet no friend is so meek and lowly–
No, not one! no, not one!

There's not an hour that He is not near us –
No, not one! no, not one!
No night so dark but His love can cheer us–
No, not one! no, not one!

Was e'er a gift like the Saviour given?
No, not one! no, not one!
Will He refuse us a home in heaven?
No, not one! no, not one!

(Johnson Oatman)

Having Jesus as our friend gives us tremendous emotional and spiritual support.

The article also made me reflect on friends who have helped and encouraged me over the years. David and Jonathan is a biblical example of such friendships: 'Jonathan said to David, Go in peace, for we have sworn friendship with each other in the name of the Lord, saying, The Lord is witness between you and me, and between your descendants and my descendants forever. Then David left, and Jonathan went back to the town'. 1 Samuel 20:42 (NIV).

I trust this encourages us today to stick close to Jesus as our greatest ever friend and to be a friend to others.

2ND FEBRUARY

THEY FOLLOW MY CALL

My sheep hear my voice, and I know them, and they follow me.

John 10:27

In John 10:27–29 Jesus outlines seven separate statements of relation to His followers:

I. THEY HEAR HIS VOICE

'My sheep hear my voice' v. 27:

> *I heard the voice of Jesus say,*
> *Come unto me and rest;*
> *lay down, O weary one,*
> *lay down your head upon my breast.*
> *I came to Jesus as I was,*
> *so weary, worn, and sad;*
> *I found in him a resting place,*
> *and he has made me glad.*

(Horatius Bonar)

2. HE KNOWS THEM:

'and I know them' v. 27

3. THEY FOLLOW ME:

'and they follow me' v. 27: Ivor Powell makes the point that 'no man can be truly united to Christ and not wish to follow Him fully.

4. HE GIVES THEM ETERNAL LIFE:

'I give them eternal life' v. 28

> *Life! life! eternal life!*
> *Jesus alone is the Giver:*
> *Life! life! abundant life!*
> *Glory to Jesus forever!*

(William Leslie)

5. THEY SHALL NEVER PERISH:

'and they will never perish' v. 28

6. NO ONE CAN SNATCH THEM OUT OF HIS HAND:

'and no one will snatch them out of my hand' v. 28

7. NO ONE CAN SNATCH THEM OUT OF MY FATHER'S HAND:

'and no one is able to snatch them out of the Father's hand' v. 29 Ivor Powell calls this 'God's great grip'.

Rejoice today in the fact that we are one of Jesus' sheep. It is just wonderful being a follower of Jesus knowing that we are safe and secure in His loving care.

> *My sheep hear My voice, and*
> *the path that I take,*
> *They follow wherever I go;*
> *My sheep know My voice and come at my call,*
> *But a stranger's voice do they not know.*
> *My sheep know My voice, and day by day*
> *They abide in the fold and go not astray,*
> *They love Me because I have*
> *made them my choice,*
> *And they follow My call for My*
> *sheep know My voice.*

(Herbert Buffum)

3RD FEBRUARY

I'LL TRUST THE GOD OF MIRACLES, GIVE TO HIM MY ALL.

Blessed is the man who trusts in the Lord, whose trust is the Lord.

Jeremiah 17:7

In discussion with a consultant regarding a building project for a ministry I am involved with his advice was that we needed to work with people that we can trust. However first and foremost to trust the Lord, not ourselves but commit everything to Him. He referenced Proverbs 3:5: 'Trust in the Lord with all your heart, and do not lean on your own understanding', and Philippians 4:6: 'do not be anxious about anything, but in everything by prayer and supplication with thanksgiving let your requests be made known to God'. I thought what a wonderful basis on which to commence a conversation regarding the project.

It is wonderful that in world of distrust that as believers we can fully trust the Lord. He is trustworthy.

The very first thing we need to do is trust the Lord for salvation in His appointed way: Repentance towards God and faith in the Lord Jesus Christ as our only Saviour. Isaiah 12 was one of my father's favourite portions of Scripture. He had it read at his funeral. Verse 2 says: 'Behold, God is my salvation; I will trust, and will not be afraid; for the Lord God is my strength and my song, and he has become my salvation'.

There are good reasons we can trust the Lord: He always tells the truth because He is 'the truth'. He loves us and is in total control of everything.

God can also be trusted because his word is true, and he keeps all his promises (John 17:17; Num. 23:19). As our verse for today informs us 'blessed is the man who trusts in the Lord, whose trust is the Lord' (Jer. 17:7), and he will be blessed because the Lord cannot lie and he will keep all of his promises. The Bible is full of what Peter calls 'precious and very great promises' that have to do with our complete salvation and entrance into the eternal kingdom of our Lord and Saviour Jesus Christ (2Pet. 2:3–11). Praise God we can truly sing: Trust in the Lord and don't despair. He is a friend so true'. Ultimately He will bring us home to heaven.

This reminded me of the following quotes and chorus that I trust will bring confidence to all those that read this today:

Few delights can equal the presence of one whom we trust utterly. (George MacDonald)

Never be afraid to trust an unknown future to a known God. (Corrie Ten Boom)

I know who holds the future, And I know he holds my hand;
With God things don't just happen ev'rything by Him is planned.
So as I face tomorrow with its problems large and small,
I'll trust the God of miracles, Give to Him my all!

(Unknown)

4TH FEBRUARY

WE WILL FOLLOW THE STEPS OF JESUS

For to this you have been called, because Christ also suffered for you, leaving you an example, so that you might follow in his steps.

1 Peter 2:21

In his first epistle Peter was writing to scattered and suffering Christians in various parts of the Roman Empire at that time. It was a letter of encouragement, assuring these dear suffering believers that one day their suffering will be turned into glory.

Against this background in 1 Peter 2:21 Peter is encouraging the saints to follow the example of Jesus particularly in the area of suffering. Of course we are not saved by following Christ's example. As sinners we need a Saviour in the person of the Lord Jesus Christ. However after our conversion we should follow in His footsteps. There are various ways that we as His believers should follow in the steps of Jesus. The following are but a few for us to consider today:

IF WE FOLLOW IN THE FOOTSTEPS OF JESUS WE:

A. WILL BE SENSITIVE: "When he saw the crowds, he had compassion for them, because they were harassed and helpless, like sheep without a shepherd'. Jesus was compassionate and sensitive to the needs of the lost. Matthew 9:36

B. WILL BE SERVING: even as the Son of Man came not to be served but to serve, and to give his life as a ransom for many' Matthew 20:28

C. WILL BE SCRIPTURAL: 'Then he said to them, these are my words that I spoke to you while I was still with you, that everything written about me in the Law of Moses and the Prophets and the Psalms must be fulfilled. Then he opened their minds to understand the Scriptures'. Luke 24:44–45. Jesus made much of the scriptures. So must we.

D. WILL BE SUPPLICANTS: 'Now Jesus was praying in a certain place, and when he finished, one of his disciples said to him, Lord, teach us to pray, as John taught his disciples' Luke 11:1. Jesus had an amazing prayer life as a study of the gospels will reveal. The disciples did not ask Jesus how to preach but how to pray. We too need to follow Jesus' steps in our prayer life.

E. WILL BE SUBMISSIVE: 'saying, Father, if it is Your will, take this cup away from Me; nevertheless not My will, but Yours, be done'. Luke 22:42. Jesus submitted to all the ways of God. So should we.

F. WILL BE WILLING TO SUFFER: 'For to this you have been called, because Christ also suffered for you, leaving you an example, so that you might follow in his steps' 1 Peter 2:21

Sweetly, Lord, have we heard Thee calling,
Come, follow Me!
And we see where Thy footprints falling
Lead us to Thee. Footprints of Jesus,
That make the pathway glow;
We will follow the steps of Jesus
Where'er they go

(Mary B. Slade)

5TH FEBRUARY

HAPPINESS IS THE LORD

Happy is that people, that is in such a case: yea,
happy is that people, whose God is the Lord.

Psalm 144:15 (KJV)

The UK government produced a happiness index of its population some years ago. Away back in 2010 the BBC reported that: The government will attempt to measure the happiness of UK citizens, The Office for National Statistics is to devise questions for a household survey, to be carried out up to four times a year.

Today they would rather use the term 'wellbeing'. The reason being that happiness can go up and down in one day. Happiness is to do with happenings. Christians should be measured more by their 'joy' levels. Christians can have the joy of the Lord even in the midst of challenging circumstances. We agree that the Bible does make positive statements about how a nation can experience true happiness: 'happy is that people, whose God is the Lord'

John Phillips commenting on this said: 'David's national goal was that his people be free from complaints and full of contentment. He realised that there was only one way for such national goals to be realised. They cannot be attained by political acumen nor by the pursuit of peace and prosperity in themselves. No humanistic policies will produce the national happiness envisioned by David—policies that leave out God. True political stability and national well-being must be related to God. Any nation that departs from God sows the seeds of its own disunity, discontentment, and dissolution. HAPPY IS THAT PEOPLE WHOSE GOD IS THE LORD. This reminds me of two songs we used to sing - the first one for adults and the other for children. Take time to read them today and make sure that your God is the Lord and that you can truly say 'Happiness is to know the Saviour' and 'I have the love of Jesus in my heart'

Happiness is to know the Savior
Living a life within His favour
Having a change in my behaviour
Happiness is the Lord!

Happiness is a new creation
Jesus and me in close relation
Having a part in His salvation
Happiness is the Lord!
Real joy is mine
No matter if teardrops start,
I've found the secret,
It's Jesus in my heart!

Happiness is to be forgiven
Living the life that's worth the living
Taking a trip that leads to heaven
Happiness is the Lord,
Happiness is the Lord,
Happiness is the Lord!

(Ira F. Stanphill)

Trust and obey, for there's no other way to be happy in Jesus, but to trust and obey (John H. Sammis).

'Give thanks in all circumstances; for this is the will of God in Christ Jesus for you' 1 Thessalonians 5:18

6TH FEBRUARY

COUNT YOUR BLESSINGS

*The blessing of the Lord makes rich, and
he adds no sorrow with it.*

Proverbs 10:22

I was greatly blessed at our Mid-Week prayer meeting by the prayer of one of the men of our Church who is in his 89th year. In tears he quoted the following words of the little chorus 'I am blessed' as a means of praising and thanking the Lord:

*'I am blessed
Every day of my life I am blessed
When I wake up in the morning
And I lay my head to rest
Every day of my life I am blessed'*

Later I read an article in one of the daily papers written by Dr Michael Mosley called 'Count your blessings': The following is an extract from it: 'Last thing at night, write down three things for which you feel grateful. There is solid science that getting into the habit of being regularly grateful can make you feel happier; lower your blood pressure, improve sleep, ease pain and even rewire your brain'. Reflecting on this at a personal level I thanked God for 1. My salvation, 2. My daily food, and 3. Soundness of mind. Then the words of the hymn 'count your many blessings' came to my mind. Let us prayerfully consider the words of this lovely hymn today:

*When upon life's billows you
are tempest tossed,
When you are discouraged, thinking all is lost,
Count your many blessings,
name them one by one,
And it will surprise you what
the Lord hath done.*

*Refrain: Count your blessings,
name them one by one;
Count your blessings, see what God hath done;
Count your blessings, name them one by one;
Count your many blessings, see
what God hath done.*

*Are you ever burdened with a load of care?
Does the cross seem heavy you
are called to bear?
Count your many blessings, ev'ry doubt will fly,
And you will be singing as the days go by.*

*When you look at others with
their lands and gold,
Think that Christ has promised
you His wealth untold;
Count your many blessings, money cannot buy
Your reward in heaven, nor
your home on high.*

*So, amid the conflict, whether great or small,
Do not be discouraged, God is over all;
Count your many blessings, angels will attend,
Help and comfort give you
to your journey's end.*

(Johnson Oatman)

Blessed is the man who remains steadfast under trial, for when he has stood the test he will receive the crown of life, which God has promised to those who love him' James 1:12

7TH FEBRUARY

PERMACRISIS

O our God, will you not execute judgment on them? For we are powerless against this great horde that is coming against us. We do not know what to do, but our eyes are on you.

2 Chronicles 20:12

Permacrisis was a word added to the Collins Corpus database in 2022. The database contains 4.5 billion entries and is the basis for the Harper Collins dictionary. They define permacrisis as 'an extended period of instability and insecurity'.

This led my mind to 2 Chronicles chapter 20 which relates the story of King Jehoshaphat when he and the nation of Judah were encountering a permacrisis.

So what did Jehoshaphat do when he encountered a permacrisis and what can we learn from the approach he took:

HE ENCOUNTERED A PERMACRISIS: An invasion of Judah by Moabites, Ammonites and Syrians. In earthly terms they didn't stand a chance v. 1–2. He went on to admit to the Lord: 'We do not know what to do' v. 12.

HE ENLISTED PRAYER: 'Then Jehoshaphat was afraid and set his face to seek the Lord, and proclaimed a fast throughout all Judah. And Judah assembled to seek help from the Lord; from all the cities of Judah they came to seek the Lord' v. 3–4.

HE EMBRACED A PROMISE v. 9: 'If disaster comes upon us, the sword, judgment, or pestilence, or famine, we will stand before this house and before you—for your name is in this house—and cry out to you in our affliction, and you will hear and save'.

They received a promise from God after they prayed: 'Thus says the Lord to you, do not be afraid and do not be dismayed at this great horde, for the battle is not your's but God's' v. 15 and 'You will not need to fight in this battle. Stand firm, hold your position, and see the salvation of the Lord on your behalf, O Judah and Jerusalem. Do not be afraid and do not be dismayed. Tomorrow go out against them, and the Lord will be with you' v. 17.

THEY EXPRESSED PRAISE and were delivered out of and from the permacrisis: 'And when they began to sing and praise, the Lord set an ambush against the men of Ammon, Moab, and Mount Seir, who had come against Judah, so that they were routed' v. 22.

Jehoshaphat and Judah focused their eyes upon the Lord: 'but our eyes are on you' v. 12. They were looking to God for deliverance, they trusted the Lord and He brought them through. Are you facing a permacrisis today? Then like Jehoshaphat and Judah:

Trust in the Lord and don't despair,
He is a friend so true!
No matter what your troubles are,
Jesus will see you through.
Sing, when the day is bright;
Sing, through the darkest night
Every day, all the way,
Let us sing, sing, sing!

8TH FEBRUARY

SAVED FROM WHAT

*For by grace you have been saved through faith. And
this is not your own doing; it is the gift of God.*

Ephesians 2:8

It is a wonderful thing to be saved
AND KNOW IT:

Saved by His pow'r, by His pow'r divine,
Saved to new life, to new life sublime!
Life now is sweet and my joy is complete,
For I'm saved, saved, saved.

(Jack P. Scholfield)

The world will mock saved people and
ask the question: Saved FROM what?
We are saved:

- FROM the wrath of God: Since,
  therefore, we have now been justified by his blood, much more shall
  we be saved by him from the wrath
  of God. Romans 5:9
- FROM our sins: She will bear a son,
  and you shall call his name Jesus,
  for he will save his people from
  their sins. Matthew 1:21.
- FROM this present evil world:
  who gave himself for our sins to
  deliver us from the present evil age,
  according to the will of our God
  and Father. Galatians 1:4
- FROM our enemies: that we should
  be saved from our enemies and
  from the hand of all who hate us.
  Luke 1:71
- FROM so great a death/deadly peril:
  He delivered us from such a deadly
  peril, and he will deliver us. On him
  we have set our hope that he will
  deliver us again. 2 Corinthians 1:10

- FROM the power of darkness: He
  has delivered us from the domain
  of darkness and transferred us to
  the kingdom of his beloved Son.
  Colossians 1:13
- FROM the Law: Its curse and
  burden: But now we are released
  from the law, having died to that
  which held us captive, so that we
  serve in the new way of the Spirit
  and not in the old way of the written code. Romans 7:6
- FROM evil men: And that we
  may be delivered from wicked
  and evil men. For not all have
  faith. 2 Thessalonians 3:2.
- FROM the bondage of corruption:
  That the creation itself will be set
  free from its bondage to corruption and obtain the freedom of
  the glory of the children of God.
  Romans 8:21.
- FROM the fear of death: And
  deliver all those who through fear
  of death were subject to lifelong
  slavery. Hebrews 2:15.
- FROM all our fears: I sought the
  Lord, and he answered me and
  delivered me from all my fears.
  Psalm 34:4.

Jesus saves me now,
Jesus saves me now;
Yes, Jesus saves me all the time;
Jesus saves me now.

(A. C. Downer)

9TH FEBRUARY

BURIED GRAINS

Truly, truly, I say to you, unless a grain of wheat falls into the earth and dies, it remains alone; but if it dies, it bears much fruit.

John 12:24

I had the privilege of serving with a mission agency called One Mission Society formerly called the Oriental Missionary Society. Lettie Cowman the wife of the founder was the second President of the mission. The following are some extracts from an article she wrote in 1944 called HARVEST SECRETS about 'BURIED GRAINS':

1. 'A cry from the heart of black slaves reached the throne of God and dark Africa stretched forth her dusky hand beseeching Him for help. God heard, but to answer their cry for help He needed a human voice. An angel could not carry to the black man the sweet story of Calvary love. A young Scotsman sat at His loom weaving when he heard a faint cry—a cry as of pain. He heard it in the night watches; he heard it in the daytime. Would he leave home, friends, all to bury himself amongst Africa's wilds? The whole wide world has the answer for David Livingstone was ploughed under on Africa's soil, and the harvest of his buried life is a multitude of blacks redeemed by the precious blood of Christ'

It is estimated that there are 115 Million evangelical Christians on the continent of Africa today.

2. 'The Lord of the harvest wanted to sow a great field with living seed in age-old China. He needed a sower. On a fine Sabbath morning in Brighton He found Hudson Taylor walking by the seashore. He spoke to him saying, if you would let me, I will walk all over China through you. And on that morn of all morns a grain of wheat fell into the ground and died. Multiplied thousands of living grains in the land of Sinim is the result—and the end is not yet!'

Hudson Taylor once said: 'China is not to be won for Christ by quiet, ease-loving men and women. The stamp of men and women we need is such as will put Jesus, China, [and] souls first and foremost in everything and at every time—even life itself must be secondary.'

Hudson Taylor was indeed 'BURIED GRAIN' and looked for workers who were prepared to become 'buried GRAIN'

It is estimated that there are around 100 million believers in China today.

3. 'Not all are commissioned literally to go forth to fields afar. A great company must stand in the homeland as rear guards. But all must become BURIED GRAINS and their consecration and surrender just as real and deep as those felt at the forefront'.

These extracts contain some quite challenging thoughts for us to consider today.

10TH FEBRUARY

O HAPPY DAY

*He who heeds the word wisely will find good, and
whoever trusts in the LORD, happy is he.*

Proverbs 16:20

2022 marked the 10th anniversary of the World Happiness Report, which uses global survey data to report how people evaluate their own lives in more than 150 countries worldwide. Over the last ten years, there has been an increased public interest in happiness.

The World Happiness Report is based on the Gallup World Poll, which surveys around 1,000 people per country in over 150 countries every year. The key question, used to create a ranking of the happiest countries in the world, asks people to evaluate their life as a whole on a scale of 0–10, from the worst possible to the best possible.

Long before The World Happiness Report was ever issued or thought about, God in His love and mercy wants us to be happy. Therefore today let us reflect on what real happiness looks like and how we can find true happiness. The only way to find happiness is through the LORD. He created us and knows us better than we know ourselves. As I thought on this my mind went to some verses of Philip Doddridge's lovely hymn:

*O happy day that fixed my choice
On Thee, my Savior and my God!
Well may this glowing heart rejoice,
And tell its raptures all abroad.*

Refrain:

*Happy day, happy day,
When Jesus washed my sins away!
He taught me how to watch and pray,
And live rejoicing every day;*

*Happy day, happy day,
When Jesus washed my sins away!*

*'Tis done, the great transaction's done;
I am my Lord's and He is mine;
He drew me and I followed on,
Rejoiced to own the call divine.*

*Now rest, my long-divided heart,
Fixed on this blissful centre, rest;
Here have I found a nobler part,
Here heavenly pleasures fill my breast.*

(Philip Doddridge)

George Muller writing about the Lord Jesus said: 'Intimate experimental acquaintance with Him will make us truly happy. Nothing else will'. True joy and true happiness comes from our faith in Jesus Christ. Joy and true happiness is everlasting because the source of it is everlasting. The following is a little acrostic using the word 'HAPPY' and the words part a little children's chorus which I trust will be helpful to you today:

H – HELP FROM GOD
A – ASSURANCE OF SALVATION
P – PLEASURES FOREVERMORE IN HEAVEN
P – POWER FROM THE HOLY SPIRIT
Y – YIELDING TO HIS WILL

*I'm inright, outright, upright, downright
Happy all the time
Since Jesus Christ came in
and cleansed my heart from sin
I'm inright, outright, upright, downright
Happy all the time*

11TH FEBRUARY

HOW MUCH I OWE

For what does the Scripture say? Abraham believed
God, and it was counted to him as righteousness.

Romans 4:3

As we read Romans 4 we learn that as believers we are counted righteous because of what Jesus achieved for us through His death and righteousness: 'That is why his faith was counted to him as righteousness. But the words 'it was counted to him' were not written for his sake alone, but for ours also. It will be counted to us who believe in him who raised from the dead Jesus our Lord, who was delivered up for our trespasses and raised for our justification' v. 22–25

This is our only hope of heaven because nothing that defileth will ever enter there. Praise God for Christ's imputed righteousness to every blood bought child of God.

It was Jesus, the righteous servant, who made it possible for many to be counted righteous, for he bore all our sins: 'Out of the anguish of his soul he shall see and be satisfied; by his knowledge shall the righteous one, my servant, make many to be accounted righteous, and he shall bear their iniquities' Isaiah 53:11.

This brings to mind verses of various hymns that make this point:

Jesus, your blood and righteousness
My beauty are, my glorious dress;
Mid flaming worlds, in these arrayed,
With joy shall I lift up my head.

Translator: John Wesley; Author: Nicolaus Ludwig, Graf von Zinzendorf (1739)

When I stand before the Throne,
Dressed in beauty not mine own.
When I see Thee as Thou art,
Love Thee with unsinning heart,
Then, Lord, shall I fully know-
Not to then—how much I owe.

Robert Murray McCheyne

At that day we pray, Lord Jesus,
To be found of Thee in peace,
Wearing not our filthy raiment,
But Thy Robe of Righteousness.

(Unknown)

God laid on Christ the iniquity of us all Isaiah 53:6, so that He was made sin and made a curse for us, by having our sin and our curse imputed to Him and laid to His account. Just as He became sin, so we when reconciled become the righteousness of God: 'For our sake he made him to be sin who knew no sin, so that in him we might become the righteousness of God' 2 Corinthians 5:21.

Surely as we consider today just something of what Christ has accomplished for us as believers, our earnest prayer about Him must be: 'MAY I KNOW YOU MORE CLEARLY, LOVE YOU MORE DEARLY, FOLLOW YOU MORE NEARLY, DAY BY DAY? AMEN'.

12TH FEBRUARY

SEEKING TO MAKE HIM KNOWN

He that believeth not is condemned already.

John3:18

The following is a testimony in the form of a poem which I found in a second hand book shop for your encouragement today.

I love to speak of Jesus—that Name how sweet it sounds
Oh, tell it out ye faithful to earth's remotest bounds
I love to speak of Jesus and what He's done for me
Twas in the year 1905, September twenty three.

I do remember well the day when on a pleasure bent
I got an invitation to a meeting in a tent
So just to please the person I decided to go in
No love for God or Christ had I, for I was dead in sin.

I was careless and indifferent whene'er I entered there
But ere that meeting ended I was almost in despair
John Chapter 3, and verse 18, was the text the speaker chose
When scenes of death and judgement before my vision rose.

Condemned already, fearful words, they fixed me to the seat
Struck terror to me when I thought' tis God I have to meet
Four weeks I struggled in the dark, and light I could not see
I longed to know how to be saved, and from my sins be free.

I then left Belfast City for the County Donegal
And the God of Grace was with me, and He overruled it all
For whilst engaged at work one day a letter I received
And as I read its contents o'er, I on the Lord believed.

H-A-T-H—those letters four were simply underlined
I just took in what God had said, and made His promise mine
Now many years have gone since then, and Christ remains the same
Eternal life He gives to those who trust His blessed Name.

And so I came to Jesus while standing on the roof
And in the good old Bible I have the blessed proof
While passing through this wicked world of sin, and woe, and strife
He that believeth on the Son HATH everlasting life.

Saved by the blood of Jesus, kept by His power alone
This my glorious privilege—seeking to make Him known
And when I see the Saviour I'll praise His blessed Name
For the love that stooped to save me from sin and death and shame.

Oh, sinners trust in Jesus, He'll make your life anew
And when at home in glory you'll praise the Saviour too
Yes, you and I together, in heavenly mansions bright
Will bless the Lord that saved us from hell's eternal night.

Oh, sinners don't reject Him, but trust Him now today
Hast thou not travelled long enough the broad and crowded way?
In grace He waits to save you from dark impending doom
And take you home to be with Him in His eternal home.

(FRANK KNOX, BELFAST)

'He that believeth on the Son hath everlasting life' John 3:36

13TH FEBRUARY

A HEAVEN-SENT VISION

*Where there is no prophetic vision the people cast off
restraint, but blessed is he who keeps the law.*

Proverbs 29:18

The word 'vision' used here in our text verse today, has to do with the Word of God. Where there is no Word of God, where there is no message of life, and as a result, the people perish. This is the primary interpretation of Proverbs 29:18. The word 'vision' is also associated with what we see with the mind's eye.

I have a copy of the 18th May 1957 edition of 'The Elim Evangel' given to me by my mother. My parents kept it as my dedication on Easter Sunday April 21st at Brookeborough Elim Church, was mentioned in it.

However, it was an article written in it regarding Vision written by Ken Smith the then Minister of Elim Church, Pontardulais that caught my attention. The following is a summary of the article which is still relevant today:

It is not much good singing 'Rescue the perishing' with your feet on the mantle shelf. Someone has said 'A task without a vision is drudgery, a vision without a task is a dream, but a task with a vision is victory'. . . . A so-called vision which does not affect our work and witness for Christ is earth-born and not heaven-sent.

He went on to point out the following aspects of vision that are necessary if we are to be effective for God:

A VISION OF THE VALUE OF A SOUL: The potentialities of a soul are immense, and Jesus Christ valued the soul of man above all else in the world.

A VISION OF THE VILENESS OF SIN: The sins of saints and sinners are vile. We must realise the loathsomeness of sin before we can be freed from its power.

A VISION OF THE VERACITY (ACCURACY) OF THE WORD OF GOD: The exhortation of Paul to Timothy was to 'Preach the Word', and it is still the need of the Church—preachers of the WORD –for the ultimate purpose of all preaching is to see the 'Living Word', by the written Word, through the spoken word.

A VISION OF THE VANITY OF THE WORLD: John's epistle commands us to 'love not the world neither the things in the world', for we are to set our heart's affections on Him.

A VISION OF THE VICTORY IN JESUS CHRIST: We are not fighting to win a battle—we must live in victory which Jesus Christ won for us two thousand years ago. John claims that it is our faith in Jesus Christ which gives us victory.

O victory in Jesus, my Savior, forever!
He sought me and bought me
with His redeeming blood;
He loved me ere I knew Him,
and all my love is due Him.
He plunged me to victory beneath
the cleansing flood

(E. M. Bartlett)

14TH FEBRUARY

GIVE ME A VISION

Where there is no vision, the people perish: but
he that keepeth the law, happy is he.

Proverbs 29:18 (KKV)

Over the years I have heard various preachers quote the late Dr Stephen F. Olford in their sermons. Indeed I have a number of his books in my study. I appreciate his insights on various spiritual topics. The following are some of his thoughts on 'Vision':

'The word 'vision' occurs some 31 times in the Old Testament and denotes that which is communicated by God to man through prophetic preaching. In the context of today's verse, it refers to the prophetic vision of God as related to man'.

Without anointed preaching the people cast off restraint. Does this remind you of our current state in the west? Olford goes on to say that 'as salt of the earth, God's people are expected to arrest corruption, and as light of the world they are commanded to dispel darkness. But 'where there is no vision' the reverse happens: people become spiritually defenceless; people become naturally defiant and people become personally destructive'.

The answer to these problems is vision. Dr Olford goes on to say that 'prophetic vision produces redemptive passion. When Jesus 'saw the multitudes, He was moved with compassion for them, because they were weary and scattered, like sheep without a shepherd' (Matt 9:36). This redemptive passion leads to responsive action. Having looked out on the multitudes Jesus said to His disciples: 'The harvest truly is plentiful, but the labourers are few. Therefore pray the Lord of the harvest to send out labourers into His harvest' (Matt 9:36–38)".

Indeed this prayer was answered because as we know these disciples were the answer to their own prayer.

Dr Olford continues: 'This is the best outworking of true vision! To have this redemptive concern slays selfishness, laziness, and carelessness in us and sends us forth to seek and to save that which is lost. Redemptive passion always leads to responsive action; vision begets venture'.

I have shared in various parts of this book that I had COVID on my 44th spiritual birthday. As I was housebound I was led to read Dr Wesley Duewel's book: 'Measure your Life: 17 ways to evaluate your life from God's perspective'. One of those measurements was: 'Measure your Life by your Vision'. He finishes off that chapter with one of his poems called: 'Give Me A Vision': The following is the first and last verse of the poem:

Give me a vision of sin's dark night,
Millions still fettered by Satan's night.
Show me the darkness where shines no light-
Show me the need of the world

Show me the Christ of eternity;
Show me Gethsemane's agony.
Show me the love of dark Calvary;
Give me His love for the world.

Lord give me redemptive passion that leads me to responsive action I pray.

15TH FEBRUARY

THE FACE OF JESUS

Those who look to him are radiant.

Psalm 34:5

On Good Friday 2022 my good 100 year old friend Alfie Kells rang me to share some thoughts with me concerning a sermon series he heard many years preciously on 'THE FACE OF JESUS', preached by the late Rev Bert Finlay. On that Good Friday morning Alfie was meditating on the scarred face of Jesus. He said that Mr Finlay had said the lovely face of Jesus was unrecognisable as He took our place, our punishment that day at Calvary. Alfie was really moved that morning as He was so thankful for what the dear Son of God accomplished on his behalf when He made that one sacrifice for sin forever on the cross as his substitute and as his sin bearer. Alfie went on to tell me that he and his dear late wife Maud had gone on to post this sermon series to various missionaries they supported in different countries around the world at that time because it is the message of the Cross that makes the difference in people's lives. It the vital aspect of the Gospel. It is where they find forgiveness for their sin and peace with God.

There's a way back to God
From the dark paths of sin;
There's a door that is open
And you may go in:
At Calvary's cross Is where you begin,
When you come as a sinner to Jesus

I see the love of my Father
In the earth, the sky and the sea
But I see it best
In the gift of his son
Who died on the cross for me.

(E. H. Swinstead)

On a later date that year when I visited Alfie who was now 101 he discussed Mr Finlay's sermon series on the 'Face of Jesus'. He recalled some of the following aspects of the Saviour's face that Mr Finlay preached his series around: His scarred face, His sad face, His smiling face and His serene face. Alfie thought there were eight in total. What a wonderful time we had meditating and discussing together this aspect of the suffering of our wonderful Lord and Saviour Jesus Christ on our behalf. It was just wonderful to spend time with a lovely old believer who really appreciated all that Jesus did on his behalf so that he could have his sins forgiven and go to heaven one day saved by His precious blood.

And while it is just wonderful when we get glimpses of something of Christ's sufferings on our behalf, the following words of Elizabeth Cecilia Clephane's hymn are also true:

But none of the ransomed ever knew
how deep were the waters crossed;
nor how dark was the night
that the Lord passed thro'
ere he found his sheep that was lost.

16TH FEBRUARY

THE FACE OF GOD

*But Jesus said to him, Judas, would you
betray the Son of Man with a kiss?*

Luke 22:48

In our devotion yesterday I shared about a discussion I had with my friend Alfie about various aspects and scriptural pictures regarding the face of Jesus. Over these next few days we will look at the face of Jesus as revealed in the Bible.

HIS SOVEREIGN FACE: I love the Christmas song written by Mark Lowry regarding the incarnation of the Lord Jesus Christ from Mary's viewpoint:

*Mary, did you know that your baby boy
Would one day walk on water?
Mary, did you know that your baby boy
Would save our sons and daughters?
Did you know that your baby boy
Has come to make you new?
This child that you delivered,
will soon deliver you*

*Mary, did you know that your baby boy
Will give sight to a blind man?
Mary, did you know that your baby boy
Will calm the storm with his hand?
Did you know that your baby boy
Has walked where angels trod?
When you kiss your little baby
You kiss the face of God*

*Mary, did you know that your baby boy
Is Lord of all creation?
Mary, did you know that your baby boy
Would one day rule the nations?
Did you know that your baby boy
Is heaven's perfect Lamb?
That sleeping child you're
holding is the great, I Am*

(Mark Lowry / Buddy Greene)

When you are looking into the face of Jesus you are not only looking into a human face but into the face of God: 'For the law was given through Moses; grace and truth came through Jesus Christ. No one has ever seen God; the only God, who is at the Father's side, he has made him known'. John 1:17–18. Jesus manifested the face of God to mankind.

It is hard to believe that on the night before His crucifixion Judas betrayed Jesus by kissing His cheek: 'Now the betrayer had given them a sign, saying, The one I will kiss is the man. Seize him and lead him away under guard'. Mark 14:44. In the culture of first-century Israel, a kiss on the cheek was a common greeting, a sign of deep respect, honour, and brotherly love. What really stands out in the way of Judas's betrayal is that Judas used such an intimate expression of love and respect to betray Jesus. One has said that Judas in kissing Jesus, 'Kissed the Door of Heaven and went to Hell'. I trust as we look at the face of Jesus that it is a look of appreciation at the one: 'who loved me and gave himself for me'. Galatians 2:20

*Looking in the face of Jesus,
Wondrous beauty there I see;
Tenderness divine abounding,
Purer love there could not be.*

(Harry Dixon Clarke)

17TH FEBRUARY

SHINE JESUS SHINE

And he was transfigured before them, and his face shone
like the sun, and his clothes became white as light.

Matthew 17:2

Yesterday we looked at the SOVEREIGN FACE of Jesus. Speaking about the face of Jesus S.D.Gordon said: 'The glory of God was in the face of Jesus as He walked quietly among men. Looking into that face men saw God. That simple, gentle, patient, pure face, with its deep peace and victory and yet its yearning -- that was God looking out into men's faces'.

Today we will look at the following scriptural pictures of the face of Jesus:

HIS SMILING FACE: The Bible doesn't specifically speak of Jesus smiling. In fact the Bible teaches us that He was a man of sorrows and acquainted with grief. And so He was. However this doesn't mean that was His posture all the time. The writer of Hebrews informs us of what God the Father said about the smile of Jesus: 'But of the Son he says. . . You have loved righteousness and hated wickedness; therefore God, your GOD, HAS ANOINTED YOU WITH THE OIL OF GLADNESS BEYOND YOUR COMPANIONS'. Hebrews 1:8–9. Many scriptures would indicate that Jesus smiled on many occasions while on earth.

The smilings of Thy face,
How amiable they are!
'Tis heav'n to rest in Thine embrace,
And nowhere else but there.

(Isaac Watts)

HIS SHINING FACE: 'The Lord bless you and keep you; the Lord make his face to shine upon you and be gracious to you; the Lord lift up his countenance upon you and give you peace'. Numbers 6:25–26. On the mountain of transfiguration Jesus took on his glorified, heavenly, majestic form. His face shone as the sun! Through his body showed his divinity. Through his human nature was shown his heavenly nature! He was confirming to the inner circle of apostles (Peter, James, and John) and later through his Word to us his authority as heaven's representative on earth.

I trust that we know the smile and shine of Jesus face today:

Lord, the light of your love is shining
In the midst of the darkness, shining
Jesus, Light of the world, shine upon us
Set us free by the truth you now bring us
Shine on me, shine on me

(Graham Kendrick)

Of all the faces of the human race,
None shine so bright as the Saviour's face.
Of all whom we love, of all whom we embrace,
There is none who can take the Master's place.
Be willing however great the price
To follow the light from the face of Christ.
The Face of Jesus
The Face of Jesus

(Elisabeth Elliot)

18TH FEBRUARY

WEEP O'ER THE ERRING ONE

And when he was come near, he beheld the city, and wept over it.

Luke 19:41

Over these past days we are considering various scriptural pictures of the face of Jesus. We have looked at the sovereign, smiling and shining face of Jesus.

Today we will consider:

HIS SAD FACE: The Bible records that Jesus shed tears on various occasions. As mentioned previously Jesus was a man of sorrows and acquainted with grief. Isaiah 53:3. The Bible records various occasions of sorrow and sadness for Jesus: In fact, one of the best known verses in the Bible referring to His sad face is John 11:35 which says 'Jesus wept'. Another time we see Jesus weep is in Luke 19:41–42: 'And when he drew near and saw the city, he wept over it, saying, Would that you, even you, had known on this day the things that make for peace! But now they are hidden from your eyes'. Here Jesus is about to enter Jerusalem. As He approaches the city, the road gives a panoramic view of the city. There Jesus is overcome with grief and weeps because He is broken- hearted that Jerusalem and His chosen people are missing out on the coming of the Messiah–an event they had anticipated for generations. Yet because they had strayed from God, they were ignorant of what was happening. It broke His heart. A missed opportunity to come to Him as Saviour and Lord.

At a mission I attended in 2010, the speaker one night made the following points including comments on Luke 19:41 which I trust will be a benefit to us today:

- A DAY THAT NEVER WILL BE RELIVED (Weeping): Luke 19:41–42
- A DEATH THAT NEVER WILL BE REPEATED (Calvary): Luke 23: 33–34:
- A DOOR THAT NEVER WILL BE RE-OPENED (When salvation's door is closed): Luke 13:22–25:
- A DECISION THAT NEVER WILL BE REGRETTED (She got to Jesus): Luke 8:43–44
- A DEBT THAT NEVER WILL BE REPAID (True Christianity a life of devotion): Luke 7:40–43:

Jesus is still concerned about the lost. Just as Jesus wept for the lost so should we. Jesus wept in the face of death, knowing that death was a result of sin. Yet we can rejoice in the fact that Jesus did something about this. He paid the debt for our sins, a debt that we never can repay. He has conquered death. It is our responsibility to tell others of this wonderful compassionate Saviour who has provided eternal life for all those who put their faith and trust in Him alone for salvation. We need to get people to Jesus before it is for ever too late.

Rescue the perishing,
Care for the dying,
Snatch them in pity from sin and the grave;
Weep o'er the erring one,
Lift up the fallen,
Tell them of Jesus the mighty to save.

(Fanny Crosby)

19TH FEBRUARY

HE SET HIS FACE

And it came to pass, when the time was come that he should be received up, he stedfastly set his face to go to Jerusalem.

Luke 9:51

HIS SET FACE: The Prophet Isaiah 700 years before Jesus came prophesied that the coming Messiah would set His face like a flint to go to Calvary: 'The Lord God has opened my ear, and I was not rebellious; I turned not backward. I gave my back to those who strike, and my cheeks to those who pull out the beard; I hid not my face from disgrace and spitting. But the Lord God helps me; therefore I have not been disgraced; therefore I have set my face like a flint, and I know that I shall not be put to shame' Isaiah 50:5–7

The ultimate purpose or reason Jesus came to earth was to go to Calvary and die on our behalf as our substitute. When the time came Jesus was determined to go to the cross:

Jesus knew He would be beaten, even on His face, and yet He trusted in God's power and plan for His life that He set His face 'like a flint.' He determined that nothing and no one, especially the devil, would stop Him from His appointed mission. The following is a part of a devotional article by Toby Powers that explains just what it meant for Jesus to 'Set His Face':

- 'This phrase 'set his face' shows us his determination.
- Though he knew what would become of him, he set his face.
- Though he knew he would be doubted, he set his face.
- Though he knew he would be rejected, he set his face.
- Though he knew he would be arrested, he set his face.
- Though he knew he would be carried from prison and to judgment, he set his face.
- Though he knew the crowd would cry 'crucify him!' he set his face.
- Though he knew all his disciples would forsake him fleeing, he set his face.
- Though he knew he would be beaten, spat upon, and mocked, he set his face.
- Though he knew he would be hanged on a rugged cross, he set his face.
- Though he knew he would thirst, he set his face.
- Though he knew he would be buried in a borrowed tomb, he set his face. . .
- Because he knew that he would rise on the third day, he set his face! Hebrews 12:1–2'.

'Wherefore seeing we also are compassed about with so great a cloud of witnesses, let us lay aside every weight, and the sin which doth so easily beset us, and let us run with patience the race that is set before us, Looking unto Jesus the author and finisher of our faith; who for the joy that was set before him endured the cross, despising the shame, and is set down at the right hand of the throne of God.'

20TH FEBRUARY

WOULD HE DEVOTE THAT SACRED HEAD FOR SINNERS SUCH AS I?

As many were astonished at you—his appearance was so marred, beyond human semblance, and his form beyond that of the children of mankind

Isaiah 52:14

Over these past days we have been looking at various aspects of the face of Jesus. We have looked at the Sovereign, Smiling, Shining, Sad and Set face of Jesus. Today we will consider:

HIS STRICKEN FACE AND SCARRED FACE: 'And the men that held Jesus mocked him, and smote him. And when they had blindfolded him, they struck him on the face, and asked him, saying, Prophesy, who is it that smote thee? Luke 22:63–64

HIS SPAT UPON, SMITTEN AND SLAPPED FACE: 'Then they spit in his face and struck him. And some slapped him' Matthew 26:67

HIS SUFFERING FACE: Never forget that Jesus was the spotless Lamb offered in sacrifice, and so even though He was made ugly by the sin of man, He was in His own perfection the most beautiful of all men. We ought never to lose the picture of His suffering face. This was none other than God manifested in flesh: 'Great indeed, we confess, is the mystery of godliness: He was manifested in the flesh' 1 Timothy 3:16

Jesus was marred beyond human likeness, He was left unrecognisable: 'As many were astonied at thee; his visage was so marred more than any man, and his form more than the sons of men' Isaiah 52:14 KJV. The face of Jesus was greatly disfigured. The question is why? The simple answer being, it was for you and me:

There was One who was willing to die in my stead,

That a soul so unworthy might live,
And the path to the cross He was willing to tread,
All the sins of my life to forgive.

Refrain: They are nailed to the cross,
They are nailed to the cross,
O how much He was willing to bear!
With what anguish and loss,
Jesus went to the cross
And He carried my sins with Him there!

(Carrie Ellis Breck)

Alas! and did my Savior bleed,
and did my Sovereign die!
Would he devote that sacred head
for sinners such as I?

Was it for crimes that I have done,
he groaned upon the tree?
Amazing pity! Grace unknown!
And love beyond degree!

Well might the sun in darkness hide,
and shut its glories in,
when Christ, the mighty maker, died
for man the creature's sin.

Thus might I hide my blushing face
while his dear cross appears;
dissolve my heart in thankfulness,
and melt mine eyes to tears.

But drops of tears can ne'er repay
the debt of love I owe.
Here, Lord, I give myself away;
'tis all that I can do.

(Isaac Watts)

21ST FEBRUARY

TURN YOUR EYES UPON JESUS

You who are of purer eyes than to see evil
and cannot look at wrong.

Habakkuk 1:13

Over these past days we have looked at various Biblical snapshots of the face of Jesus. Today we are looking at two very solemn pictures of His face:

HIS SECRET FACE: What do we mean by His secret face? Jesus withholds the view of His lovely face from the sinner and the godless: 'There is no one who calls upon your name, who rouses himself to take hold of you; for you have hidden your face from us, and have made us melt in the hand of our iniquities'. Isaiah 64:7. 'Then my anger will be kindled against them in that day, and I will forsake them and hide my face from them, and they will be devoured. And many evils and troubles will come upon them, so that they will say in that day, Have not these evils come upon us because our God is not among us? And I will surely hide my face in that day because of all the evil that they have done, because they have turned to other gods'. Deuteronomy 31:17–18. It does suffice to say that the Lord turns His face away from sin, iniquity and transgressions. And yet God in His mercy promises to turn His face towards us again if we would only turn again to Him 'for if you return to the Lord, your brothers and your children will find compassion with their captors and return to this land. For the Lord your God is gracious and merciful and will not turn away his face from you, if you return to him'. 2 Chronicles 30:9.

HIS STERN FACE: In our modern world we often look upon sin lightly. This is not so with Jesus. 'For the eyes of the Lord are on the righteous, and his ears are open to their prayer. But the face of the Lord is against those who do evil' I Peter 3:12. There are many other scriptures that reference the fact that God set a stern face against evildoers. The Lord Jesus takes sin seriously. He deals with sin. Ultimately God will judge sin: 'because he has fixed a day on which he will judge the world in righteousness by a man whom he has appointed; and of this he has given assurance to all by raising him from the dead' Acts 17:31.

Today as believers we can rejoice that we have the approving smile of Jesus' face upon us. If per chance you are reading this and you are living in sin why not turn to Him today and He will no longer hide His face from you but will save you and redeem you and bring you under His smile of approval:

O soul are you weary and troubled
No light in the darkness you see
There's light for a look at the Savior
And life more abundant and free

(Helen H. Lemmel)

22ND FEBRUARY

SEEK MY FACE

*You have said, Seek my face. My heart says
to you, Your face, Lord, do I seek.*

Psalm 27:8

Today we will look at another biblical portrait of the face of Jesus. Well could Harry Dixon Clarke write:

*Looking in the face of Jesus,
Wondrous beauty there I see;
Tenderness divine abounding,
Purer love there could not be.*

HIS SOUGHT FACE: The bible points out repeatedly that if we are earnest about seeking Jesus He will be found: 'You will seek me and find me, when you seek me with all your heart' Jeremiah 29:13. In terms of our Salvation we need to seek the Lord now: 'Seek the Lord while he may be found; call upon him while he is near' Isaiah 55:6. Jesus has promised that He will turn no one away.

As believers we need to seek the Lord's face continually: 'Seek the Lord and his strength, seek his face continually' I Chronicles 16:11 KJV. We can seek God's face through His Word, through prayer, through worship.

*Lord Jesus Christ, we seek Thy face;
Within the veil we bow the knee;
Oh, let Thy glory fill the place,
And bless us while we wait on Thee.*

(Alexander Stewart)

We to seek the Lord for revival: There is no doubt that from a Christian's perspective there is a great need for revival in the UK and Ireland.

Some years ago I did an M. A in Theology. My dissertation was based on the following question: 'Is it possible for the church in Ireland to experience revival in the 21st century?'. Sometime after this I attended a conference where Harold Vaughan was speaking on revival. He asked the following question: 'Is revival possible today?' He answered this question with just one word: 'Absolutely'. This was the conclusion that came out of the dissertation I undertook but with a lot more words!

Harold made the following comments in seeking the Lord's face for revival today from 2 Chronicles 7

CIRCUMSTANCES WHERE GOD CAN WORK: 'Then the Lord appeared to Solomon in the night and said to him: I have heard your prayer and have chosen this place for myself as a house of sacrifice. When I shut up the heavens so that there is no rain, or command the locust to devour the land, or send pestilence among my people' v. 12–13. God can work where there is disobedience, drought (Spiritual), destruction and disease (sin of all sorts)

CONDITIONS FOR GOD TO WORK: 'if my people who are called by my name humble themselves, and pray and seek my face and turn from their wicked ways' v. 14. If my people get: Humble, Hungry and Honest

CONSEQUENCES WHEN GOD WORKS: 'then I will hear from heaven and will forgive their sin and heal their land'.

Let us earnestly seek the Lord's face for revival in our land today.

23RD FEBRUARY

FACE TO FACE WITH CHRIST MY SAVIOUR

They will see his face.

Revelation 22:4

Over these past days we have looked at various pictures or portraits of the face of Jesus. As we looked through Scriptures for brief glimpses into some of the facial expressions of Jesus we looked at His: Sovereign; Smiling; Shining; Sad; Set; Stricken; Scarred; Slapped; Smitten; Spat upon; Secret; Stern and Sought face. Today we are going to look at: HIS SEEN FACE:

Oh, the soul thrilling rapture
when I view His blessed face,
And the lustre of His kindly beaming eye;
How my full heart will praise Him
for the mercy, love and grace
That prepared for me a mansion in the sky.

(Fanny Crosby)

During Lockdown in the Covid-19 pandemic period, face - to - face meetings by in large stopped. We commenced communicating by mobile or landline. For me Zoom Meetings became a regular feature. While I praised God for modern technology there is still nothing better than communicating face to face in person. In a face-to-face meeting those involved are in each other's physical presence, and in each other's sight, directly connecting with each other, and in close enough proximity to discern facial expressions.

Each individual believer will one day see Jesus face to face. The thought of looking in the face of Jesus has been the theme of many hymns over the years. As we conclude our thoughts on the face of Jesus let us rejoice and consider the following verses of hymns that reflect this tremendous truth:

Looking in the face of Jesus,
Hope and comfort there I see,
Giving me that blest assurance
That He will return for me.
On that day I shall be like Him
Clothed in immortality,
When I rise in His own likeness
Living on, His life in me.

(Harry Dixon Clarke)

By and by when I look on His face,
Beautiful face, thorn-shadowed face;
By and by when I look on His face,
I'll wish I had given Him more
More, so much more —
More of my love than I e'er gave before.
By and by when I look on His face,
I'll wish I had given Him more.

(Grace Reese Adkins)

What a day that will be,
When my Jesus I shall see,
And I look upon His face,
The One who saved me by His grace;
When He takes me by the hand,
And leads me through the Promised Land,
What a day, glorious day that will be.

There'll be no sorrow there,
No more burdens to bear,
No more sickness, no pain,
No more parting over there;
And forever I will be,
With the One who died for me,
What a day, glorious day that will be.

(Jim Hill)

24TH FEBRUARY

JESUS LIVES

*But he laid his right hand on me, saying, Fear
not, I am the first and the last, and the living one.
I died, and behold I am alive for evermore.*

Revelation 1:17–18

Jesus is a living person and not just an historical character. Other religions reverence the memory, treasure the relics, and study the teachings of their long-since dead founders. Christianity is totally different. Our founder is alive. We can sing with assurance that:

*I serve a risen Saviour
He's in the world today.
I know that He is living,
Whatever men may say.*

*I see His hand of mercy;
I hear His voice of cheer;
And just the time I need Him
He's always near.*

*He lives, He lives, Christ Jesus lives today!
He walks with me and talks with me
along life's narrow way.
He lives, He lives, salvation to impart!
You ask me how I know He lives?
He lives within my heart.*

(A. H. Ackley)

Jesus is the first who has risen triumphant over death and the grave. The Lord Jesus is the first begotten from the dead. Death could not hold Him. Death hath no more dominion over Him. And here is the great truth for us today - everyone who trusts in Him as Saviour and Lord has eternal life and will live eternally. Jesus said: 'Because I live, you also will live'. John 14:19

Because Jesus lives we have 1. His presence to surround us; 2. His peace to secure us; 3. His power to strengthen us; 4. His purpose to stir us; and 5. His promise to satisfy us.

The following is one part of the story behind the hymn: 'I serve a risen Saviour': In 1933, Alfred Ackley, a musician and preacher, wrote the famous hymn 'He Lives'. At the time, Ackley was challenged by a young Jewish student who was confused as to why Christians worshipped someone who had died centuries earlier. In response, Ackley is quoted as saying, He lives, I tell you, He is not dead but lives here and now! Jesus Christ is more alive today than ever before. I can prove it by my own experience, as well as the testimony of countless thousands.

Motivated by the student's questions, Ackley wrote this lovely hymn. His refrain is so encouraging, reminding us all that Jesus rose from the dead as promised and remains alive today in the heart of every believer.

Can you say today: You ask me how I know He lives? He lives within my heart. If you can why not share your testimony using the words of the chorus of Bill and Gloria Gaither's lovely song:

*Because He lives, I can face tomorrow,
Because He lives, all fear is gone;
Because I know He holds the future,
And life is worth the living,
Just because He lives!*

25TH FEBRUARY

GOD IS SO GOOD

Oh, how abundant is your goodness.

Psalm 31:19

One of the wonderful lessons I learned while serving the Lord with a Mission Agency was the need for a team of supporters. Those who support you in prayer, finance, encouragement and advice. One of these is my friend Alfie Kells. At the time of writing this he is in his 102nd year and is of sound mind and alert mentally. On one of my visits with him he repeated on at least three occasions: 'God is so good'. He was particularly referring to the goodness of God towards him since he met Jesus in a saving way some 60 years earlier. After visiting Alfie I always come away blessed and refreshed and often reflected and meditated on the things we spoke about from the Scripture, about following Jesus and about various Mission outreaches Alfie was involved with over the years. On this occasion I came away thinking about God's goodness. I found myself singing and reflecting on the words of the following songs:

God is so good,
God is so good,
God is so good,
He's so good to me.

(Paul Makai)

I love You, Lord
Oh Your mercy never fails me
All my days, I've been held in Your hands
From the moment that I wake up
Until I lay my head
Oh, I will sing of the goodness of God

'Cause all my life You have been faithful
And all my life You have been so, so good
With every breath that I am able
Oh, I will sing of the goodness of God

(Ed Cash, Ben Fielding, Jason Ingram, Brian Johnson, and Jenn Johnson)

Let us thank God for the following two aspects of His goodness today: The first being the goodness of God that led us to repentance: 'Or despisest thou the riches of his goodness and forbearance and longsuffering; not knowing that the goodness of God leadeth thee to repentance?' Romans 2:4 KJV. Both Alfie and I rejoice in the fact that God led us to repentance. There was a time in our life's experience when we recognised we were sinners and in need of a Saviour. We put our faith and trust in Him alone for salvation.

The second is for every good and perfect gift He has given to us since: 'Every good gift and every perfect gift is from above, coming down from the Father of lights, with whom there is no variation or shadow due to change'. James 1:17. Lehman Strauss commenting on this verse said: 'God is the Author of all that is good. Solicitation to do wrong comes from men and Satan but never from God. He is not the source of our sin and sufferings. Behind every mercy and blessing stands God, the Giver of every good and perfect gift. He is a great giver'.

26TH FEBRUARY

HOW GOOD IS THE GOD WE ADORE

*Oh give thanks to the Lord, for he is good, for
his steadfast love endures forever!*

Psalm 107:1

Yesterday I shared about my friend Alfie Kells aged 101 and how he expressed to me on one of my visits the goodness of God throughout his long life. 'How good is the God we adore' was one of the songs the Lord brought to my mind when reflecting on the goodness of God that Alfie testified to. The writer of the hymn was Joseph Hart, an unbeliever. He had periods in his life where he lived in outward sin, and periods where he lived an outwardly moral life but inwardly committed the sin of self-righteousness, trusting his own works to save him. Then, for a time, he asserted that it didn't matter how you live, as long as you believed God. During this period of his life, Hart wrote a pamphlet titled, 'The Unreasonableness of Religion' against John Wesley. In 1757, at the age of 45, Joseph Hart was saved by God's grace through the preaching of George Whitefield. He repented of his past self-righteousness, repudiated his pamphlet and apologised to Wesley, and began a life of service to the Lord that lasted for 11 years until the Lord took him Home. (Source: Jon Gleason)

How good is the God we adore!
Our faithful, unchangeable friend:
his love is as great as his pow'r
and knows neither measure nor end.
For Christ is the first and the last;
his Spirit will guide us safe home;
we'll praise him for all that is past
and trust him for all that's to come.

(J. Hart)

Like Alfie and Joseph Hart we too can say 'How good is the God we adore' when we think of His great love towards us in sending Jesus to be our Saviour.

God's goodness is one of His divine attributes. It is a part of His very nature as God. Therefore, being good, showing His goodness, is as much what God is as what God does:

THE LORD IS GOOD—TRUST HIM
The Lord is good to all, and his mercy is over all that he has made. Psalm 145:9

THE LORD IS GOOD—TELL OF HIM
For the Lord is good; his steadfast love endures forever, and his faithfulness to all generations. Psalm 100:5

THE LORD IS GOOD - TRY HIM
Oh, taste and see that the Lord is good! Blessed is the man who takes refuge in him! Psalm 34:8

THE LORD IS GOOD –THANK HIM
The Lord is good, a stronghold in the day of trouble; he knows those who take refuge in him. Nahum 1:7

27TH FEBRUARY

SIN AT THE DOOR

*If you do well, will you not be accepted? And if you
do not do well, sin is crouching at the door.*

Genesis 4:7

As recorded in Genesis 3 sin entered the world through the fall: 'Therefore, just as sin came into the world through one man, and death through sin, and so death spread to all men because all sinned' Romans 5:12. Cain was the first human ever to be born on earth after the fall of his parents Adam and Eve. Adam's sin was imputed to the entire human race so that each person is born in sin. Sometime later Abel was born. He too was born a sinner.

However Adam and Eve had instructed their family how to approach God in worship. After the fall God provided the clothing of animal skins after His judgement of their sin. God taught Adam and Eve the symbolism of those skins, revealing to them that the way out of judgement and back into a right relationship with Him would be through the blood of a prescribed sacrifice. The two boys would have been taught this and knew it. However we read that: 'In the course of time Cain brought to the Lord an offering of the fruit of the ground, and Abel also brought of the firstborn of his flock and of their fat portions. And the Lord had regard for Abel and his offering, but for Cain and his offering he had no regard. So Cain was very angry, and his face fell. The Lord said to Cain, Why are you angry, and why has your face fallen? If you do well, will you not be accepted? And if you do not do well, sin is crouching at the door. Its desire is contrary to you, but you must rule over it'.

Abel came in the God appointed way, Cain came in his own way. The phrase 'sin crouching at the door' depicts a wild animal such as a lion, ready to pounce on you. This is the word picture about the attack of sin. This word picture is not a literal door, but portrays Cain's heart as a door. Cain wanted salvation on his terms. Abel accepted God's way of salvation. As a result of his sin Cain ended up murdering his brother. The words of the following song remind us that:

Sin will take you farther than you want to go
Slowly and wholly taking control
Sin will keep you longer than you want to stay
Sin will cost you far more
than you want to pay.

God made provision for Cain before and after he made the wrong sacrifice. Cain rejected. Today we thank God and accept the provision He has made in Christ for our sin: 'In him we have redemption through his blood, the forgiveness of our trespasses, according to the riches of his grace' Ephesians 1:7.

28TH FEBRUARY

THE DOOR OF SALVATION

*I am the door. If anyone enters by me, he will be
saved and will go in and out and find pasture.*

John 10:9

Speaking about our salvation Jesus did not say He was 'a' door, rather He called Himself 'The Door'. Jesus communicated in very simple everyday language. Doors are something we are all very familiar with and they are an essential part of everyday life. You cannot get into physical structures without them. Likewise, heaven has a door, salvation has a door, and a relationship with God requires a door. Jesus makes it clear that there is a door into heaven and that He is that Door. He also made it clear that there is only one Door to Heaven and He is that Door. As individuals we do not have access through certain doors. Some doors read: 'Keep Out' 'Staff Only' or 'Only Authorized Personnel' etc. etc. The message is clear, we are not to try to enter those doors. However this door is inviting. Jesus makes it clear that He is the Door of salvation and it is open for everyone. It is for the 'Whosoever'. All have need of this door and all have access. Let us praise God today for 'The Door' of Salvation, the Lord Jesus Christ Himself. If per chance you are reading this and you have never entered this Door why not today.

I am the Door, I am the Door;
By Me if any man enter in,
He shall be saved,
he shall be saved,
he shall be saved.

(Unknown)

I am the door; if any man by Me shall enter in,
He shall be saved, and shall go

forth a conqu'ror over sin.
In pastures green his soul shall
feed, beside still waters lie,
And nothing shall he ever need,
for God is his supply.

Refrain: I am the door, I have one
fold, and all who dwell in Me
And I in them are in My fold;
their spirits all agree.

I am the door; I know My sheep
and I am known of Mine;
Within My book their names I
keep, My fold is all divine.
Though robbers create other folds
to lead My sheep astray,
And many say, 'Lo, here; lo,
there,' I yet remain the Way.

I'm the good Shepherd, hear My
voice and follow me today;
Leave all behind and make thy
choice within My fold to stay.
I'll join your heart to all My sheep
whose names are kept above;
With them thy soul shall find
delight in My redeeming love.

I am the way, the truth, the life;
in Me ye are complete;
My Spirit brings an end of strife,
and pleasures pure and sweet.
Why not throw off the yokes of men
and leave their folds behind?
Yoke up with Me and learn of Me,
and rest your souls shall find.

(Harlan D. Sorrell)

29TH FEBRUARY

THE DOOR OF SURRENDER:

But if the slave plainly says, I love my master, my wife, and my children; I will not go out free, then his master shall bring him to God, and he shall bring him to the door or the doorpost. And his master shall bore his ear through with an awl, and he shall be his slave forever.

Exodus 21:5–6

This short passage is in the middle of several chapters of regulations that God gave the people of Israel. He gave Moses these regulations to govern the people so that they would be blessed in the land He promised to bring them into . . . Laws to keep them safe and prosperous. It should be noted that slavery allowed under Jewish law was different from slavery as we think of it. In reality it was a provision to save people. For example if a farmer lost all his crops and couldn't pay his debts he could be ruined for life. Since there was no social security, his family might starve because they could not afford food. This provision of the law made it possible for this person to sell himself into slavery in order to pay off his debts and have a new start. And the law guaranteed him that new start, because the terms of slavery were limited. He would serve for 6 years, but in the 7th year he had to be released.

In this we see a picture of true surrender or submission. The law of the slave guaranteed freedom after six years. However the slaves themselves could choose permanent servitude because they loved their master who had treated them so well. The law allowed them to remain a slave of their good master. While they were legally free they could choose to stay. If they made that choice, there was a ceremony performed to make it official. The master would bring them before the judges of the people and together they would tell them of their decision. And the master would stand the person up against the door-post of his house, and he would take an 'awl', and he would drive it through the lobe of their ear and into the door-post. They would be free men—but committed slaves of love for the rest of their lives.

This is a picture of when Jesus sets a sinner free: 'So if the Son sets you free, you will be free indeed' John 8:36. Jesus does set every sinner who comes to Him for salvation free from the law and bondage. Yet as an act of our love we should surrender our lives totally to Him.

I love, I love my Master,
I will not go out free,
For He is my Redeemer;
He paid the price for me.
I would not leave His service,
It is so sweet and blest;
And in the weariest moments
He gives the truest rest.

(Francis R. Havergal)

1ST MARCH

A DOOR OF SERVICE

I know your works. Behold, I have set before you an open door,
which no one is able to shut. I know that you have but little power,
and yet you have kept my word and have not denied my name.

Revelation 3:8

There are three aspects to this open door for service, found in Revelation 3:8:

- THE MASTER OF THIS DOOR: OUR SAVIOUR: 'I Know your Works'. 'I have set before you an open door'. The 'I' referred to is none other than the risen exalted Lord Jesus.
- THE MINISTRY OF THIS DOOR: OUR SERVICE: 'your work'.
- THE MESSAGE OF THIS DOOR: OUR SUCCESS: 'which no one is able to shut'. If God calls you to a work and you are obedient, He will bring you the success He wants for His glory.

Lehman Strauss commenting on this verse said: 'While it is true Christ opens the door for us, He will not enter it for us. It is His part to open the door. It is ours to enter. Paul was alert to the many doors Christ opened for him. He said: 'for a wide door for effective work has opened to me, and there are many adversaries' 1 Corinthians 16:9. 'When I came to Troas to preach the gospel of Christ, even though a door was opened for me in the Lord' 2 Corinthians 2:12. It was Paul's prayer that he would never force his way ceremoniously in through doors which the Lord never opened: At the same time, pray also for us, that God may open to us a door for the word, to declare the mystery of Christ, on account of which I am in prison Colossians 4:3. Any man of God in the will of God will find an open door for Christian service, and there is no power on earth or hell that can shut the door which God has opened'.

Dear reader is there a door God has opened for, you to walk through. Christ has opened up many doors of service. But will you walk through yours today. Remember doors do shut including doors into schools, into institutions and into various countries around the world. Will you arise today and step through the door of service that is still open for you.

God Has Set An Open Door,
An Open Door No One Can Shut
The Devil Tries, Temptation Comes
But, God Has Set A Door
No One Can Shut

(Unknown)

In the things familiar we find security
Resisting all the changes that
days and years can bring
When God decides to lead you
through an open door
Inviting you to walk in realms
you've never known before

Beyond the open door is a new
and fresh anointing
Hear the Spirit calling you to go
Walk on through the door for
the Lord will go before you
Into a greater power you've never known before

(Unknown)

2ND MARCH

A SPECIFIC DOOR

*For a wide door for effective work has opened
to me, and there are many adversaries.*

1 Corinthians 16:9

Paul is speaking in verse 9 of 1 Corinthians 16 about a specific opportunity of service for him at Ephesus: 'a wide door . . . has opened to ME'. According to scholars the words 'to me' comes from the Greek word 'moi', which means 'uniquely to me'. God used this verse to me to confirm a specific role He was calling me too for a specific time.

Paul called his door of opportunity at Ephesus 'wide' because it was great and challenging. He called it 'effective' because it promised many opportunities for work. He called it a 'door' because it was an opening of providential, dive arrangement and appointments.

Paul's accomplishment in Ephesus was no doubt one of his greatest works. During the three years that he lived and worked in Ephesus, Paul established one of the greatest churches in world history. The revival that swept through the city was so massive that the church of Ephesus soon became the largest and most influential church in the first century.

Paul also noted that there is never an opportunity without an adversary. Success always generates opposition. Paul accepted the opportunities and ignored the adversaries. To Paul the opportunities were more important than the problems.

God does open up specific and unique opportunities for his children to serve Him. It could be as a Sunday School teacher, a youth worker, a teacher, serving in a church leadership role, hospitality, catering team in the church, a caretaking role in the church building, a preacher, a teacher, a missionary in the homeland or overseas. And the list goes on.

What a work to do for Jesus!
Work for you and work for me,
Work for all who trust His merit,
All who would His glory see;
Though we fill a lowly station,
And our talent be but small,
Though we are but young disciples,
We must heed the Saviour's call.

What a work to do for Jesus
And the perishing around,
Souls that by His blood are ransomed,
Telling them the joyful sound!
Oh, the lost and dying millions,
Wandering from God astray,
You and I may help to lead them,
In the straight and narrow way.

What a work to do for Jesus,
Work for heart and hand and brain!
Sowing aye, beside all waters,
Precious seeds of golden grain;
Going forth in life's glad morning,
Happy with the Master's love,
And at eve returning, laden
For the Welcome Home above.

Oh, the sacred inspiration,
Blest each heart by grace made free,
From the cross and from the garden,
This I freely do for Thee!
Can our lips be dumb in silence,
All unmoved by Love's bequest?
Can we close our eyes in slumber?
Can we fold our hands to rest?

(A. Parke Burgess)

3RD MARCH

THE SURPRISING DOOR

*And when he knocked at the door of the gateway, a servant
girl named Rhoda came to answer. Recognizing Peter's voice,
in her joy she did not open the gate but ran in and reported
that Peter was standing at the gate. They said to her, You are
out of your mind. But she kept insisting that it was so, and
they kept saying, It is his angel! But Peter continued knocking,
and when they opened, they saw him and were amazed.*

Acts 12:13–16

The context around our verse today is Peter's miraculous escape from prison in answer to prayer. The setting of this story shows us that the early church was being persecuted due to political pleasure and posturing. The leaders of Jerusalem found it to be popular to kill Christians. The thirst for popularity could be achieved by publically persecuting church leaders. In Acts 12:1–5 we learn that: 'About that time Herod the king laid violent hands on some who belonged to the church. He killed James the brother of John with the sword, and when he saw that it pleased the Jews, he proceeded to arrest Peter also. This was during the days of Unleavened Bread. And when he had seized him, he put him in prison, delivering him over to four squads of soldiers to guard him, intending after the Passover to bring him out to the people. So Peter was kept in prison, but earnest prayer for him was made to God by the church.

God answers the prayers of the Church and releases Peter who immediately goes to the house of Mary where the special prayer meeting was being held. He knocked the door, but those praying were taken totally by surprise. They couldn't believe that God had answered their prayers in such a short time and in such an awesome way. God is able to do exceedingly beyond anything we can ask or think.

Here are some thoughts about the praying of this group of people which brought such a great result:

IT WAS POINTED PRAYER: ' but earnest prayer for him was made to God by the church' v. 5. Their prayer was specific and it was to the point.

IT WAS PERSISTENT PRAYER: 'but prayer was made without ceasing' v. 5 KJV. When he realized this, he went to the house of Mary, the mother of John whose other name was Mark, where many were gathered together and were praying v. 12.

IT WAS PARTNERSHIP IN PRAYER: 'where many were gathered together and were praying' v. 12.

IT WAS PATIENCE IN PRAYER: 'But Peter continued knocking, and when they opened, they saw him and were amazed'. They kept on praying even after Peter's release and were surprised 'amazed' by God.

We should be praying much for the persecuted church today. And pray believing for some amazing surprises in answer to those prayers.

The angel fetched Peter out of prison, but it was prayer fetched the angel.
Thomas Watson

4TH MARCH

THE SELL-OUT DOOR

Now the betrayer had given them a sign, saying, The one I will kiss is the man; seize him. And he came up to Jesus at once and said, Greetings, Rabbi! And he kissed him.

Matthew 26:48–49

Judas has been described as one who kissed 'The Door' to Heaven and went to Hell. What a tragedy. It would have been better for Judas if he had not been born. It would be better to never live, than to die without Christ. Are you a child of God? Are you real? Not religious, but saved. Have you turned to Christ alone? Jesus died for you and me.

When you look at Judas's story you find out about:

- His Potential: No man in human history had a greater opportunity for success and happiness than did Judas Iscariot.
- His Position: He was a disciple. He had close contact with Jesus. He knew His teachings, seen His miracles.
- His Pretending: He looked like the others but he was false. This was Luke's assessment of him: 'and Judas the son of James, and Judas Iscariot, who became a traitor' Luke 6:16. John's view of him was equally bad: 'He said this, not because he cared about the poor, but because he was a thief,' John 12:6. A traitor and a thief.
- His Peril: He disregarded all that Christ taught including the consequences of his sin and actions. He betrayed the Saviour for 30 pieces of silver. The consequences were terrible: 'he departed, and he went and hanged himself' Matthew 27:3–5.

If Judas had turned to the cross instead of taking his own life, he could have been forgiven - but he wasn't going to, and he didn't. He will stand before Christ again one day with no excuse. It would have been better if he never had been born. The message today is: Be a genuine follower of Jesus.

Jesus said, I'm the Way,
The Truth, the Life, the Door.
All those who hear My words,
Find the life they've searched for.

He chose Twelve Disciples,
And sent them forth to preach.
Equipped for every task,
His gospel they did teach.

But one did not believe
The kingdom he proclaimed.
He was one of the Twelve,
And Judas was his name.

So he devised a plan.
For a price, he'd betray,
The One who proved to be,
The Truth, the Door, the Way.

A kiss would be the sign,
The enemies would know.
"Hold Him fast and bind Him,
And do not let Him go."

Judas said, 'Hail Master,'
And kissed Him as before.
He sealed his fate that day,
As he kissed Heaven's door.

Let this be a warning.
You know the story well.
Judas kissed heaven's door,
And sent his soul to hell.

(Ken Blue)

5TH MARCH

THE SUPPLICATION DOOR

*But when you pray, go into your room and shut the
door and pray to your Father who isw in secret. And
your Father who sees in secret will reward you.*

Matthew 6:6

The disciples observed the prayer life of Jesus. They asked Jesus to teach them how to pray. In this section of Matthew called the 'Beatitudes' Jesus shares teaching on the importance of a private, personal and powerful prayer life with the Heavenly Father. He goes on to give them a model prayer or the disciples' prayer. Jesus taught them and by extension us the following important instruction about our private prayer life:

- THE PRIORITY ON PRAYER: 'when you pray', not 'if' you pray.
- THE PLACE OF PRAYER: 'go into your room'. We need a place to pray. I used to sit under the ministry of a Pastor who often said in regards to praying 'steal away home to Jesus'. In other words get alone with the Lord in the place of prayer. I have found it to be good advice over the years.
- THE PRIVACY OF PRAYER: 'go into your room and shut the door'. Corporate prayer is essential and beneficial. However daily private prayer alone with God is also essential in our Christian life and walk.
- THE PERIOD OF PRAYER: Jesus doesn't specify a definite time, but don't rob God of time set aside to be in His presence.
- THE PLAN OF PRAYER: We need to thank God, confess our sins, ask in prayer and intercede for others. In the context of Matthew 6:6, Jesus taught the disciples' prayer

in verses 9 to 13. I pray this prayer on a regular basis.

The following are some helpful ways you can use to break the prayer down into various prayer and praise points:

- GOD'S PERSON: Our Father.
- GOD'S PURPOSES: Thy Kingdom come.
- GOD'S PROVISION: Give us . . . our daily bread.
- GOD'S PARDON: Forgive us our debts.
- GOD'S PURITY: Lead us not into temptation.
- GOD'S PROTECTION: Deliver us from evil.
- GOD'S POWER: Yours is the Kingdom.

(John Phillips)

- ADOPTION: Our Father in heaven.
- ADORATION: hallowed be your name.
- ANTICIPATION: Your kingdom come.
- ASPIRATION: your will be done, on earth as it is in heaven.
- PROVISION: Give us this day our daily bread.
- PARDON: and forgive us our debts, as we also have forgiven our debtors.
- PROTECTION: And lead us not into temptation, but deliver us from evil.
- PRAISE: For yours is the kingdom, and the power, and the glory, for ever. Amen.

(Timothy Cross)

6TH MARCH

THE SHAKEN DOOR

Suddenly there was a great earthquake, so that the foundations of the prison were shaken. And immediately all the doors were opened, and everyones bonds were unfastened. When the jailer woke and saw that the prison doors were open, he drew his sword and was about to kill himself, supposing that the prisoners had escaped.

Acts 16:26–27

This incident happened soon after Paul and his fellow-worker were given a clear calling into Europe: 'A vision appeared to Paul in the night: a man of Macedonia was standing there, urging him and saying, Come over to Macedonia and help us.' Acts 16:9. In fact the door into Asia closed and the door into Europe opened. John Phillips commenting on this event said: 'This vision marks one of the most important turning points in history. It turned Paul westward into Europe and resulted in the evangelisation of the west. Europe became, as a result, the great centre of Christianity'. Sadly this is not the case today.

Back to our verses. Not long after this Paul and Silas found themselves beaten and in a prison cell in Philippi singing at mid-night. You may ask how they could do this after such clear direction from the Lord. The answer being that they knew they were in the centre of God's will. This led to one of the great questions in Scripture: 'What must I do to be saved?' Then the glad answer: 'believe on the Lord Jesus Christ and you shall be saved'. There was a revival in the jail cell:

- A time of prayer: About midnight Paul and Silas were praying v. 25.
- A time of praise: and singing hymns to God, and the prisoners were listening to them v. 25.
- A time of power to: Release: v. 26; Restrain: v. 27–28; Redeem: v. 29–34; Require; v. 35–40.

A believer, free from care,
May in chains, or dungeons, sing,
If the Lord be with him there;
And be happier than a king:
Paul and Silas, thus confined,
Tho' their backs were torn by whips,
Yet possessing peace of mind,
Sang His praise with joyful lips.

Suddenly the prison shook,
Open flew the iron doors;
And the jailer, terror struck,
Now his captives' help implores:
Trembling at their feet he fell,
Tell me, sirs, what must I do
To be saved from guilt and hell?
None can tell me this but you.

Look to Jesus, they replied.
If on Him thou canst believe,
By the death which He has died,
Thou salvation shalt receive.
While the living word he heard,
Faith sprang up within his heart;
And, released from all he feared,
In their joy his soul had part.

Sinners, Christ is still the same,
O that you could likewise fear!
Then the mention of His name
Would be music to your ear:
Jesus rescues Satan's slaves,
His dear wounds still plead, Forgive!
Jesus to the utmost saves;
Sinners, look to Him and live.

(John Newton)

7TH MARCH

STANDING AT THE DOOR

Behold, I stand at the door and knock. If anyone hears my voice and opens the door, I will come in to him and eat with him, and he with me.

Revelation 3:20

Primarily Rev 3:20 is a picture of Jesus standing outside the Laodicea church seeking entrance. He is pleading for individuals to give Him His rightful place. Yet it is also in order to look at this verse from an evangelistic point of view.

Holman Hunt's famous painting known as 'The Light of the World' is in St Paul's Cathedral in London. The Cathedral's webpage describes the painting as follows: 'The door represents the human soul: its lack of handle, the rusty nails and its hinges overgrown with ivy are intended to show that it has never been opened—and the figure of Christ is asking for permission to enter. The writing beneath the picture is taken from Revelation 3:20 'Behold! I am standing at the door, knocking; if you hear my voice and open the door, I will come in to you and eat with you, and you with me.'

When the painting was first displayed, critics came to comment on its work. One of them said to Mr Hunt, you have painted a masterpiece, but you made a serious mistake. You have painted a door without a handle. Mr Hunt replied: 'That's no mistake, the handle is on the inside'.

Many preachers have used this verse as a gospel text over the years: The hymn writer M. B. C. Slade put it as follows:

Who at my door is standing,
Patiently drawing near,
Entrance within demanding?
Whose is the voice I hear?

Refrain

Sweetly the tones are falling;
"Open the door for me!
If thou wilt heed My calling,
I will abide with thee."

Lonely without He's staying:
Lonely within am I;
While I am still delaying,
Will He not pass me by?

All through the dark hours dreary,
Knocking again is He;
Jesus, art Thou not weary,
Waiting so long for me?

Door of my heart, I hasten!
Thee will I open wide.
Though He rebuke and chasten,
He shall with me abide.

Today let us apply Horatius Bonar's (1808 - 1889) comments about this verse to our churches' individual lives: 'O Church of God, keep Him not out. How much you lose! For His absence, no outward prosperity, nor riches, nor numbers, can compensate. If He be kept out, all is sadness, and leanness, and poverty. If He be admitted, all is well. Happy the Church with which Christ is daily feasting. Happy the soul in which He has come to dwell, and who, in daily communion by faith, tastes the Bridegroom's love!'

8TH MARCH

THE SENTENCING DOOR

Do not grumble against one another, brothers, so that you may not be judged; behold, the Judge is standing at the door.

James 5:9

We are exhorted in this verse not to Judge one another. We must leave all judgement until the Judge comes, who, at His appearing, will judge the quick and the dead.

Vengeance will be meted out by Him at that day. If we take into our own hands the matter of judging, we will ourselves be judged for so doing (Matthew 7v 1). Jesus alone is qualified to judge in all matters: 'because he has fixed a day on which he will judge the world in righteousness by a man whom he has appointed; and of this he has given assurance to all by raising him from the dead' Acts 17:31.

He will not let sin go unpunished. Unlike us He is completely fair and just in Judgement: 'But because of your hard and impenitent heart you are storing up wrath for yourself on the day of wrath when God's righteous judgement will be revealed. He will render to each one according to his works: to those who by patience in well-doing seek for glory and honour and immortality, he will give eternal life; but for those who are self-seeking and do not obey the truth, but obey unrighteousness, there will be wrath and fury. Romans 2:5–8.

Whether we believe in Him or not, we will all meet Jesus Christ. He is unavoidable; He cannot be deceived, disputed, or discredited. Adrian Rogers says, 'If you don't meet Him as Saviour, you will meet Him as Judge.' Today Jesus is our Saviour, however if we reject Him in life then one day we will meet Him as judge.

Adrian Rogers puts it as follows:' I'm not going to stand before the great white throne, and I'll tell you why: I settled out of court. I have given my heart to Jesus Christ and, on that cross, He took my sin and my judgement. Through the blood of Jesus, our sins can be buried in the grave of God's forgetfulness, never to be brought up against us again'.

The wrath of God that was our due,
Upon the Lamb was laid;
And by the shedding of His blood,
The debt for us was paid.
How calm the Judgement hour shall pass
To all who do obey
The Word of God, and trust the blood,
And make that Word their stay!

(D. W. Whittle)

As believers we will stand before God at the Judgement Seat of Christ and give an account for our lives. At the 'Bema' seat we will be given rewards accordingly: 'For we must all appear before the judgment seat of Christ, so that each one may receive what is due for what he has done in the body, whether good or evil' 2 Corinthians 5:10. Let us keep short accounts with God and be fervent in His service.

9TH MARCH

THE SIDE DOOR

*Make a roof for the ark, and finish it to a cubit
above, and set the door of the ark in its side. Make
it with lower, second, and third decks.*

Genesis 6:16

In Genesis chapters 6–10, we are introduced to Noah. Noah's grandfather was Methuselah and Enoch was his great grandfather. His father Lamech named him Noah because it meant 'a resting place.' He sensed from the Lord that his son Noah would provide unusual strength and comfort to his generation. Noah lived in a period of moral chaos and spiritual darkness. Jesus likened the time he lived in as comparable to that of Sodom. God told Noah that he was going to judge and destroy the world at that time due to their sin: 'And God said to Noah, I have determined to make an end of all flesh, for the earth is filled with violence through them. Behold, I will destroy them with the earth'. God therefore told Noah to build an Ark to save himself and all who entered it with him from the coming judgement. Noah's legacy is recorded in Hebrews 11:7, 'by faith Noah...prepared an ark to the saving of his house'. For 120 years, Noah constructed this ark on dry ground with no clouds on the horizon. While he laboured and preached, the world laughed, played and mocked. But the storm did come and all the people in the world at that time perished. Those that came into the Ark were saved. The Ark is a lovely type of Christ. God is going to judge the world again. Those who die in their sin will be forever separated from God in hell. Those who are in Christ (In the Ark) will be saved and spend eternity in heaven.

*God looked down upon the
world many years ago
He saw the awful sin of man about to overflow
Only Noah was righteous, only
Noah walked with God
Only Noah believed Him when
He said there'd be a flood*

*Now God told Noah to build an
ark: 'Build it big and wide
Round up all the animals and
put them safe inside
Then come in with all your folk
and I will close the door
And in the morning this world will be no more'*

*Are you in the ark? Or are you outside?
O don't hesitate, you'll be too late
The door's open wide*

*Now people stood outside the
door just like they do today
They fell about all laughing
at Noah's funny ways
'Ha! Noah's built himself an ark
to sail it on dry ground'
Meanwhile up above them
the sky began to frown*

*Forty days and forty nights the
rain came tumbling down
Everyone inside the ark was
warm and safe and sound
Only those outside now they
weren't laughing any more
Rain and tears were mingled as
they scratched upon the door*

(Len Magee)

10TH MARCH

THE SHELTERING DOOR:

Then they shall take some of the blood and put it on the two doorposts and the lintel of the houses in which they eat it.

For the Lord will pass through to strike the Egyptians, and when he sees the blood on the lintel and on the two doorposts, the Lord will pass over the door and will not allow the destroyer to enter your houses to strike you.

Exodus 12:7, 23

When we understand that everything that comes into our home goes through a door we can appreciate the symbolic dimension of this event in Exodus about covering the 'doorposts' with blood. The symbolism in this door is very powerful and of utmost importance. Only those homes where the entrance was covered by the blood of the sacrificial lamb were spared the destructive death angel.

The Passover in Egypt is a prophetic picture of what was to be accomplished by the sacrificial death of Jesus on the cross: 'For Christ, our Passover lamb, has been sacrificed' 1 Corinthians 5:7. Christ is the true Passover. It is His blood that finally assures us of eternal redemption.

The way that Israel was instructed to apply the blood of the lamb is a wonderful pattern for us. The Jews were slaves in Egypt, but God said, 'You're my chosen people. I will bring you out.' On the night called 'Passover', He did just that and headed them toward Canaan, their homeland.

When Pharaoh refused to release God's people, a series of plagues descended on Egypt to get Pharaoh to turn them loose. Nothing worked until God sent the final plague: the death angel. The firstborn in every family would be slain... unless a particular family had put the blood of a lamb upon the doorposts of their house. God had said, when I see the blood, I will *pass over* you'. Passover is all about a perfect lamb. The lamb that each Jewish household was to prepare foretold the Lamb of God, Jesus Christ. The lamb was spotless, sacrificial, saving and shared. A picture of Jesus: 'The Lamb of God'.

Its blood upon Jewish doors saved God's people from the death angel and secured their freedom from Egypt. This same blood depicted our salvation through Jesus' death on the cross.

Our Lamb is slain, the Paschal Lamb,
Of which the old is but a token;
Though shadowed in the midnight past,
There's not a word has e'er been broken.

I'm under the blood, the passover blood,
The Lamb was 'slain from the foundation;'
It points to the side of Jesus, who died,
And purchased for us salvation.

I'll ne'er forget when first, by faith,
I saw my Saviour, bleeding, dying;
And there again, for Perfect Love,
I plunged into the fountain, crying.

There's sweet repose beneath the cross,
And safety when the blood doth cover;
For God has spoken in his Word,
'When I see the blood, I will pass over'

(Henry L. Gilmour)

11TH MARCH

THE SHARING DOOR

At the same time, pray also for us, that God may open to us a door for the word, to declare the mystery of Christ, on account of which I am in prison.

Colossians 4:3

In his book on Colossians called 'Christ above all' Dr David Jeremiah said: 'Now as we're coming to chapter 4, Paul turns his attention from inside the church to those who are outside. Paul was an evangelist who wanted his churches to be magnetic. He wanted believers to share their faith and lead others to the hope of Jesus Christ'.

This reminds me of a verse of a chorus
we used to sing as children:
Telling others, telling others
My life's work is telling others,
Since the Lord saved me
I am as happy as can be,
My life's work is telling others.

(Seth Sykes)

In our verse today Paul was asking for two things 1. An open door for the word and 2. The ability to clearly proclaim the mystery of Christ. We too should be praying for opportunities to share the gospel. Open doors in scripture, just as today speaks of new opportunities, especially in relation to sharing the message of the gospel:

- 'And when they arrived and gathered the church together, they declared all that God had done with them, and how he had opened a door of faith to the Gentiles' Acts 14:27

- 'For a wide door for effective work has opened to me, and there are many adversaries' 1 Cor 16:9
- 'When I came to Troas to preach the gospel of Christ, even though a door was opened for me in the Lord' 2 Cor 2:12

Let us pray for opportunities for ourselves and others to share Christ:

Give me a passion for souls, dear Lord,
A passion to save the lost;
O that Thy love were by all adored,
And welcomed at any cost.

Refrain:

Jesus, I long, I long to be winning
Men who are lost, and constantly sinning;
O may this hour be one of beginning
The story of pardon to tell.

Though there are dangers untold and stern
Confronting me in the way,
Willingly still would I go, nor turn,
But trust Thee for grace each day.

How shall this passion for souls be mine?
Lord, make Thou the answer clear;
Help me to throw out the old Life-Line
To those who are struggling near.

(Herbert G. Tovey)

12TH MARCH

THE SPLENDOUR DOOR

After this I looked, and behold, a door standing open in heaven! And the first voice, which I had heard speaking to me like a trumpet, said, Come up here, and I will show you what must take place after this.

Revelation 4:1

Many scholars divide the book of Revelation into three sections as outlined in chapter 1:19: Write therefore the things that you have seen, those that are and those that are to take place after this.

- Section 1: 'the things that you have seen' takes in Chapter 1.
- Section 2: 'those that are' includes chapters 2 to 3.
- Section 3: Chapters 4 to 22.

In this section the Lord reveals future events to take place after the true Church has been taken out of the earth.

In verse 1 of chapter 4 John is taken up into Heaven through an 'Open Door' and he is amazed at the splendour of what he sees. John Phillips commenting on this verse said that three things were impressed indelibly upon his mind: an unforgettable throne, an unforgettable throng, and an unforgettable thrill. One day every true child of God will go through those open doors and experience these blessings for themselves. Today we will just concentrate on the One on the Throne. It is mentioned 14 times in Chapter 4. One day we will see the Lord on the throne in all His glory:

The splendour of a King
Clothed in majesty
Let all the earth rejoice
All the earth rejoice

He wraps Himself in light
And darkness tries to hide
And trembles at His voice
Trembles at His voice

Refrain:

How great is our God
Sing with me
How great is our God
And all will see
How great, how great is our God

Age to age He stands
And time is in His hands
Beginning and the end
Beginning and the end

The Godhead Three in One
Father, Spirit, Son
The Lion and the Lamb
The Lion and the Lamb

Name above all names
Worthy of our praise
My heart will sing
How great is our God

Name above all names
You are worthy of our praise
And my heart will sing
How great is our God

(Chris Tomlin)

13TH MARCH

THE SOVEREIGN DOOR

I am the door.

John 10:9

I was sharing with my daughter and son-in-law about the various doors of the Bible about which I was writing little devotions using the letter 'S' as a means of alliteration. My eleven year old grandson Noah asked if I had written about the 'Sovereign' door.

Today I want to share about the 'Sovereign Door'. 'I AM' is one of the titles of God. When the Lord appeared to Moses in Exodus He used this name: 'God said to Moses, I am who I am' Exodus 3:14. The Dutch theologian Herman makes the following comments regarding this name: 'The One who appears to Moses is not a strange God, but is the God of the fathers, the Unchangeable, the Immutable One who never leaves nor forsakes His people but ever seeks His own and ever saves them, who is unchangeable in His grace, His love, in His succour, who will be what He is, since He ever remaineth Himself'. In reality when Jesus said 'I am' he was saying: 'I Am God the Sovereign one'.

Charles J Roll puts it like this: 'the name, I AM THAT I AM, conveys to us a glimpse of the infinities centered in Deity. The name suggests I am the continual One continually, I am the constant One constantly, I am the perfect One perpetually, I am the steadfast One steadfastly, I am the presiding One permanently, I am the essential One eternally, I am the excellent One everlastingly. After that all one can say is praise God for the 'Sovereign Door', the only door to Heaven and home. But what a secure and certain door.

'I am the door,' come in, come in,
And leave without thy load of sin;
The night is dark, the storm is wild,
O venture in, thou stranger child,
O venture in, thou stranger child.

'I am the door,' come gently knock
And I will loose the heavy lock,
That guards my Father's precious fold:
Come in from darkness and from cold,
Come in from darkness and from cold.

'I am the door,' no longer roam;
Here are thy treasures, here thy home;
I purchased them for thee and thine,
And paid the price in blood of mine,
And paid the price in blood of mine.

'I am the door,' my Father waits
To make thee heir of rich estates;
Come dwell with him, and dwell with me,
And thou my Father's child shall be,
And thou my Father's child shall be.

'I am the door,' come in, come in,
And everlasting treasures win;
My Father's house was built for thee,
And thou shalt share his home with me,
And thou shalt share his home with me.

(Dwight Willams)

14TH MARCH

THE SELECT DOOR

Strive to enter through the narrow door. For many, I tell you, will seek to enter and will not be able.

Luke 13: 24

There are two main points to consider in regards to Luke 13:24. First, there is only one way to be saved (the door is narrow). Second, many seek to enter incorrectly. There are not many paths to God, but One: Jesus Christ. Peter preached that 'salvation is found in no one else, for there is no other name under heaven given to mankind by which we must be saved' (Acts 4:12). Jesus Himself said, 'I am the way, and the truth, and the life. No one comes to the Father except through me' (John 14:6). The door is narrow, but it is open.

The door is narrow, it is open, and it must be entered correctly. You enter the door by striving according to God's Word. Jesus isn't talking about salvation by works or human effort. But He is talking about our attitude toward it (Ephesians 2:8–9). Strive means that we intentionally struggle to resist the wrong ways of 'salvation' and to trust completely in Jesus Christ for our salvation. The many who fail to enter are striving in vain because they are seeking to enter through their own goodness. They have 'zeal for God, but not according to knowledge. For, being ignorant of the righteousness of God, and seeking to establish their own, they did not submit to God's righteousness' (Rom 10:2–3). Therefore, they are not able to enter the narrow door.

Jesus says 'strive to enter through the narrow door' because the door will not always be open. Jesus says, 'when once the master of the house has risen and shut the door, and you begin to stand outside and to knock at the door, saying, 'Lord, open to us,' then he will answer you, 'I do not know where you come from'" (Luke 13:25). We are currently living in the age of grace in which 'everyone who calls upon the name of the Lord will be saved' (Rom 10:13) therefore we must 'seek the LORD while he may be found; call upon him while he is near' (Isaiah 55:6). We live in a favourable time for salvation.

But this age of grace will one day come to an end when the Master of the house (Jesus) shall shut the door of salvation. Strive to enter the narrow door while it is open, commit your life to Jesus Christ today.

Strait is the gate and narrow is the way
That leadeth unto life above;
Strive to enter in, oh, strive to enter in!
Come to a Saviour's love.

(Fanny Crosby)

15TH MARCH

THE SENDING DOOR

On the evening of that day, the first day of the week, the doors being locked where the disciples were for fear of the Jews, Jesus came and stood among them and said to them, Peace be with you.

John 20:19

Thomas was not present at this meeting. Many years ago, commenting on Thomas not being at this meeting a preacher made the point that we shouldn't miss attending church on the Lord's Day or the Mid-week Prayer and Bible study meetings as we might well miss having an encounter with the risen Lord Jesus Christ. Ivor Powell points out several things happened at this meeting:

1. The disciples looked at the Lord and discovered a new PEACE: 'Jesus came and stood among them and said to them, Peace be with you':

Oh, the peace the Savior gives!
Peace I never knew before;
And my way has brighter grown
Since I've learned to trust Him more

(Francis A. Blackmer)

2. They recognised the way of PARDON: 'When he had said this, he showed them his hands and his side' John 20:20.

3. They experienced PLEASURE: 'Then the disciples were glad when they saw the Lord' John 20:20.

So in gladness I go on,
Till the Master's work is done,
Trusting in atoning blood,
Walking in the love of God

(Elisha A. Hoffman)

There is pardon, peace, and pow'r.
And purity and Paradise;
With all of these in Christ for me,
Let joyful songs of praise to Him arise!

(D. W. Whittle)

Then the Lord gave them one great aspect of His great commission: 'As the Father has sent me, even so I am sending you' John 20:21. God is a sending God. As you study the great commission you learn that God the Father, God the Son; God the Holy Spirit and the local Church are all involved in sending out missionaries.

From Jesus flows our mission, the mission of the church, until he comes again. Jesus sends us into the world. That may be at home or abroad. We can send through our prayers, our purse and person.

Hudson Taylor said, 'The Great Commission is not an option to be considered; it is a command to be obeyed.' Every single Christian is under personal orders from Jesus Christ himself to spread the gospel in some way. John Piper reminds us that there are three responses to the Great Commission: 'Go, send, or disobey'.

16TH MARCH

THE SCEPTICAL DOOR

Eight days later, his disciples were inside again, and Thomas was with them. Although the doors were locked, Jesus came and stood among them and said, Peace be with you.

John 20:26

After the disciples met Jesus after the resurrection as recorded in John 20:19–23, they informed Thomas who wasn't present on this occasion of their meeting. Thomas responded by saying: 'Unless I see in his hands the mark of the nails, and place my finger into the mark of the nails, and place my hand into his side, I will never believe' John 20:25. Thomas was sceptical meaning: one that is not easily convinced or one having doubts or reservations. However eight days later Jesus appeared to the disciples again. On this occasion Thomas was present. The following is Thomas's response: 'Then he said to Thomas, Put your finger here, and see my hands; and put out your hand, and place it in my side. Do not disbelieve, but believe. Thomas answered him, My Lord and my God' John 20:27–28.

F. B. Meyer commenting on this said: 'Thomas was left for a whole week. Day after day he heard the repeated story of Christ's appearances; and waited for Him to come again; and became more and more confirmed in his sad presentiment that the whole story was a myth. How great must have been the anguish during those days, as he tossed between hope and fear, saw on other faces the light which he might not share, and thought that the Master, if really living, was neglectful of his friend! At last Jesus came, not to anathematise (condemn) or exclude him, not to break the bruised reed or quench the smoking flax, but to restore him, and to lift on him the light of His countenance'.

Meyer commenting on Jesus response to Thomas wrote: 'He suited Himself to his needs. He was willing to give proofs. He said to Thomas: Put your finger here, and see my hands; and put out your hand, and place it in my side. Thomas responded by saying: My Lord and my God!' Meyer continues: 'Ah, Thomas, in that glad outburst of thine, thou reachedst a higher level than all the rest; and thou art not the last man who seemed a hopeless and helpless wreck, unable to exercise the faith that seemed so natural to others, under the teaching of Jesus, has been enabled to assume a position to which none of his associates could aspire!'.

We may not touch his hands and side,
nor follow where he trod;
but in his promise we rejoice
and cry, 'My Lord and God!'

Help then, O Lord, our unbelief;
and may our faith abound
to call on you when you are near,
and seek where you are found.

(Henry Alford)

'Blessed are those who have not seen and yet have believed' John 20:29.

17TH MARCH

KEEP SOWING ON

*He who goes out weeping, bearing the seed for sowing, shall
come home with shouts of joy, bringing his sheaves with him.*

Psalm 126:6

I had the privilege of serving the Lord full-time in Mission work for 15 years. This continues in my retirement. With the Lord there is no retirement in this life, He just re-tyres us. He brings us into other seasons and phases of service.

One of the things the Lord graciously allowed us to be involved in was mass evangelism in Ireland. One gospel initiative was to send a piece of gospel literature into every home in N Ireland called 'Into Every Community for Christ'. The other was being part of resourcing and planning a national evangelistic endeavour in the Republic of Ireland through local evangelical churches called 'What's the Story?' Some would call this abundant gospel sowing.

After such initiatives 'hindsight' type of people would ask was it any use, was it 'value for money' etc. etc. When this happens the Lord reminds me of Psalm 126 v. 6: 'He who goes out weeping, bearing the seed for sowing, shall come home with shouts of joy, bringing his sheaves with him'.

As believers we are to be constantly doing this by our Life, our Lips and by Literature (certainly the written Word of God). I recently listened to a sermon preached by Dr David Jeremiah: He shared three ways of witnessing: Show the Gospel, Share the Gospel, and Support the Gospel (and can I add what I would call Supplicate the Gospel)

So today keep on Sowing and leave the results to God:

*Keep sowing on! What God hath planned
We may not know or understand,
Yet let us with unwearied hand
Keep sowing at His command*

*Keep sowing on with faith and prayer,
All times, all weather, everywhere;
Nor ever yielding to despair:
For grain that dies, much grain will bear.*

*Keep sowing on—it is the way,
Keep sowing on by night and day;
Nor ever from your toiling stay
From early morn till evening grey*

*Keep sowing on though winds may blow,
Your seed be covered with the snow;
Keep sowing on, for this you know,
That grain He gives shall surely grow.*

*Keep sowing on, though naught appears
Of scattered seed of other years;
Keep sowing on in face of fears,
For they shall reap who sow in tears.*

*Keep sowing on! The precious grain
That long unseen has dormant lain,
Though seeming lost, shall spring again;
A rich reward for all your pain.*

*Keep sowing on—you can't go wrong;
So drop the seed with faith more strong,
With patient hand—twill not be long
Till harvest come with harvest song.*

(Unknown)

18TH MARCH

ONE MESSAGE

But we preach Christ crucified.

1 Corinthians 1:23

In the 1st year of my retirement a number of momentous events happened in the UK. Not least of these was the death of Queen Elizabeth II on the 8th September at Balmoral Castle in Scotland. The Queen was on the throne for all of my life to that date. Interestingly it was reported that Balmoral Castle is the place where the Queen was 'most happy'. It was also reported that it was the Queen's 'favourite home'. Therefore it was wonderful that the Queen could spend her last days on earth there.

Opposite the main entrance to Balmoral Castle is the Crathie Kirk. The Church where the Queen and members of the Royal Family attended while visiting Balmoral.

My wife and I while on holiday in Scotland did a tour around Crathie Kirk which was open to the public. One of the things that caught my eye was a plaque at the front door entrance which contained the following Scriptures: 1 Corinthians 1:23; Timothy 2:5, and Galatians 1:7–8, 12. These verses contain truths that would enlighten anyone who reads them including the then Queen on the throne to her most humble or poorest subject.

Today we will reflect on the first verse: 'But we preach Christ crucified' 1Corinthians 1:23. Roy L. Laurin commenting on 1 Corinthians 1:22–25 points out that there are three things about the substance of preaching Christ Crucified:

1. THE REACTION: There is a twofold reaction. The Jews require a sign and the Greeks seek after wisdom. However the way to God is neither religious pageantry nor mental culture. It is the way of spiritual biology which requires birth into a new life. That life is inherent in the cross, for Christ's death released His life so that what was once His becomes ours,

2. THE RESULT: To the unregenerate it may be either a stumbling block or foolishness. But to the regenerate, whether Jew or Greek, it is the power of God and the wisdom of God. He is God's power for empowering the human nature. He is God's wisdom for the enlightenment of the human mind.

3. THE REASON: Here is a gospel which seems foolish to men, yet it is wiser than their wisdom. It seems weakness to men, yet it is stronger than any power men possess. Here is the way of salvation'.

Today rejoice in the fact that the way of the Cross leads home to heaven. Whether that be the monarch on the throne or any of their subjects. We preach Christ crucified.

We preach Christ who was crucified
and risen from the grave
We preach Christ the only one
who has the strength to save
The message we proclaim is
the power of His Name
We preach Christ

(Unknown)

19TH MARCH

ONE MEDIATOR

For there is one God, and there is one mediator
between God and men, the man Christ Jesus.

1 Timothy 2:5

On the 8th of September 2022 the Royal communications made the following statement. The Queen died peacefully at Balmoral this afternoon. As the Queen had been on the throne for all of my life I felt her death deeply and therefore for me it was a time of reflection. One of the things I reflected on was a plaque which I once read at the entrance to Crathie Kirk, the Church the Queen attended while in residence at Balmoral. The plaque contained verses of Scriptures with tremendous truths for all who read them. We will consider the second verse today: 1 Timothy 2:5.

In my study I have a small commentary on 1&2 Timothy and Titus written by Maurice Flanigan. Maurice was an Elder in the Church of which I am a member. Maurice went to be with the Lord on the very first month of the COVID 19 pandemic lockdown in the UK.

Here is what Maurice wrote about this verse: 'There is only one person through whom we can come to God. Our mediator is the man Christ Jesus. A mediator is someone who acts as a go-between for two parties in order to bring peace and reconciliation. In order to be a good mediator you need to know and understand both sides. Our Lord as God's divine Son took on human flesh and lived among men. He is uniquely equipped to fulfil this role and indeed is the only one who can. Whether we are sinners or saints the only way to God is through Him.

Since the fall, man is separated from God because of sin. He needs someone to intervene on his behalf. That's why our Lord died at Calvary. It was that He might redeem us back to God. As believers, we have access to God and approach Him in and through our Lord Jesus Christ. This is a wonderful privilege. We can bring all our requests and petitions to the One who sits at the right hand of the Father interceding on our behalf.

It should thrill our souls to know that the God of Heaven who is sovereign over all can be approached by the most ordinary of people. What a privileged people we are! We need to appreciate in a new way what it means for the Lord to be our mediator.

On the cross He shed His precious blood for me
Jesus is the great Mediator;

From the grave He rose with saving victory
Jesus is the great Mediator.

Earthly creeds may fail and kingdoms pass away
Jesus is the great Mediator;

Countless worlds forever shall His word obey
Jesus is the great Mediator.

(Charles Hutchinson Gabriel)

20TH MARCH

ONE GOSPEL

But there are some who trouble you and want to distort the gospel of Christ. But even if we or an angel from heaven should preach to you a gospel contrary to the one we preached to you, let him be accursed. For I did not receive it from any man, nor was I taught it, but I received it through a revelation of Jesus Christ.

Galatians 7–8, 12

There have been several centres of worship in Crathie from the 6th Century. A new, simple building typical of Scottish Presbyterian churches of the time was built on the site of the present church in 1805. It was to this church that Queen Victoria came in 1848 on coming to Balmoral Castle. This began the custom, which continues to this day, of members of the Royal Family and their guests worshipping with local people in the parish church. The current church was completed and dedicated in 1895. My wife and I visited this church while on holiday some years ago.

The verses we will reflect on today are found on a plaque at the entrance of Crathie Kirk, the Church. I trust the late Queen Elizabeth II, our current King Charles III and the Queen Consort along with other members of the Royal family will have read and taken note of the meaning of these tremendous portions of God's Word.

The churches of Galatia had come under severe doctrinal attack. The assault was in the form of trying to turn members of the churches from the fundamental truth of justification in Christ alone. Paul is pointing out to the Galatian believers that salvation was by grace alone and not by works. False teachers were guilty of changing the Gospel of grace to a gospel of works.

Let's consider the following simple way to explain the Gospel:

THE PROBLEM: Sin: 'for all have sinned and fall short of the glory of God' Romans 3:23;

THE PENALTY: Death: 'For the wages of sin is death, but the free gift of God is eternal life in Christ Jesus our Lord' Romans 6:23;

THE PRICE: Fully paid: 'For Christ also suffered once for sins, the righteous for the unrighteous, that he might bring us to God, being put to death in the flesh but made alive in the spirit' 1 Peter 3:18;

THE PLEA: Repent: 'No, I tell you; but unless you repent, you will all likewise perish' Luke 13:3;

THE POSSIBILITY: New life: 'Therefore, if anyone is in Christ, he is a new creation. The old has passed away; behold, the new has come' 2 Corinthians 5:17;

THE PROMISE: No condemnation: 'There is therefore now no condemnation for those who are in Christ Jesus' Romans 8:1.

Great is the gospel of our glorious God,
Where mercy met the anger of God's rod;
A penalty was paid and pardon bought
And sinners lost at last to him were brought:

(William Vernon Higham)

21ST MARCH

YOURS IN HIS GRIP

I give them eternal life, and they will never perish, and no one will snatch them out of my hand. My Father, who has given them to me, is greater than all, and no one is able to snatch them out of the Father's hand.

John 10:28–29

One of the workers with the Mission that I had the privilege of serving with signs off their prayer letter with the words 'Yours in His grip'.

Ivor Powell describes John 10:28–29 as 'God's Great Grip' and 'The Double Grip'.

He goes on to say: 'We do well to remember that eternal life is eternal life. When a man becomes a child of God, he becomes one forever. If the priceless treasure disappears after one month, it can hardly be eternal'.

He adds: 'This is the reason why the Saviour spoke of the double grip. He said... no one will snatch them out of my hand ... and no one is able to snatch them out of the Father's hand'.

John MacArthur commenting on John 10 makes the following seven points about our security in Christ:

Christ's words reveal seven realities that bind every true Christian forever to God.

FIRST, believers are HIS SHEEP, and it is the duty of the Good Shepherd to protect HIS FLOCK. 'This is the will of Him who sent Me,' Jesus said, 'that of all that He has given Me I lose nothing, but raise it up on the last day' (6:39). To insist that a true Christian can somehow be lost is to deny the truth of that statement. It is also to defame the character of the Lord Jesus Christ—making Him out to be an incompetent shepherd, unable to hold on to those entrusted to Him by the Father.

SECOND, Christ's sheep hear only HIS VOICE and FOLLOW only Him. Since they will not listen to or follow a stranger (10:5), they could not possibly wander away from Him and be eternally lost.

THIRD, Christ's sheep have ETERNAL LIFE. To speak of eternal life ending is a contradiction in terms.

FOURTH, Christ gives eternal life to His sheep. Since they did nothing to earn it, they can do nothing to lose it.

FIFTH, Christ promised that His sheep WILL NEVER PERISH. Were even one to do so, it would make Him a liar.

SIXTH, no one—not false shepherds (the thieves and robbers of v. 1), or false prophets (symbolized by the wolf of v. 12), nor even the Devil himself—is powerful enough to SNATCH Christ's sheep out of HIS HAND.

FINALLY, Christ's sheep are held not only in His hand, but also in the hand of the Father, who is greater than all; and thus no one is able to snatch them out of His hand either. Infinitely secure, the believer's 'life is hidden with Christ in God' (Col. 3:3).

Let's rejoice in God's great grip on our lives as believers today

22ND MARCH

INVITATION TO GET YOUR STATE PENSION

The years of our life are seventy, or even by reason of strength eighty; yet their span is but toil and trouble; they are soon gone, and we fly away.

Psalm 90:10

On this date (28th October) I received an official letter from the Northern Ireland Pension Centre inviting me to apply for the State Pension commencing on my 66th birthday (24th February of the next year). Interesting on the first day of the same week, the Lord's Day our Pastor spoke from Psalm 90.

In that Psalm Moses the man of God inspired by the Holy Spirit points out that: 'The years of our life are seventy, or even by reason of strength eighty; yet their span is but toil and trouble; they are soon gone, and we fly away' v. 10. In verse 12 he goes on to exhort: 'So teach us to number our days that we may get a heart of wisdom'.

While recognising that a lot more of my earthly life lies behind me than in front of me, I still praise God that the best is yet to come. I still have the privilege of serving Him for as long or as short a period that He has left for me on this scene of time and then to be with Him in that lovely place called Heaven throughout the countless years of eternity. What a hope.

Why can I say this? On the letter I received it gave me what they call a 'Unique Invitation Code'. This made the point that it was unique to me. The Lord Jesus gave me an unique invitation: 'Come now, let us reason together, says the Lord: though your sins are like scarlet, they shall be as white as snow; though they are red like crimson, they shall become like wool. Isaiah 1:18; 'Come to me, all who labour and are heavy laden, and I will give you rest' Matthew 11:28; 'All that the Father gives me will come to me, and whoever comes to me I will never cast out' John 6:36–38.

I accepted this lovely invitation on the 9th October 1978. From then on I can say that:

Once I was lost in sin's degradation,
Jesus came down to bring me salvation,
Lifted me up from sorrow and shame,
Now I belong to Him.

Now I belong to Jesus,
Jesus belongs to me,
Not for the years of time alone,
But for eternity.

(Norman J. Clayton)

23RD MARCH

THE TRIPLE LOCK V. THE DOUBLE GRIP

*My sheep hear my voice, and I know them, and they follow me. I give
them eternal life, and they will never perish, and no one will snatch
them out of my hand. My Father, who has given them to me, is greater
than all, and no one is able to snatch them out of the Fathers hand.*

John 10:27–29

Yesterday I shared about an invitation I received to apply for my state pension. At the time of writing this there is speculation that the government is going to remove their 'triple lock' pledge regarding pensions.

The triple lock is a government policy designed to ensure people's pensions are not impacted by gradual rises in the cost of living over time. In practice, it means that the state pension must rise by whichever of the following three things is highest: Average earnings. Inflation. 2.5%.

This reminds me of comments made in Psalm 20:7: 'Some trust in chariots and some in horses, but we trust in the name of the Lord our God'. Some trust Government; some trust Gold; but as believers we trust God. How true. You cannot trust promises governments make. But you can trust in the name of the Lord our God: 'For all the promises of God find their Yes in him. That is why it is through him that we utter our Amen to God for his glory' 2 Corinthians 1:20. We can stand on the promises of God:

Standing on the promises of Christ my King,
Through eternal ages let His praises ring,
Glory in the highest, I will shout and sing,
Standing on the promises of God.

Standing, standing,
Standing on the promises of God my Savior;
Standing, standing,
I'm standing on the promises of God.

(Russell Kelso Carter)

Just as I was thinking about the triple lock the Lord brought to my mind the promise of His 'Double Grip': 'no one will snatch them out of my hand' and 'no one is able to snatch them out of the Father's hand'. I do praise God for His great grip.

Safe in the hands of God who made me,
What can there be that I should fear?
God is my light and my salvation,
Strong is his help when foes are near.

(Michael Perry)

24TH MARCH

I'M DEPENDING ON THE BLOOD

*But with the precious blood of Christ, like that
of a lamb without blemish or spot.*

1 Peter 1:19

The Bible refers to the blood of the Lord Jesus Christ as precious—1 Peter 1:18–19. The blood of Jesus is precious because it is royal blood, it is the very blood of God: 'care for the church of God, which he obtained with his own blood' Acts 20:28. It is the blood of the divine-human one. Through the blood of Jesus we have redemption. That is we have been bought back out of the slave market of sin, resulting in the fact we will be one day in heaven: 'And they sang a new song, saying, Worthy are you to take the scroll and to open its seals, for you were slain, and by your blood you ransomed people for God from every tribe and language and people and nation' Revelation 5:9. Therefore our only hope of being in Heaven is through the merits of the precious blood of Christ. Through the blood we have: forgiveness of sin, peace with God, nearness to God, on-going cleansing for sin as we walk in the light as He is in the light. Not only are we saved through the blood and given eternal life now, but the Lamb that was slain will be the very centre of Heaven's throne when one day we go to be with the Lord which is far better. As believers in Christ we can say; 'I'm depending on the blood':

On the golden streets of heaven all men hope to walk someday,
Yet so many are not willing to accept the living way;
But while others build on good works or opinions if they may,
Hallelujah! hallelujah! I'm depending on the blood.

In the soul-cleansing blood of the Saviour, I've been wash'd in the crimson flood;
Tho' the world may say There is hope some other way, I'm depending on the blood.

Some will tell us that God's mercy is their only hope and plea,
That a soul He could not punish thro'out all eternity;
But I read that my dear Saviour died for sinners just like me,
Hallelujah! hallelujah! I'm depending on the blood.

As we look back thro' the ages where the kings and prophets trod,
We may see their altars reeking with the sacrifice and blood;
But those types were only pointing to the Paschal Lamb of God,
Hallelujah! hallelujah! I'm depending on the blood.

'Tis the burden of that chorus over on the streets of light,
That the blood from Calv'ry's mountain hath wash'd all their garments white;
So I'll shout along life's pathway till I reach that land so bright,
Hallelujah! hallelujah! I'm depending on the blood.

(Johnson Oatman, Jr.)

25TH MARCH

THE WORD OF GOD AND PRAYER

*If you abide in me, and my words abide in you, ask
whatever you wish, and it will be done for you.*

John 15:7

While serving the Lord in a UK role, I had the privilege of going to speak at Churches, Prayer Group meetings or attend missionary conferences in various areas. In my free time I would visit various Christian heritage sites in that area. One such was the James Hudson Taylor Trail (1832–1905), Pioneer Missionary to China, in Barnsley. Hudson Taylor was the founder of the China Inland Mission known as OMF today. Followers of Jesus must make the Word of God and prayer key priorities in their lives and Christian experience.

The following are some thoughts of Hudson Taylor based on John 15:7 and 1 Kings 18:36–38: on how the Word of God is necessary to prayer: '. . . I have done all these things at your word. Answer me, O Lord, answer me. . . Then the fire of the Lord fell'. The verse before us shows the important connection existing between a full knowledge of the Word of God and successful prayer. Those prayers only will be answered which are in harmony with the revealed will of God. Many of us have heard earnest, but ignorant, believers praying for things clearly contrary to the revealed purposes of God. Again a full knowledge of the Word will often bring to our recollection appropriate promises, and thus enable us to pray with faith and confidence. Abiding in Christ and feeding upon His Word will lead to a Christ-like walk, which will assure our hearts before God. We must take time to be holy. It is not so much the quantity of Scripture we read, as the subjects for meditation which we find in it, that measure the nourishment we gain. On the other hand, our reading must not be too limited; for as the whole Paschal Lamb was to be eaten, so the whole Word of God is profitable and necessary 'that the man of God may be complete, equipped for every good work'. We would earnestly recommend the consecutive reading of the whole Word of God to all who do not so read it; and all who are able to do so that the whole Bible be read over in the course of a year. Where this cannot be done prayerfully and thoughtfully, rather let a shorter portion be taken for daily reading, still going through the whole Bible consecutively'.

*What would He think of me
If when I saw Him, I should say
'I was too busy every day
To read what Thou didst write to me;
I really hadn't time for Thee!'*

(Martha Snell Nicholson)

(Margaret Snell Nicholson was a woman who suffered from four incurable diseases. She struggled with pain more than thirty-five years, an invalid, bound to her bed. Her spirit was so transcendently triumphant through those many weary years, that she wrote some of the finest Christian poetry which has ever been written)

26TH MARCH

THE SECOND COMING DOOR

And while they were going to buy, the bridegroom came, and those who were ready went in with him to the marriage feast, and the door was shut.

Matthew 25:10

The story of the ten virgins as found in Matthew 25:1–13 is based around being ready for the Lord's return. Five of the ten were ready, five were not. Jesus taught distinctly that He was coming again: We find the certainty of His coming in John 14:1–3: 'Let not your hearts be troubled. Believe in God; believe also in me. In my Father's house are many rooms. If it were not so, would I have told you that I go to prepare a place for you? And if I go and prepare a place for you, I will come again and will take you to myself, that where I am you may be also'. The uncertainty of the time of His coming in Matthew 24:36: 'But concerning that day and hour no one knows, not even the angels of heaven, nor the Son, but the Father only'. The necessity of preparedness for His coming in Matthew 25:13: 'Watch therefore, for you know neither the day nor the hour'. The blessedness of the prepared in Matthew 25:10. And the wretchedness of the unprepared as found in Matthew 25:1–13. Those who had not being born again. Yes, perhaps went to church with the rest, kept good company but not saved. They had no oil in their lamps speaking of the indwelling Holy Spirit: Those five virgins who went in could sing:

'Soon as my all I ventured
on the atoning blood,
The Holy Spirit entered, and
I was born of God'

(Hugh Bourne)

Sadly those who were not born again of the Spirit of God were shut out. John 3:7 clearly teaches that you cannot enter heaven unless you are born again.

Ere that solemn hour of doom,
When the Son of man shall come,
Bidding quick and bidding dead
Rise to meet their risen Head,
Church of Jesus, hear the Word
Of thine own eternal Lord.

Virgins ten with joyous feet
Went the Bridegroom forth to meet;
Wise with heavenly wisdom, five
Kept with oil their lamps alive;
Five with earth-born folly dim
Scorned with oil their lamps to trim.

While the Bridegroom yet delayed,
Slumber bowed each virgin head;
Sudden rose the midnight cry—
Lo, the Bridegroom draweth nigh!
Leapt to life that virgin train,
Trimmed their dying lamps amain.

Vainly now for oil ye cry,
Foolish virgins, hence, and buy;
Fast thy speed—when lo! the door
Closes on them evermore:
Stern the voice which stuns each heart,
'Hence, I know you not, depart.'

Church of Jesus, rise and pray,
Dark that hour, and nigh that day;
Woe, ye hypocrites, to you,
Trim you saints, your lamps anew;
For the Bridegroom watch and wait,
Jesus Christ is at the gate.

William Dickinson

27TH MARCH

CHRIST'S FIRST AND LAST SUBJECT

From that time Jesus began to preach, saying,
Repent, for the kingdom of heaven is at hand.

Matthew 4:17

Beside Matthew 4:17 in my Bible I have the following CH Spurgeon quote: 'Christ's first and last subject'. This led me to Luke 24:47: 'and that repentance for the forgiveness of sins should be proclaimed in his name to all nations, beginning from Jerusalem'. Before going back to heaven Jesus told His disciples to preach the need of repentance. In Luke 13:1–5 people were pointing out to Jesus two groups of people who came to a terrible end. They suggested that they came to such a bad end because of their lifestyle. Jesus pointed out to these folk in both verse 3 and 5 that: 'unless you repent, you will all likewise perish'. Paul pointed out to his audience in Athens the absolute need for repentance: 'The times of ignorance God overlooked, but now he commands all people everywhere to repent'. Again in Acts 20:21 Paul reminded the Ephesus church of how he had preached to them the way of salvation: 'testifying both to Jews and to Greeks of repentance toward God and of faith in our Lord Jesus Christ'.

Elisha A. Hoffman in his hymn: 'Where will you spend eternity' put it like this:

Repent, believe, this very hour,
Trust in the Saviour's grace and power,
Then will your joyous answer be,
Saved thro' a long eternity!
Eternity! eternity!
Saved thro' a long eternity!

In Luke 15 verses 7 and 10 Jesus pointed out that when a person repents there is rejoicing in heaven: ' I tell you, there will be more joy in heaven over one sinner who repents'.

I have built up quite a library of books over the years purchased in 'Charity shops'. Sometimes the books still contain book markers, notes and various other materials left in them by their previous owners. I found the following little note regarding repentance in one of the books:

'There are at least seven parties who rejoice at the repenting of a soul:

- The Father Luke 15:32
- The Son Luke 15:6
- The Holy Spirit: Luke 15:9
- The Angels Luke 15:10
- The Loved Ones: Luke 15:6
- The Church Luke 15:3
- The one who repents: Acts 8:8,39

When a sinner comes as a
sinner may, there is joy;
When he turns to God in the
Gospel way, there is joy'.

28TH MARCH

LITTLE FOXES

Catch the foxes for us, the little foxes that spoil the vineyards, for our vineyards are in blossom.

Song of Solomon 2:15

A fellow worker in ministry shared with me some issues he had with worries, doubts and fears about the future. While speaking to him the words 'the little foxes that spoil the vineyards' came to my mind.

The little foxes referred to here are the little things which could cause problems between the Shulammite and Solomon. Dr David Jeremiah commenting on this verse said: 'Foxes of Bible times were closely related to jackals. In the Book of Judges, Samson tied a number of these together, lighting their tails and sending them out to spoil the fields of the Philistines. Foxes and crops did not go together. The queen would have known about their danger to the vineyards. Little foxes were the worst. Large groups of them would descend on a field or orchard and destroy it. In this text, the animals are used as metaphors of little problems that creep into marriages and destroy the sweetness there'.

Likewise there are little things that can come between us and our heavenly bridegroom that can destroy sweet fellowship with Him. Here are some little things in the Bible we need to watch out for that could spoil our relationship with Jesus:

LAZINESS IN SERVING HIM: 'A little sleep, a little slumber, a little folding of the hands to rest, and poverty will come upon you like a robber, and want like an armed man' Proverbs 6:10–11.

ACTING FOOLISHLY CONCERNING OUR WALK WITH JESUS: 'so a little folly outweighs wisdom and honour. Ecclesiastes 10:1.

LACK OF FAITH IN GOD TO MEET OUR EVERY NEED: 'But if God so clothes the grass of the field, which today is alive and tomorrow is thrown into the oven, will he not much more clothe you, O you of little faith?' Matthew 6:30.

OUR TOTAL LOVE FOR JESUS: 'Therefore I tell you, her sins, which are many, are forgiven—for she loved much. But he who is forgiven little, loves little' Luke 7:47. Jesus rebuked the church at Ephesus for leaving their first love: 'But I have this against you, that you have abandoned the love you had at first' Revelation 2:4.

WE ARE NOT TO TOLERATE THE LITTLE SINS IN OUR LIVES: 'A little leaven leavens the whole lump' Galatians 5:9. In the Bible leaven is a type of sin. We are to keep short accounts with God. We are not to be unthankful for all the little things God does for us. Little is much when God is in it: 'For who hath despised the day of small things?' 1 John 2:1.

These are but some of the little foxes that can spoil the sweet fellowship between us and our Lord.

29TH MARCH

AN INSTRUMENT IN HIS HANDS

*To the weak I became weak, that I might win
the weak. I have become all things to all people,
that by all means I might save some.*

1 Corinthians 9:22

Denzil McIlfatrick was a member of the UK Board of the Missionary Agency I served with from 2007 to 2022. Denzil originally came from Co Fermanagh the County I was born and brought up in. Denzil was a very faithful and supportive friend to me over the years.

The following is an account of Denzil's conversion at a mission held in Enniskillen and a correspondence between the evangelist and Denzil ten years later. The Rev W P Nicholson was invited to conduct a mission in Enniskillen from 2nd -23rd February 1947. On the night of the 21st February Denzil who was attending the Mission came to a saving knowledge of the Lord Jesus Christ after listening to Mr Nicholson's message that evening based on Genesis 6:3: 'My Spirit shall not always strive with man'. Over 200 people indicated that they had been converted as a result of the mission. Many of these converts became involved in various aspects of Christian work thereafter. Three of the converts went as missionaries to Africa.

Ten years after the mission it was decided to have a special reunion meeting of the converts. Denzil decided to write to Mr Nicholson to share about this special meeting. The following is the reply Denzil received back from the Rev Nicholson in response to his letter dated 1st March 1957:

'Dear Brother McIlfatrick

Your good, heart-cheering letter received and read with interest. It filled my heart with gratitude to God for allowing me to be an instrument in His hands of leading you to Jesus Christ as Saviour. God bless you and keep you from ever getting used to men going down to hell, but by all means win some. It is so easy these days to become lukewarm. There is no substitute for a Spirit-baptised, sanctified experience if we are to live holy lives of victory and satisfaction and successful, soul-winning service. Keep nothing back from the Lord Jesus. Let Him have all, always, Jesus never fails, Never! Hallelujah! May you ever be a terrible nuisance to the devil and a delight to God.

Maranatha! Hallelujah!

Yours restfully busy,
Wm P. Nicholson'

The cry of my heart today is: 'Lord do it again'. Grant that in our day and generation we will never get used to people going to hell, but we too by all means, all the time, will be involved in reaching the lost.

*Rescue the perishing, Care for the dying,
Snatch them in pity from sin and the grave;
Weep o'er the erring one, lift up the fallen,
Tell them of Jesus the mighty to save.*

(Fanny Crosby)

30TH MARCH

I MUST GO ON

Jesus said to him, "No one who puts his hand to the plough and looks back is fit for the kingdom of God.

Luke 9:62

James Kyle Paisley was a Baptist Pastor in N Ireland. He was born in 1891 and died in 1973. He had two well-known sons in Christian service, Harold Paisley an evangelist with the Brethren and Ian Paisley a famous politician and Free Presbyterian Minister.

Today I want to share with you a poem written many years ago by Pastor Paisley entitled 'I must go'. I trust it will be an encouragement for us to go through with God our vows to pay our all upon the alter lay:

I MUST GO ON:
My hand is put to the plough;
The wind blows cold; the sluggard leaves the sod unturned;
Nor cares that in the time of harvest he must beg!
But I have seen another Ploughman, spite of wind and snow,
Plough an unbending furrow to the end;
And ceaseless in His toil, break fallow Ground.
And though the mist and murk of unpropitious days
Lay up in store the summer's golden harvest joy
That Ploughman is the Master of my soul;
Therefore, in spite of storm and stress, like Him, I MUST GO ON!

I MUST GO ON:
I have in conscience drawn the sword;
The fight is hard; the armed Ephraimites may flee
And fill the streets of Gath and Askelon with mirth;
But I have seen a Warrior take the field alone,
Unsheath his sword against infernal foes,
And, though forsaken of the men He came to save,
Pour out His blood to win for them the victor's crown.
That warrior is the Captain of my soul,
And I though I should stand alone, like Him, I MUST FIGHT ON!

AND I MUST LOVE:
My heart is longer not my own.
The world allures, and fickle hearts may turn aside,
Nor care that ashes mark the place of yester's flame;
But I have seen a Lover, a spite of scorn and hate,
Love through an agony of blood and tears;
And ceaseless in His love for e'en His enemies,
Lay down His life, forsaken of earth and sky,
And rising, win a bride, and ring the marriage bells!
That Lover is the Lover of my soul;
And I, unto the endless end, like Him, I TOO MUST LOVE!

31ST MARCH

PRIDE REBUKED

But he gives more grace. Therefore it says, God opposes the proud but gives grace to the humble. Submit yourselves therefore to God. Resist the devil, and he will flee from you.

James 4:6–7

All through scripture we are warned against pride.

'Pride's ultimate goal is to preserve self, to protect self, and to promote self. It may take many different forms, but ultimately it must preserve, protect, and promote self. It is then robbing God of the glory that belongs solely to Him and to Him alone. Pride was birthed with original sin when Lucifer attempted to ascribe glory to himself that was God's alone. And pride continues to be the great divide between God and man today' Jeff Redlin.

In contrast as followers of Jesus we are encouraged to be humble.

I have a booklet on revival written in 1967 which carries a small article called 'Pride Rebuked'. It makes the point that the life and death of our Lord Jesus Christ are a standing rebuke to every form of pride:

- Pride of birth: 'Is not this the carpenter's son?'
- Pride of wealth: 'The Son of man hath not where to lay His head'.
- Pride of personal appearance: 'He hath no form nor comeliness'.
- Pride of reputation: 'Made Himself of no reputation'.
- Pride of superiority: I am . . . As one who serveth'.
- Pride of ability: 'I can of mine own self do nothing'.
- Pride of will: 'I seek not mine own will'.
- Pride of resentment: 'Father, forgive them'.

Purge me from every sinful blot,
My idols all be cast aside,
Cleanse me from every evil thought,
From all the filth of self and pride.

Give me a new, a perfect heart,
From doubt, and fear, and sorrow free,
The mind which was in Christ impart,
And let my spirit cleave to Thee.

(Charles Wesley)

Lord, bend that proud and stiff-necked I,
Help me to bow the head and die,
Beholding Him on Calvary,
Who bowed His head for me.

(African Hymn)

1ST APRIL

DON'T BE A FOOL

The fool says in his heart, there is no God. They are corrupt,
they do abominable deeds; there is none who does good.

Psalm 14:1

Today is known as 'April Fools' day. In Florida, an atheist created a case against the upcoming Easter and Passover holy days. He hired an attorney to bring a discrimination case against Christians, Jews and observances of their holy days.

The argument was that it was unfair that atheists had no such recognized days. The case was brought before a judge. After listening to the passionate presentation by the lawyer, the judge banged his gavel declaring, 'Case dismissed'.

The lawyer immediately stood objecting to the ruling saying, 'your honour, how can you possibly dismiss this case? The Christians have Christmas, Easter and others. The Jews have Passover, Yom Kippur and Hanukkah, yet my client and all other atheists have no such holidays'.

The judge leaned forward in his chair saying, 'But you do. Your client, counsel, is woefully ignorant'. The lawyer said, 'Your Honour, we are unaware of any special observance or holiday for atheists'.

The judge said, 'The calendar says April 1st is April fool's Day. Psalm 14:1 states, the fool says in his heart, there is no God. Thus, it is the opinion of this court, that if your client says there is no God, then he is a fool. Therefore, April 1st is his day. Court is adjourned'.

Human Folly is a regular theme throughout the Bible. Its definition is most serious. Fools cannot be serious and will not be taught: 'The fear of the Lord is the beginning of knowledge; fools despise wisdom and instruction' Proverbs 1:7. They meddle in other peoples' affairs: 'It is an honour for a man to keep aloof from strife, but every fool will be quarrelling' Proverbs 20:3. And of course the Bible teaches that the fool says in his heart that there is no God'. Despite many infallible proofs many still do not believe. We know that every effect must have an adequate cause. The world is here because it has been put here. The existence of the universe, its design and order tell us that there is an almighty and all-wise God.

There is a God, all nature cries
I see it painted on the skies;
I see it on the flowering spring,
I hear it when the birdlings sing,
I see it in the flowing main,
I see it on the fruitful plain,
I see it stamped on hail and snow,
I see it where the streamlets flow;
I see it in the clouds that soar,
I hear it when the thunders roar;
I see it when the morning shines,
I see it when the day declines;
I see it at the mountain height,
I see it in the smallest mite,
I see it everywhere abroad;
I feel—I know—there is a God

(Unknown)

2ND APRIL

JESUS A HISTORICAL FIGURE

He presented himself alive to them after
his suffering by many proofs.

Acts 1:3

Some years ago a leading surgeon, the son of one of the Elders in the church of which I am a member gave a talk at the church on a Good Friday evening on the death of Jesus from a medical perspective. It was one of those presentations that I will never forget. It gave me another perspective on what it meant to my lovely Lord and Saviour to bear away my sin. The surgeon at the outset made us aware that he was taking most of his medical points from an article that had been published in JAMA. JAMA is the most widely circulated general medical journal in the world, with more than 290,000 recipients of the print journal, more than 1.6 million recipients of electronic tables of contents and alerts, and over 34 million annual visits to the journal's website. Later I sourced the article through a web search. Over the next few days I want to take extracts from the article to share with you some of the agony Jesus went through to purchase our redemption and secure our salvation.

The first thing the writer of the article did was to establish the fact that there was indeed an historical person called Jesus Christ who was crucified: 'The life and teachings of Jesus of Nazareth which have formed the basis for a major world religion (Christianity), have appreciably influenced the course of human history, and, by virtue of a compassionate attitude toward the sick, also have contributed to the development of modern medicine. The eminence of Jesus as a historical figure and the suffering associated with his death has stimulated us to investigate, in an interdisciplinary manner, the circumstances surrounding his crucifixion'. After analysing the reliability and accuracy of various ancient manuscripts they conclude that indeed there was a historical Jesus Christ: 'When taken in concert—the extensive and early testimony of both Christian proponents and opponents, and their universal acceptance of Jesus as a true historical figure; the ethic of the gospel writers, and the shortness of the time interval between the events and extant manuscripts; and the confirmation of the gospel accounts by historians and archaeological findings— ensure a reliable testimony from which a modern medical interpretation of Jesus' death may be made'.

Quite an endorsement from a world renowned medical journal. Our Lord Jesus Christ is a historical figure who lived and died and praise God rose again, and is alive today. And that's a fact.

Tell me the story of Jesus,
write on my heart every word;
tell me the story most precious,
sweetest that ever was heard
Tell of the cross where they nailed Him,
writhing in anguish and pain;
tell of the grave where they laid Him,
tell how He liveth again.

(Fanny Crosby)

3RD APRIL

DARK GETHSEMANE

*And he came out and went, as was his custom, to the Mount
of Olives, and the disciples followed him. And when he came
to the place, he said to them, 'Pray that you may not enter into
temptation'. And being in agony he prayed more earnestly; and his
sweat became like great drops of blood falling down to the ground.*

Luke 22: 39–40, 44

It is worth noting that Luke alone describes the fact that the 'sweat of Jesus became like great drops of blood falling down to the ground'. He was a doctor. An article in the top medical journal JAMA states there in the section on Gethsemane as follows: 'After Jesus and his disciples had observed the Passover meal in an upper room in a house in southwest Jerusalem, they travelled to the Mount of Olives, northeast of the city. . . . At nearby Gethsemane, Jesus, apparently knowing that the time of his death was near, suffered great mental anguish, and, as described by the physician Luke, his sweat became as blood. Although this is a very rare phenomenon, bloody sweat may occur in highly emotional states in persons with bleeding disorders. As a result of haemorrhage into the sweat glands, the skin becomes fragile and tender. Luke's description supports the diagnosis of hematidrosis'.

The late John Blanchard comments: 'When the Last Supper was over, Jesus went with His disciples to the Mount of Olives. Here, He left the disciples for a while to pray alone. His prayer was simple, yet tremendously profound and we are on holy ground in trying to grasp its full meaning. Because He was truly human He actually shrank from the terrible death which faced Him the next morning; so He prayed that God should deliver Him from it 'if you are willing'. Yet because His will was totally submitted to the will of God, He added 'yet not my will, but yours be done'. Here is a model prayer, showing that God constantly requires our submission to His sovereignty. Even with the comfort of an angel the agony of the experience was so great for Jesus that blood oozed from His pores and mingled with the sweat that dropped from His face'.

*The hour in dark Gethsemane
I never shall forget,
When Christ alone the battle fought,
In grief and bloody sweat.*

*Gethsemane, Gethsemane,
I must remember thee,
Where God's eternal son I saw
In prayer on bended knee.*

*When I among thy solemn trees,
In spirit gazed around;
I saw the burden of my sin
On him with judgment bound.*

*I saw him tempted to despair,
By anguish, grief, bent low;
The depth of pain he suffered there
No man can fully know.*

*If ever, Lord, my love to thee
Should cold and fruitless be,
O show me in Gethsemane
Thy suffering there for me.*

(Edward Payson Hammond)

4TH APRIL

TRIALS

When day came, the assembly of the elders of the people gathered together, both chief priests and scribes. And they led him away to their council.

Luke 22:66

Then the whole company of them arose and brought him before Pilate.

Luke 23:1

Today we continue to look at the suffering of Jesus at the time of His death, from a medical point of view as outlined in an Article in JAMA, as He faced various trials, both Jewish and Roman before His sentence to be crucified.

'Soon after midnight, Jesus was arrested at Gethsemane by the temple officials and was taken first to Annas and then to Caiaphas, the Jewish high priest for that year. Between 1am and daybreak, Jesus was tried before Caiaphas and the political Sanhedrin and was found guilty of blasphemy. The guards then blindfolded Jesus, spat on him, and struck him in the face with their fists. Soon after daybreak, presumably at the temple, Jesus was tried before the Sanhedrin and again was found guilty of blasphemy, a crime punishable by death'. It is worth stopping at this point to consider the sufferings of Jesus at these trials. And why? Well it was for me, yes, all for me my Saviour suffered so.

'Since permission for an execution had to come from the governing Romans, Jesus was taken early in the morning by the temple officials to the Praetorium of the Fortress of Antonia, the residence and governmental seat of Pontius Pilate, the procurator of Judea. However, Jesus was presented to Pilate not as a blasphemer but rather as a self-appointed king who would undermine the Roman authority. Pilate made no charges against Jesus and sent him to Herod Antipas, the tetrarch of Judea. Herod likewise made no official charges and then returned Jesus to Pilate. Again Pilate could find no basis for a legal charge against Jesus, but the people persistently demanded crucifixion. Pilate finally granted their demand and handed over Jesus to be flogged (scourged) and crucified'.

The article then goes on to give a description of the Saviour's health up to this point: 'The rigors of Jesus' ministry (that is, travelling by foot throughout Palestine) would have precluded any major illness or a weak general constitution. Accordingly, it is reasonable to assume that Jesus was in good physical condition before his walk to Gethsemane. However, during the 12 hours between 9 pm Thursday and 9 am Friday, he had suffered great emotional stress, abandonment by his closest friends (the disciples), and a physical beating (after the first Jewish trial). Also, in the setting of a traumatic and sleepless night, he had been forced to walk more than 2.5 miles to and from the sites of the various trials'.

But none of the ransomed ever knew
How deep were the waters crossed;
Nor how dark was the night
the Lord passed thro'
Ere He found His sheep that was lost.

(Elizabeth Cecilia Clephane)

5TH APRIL

SCOURGING

Then Pilate took Jesus and flogged him.

John 19:1

I made my first visit to Israel on a trip organised by the late Hedley Murphy. We visited many biblical sites throughout Israel and its capital Jerusalem. One of the places Hedley took us to see, which had a major impact on my life, was a scourging chamber.

I am going to let a report on the death of Christ in an article in JAMA about the death of Jesus from a medical perspective, explain what it meant to be scourged. As we read this account consider the fact that:

It was for me, yes, all for me,
O love of God, so great so free!
O wondrous love, I'll shout and sing,
He died for me, my Lord and King!

(John M. Whyte)

'Flogging was a legal preliminary to every Roman execution and only women and Roman senators or soldiers (except in cases of desertion) were exempt. The usual instrument was a short whip (flagellum or flagellum) with several braided leather thongs of variable lengths, in which small iron balls or sharp pieces of sheep bones were tied at intervals. Occasionally, staves also were used. For scourging, the man was stripped of his clothing, and his hands were tied to an upright post. The back, buttocks, and legs were flogged either by two soldiers (lictors) or by one who alternated positions. The severity of the scourging depended on the disposition of the lictors and was intended to weaken the victim to a state just short of death. After the scourging, the soldiers often taunted their victims'. The article then goes on to explain the medical aspects of scourging: 'As the Roman soldiers repeatedly struck the victim's back with full force, the iron balls would cause deep contusions, and leather thongs and sheep bones would cut into the skin and subcutaneous tissues. Then, as the flogging continued, the lacerations would tear into the underlying skeletal muscles and produce quivering ribbons of bleeding flesh. Pain and blood loss generally set the stage for circulatory shock. The extent of blood loss may well have determined how long the victim would survive on the cross'.

I want us to pause again and just consider who was being scourged. It was God manifested in the flesh, the Son of God, the second person of the trinity. The article goes on to explain the scourging of Jesus: 'At the Praetoriun, Jesus was severely whipped. The severe scourging, with its intense pain and appreciable blood loss, most probably left Jesus in a preshock state. Moreover, hematidrosis had rendered his skin particularly tender. The physical and mental abuse meted out by the Jews and the Romans, as well as the lack of food, water, and sleep, also contributed to his generally weakened state. Therefore, even before the actual crucifixion, Jesus' physical condition was at least serious and possibly critical'.

6TH APRIL

CRUCIFIED, CRUCIFIED

There they crucified him.

John 19:18

Crucified! Crucified!
And nailed upon the tree!
With pierced hands and feet and side!
For you! For me!

(C. Austin Miles)

Today we continue reflecting on the death of our lovely Lord Jesus from a medical point of view as outlined in a reputable medical journal: 'Crucifixion probably first began among the Persians. Alexander the Great introduced the practice to Egypt and Carthage, and the Romans appear to have learned it from the Carthaginians. Although the Romans did not invent crucifixion they perfected it as a form of torture and capital punishment that was designed to produce a slow death with maximum pain and suffering. It was one of the most disgraceful and cruel methods of execution and was usually reserved only for slaves, foreigners, revolutionaries, and the vilest of criminals. Roman law usually protected Roman citizens from crucifixion, except perhaps in the case of desertion by soldiers'.

They go on to explain that: 'The major pathophysiologic effect of crucifixion, beyond the excruciating pain, was a marked interference with normal respiration, particularly exhalation ... The onset of muscle cramps or tetanic contractions, due to fatigue and hypercarbia, would hinder respiration further'.

The article then goes on to comment on the crucifixion of Jesus in particular: 'After the scourging and mocking, at about 9am, the Roman soldiers put Jesus' clothes back on him and led him and two thieves to be crucified. Jesus apparently was so weakened by the severe flogging that he could not carry the patibulum from the Praetorium to the site of crucifixion. Simon of Cyrene was summoned to carry Christ's cross, and the processional then made its way to Golgotha (or Calvary), an established crucifixion site. Here, Jesus' clothes, except for a linen loincloth, again were removed, thereby probably reopening the scourging wounds. He then was offered a drink of wine mixed with myrrh (gall) but, after tasting it, refused the drink. Finally, Jesus and the two thieves were crucified. Although scriptural references are made to nails in the hands, these are not at odds with the archaeological evidence of wrist wounds, since the ancients customarily considered the wrist to be part of the hand. . . . The soldiers and civilian crowd taunted Jesus throughout the crucifixion ordeal, and the soldiers cast lots for his clothing. Christ spoke seven times from the cross. Since speech occurs during exhalation, these short, terse utterances must have been particularly difficult and painful. At about 3 pm that Friday, Jesus cried out in a loud voice, bowed his head, and died. The Roman soldiers and onlookers recognised the moment of death'.

Dying for me, dying for me,
There on the cross He was dying for me;
Now in His death my redemption I see,
All because Jesus was dying for me

(Gladys Watkin Toberts)

7TH APRIL

ONE DAY THEY NAILED HIM TO DIE ON THE TREE

*For I delivered to you as of first importance what I also
received: that Christ died for our sins in accordance
with the Scriptures, that he was buried.*

1 Corinthians 15:3–4

Today we look at the death of Jesus as outlined from a medical point of view as recorded in an article in the world renowned medical journal JAMA:

'Jesus' death after only six hours on the cross surprised even Pontius Pilate. The fact that Jesus cried out with a loud voice and died suggests the possibility of a catastrophic terminal event. One popular explanation has been that Jesus died of cardiac rupture. . . . However, another explanation may be more likely. Jesus' death may have been hastened simply by his state of exhaustion and by the severity of the scourging, with its resultant blood loss and preshock state. The fact that he did not carry his patibulum supports this interpretation. The actual cause of death, like that of other crucified victims, may have been multifactorial and related primarily to hypovolemic shock, exhaustion asphyxia, and perhaps acute heart failure. A fatal cardiac arrhythmia may have accounted for the apparent catastrophic terminal event. Thus, it remains unsettled whether Jesus died of cardiac rupture or of cardiorespiratory failure. However, the important feature may not be how he died but rather whether he died. Clearly, the weight of historical and medical evidence indicates that Jesus was dead before the wound to his side was inflicted and supports the traditional view that the spear thrust between his ribs, probably perforated not only the right lung but also the pericardium and heart and therefore ensured death. Accordingly, interpretations based on the assumption that Jesus did not die on the cross appear to be at odds with modern medical knowledge'. Quite an amazing account from a secular medical journal.

Of course as you turn to scripture you find the real reason and cause of the death of Jesus: 'For one will scarcely die for a righteous person— though perhaps for a good person one would dare even to die— but God shows his love for us in that while we were still sinners, Christ died for us' Romans 5:7–8.

One day they led Him up Calvary's mountain,
One day they nailed Him to die on the tree;
Suffering anguish, despised and rejected;
Bearing our sins, my Redeemer is He.

Living, He loved me; dying, He saved me;
Buried, He carried my sins far away;
Rising, He justified freely forever:
One day He's coming—O glorious day!

One day they left Him alone in the garden,
One day He rested, from suffering free;
Angels came down o'er His tomb to keep vigil;
Hope of the hopeless, my Saviour is He.

(John Wilbur Chapman)

8TH APRIL

THE EMPTY TOMB

*Now on the first day of the week Mary Magdalene came
to the tomb early, while it was still dark, and saw that
the stone had been taken away from the tomb.*

John 20:1

On the first Easter morning angels invite us to inspect the empty tomb of the Lord Jesus Christ. Matthew's account reads as follows: 'But the angel said to the women, do not be afraid, for I know that you seek Jesus who was crucified. He is not here, for he has risen, as he said. Come, see the place where he lay' Matthew 28:5–6.

Today let us note:

1. THE TOMB'S CONSTRUCTION: It was cut out of the rock. The Rock of Ages Himself was buried in the cleft of the rock.

2 THE TOMB'S COST: Spurgeon describes it as follows: 'It is no common grave; it is not an excavation dug out by the spade for a pauper in which to hide the last remains of his miserable and over wearied bones. It is a princely tomb. Stand here, believer, and ask why Jesus had such a costly sepulchre. He had no elegant garments; he wore a coat without seam, woven from the top throughout, without an atom of embroidery. He owned no sumptuous palace, for he had not where to lay his head. His sandals were not rich with gold, or studded with brilliants. He was poor. Why, then, does he lie in a noble grave? We answer, for this reason: Christ was unhonoured till he had finished his sufferings; Christ's body suffered contumely, shame, spitting, buffeting, and reproach, until he had completed his great work; he was trampled underfoot, he was despised and rejected of men; a man of sorrows, and acquainted with grief; but the moment he had finished his undertaking, God said, No more shall that body be disgraced; if it is to sleep, let it slumber in an honourable grave; if it is to rest, let nobles bury it; let Joseph, the councillor, and Nicodemus, the man of Sanhedrim, be present at the funeral; let the body be embalmed with precious spices, let it have honour; it has had enough of contumely, and shame, and reproach, and buffeting; let it now be treated with respect. Christian, dost thou discern the meaning; Jesus after he had finished his work, slept in a costly grave, for now his Father loved and honoured him, since his work was done'.

3. THE TOMB'S CONTENTS: The grave clothes were found in the tomb, not the body. Clothes came through sin which makes naked and causes shame. Jesus left behind the clothes, the fruit of sin, because He had conquered sin forever.

*Risen Saviour, Rock of Ages
Who my sins and sorrows bore,
How the thought my fear assuages
Thou dost live for evermore.*

(Unknown)

9TH APRIL

UP FROM THE GRAVE HE AROSE

That he was buried, that he was raised on the
third day in accordance with the Scriptures.

1 Corinthians 15:4

One day the grave could conceal Him no longer,
One day the stone rolled away from the door;
Then He arose, over death He had conquered,
Now is ascended, my Lord ever more!

(J. Wilbur Chapman)

Over the past number of days we have been looking at the suffering and death of the Lord Jesus Christ from a medical perspective. But today we are going to look at what happened on the third day and what that means to us today.

Herbert Lockyer comments: 'If the Cross was what men thought about Jesus, the resurrection was what God thought about him'.

The scripture and Jesus are clear about what it means: 'Yet a little while and the world will see me no more, but you will see me. Because I live, you also will live' John 14:19. The resurrection is one of the most important doctrines of scripture. Paul makes it clear that the resurrection of Jesus from the dead is vitally connected with the work of salvation in the individual soul: 'if you confess with your mouth that Jesus is Lord and believe in your heart that God raised him from the dead, you will be saved' Romans 10:9. Therefore, the resurrection is of paramount importance.

So what does the resurrection mean to us as believers today: 'Who shall bring any charge against God's elect? It is God who justifies. Who is to condemn? Christ Jesus is the one who died—more than that, who was raised—who is at the right hand of God, who indeed is interceding for us' Romans 8:33–34. God has cleared us of all guilt on the ground of Christ's death and resurrection. 'Consequently, he is able to save to the uttermost those who draw near to God through him, since he always lives to make intercession for them' Hebrews 7:25. By His death He saved us and by His life He keeps us. On the basis of the resurrection of our Lord Jesus Christ, Paul argues that every man who has died will live again. Those who are believers will be raised with Christ: 'In a moment, in the twinkling of an eye, at the last trumpet. For the trumpet will sound, and the dead will be raised imperishable, and we shall be changed' 1 Corinthians 15:52. Their bodies will be changed to become like His glorious body. What a glad prospect of every blood bought, born again child of God.

Up from the grave he arose;
with a mighty triumph o'er his foes;
he arose a victor from the dark domain,
and he lives forever, with his saints to reign.
He arose! He arose! Hallelujah! Christ arose!

(Robert Lowry)

10TH APRIL

POWER STRUGGLE

For we do not wrestle against flesh and blood, but against the rulers, against the authorities, against the cosmic powers over this present darkness, against the spiritual forces of evil in the heavenly places.

Ephesians 6:12

The following is an extract from an Easter edition of an OMS magazine dated 1963: 'The day Christ died was a great day for death, the grim reaper. It seemed so easy:

- To buy Him for thirty pieces of silver.
- To catch Him without a struggle.
- To accuse Him and not have to worry about a successful defence in His favour.
- To force Pilate into a corner.
- To raise a rabble, stage a demonstration, and finally push His execution through.

Even the stone seemed to symbolize power and authority beyond challenge. And death stood guard with the Romans. How could anything be more secure, more hopeless, more final? All the components of human power had been marshalled to eliminate Jesus Christ from the life and affairs of human society. But, while the Romans paced back and forth outside the tomb, Omnipotent Power was at work inside! Matthew records, 'And behold, there was a great earthquake, for an angel of the Lord descended from heaven and came and rolled back the stone and sat on it' Matthew 28:2. The amazing fact was revealed—Jesus was already gone, on His way to Galilee. Now, it was a great day for Life—resurrection Life! Jesus Christ was back—this time forever and ever—to be faced and reckoned with at the consummation of history. Today, twenty centuries later, it seems that we are facing the same diabolically successful forces on many frontiers of the Gospel war. But we must remember that the real power struggle is being waged invisibly—on the inside of those so called closed situations as outlined in Ephesians 6:12. In this struggle, divine forces operate according to the supernatural law, like:

- Rolling a stone back by an angel.
- Escaping from grave clothes . . . leaving them neatly folded at the head of the bier.
- And putting fear in brawny soldiers until they did shake and became as dead men.

In this invisible power struggle we should remind ourselves that it is evolving according to a prophetic pattern:

First, through the miracle of regeneration: Ephesians 1:19–20. In this conquest of death by sin, the slaves are being ransomed and set free and the power of Satan is being broken.

Second, the Kingdom is being extended throughout the whole earth giving us a foretaste of the day when 'the earth shall be full of the knowledge of the Lord, as the waters cover the sea' Isaiah 11:9.

Third, by the cataclysmic consummation of the struggle, when our Lord Jesus Christ comes again as outlined in: 1 Corinthians 15: 24–25, 28.

So at this Eastertime, let us be thankful that we know the outcome of the power struggle'.

11TH APRIL

GOD'S WORD

Your word is a lamp to my feet and a light to my path.

Psalm 119:105

To follow Jesus requires reading, studying and applying God's Word to our lives. God's Word:

SAVES: 'receive with meekness the implanted word, which is able to save your souls' James 1:21.

SANCTIFIES: 'Sanctify them in the truth; your word is truth' John 17:17.

STABLISHES: 'rooted and built up in him and established in the faith, just as you were taught, abounding in thanksgiving' Colossians 2:7.

STRENGTHENS: 'No unbelief made him waver concerning the promise of God, but he grew strong in his faith as he gave glory to God' Romans 4:20.

SHINES: 'Your word is a lamp to my feet and a light to my path' Psalm 119:105.

SPEAKS: 'You shall teach them diligently to your children, and shall talk of them when you sit in your house, and when you walk by the way, and when you lie down, and when you rise' Deuteronomy 6:7.

Therefore:

RECEIVE GOD'S WORD WITH FAITH: 'For good news came to us just as to them, but the message they heard did not benefit them, because they were not united by faith with those who listened' Hebrews 4:2.

STORE IT IN THE HEART: 'I have stored up your word in my heart, that I might not sin against you' Psalm 119:11.

BE HEARERS AND DOERS OF THE WORD: 'But be doers of the word, and not hearers only, deceiving yourselves' James 1:22.

HOLD FAST TO IT: 'holding fast to the word of life, so that in the day of Christ I may be proud that I did not run in vain or labour in vain' Philippians 2:16.

MEDITATE IN IT: 'but his delight is in the law of the Lord, and on his law he meditates day and night' Psalm 1:2.

RIGHTLY DIVIDE IT: 'Do your best to present yourself to God as one approved, a worker who has no need to be ashamed, rightly handling the word of truth' 2 Timothy 2:15.

PREACH IT: 'preach the word; be ready in season and out of season; reprove, rebuke, and exhort, with complete patience and teaching' 2 Timothy 4:2.

ADORN IT: 'not pilfering, but showing all good faith, so that in everything they may adorn the doctrine of God our Saviour' Titus 2:10.

Ev'ry promise in the book is mine,
Ev'ry chapter, ev'ry verse, ev'ry line;
All are blessings of His love divine,
Ev'ry promise in the book is mine.

(Unknown)

12TH APRIL

ROPE HOLDERS

When many days had passed, the Jews plotted to kill him, but their plot became known to Saul. They were watching the gates day and night in order to kill him, but his disciples took him by night and let him down through an opening in the wall, lowering him in a basket.

Acts 9:23–25

Immediately after Paul was converted he started preaching the Gospel. Enraged by Paul's bold, fearless preaching of Jesus as the Messiah, the unbelieving Jews in Damascus plotted to take his life. With the help of fellow Christians, who let him down in a basket through a window in the city's wall, Paul escaped from Damascus and fled to Jerusalem. None of the people holding the ropes of the basket are identified. Today we call such people 'Rope Holders'. They are those who are faithfully holding the ropes for God's servants. We can hold the ropes personally, prayerfully, and privately for frontline Christian workers and missionaries.

When William Carey, the Father of Modern Missions, was leaving for India as a missionary, he told a group of interested friends, 'Saving souls can be likened to a man drowning in a deep well and a volunteer can do nothing unless there are people who will hold the rope for him to be lowered till he reaches the drowning man, and then pull them up to safety'. Carey adds, 'I will go to India as a volunteer to seek sinners drowning in the well of sin. But I can't do it alone. I need rope-holders. Will you be my rope-holders?'

Missionary work is a partnership. We cannot fulfil the Great Commission without those that go, and they cannot go unless we send them.

Down beneath the mighty ocean
Divers plunge for treasures rare,
But men hold the ropes above them
So they breathe the upper air;
Seeking pearls of richest value,
Braver hearts have dared to go;
But our hands must every moment
Hold the ropes that reach below

So amid the heathen darkness
There are heroes, true and brave,
Shrinking not from death or danger,
Bearing all to help and save,
But they cry, 'Oh, do not leave us
Mid these dreadful depths to drown,
Let us feel your prayers around us;
Hold the ropes as we go down'.

Who can understand the darkness
Of those realms of sin and death?
E'en the very air is tainted
With the dragon's breathe.
But across the wildest billows,
Love can reach to distant lands,
Underneath the darkest surges
Prayer can hold a brother's hand

Was it only for your brother
Jesus spake His last commands?
Is there naught for you to suffer
For those lost and Christless lands?
If you cannot go to save them,
There are those whom you can send:
And with loving hearts to help them,
Hold the ropes while they descend.

(Unknown)

13TH APRIL

WE ARE HOLDING THE LINE

*But I was let down in a basket through a window
in the wall and escaped his hands.*

2 Corinthians 11:33

Rope holders are those who support missionaries and Christian workers who are at the frontline. I read of a Church in the 1940s, who at the farewell service of a missionary family they were sending out to the mission field, brought them to the front and tied a rope around them and pulled it tight. Then the entire Church family took hold of part of the rope firmly. With tears flowing on many of their faces facing the Pastor said: 'We will be holding the rope in prayer and with our purses for you!'

Can I challenge you to become an intentional rope holder if you are not already?

'But his disciples took him by night and let him down through an opening in the wall, lowering him in a basket' Acts 9:25.

'How do you think that basket Paul was in got him to the ground? God could have suspended the law of gravity, but He didn't. No, that basket was let down by human hands. More than likely there were four men who climbed up on a wall of obscurity at night and let Paul down. Have you ever noticed how God used 'rope holders' all through the Bible?

- In Mark 2: Four men carried their friend to Jesus. Rope Holders!
- In John 6: A little boy gives his lunch to Jesus to begin the miracle of feeding 5000. Rope Holders!
- In Mark 14: A woman does 'what she could' to anoint the body of Jesus. Rope Holders!' (Steve Foster).

Christians 'hold the rope' by supporting the missions programmes of their local churches. In addition to prayer and sacrificial giving, there are many other ways Christians can get involved in missions, including correspondence, mission trips, serving on the missions committee or taking an interest in a specific missionary or missionary family, or an MK (missionary kid).

Keep holding the ropes out there for fellow believers, for those in missionary service, for your spiritual leaders and for loved ones who've not yet submitted their hearts to Christ.

*Saul of Tarsus murdered Christians
But met the Lord while on his way.
God changed his name from Saul to Paul
With his own friends he could not stay.
Old friends, now foes, desired to kill him
They watched the gates both night and day
But Paul was let down in a basket
With disciples' help he got away.
Hold the rope for friend and stranger
Hold the rope for family.*

*You never know who's in your basket
Or where they'll spend eternity
I once was lost with no direction
Stumbling around I could not see
But praise the Lord I found salvation
Someone held the rope for me.
Hold the rope of prayer for sinners
Hold the rope so faithfully
Let Christ in you, the Hope of Glory
Shine for all the world to see*

(Dee Dee Hall)

14TH APRIL

THE GREATEST SAVE

The saying is trustworthy and deserving of full acceptance, that Christ Jesus came into the world to save sinners, of whom I am the foremost.

1 Timothy 1:15

Gordon Banks' status as England's greatest goalkeeper may have been secured at the 1966 World Cup but it was a spectacular save to deny Pele in Mexico four years later that he became best remembered for. This save has been described as 'football's greatest ever save'.

However Graham Daniels the General Director of Christians in Sport (at the time of writing this devotional) explains that 'the greatest save in history was when Jesus came into the world, both fully man and fully God, to save people from their sins'. The Bible says: 'She will bear a son, and you shall call his name Jesus, for he will save his people from their sins' Matthew 1:21. The name Jesus means 'Jehovah saves' or 'Jehovah delivers'. Thus His name proclaims His deity and His office. He can save any kind of sinner, from any kind of sin, under any kind of circumstances. In any kind of place, for any length of time, and at any time.

'Consequently, he is able to save to the uttermost those who draw near to God through him, since he always lives to make intercession for them' Hebrews 7:25. John Owen points out that saving us to the uttermost means that Christ 'will not bring about part of our salvation and leave what remains to ourselves and to others....

Whatever belongs to our entire, complete salvation, he is able to effect it'. Christ does not leave us to ourselves but brings about our whole salvation, from its beginning at regeneration to its culmination in our glorification in heaven. Now to me that's 'the greatest save ever'.

Jesus is:

- Able to save (Hebrews 7:25).
- willing to save: 'The Lord is not slow to fulfil his promise as some count slowness, but is patient toward you, not wishing that any should perish, but that all should reach repentance' 2 Peter 3:9.
- Ready to save: 'The Lord will save me' Isaiah 38:20.
- Seeking to save: 'For the Son of Man came to seek and to save the lost' Luke 19:10.

Saved by His pow'r, by His pow'r divine,
Saved to new life, to new life sublime!
Life now is sweet and my joy is complete,
For I'm saved, saved, saved.

He saves me from ev'ry sin and harm,
Secures my soul each day;
I'm leaning strong on His mighty arm—
I know He'll guide me all the way.

(Jack P. Scholfield)

15TH APRIL

LORD JESUS CHRIST, THE CHURCH'S HEAD:

And he is the head of the body, the church. He is the beginning, the firstborn from the dead, that in everything he might be pre-eminent

Colossians 1:18

'For the husband is the head of the wife even as Christ is the head of the church, His body, and is himself its Saviour' Ephesians 5:23.

Today I want us to reflect on the fact that the Lord Jesus Christ is the only Head of the Church as expressed through the following hymns:

Lord Jesus Christ, the Church's head,
you are her one foundation;
in you she trusts, before you bows,
and waits for your salvation.
Built on this rock secure,
your Church shall endure
though all the world decay
and all things pass away.
O hear, O hear us, Jesus!

(Johann Mentzer)

Christ is made the sure foundation,
Christ, our head and cornerstone,
chosen of the Lord and precious,
binding all the Church in one;
holy Zion's help forever
and our confidence alone.

(J. M. Neale)

HEAD of thy church triumphant,
We joyfully adore thee;
Till thou appear, Thy members here
Shall sing like those in glory.

We lift our hearts and voices
With blest anticipation,
And cry aloud, And give to God
The praise of our salvation.

(Charles Wesley)

LORD Jesus Christ, our living Head,
How bright Thy glories shine!
Unique in Thy humanity:
Eternally divine.

Thou wast before created things,
Of all the Author Thou;
Upholder of the universe,
To Thee as God we bow.

The creature mind, howe'er sublime,
Thine essence cannot know,
Yet we to Thee in majesty,
With reverence bend low.

But in Thy manhood's glorious state
Our thankful hearts rejoice;
For of Thy body, Lord, are we,
Of love divine the choice.

Great source of wisdom, power and food,
All riches from Thee flow;
Thou on Thy church, Thy fullness here,
All treasure dost bestow.

So unto Thee, our glorious Head,
Love's tribute now we bring,
In nearness here to Thee on high
In heavenly measures sing.

(C. C. Elliott)

16TH APRIL

THE LORD IS MY SHEPHERD

The Lord is my shepherd; I shall not want.

Psalm 23:1

As His children not only is the Lord our Saviour but He is also our Shepherd. Dick Keogh, founder of the Cherith Gospel Outreach Trust, and I had a business meeting with a bank official in Thurles Co Tipperary. In the course of the meeting the young bank official asked Dick what Cherith Gospel outreach was all about. The Lord graciously opened up an opportunity for Dick to share his testimony. Dick came from the same religious background as the bank official. Dick explained that salvation was not found in a church or religious institution or in good works. Dick asked the question that if these things could save us why had Jesus to die on the Cross? The young bank official said that Dick had made a very good point. Dick went on to explain what the Lord meant to him. Jesus was both his Saviour and also his Shepherd. He shared just two verses of Scripture: 'For God so loved the world, that he gave his only Son, that whoever believes in him should not perish but have eternal life'. John 3:16. and 'The Lord is my shepherd; I shall not want'. Psalm 23:1.

The young man was getting married within two weeks of our conversation. Dick encouraged him to get a Bible and to trust Christ as His own personal Saviour by repentance and faith in Christ alone. The young man could then start off his married life with the Shepherd that had looked after Dick and Mary in their marriage ever since they trusted Him some forty years previous.

I relate all this to make the point that as believers we not only have a wonderful Saviour who died in our guilty room and stead at Calvary but also as the risen exalted Saviour we have a Shepherd to guide us through life. As Christians we can truly say: 'The Lord is MY Shepherd':

In the words of Leonard Weaver's hymn we too can say:

I have a Shepherd, One I love so well;
How He has blessed me tongue can never tell;
On the cross He suffered, shed
His blood and died,
That I might ever in His love confide.

Refrain:

Following Jesus, ever day by day,
Nothing can harm me when He leads the way;
Darkness or sunshine, whate'er befall—
Jesus, the Shepherd, is my All in All.

Pastures abundant doth His hand provide,
Still waters flowing ever at my side,
Goodness and mercy follow on my track,
With such a Shepherd nothing can I lack.

When I would wander from the path astray,
Then He will draw me back into the way;
In the darkest valley I need fear no ill,
For He, my Shepherd, will be with me still.

17TH APRIL

MIDDAY AND MIDNIGHT

At midday, O king, I saw on the way a light from heaven, brighter than the sun, that shone around me and those who journeyed with me.

Acts 26:13

God dealt with Paul at all times of the day. Paul was converted at midday and what a mighty conversion it was. Previous to his conversion he persecuted the church: 'But Saul was ravaging the church, and entering house after house, he dragged off men and women and committed them to prison'. Not only was he happy with ravaging the church at Jerusalem but at the time of his conversion he was on his way to Damascus to do the same to them. However on his journey Jesus met with Saul who would become the mighty missionary Paul: 'I heard a voice saying to me in the Hebrew language, 'Saul, Saul, why are you persecuting me? It is hard for you to kick against the goads'. And I said, 'Who are you, Lord?' And the Lord said, 'I am Jesus whom you are persecuting. But rise and stand upon your feet, for I have appeared to you for this purpose, to appoint you as a servant and witness to the things in which you have seen me and to those in which I will appear to you". Paul was saved at midday.

Later Paul, now a servant of the Lord, had a vision: 'And a vision appeared to Paul in the night: a man of Macedonia was standing there, urging him and saying, Come over to Macedonia and help us' Acts 16:9. And he did. He was obedient to the voice of God. Paul was a world Christian. He entered Europe with the Gospel.

He wasn't long in Europe until he and Silas ended up in prison for preaching the Gospel. And how did he respond: 'About midnight Paul and Silas were praying and singing hymns to God, and the prisoners were listening to them'. Acts 16:25. How and why could they do this? Because they knew they were in the centre of God's will.

As his people we need a vision of Himself; then a vision of the world and its need; and then, for those who obey and come into line with God's will, there is a song in the heart, whether it be at midday or midnight.

Lord, Thou hast made Thyself to me
A living, bright reality,
More present to faith's vision keen
Than any earthly object seen;
More dear, more intimately nigh
Than e'en the closest earthly tie

(Charlotte Elliott)

Hudson Taylor had the words of the verse of this song written by Charlotte Elliott on a paper slip, which he used as a marker for his diary. They revealed his heart's desire. Roger Carswell commenting on the same verse said: 'I understand that Dr Lloyd Jones prayed this prayer every day'.

Let it be our response today.

18TH APRIL

WAR-WIN-WORSHIP

*They will make war on the Lamb, and the Lamb will
conquer them, for he is Lord of lords and King of kings,
and those with him are called and chosen and faithful.*

Revelation 17:14

A CALL TO WAR: 'They will make war on the Lamb'.

Part of the Christian life is that of battle and conflict. The Christian life is not for 'softies'. For each Christian there is a call to war:

> *Onward, Christian soldiers,*
> *marching as to war,*
> *With the cross of Jesus*
> *going on before!*
>
> *Christ, the royal Master,*
> *leads against the foe;*
> *Forward into battle,*
> *see his banner go!*

(S. Baring-Gould)

Therefore we need to recognise that when we become true Christians the war begins. We are up against the world, the flesh and the devil. 'For all that is in the world—the desires of the flesh and the desires of the eyes and pride of life—is not from the Father but is from the world'. 1 John 2:16. 'Be sober-minded; be watchful. Your adversary the devil prowls around like a roaring lion, seeking someone to devour' 1 Peter 5:8. Someone has rightly said: 'Never expect to sin, never excuse sin and never excite sin'. We are in a constant battle.

A CALL TO WIN: 'and the Lamb will conquer them'

Here is the secret of victory. This refers to the death of Christ. Christ defeated Satan at Calvary. He paid the price for our sins at Calvary. 'But he was pierced for our transgressions; he was crushed for our iniquities; upon him was the chastisement that brought us peace, and with his wounds we are healed. All we like sheep have gone astray; we have turned—every one—to his own way; and the Lord has laid on him the iniquity of us all.' Isaiah 53:5–6. When our Lord Jesus Christ cried 'It is finished', it was not a cry of despair, it was not a cry of one dying on the Cross as if all were lost, but the triumphant shout of the Son of God who died to accomplish the work of salvation. It is because the Lamb is triumphant that we may be victorious too. 'And they have conquered him by the blood of the Lamb' Revelation 12:11.

A CALL TO WORSHIP: 'he is Lord of lords and King of kings', and those who are with Him 'are called and chosen and faithful'. Here we find the place of triumph at the feet of the Lord of Lords and King of Kings.

> *On the vict'ry side, on the vict'ry side,*
> *In the ranks of the Lord are we;*
> *On the vict'ry side we will boldly stand,*
> *Till the glory-land we see.*

(Fanny Crosby)

19TH APRIL

MAD?

And many of them said, He hath a devil, and is mad; why hear ye him.

John 10:20

Paul, thou art beside thyself; much learning doth make thee mad.

Acts 26:24

And they said unto her, Thou art mad. But she constantly affirmed that it was even so. Then said they, It is his angel.

Acts 12:15

The world thinks that one that is an out-and-out Christian is mad. And it has always been so. Jesus, Paul and Rhoda were all called mad.

Jesus was called mad because He spoke of His Cross. The world neither understands nor wants to know about the Cross of Christ. Paul understood this. Writing to the Church at Corinth he said: 'but we preach Christ crucified, a stumbling block to Jews and folly to Gentiles' 1 Corinthians 1:23. Religious people and people of the world would reduce the Christian Faith to a code of ethics and good living. In cutting out the Cross they present a message that is valueless for the souls of men.

I must needs go home by the way of the cross,
There's no other way but this;
I shall ne'er get sight of the gates of light,
If the way of the cross I miss

(Jessie Brown Pounds)

Because He lives, I can face tomorrow,
Because He lives, all fear is gone;
Because I know He holds the future,
And life is worth the living,
Just because He lives!

(Bill & Gloria Gaither)

PAUL WAS CALLED MAD BECAUSE HE PROCLAIMED THE RESURRECTION. He declared before Festus and Agrippa 'that the Christ must suffer and that, he should be the first to rise from the dead' Acts 26:23. Festus' response was: 'Paul, thou art beside thyself; much learning doth make thee mad' Acts 26:24.

RHODA WAS CALLED MAD BECAUSE SHE BELIEVED GOD ANSWERED PRAYER. When Peter was delivered from prison as recorded in Acts 12, Rhoda was accused of being mad when she told the others at the prayer meeting that he was at the door. Praise God we serve a risen exalted Saviour who intercedes on our behalf. We have a great God who not only hears but answers prayer.

The only one we want to be mad today is that old serpent the devil. He is mad because we have been redeemed and he has no longer any power over the believer.

God answers pray'r in the morning,
God answers pray'r at noon;
God answers pray'r in the ev'ning,
To keep your heart in tune.

(Unknown)

The devil is mad, and I am glad, (x3)
He lost the soul that he thought he had
All my sins are washed away, I've been redeemed.

(Unknown)

20TH APRIL

THE BODY FOR GOD

*I appeal to you therefore, brothers, by the mercies of
God, to present your bodies as a living sacrifice, holy and
acceptable to God, which is your spiritual worship.*

Romans 12:1

Data genetics have calculated that the value of an average human body in chemical terms is 160 US dollars. Paul outlines in Romans 12:1 the value of a body yielded to God:

THE APPEAL TO YIELD YOUR BODY TO GOD: 'I appeal to you therefore, brothers'. Paul isn't shouting out orders. He's not commanding and demanding. He's encouraging believers to present their bodies to God.

THE ARGUMENT FOR YIELDING YOUR BODY TO GOD: 'by the mercies of God'. Paul is pinning his argument on the mercies of God. He is not telling the people to present themselves a living sacrifice to God without giving them the reason. The call to action is powerless without the believers seeing the mercies of God. It reminds us of Jeremiah's words of praise in the book of Lamentations: 'the steadfast love of the Lord never ceases; His mercies never come to an end, they are new every morning; great is your faithfulness'.

A debtor to mercy alone,
Of covenant mercy I sing;
Nor fear, with Thy righteousness on,
My person and offering to bring.

The terrors of law and of God
With me can have nothing to do;
My Saviour's obedience and blood
Hide all my transgressions from view

(Augustus M. Toplady)

THE ABANDONMENT OF YOUR BODY TO GOD: 'to present your bodies as a living sacrifice, holy and acceptable to God': CT Studd (Charles Thomas Studd 1860–1931 was an English missionary who faithfully served his Saviour in China, India, and Africa) put it this way, 'If Jesus Christ be God and died for me, then no sacrifice can be too great for me to make for him'.

THE ALLEGIANCE OF YOUR BODY TO GOD: 'which is your spiritual worship'. Isaac Watts, a great hymn writer of the 17th-18th century, wrote from His view of God these words: 'Love so amazing, so divine, demands my soul, my life, my all'.

When I survey the wondrous cross
On which the Prince of glory died,
My richest gain I count but loss,
And pour contempt on all my pride.

Forbid it, Lord, that I should boast,
Save in the death of Christ my God!
All the vain things that charm me most,
I sacrifice them to His blood.

See from His head, His hands, His feet,
Sorrow and love flow mingled down!
Did e'er such love and sorrow meet,
Or thorns compose so rich a crown?

Were the whole realm of nature mine,
That were a present far too small;
LOVE SO AMAZING, SO DIVINE,
DEMANDS MY SOUL, MY LIFE, MY ALL.

(Isaac Watts)

21ST APRIL

SHINE OUT THROUGH MY LIFE EACH DAY

Again Jesus spoke to them, saying, I am the light of the world. Whoever follows me will not walk in darkness, but will have the light of life.

John 8:12

THE SOURCE OF LIGHT: The source of all spiritual light is Christ. He is not a mere reflector or conveyor of light, but the very essence and source of it. It was the Son of God the 'Great I Am' that said 'I Am the light of the world'.

THE COURSE OF LIGHT: 'Whoever follows me will not walk in darkness'. Follow the course of light and you will find it dispels darkness. When we yield ourselves to Christ; when we open our hearts to His incoming, so that He who is the Light of the world floods our soul with light, there is one thing that will happen: darkness of sin vanishes. Nor will it return as long as the Light of the world indwells and controls us. If you let Christ in and let Him take control of your life and you follow Him, then the darkness of sin and unbelief must go.

I wandered so aimless life filled with sin
I wouldn't let my dear saviour in
Then Jesus came like a stranger in the night
Praise the Lord I saw the light.

CHORUS:

I saw the light I saw the light
No more darkness no more night
Now I'm so happy no sorrow in sight
Praise the Lord I saw the light.

Just like a blind man I wandered along
Worries and fears I claimed for my own
Then like the blind man that God gave back his sight
Praise the Lord I saw the light.

I was a fool to wander and stray
Straight is the gate and narrow the way
Now I have traded the wrong for the right
Praise the Lord I saw the light.

(Hank Williams)

THE FORCE OF LIGHT: 'but will have the light of life'. Once the light of life comes into your life to dwell, the darkness will go, and then we must go out into the world to shine. There is much darkness around us. The darkness of unbelief and sin and indifference. The Lord wants us to be light to others. Jesus gives us the conditions of doing so: 'Whoever follows me will not walk in darkness, but will have the light of life'. We are to follow Christ and in so doing He will shine through us as He promised to do, the Light of Life.

Finding, following, keeping, struggling,
Is He sure to bless?
Saints, apostles, prophets, martyrs,
Answer, Yes.

(St. Stephen of Mar Sabas;
Translator: J. M. Neale)

Shine, shine in my heart, I pray,
Shine out through my life each day;
Sun of righteousness, Light of truth,
Shine in Thy glory in me.

(Charles W. Naylor)

22ND APRIL

FOR-WITH-IN-THROUGH

You are the Christ, the Son of the living God.

Matthew 16:16

The word Christ is from the similar-sounding Greek word '*Christos*', which describes the divine Son of God, the Anointed King, and the 'Messiah' who is positioned and purposed by God to be the deliverer of all people in a way that no regular person, prophet, judge, or ruler could be. Of course that person was Jesus. His full title being the Lord Jesus Christ.

The following are four truths about Christ that are true of every Christian:

CHRIST FOR ME: This was demonstrated at the Cross: 'Christ died for our sins in accordance with the Scriptures' 1 Corinthians 15:3. Christ for me on the Cross of Calvary is the place where life for the Christian begins. The Cross demonstrates that Christ is for me.

CHRIST WITH ME: From the moment we come to the Cross and repent of our sins and trust Him as our Lord and Saviour we have the assurance that Christ is with us. In fact he promises never to leave us or forsake us: 'for he has said, I will never leave you nor forsake you. So we can confidently say, The Lord is my helper; I will not fear; what can man do to me? Hebrews 13:5–6. Believer are you finding it hard today?. Christ will be with you. Trust Him to see you through. He will be by your side.

CHRIST IN ME: 'To them God chose to make known how great among the Gentiles are the riches of the glory of this mystery, which is Christ in you, the hope of glory' Colossians 1:27. The truth is that you cannot live what we have not got. We cannot live a life we do not possess. We cannot be Christians apart from Christ. Jesus said you must be born again. When we come to Him we receive a new life. He comes to indwell us by His Spirit, and it is 'Christ in you' that makes the Christian experience possible.

CHRIST THROUGH ME: Jesus Christ wants to live His life in us—to express His life through us to others.

Christ Is The Answer To My Every Need;
Christ Is The Answer, He Is My Friend Indeed.
Problems Of Life My Spirit May Assail,
With Christ My Saviour
I Need Never Fail,
For Christ Is The Answer To My Need

(Unknown)

Let the beauty of Jesus be seen in me,
All his wonderful passion and purity,
O thou Spirit divine, all my nature refine,
Till the beauty of Jesus be seen in me.

(Albert W. T. Orsborn)

23RD APRIL

THE HOUR IS COMING

But the hour is coming, and is now here, when the true worshipers will worship the Father in spirit and truth, for the Father is seeking such people to worship him.

John 4:23

My good friend Dick Keogh has written many Gospel tracts and pamphlets over the years which have been and are being used of God in evangelism and discipleship in many countries of the world. One of his booklets is called 'New Life in Luke'. It contains the Gospel of Luke and some Bible lessons.

The following is an extract from one of the lessons entitled 'The hour is coming':

- The hour is coming when you will have to leave your family, friends and neighbours behind.
- The hour is coming in which you will have to leave all of your plans, aspirations and dreams behind.
- The hour is coming in which you will leave all of your wealth, property and possessions behind. You may be prosperous and popular, but 'what shall it profit a man, if he shall gain the whole world, and lose his own soul?'
- The hour is coming in which many will understand what the Lord meant when He said, 'I have called, and ye refused; I have stretched out my hand, and no man regarded. When I called ye did not answer. And ye will not come to me, that ye might have life'
- The hour is coming in which you will no longer have the opportunity to respond to God's offer of salvation. 'the Lord said, 'My Spirit shall not always strive with man'

- The hour is coming in which you will die. 'What man is he that liveth, and shall not see death?
- The hour is coming in which you will stand before the Judgement Seat of God. 'It is appointed unto men once to die, but after this the judgement'
- The hour is coming in which 'all that are in the graves shall hear his voice, and shall come forth; they that have done good, unto the resurrection of life; and they that have done evil, unto the resurrection of damnation'
- The hour is coming in which the resurrected multitude will hear God, the righteous judge, passing sentence. To those who died in the faith (who were trusting Christ as Saviour) He will say, 'Come, ye blessed of my Father, inherit the kingdom prepared for you from the foundation of the world'. To those who died in their sins (who refused or rejected God's offer of salvation) He will say, 'Depart from me, ye cursed, into everlasting fire, prepared for the devil and his angels'. What will God say to YOU on Judgement Day?

SOMETHING TO CONSIDER: The hour is coming when your opportunity to receive Christ as your Saviour will have passed and it will be too late.

24TH APRIL

THE DOOMSDAY CLOCK

And there will be signs in sun and moon and stars, and on the earth distress of nations in perplexity because of the roaring of the sea and the waves

Luke 21:25

As I was reading this verse it reminded me of the signs of the end times as outlined by Jesus. Of course Jesus also said: 'But concerning that day and hour no one knows, not even the angels of heaven, nor the Son, but the Father only'. Matthew 24:36. We do not know when Jesus is coming but we can discern the times.

However when I was reading our verse for today the 'Doomsday Clock' came to my mind. Founded in 1945 by Albert Einstein and University of Chicago scientists who helped develop the first atomic weapons in the Manhattan Project, the Bulletin of the Atomic Scientists created the Doomsday Clock two years later, using the imagery of apocalypse (midnight) and the contemporary idiom of nuclear explosion (countdown to zero) to convey threats to humanity and the planet. The Doomsday Clock is set every year by the Bulletin's Science and Security Board in consultation with its Board of Sponsors, which includes 10 Nobel laureates. The Clock has become a universally recognized indicator of the world's vulnerability to global catastrophe caused by manmade technologies.

The following is the assessment of the 'Doomsday Clock' for 2023, the year of writing this devotional:

'A time of unprecedented danger: It is 90 seconds to midnight.

This year, the Science and Security Board of the Bulletin of the Atomic Scientists moves the hands of the Doomsday Clock forward, largely (though not exclusively) because of the mounting dangers of the war in Ukraine. The Clock now stands at 90 seconds to midnight—the closest to global catastrophe it has ever been.

The war in Ukraine may enter a second horrifying year, with both sides convinced they can win. Ukraine's sovereignty and broader European security arrangements that have largely held since the end of World War II are at stake. Also, Russia's war on Ukraine has raised profound questions about how states interact, eroding norms of international conduct that underpin successful responses to a variety of global risks.

And worst of all, Russia's thinly veiled threats to use nuclear weapons remind the world that escalation of the conflict—by accident, intention, or miscalculation—is a terrible risk. The possibility that the conflict could spin out of anyone's control remains high'.

The truth for today is that Jesus is coming again and even the world acknowledges that this age could come to an end at any time. Jesus put it like this: 'Now when these things begin to take place, straighten up and raise your heads, because your redemption is drawing near' Luke 21:28.

The day approaches; Jesus soon is coming.
Redeem the time; it must not slip away.
Lord, make us ready for the cry: 'Behold Him!'
By using every moment of each day.

(Unknown)

25TH APRIL

Make me to know your ways, O Lord; teach me your paths.

Psalm 25:4

The Bible has much to say about paths in life. Our path refers to the way we live and what we decide to do with our limited time on earth. The following are just a few verses about paths that I trust will be helpful and an encouragement to you today:

PROVERBS 3:5–6: Trust in the Lord with all your heart, and do not lean on your own understanding. In all your ways acknowledge him, and he will make straight your paths.

In these verses we see: 1. A trusting confidence in God: Trust in the Lord with all your heart; 2. A total commitment to God: In all your ways acknowledge him; 3. A thrilling confidence from God: and he will make straight your paths.

PSALM 16:11: You make known to me the path of life; in your presence there is fullness of joy; at your right hand are pleasures for evermore.

In this verse we see: 1. The path of life; 2. The presence of joy; 3. The pleasures of eternity.

PSALM 119:105: Your word is a lamp to my feet and a light to my path.

Dean Burgon commenting on the Bible said: 'The Bible is none other than the voice of Him that sitteth on the throne. Every book of it, every chapter of it, every verse of it, every syllable of it, every letter of it, is the direct utterance of the Most High'.

JEREMIAH 6:16: Thus says the Lord: Stand by the roads, and look, and ask for the ancient paths, where the good way is; and walk in it, and find rest for your souls. But they said, we will not walk in it.'

In this verse, we are given the image of a traveller who comes to a fork or junction in the road. He has the opportunity to go anyway he desires, but God tells him to 'ask for the ancient paths, where the good way is'. Instead of just travelling blindly on, this traveller is to stop and ask directions. How might we do this:

- STAND: Stand by the roads;
- SEE: and look;
- SAY: ask for the ancient paths, where the good way is;
- SOJOURN: and walk in it;
- SAFETY: and find rest for your souls;
- STUBBORNNESS: But they said, we will not walk in it.

Today let us not be stubborn but obedient and walk in the path God has for us

He will show me the pathway of life,
Leading up to a fullness of joy
At the right hand of the throne,
When this dreary life is done
Not a care shall my peace destroy.

(Thomas P. Westendorf)

Ask for the old paths, walk in the old paths;
Christ and the prophets trod the way before:
Ask for the old paths, walk in the old paths,
Leading away to the better shore.

(F. E. Belden)

26TH APRIL

LIFE BEGINS AT FORTY

For the man on whom this sign of healing was performed was more than forty years old.

Acts 4:22

This verse refers to the lame man that was healed at the gate Beautiful while Peter and John were on their way to pray. Luke records the miraculous healing of this man in Acts 3:1–11. By many it was assumed that this man was beyond help, hope and healing. He was lame from birth, he lay daily at the gate Beautiful, he was a beggar and at this stage he was forty years old. But nothing is impossible with our God. Never give up hope in a hopeless situation. The man asked of Peter and John money but they gave him so much more. The lame was healed and could walk and leap and as a result was praising God. From that day forward his life was changed forever. It is said that life begins at forty—well it definitely did for this man:

We see here the type of men that God uses to see lives changed in Jesus name: What type of men were Peter and John:

THEY WERE PARTNERS: 'Now Peter and John were going up to the temple at the hour of prayer' Acts 3:1. They were together. They were united. That is where God commends a blessing.

THEY WERE PRAYER WARRIORS: 'at the hour of prayer' Acts 3:1; 'And when they had prayed, the place in which they were gathered together was shaken, and they were all filled with the Holy Spirit and continued to speak the word of God with boldness' Acts 4:31. They were men living in revival.

THEY WERE PREPARED: When challenged they were always prepared: 'always being prepared to make a defence to anyone who asks you for a reason for the hope that is in you' 1 Peter 3:15. They were prepared to come before the religious leaders and courts to defend Christ: Acts 3:13, 22, 24–25.

THEY WERE POWER-FILLED: 'Then Peter, filled with the Holy Spirit' Acts 4:8. 'Now when they saw the boldness of Peter and John, and perceived that they were uneducated, common men, they were astonished. And they recognized that they had been with Jesus' Acts 4:13.

Peter and John went to pray
They met a lame man on the way
He asked for alms and held out his palms
And this is what Peter did say

Silver and gold have I none
But such as I have give I thee
In the name of Jesus Christ of Nazareth,
rise up and walk

He went walking and leaping
and praising God
Walking and leaping and praising God
In the name of Jesus Christ of Nazareth,
rise up and walk

(Unknown)

27TH APRIL

FOOT AND MOUTH

Because, if you confess with your mouth that Jesus is Lord and believe in your heart that God raised him from the dead, you will be saved

Romans 10:9

'He will guard the feet of his faithful ones'

1 Samuel 2:9

The last major outbreak of 'Foot and Mouth' disease in the UK was in 2001. I can remember it well for at that time I was working in the agricultural industry. There were 2,000 cases of the disease in farms across most of the British countryside. Over 6 million cows and sheep were killed in an eventually successful attempt to halt the disease.

I have some notes from that time on 'Foot and Mouth' from a spiritual context: The Foot by nature and by grace, and the Mouth by nature and grace:

THE MOUTH BY NATURE:

• Is full of cursing and deceit: Psa 10:7
• Speaks proudly: Psa 17:10
• Is given to evil: Psa 50:19
• Speaks vanity: Psa 144:8
• Pours out foolishness: Prov 15:2
• Ends in destruction: Prov 18:7

THE MOUTH BY GRACE:

• Cries unto the Lord: Psa 66:17
• Is filled with praise: Psa 71:8
• Shows His righteousness: Psa 71:15
• Is a well of life: Prov 10:11
• Is satisfied: Prov 18:20
• Confesses the Lord Jesus: Rom 10:9

THE FEET BY NATURE:

• Were almost gone: Psa 73:2
• Run to evil: Prov 1:16
• Run to mischief: Prov 6:18

• Are sunk in the mire: Jer 32:35
• Slide in due time: Deut 32:35

THE FEET BY GRACE:

• Are washed: John 13:10
• Kept: 1 Sam 2:19
• Are set upon a Rock: Psa 40:2
• Cannot be moved: Psa 66:9
• Are shod with the Gospel: Eph 6:15
• Bring the Gospel: Rom 10:15
• Will bruise Satan: Rom 16:20

Take my feet and let them be
Swift and beautiful for Thee,
Swift and beautiful for Thee.

Take my lips, and let them be
Filled with messages from Thee,
Filled with messages from Thee.

(Frances Ridley Havergal)

May the words of my mouth
and the meditation of my heart be pleasing,
be pleasing in Thy sight, O Lord,
my Rock and my Redeemer.

(Unknown)

I'm pressing on the upward way,
New heights I'm gaining every day;
Still praying as I onward bound,
Lord, plant my feet on higher ground.

(Johnson Oatman Jr.)

28TH APRIL

GUIDE ME O, THOU GREAT JEHOVAH

You guide me with your counsel.

Psalm 73:24

My father often quoted the first part of William Williams great hymn 'Guide Me, O Thou Great Jehovah' while praying. We all need God's guidance in our Christian journey. And we are promised guidance in God's Word. As a Christian, God must be our only guide. The Psalmist puts it as follows: 'For you are my rock and my fortress; and for your name's sake you lead me and guide me' Psalm 31:3; and 'He restores my soul. He leads me in paths of righteousness for his name's sake' Psalm 23:3.

You may ask the question how does He guide us:

1. BY HIS WORD: 'Your word is a lamp to my feet and a light to my path' Psalm 119:105;

2. BY HIS SPIRIT: 'And I will give them one heart, and a new spirit I will put within them. I will remove the heart of stone from their flesh and give them a heart of flesh' Ezekiel 11:19, 'When the Spirit of truth comes, he will guide you into all the truth' John 16:13;

3. BY HIS PROVIDENCE: 'The steps of a man are established by the Lord, when he delights in his way' Psalm 37:23;

4. BY HIS EYE: 'I will instruct you and teach you in the way you should go; I will counsel you with my eye upon you' Psalm 32:8: 'His eye is on the sparrow, And I know he watches me' Civilla D. Martin;

5. 'BY HIS COUNSEL: Psalm 73:24;

6. BY HIS VOICE: 'And your ears shall hear a word behind you, saying, This is the way, walk in it, when you turn to the right or when you turn to the left' Isaiah 30:21;

7. BY GODLY COUNSEL: 'Where there is no guidance, a people falls, but in an abundance of counsellors there is safety' Proverbs 11:14.

These are but some of the ways God guides us.

Guide me, O thou great Jehovah,
pilgrim through this barren land.
I am weak, but thou art mighty;
hold me with thy powerful hand.
Bread of heaven, bread of heaven,
feed me till I want no more;
feed me till I want no more.

Open now the crystal fountain,
whence the healing stream doth flow;
let the fire and cloudy pillar
lead me all my journey through.
Strong deliverer, strong deliverer,
be thou still my strength and shield;
be thou still my strength and shield.

When I tread the verge of Jordan,
bid my anxious fears subside;
death of death and hell's destruction,
land me safe on Canaan's side.
Songs of praises, songs of praises,
I will ever give to thee;
I will ever give to thee.

(William Williams)

29TH APRIL

ALL THE WAY MY SAVIOUR LEADS ME

He leads the humble in what is right, and
teaches the humble his way.

Psalm 25:9

Yesterday we looked at how God guides us. Today we will take a look at where He guides us. I trust our testimony is like that of Fanny Crosby: 'All the way my Savior leads me–Cheers each winding path I tread'.

GOD GUIDES US INTO ALL TRUTH: 'Send out your light and your truth; let them lead me; let them bring me to your holy hill and to your dwelling' Psalm 43:3.

HE LEADS US INTO THE WAY OF PEACE: 'to give light to those who sit in darkness and in the shadow of death, to guide our feet into the way of peace' Luke 1:79.

GOD LEADS US TO REPENTANCE: 'realising that God's kindness is intended to lead you to repentance' Rom 2:4.

IN THE WILDERNESS: 'Then he led out his people like sheep and guided them in the wilderness like a flock' Psa 78:2. Are you experiencing a period in the wilderness, a dry period? Then hold on to God and He will bring you through.

HE LEADS US TO SPRINGS OF WATER: 'they shall not hunger or thirst, neither scorching wind nor sun shall strike them, for he who has pity on them will lead them, and by springs of water will guide them' Isaiah 49:10.

HE PROMISES TO GUIDE US CONTINUALLY: 'And the Lord will guide you continually' Isaiah 58:11.

HE WILL LEAD US SAFELY HOME TO GLORY: 'You guide me with your counsel, and afterward you will receive me to glory' Psalm 73:24.

All the way my Savior leads me–
What have I to ask beside?
Can I doubt His tender mercy,
Who through life has been my guide?
Heav'nly peace, divinest comfort,
Here by faith in Him to dwell!
For I know, whate'er befall me,
Jesus doeth all things well;
For I know, whate'er befall me,
Jesus doeth all things well.

All the way my Savior leads me–
Cheers each winding path I tread,
Gives me grace for ev'ry trial,
Feeds me with the living bread.
Though my weary steps may falter
And my soul athirst may be,
Gushing from the rock before me,
Lo! a spring of joy I see;
Gushing from the rock before me,
Lo! a spring of joy I see.

All the way my Savior leads me–
Oh, the fullness of His love!
Perfect rest to me is promised
In my Father's house above.
When my spirit, clothed immortal,
Wings its flight to realms of day,
This my song through endless ages:
Jesus led me all the way;
This my song through endless ages:
Jesus led me all the way.

(Fanny Crosby)

30TH APRIL

THE RELEVANCE OF THE BIBLE

And we also thank God constantly for this, that when you received the word of God, which you heard from us, you accepted it not as the word of men but as what it really is, the word of God, which is at work in you believers.

1 Thessalonians 2:13

I have a little book written by the late Ian R.K. Paisley entitled 'Why I believe the Bible is the Word of God . . .', which he wrote as a young minister. In it Dr Paisley makes the point that the Bible is the most practical of all books. That it is a book for all peoples.

I found the following extracts to be helpful and encouraging: 'The message of the Bible is the most practical message ever embalmed in writing. There is not an experience known to pilgrims of this planet for which the Bible has not a word either of direction or correction. It prescribes for all cases ever known or ever to be known by man'. He then goes on to say that the Bible is relevant for ages. He points out that according to Philo there are seven stages of man's development: Infancy, childhood, youth, adolescence, manhood, decline and senility. Mr Paisley continues to comment that: 'In every stage of man's physical and spiritual history the Bible has a message which is adaptable to all.

How children delight in the stories of the Bible. All classes and conditions of young folk find something fascinating and appealing in the immortal records of Bible history. . ... Children have more than enough to go on with in these great Bible histories which are able to make them wise unto salvation.

When innocency is scarred with sin and upon the horizon of expectant youth there breaks the storm of irresistible temptation, wherewithal shall a young man cleanse his way but by taking heed thereto according to Thy Word.

In the trials and tribulations of life's rugged pathway, in joys and pleasures of life's sunshine the Bible has always a message suitable to our experience and need.

In old age the Bible still has a fresh message for our tired hearts, while the silence of death itself is broken with the assurance from the sweetest lips that ever spake, 'certainly I will be with you'.

To this I add a hearty Praise the
Lord for the Grand Old Book.
The Grand Old Book
You Find The Words Of Comfort
Wherever You May Look
In Sorrow Or In Pain
His Promises Are Plain
So Keep On Believing
In The Grand Old Book

(Unknown)

1ST MAY

JUSTIFIED FREELY THROUGH CALVARY'S LOVE

The righteous shall live by his faith.

Habakkuk 2:4

When John Wesley became an evangelical Christian in 1738, his new understanding of justification by faith alone was directly influenced by Martin Luther, passed down to him through the Moravians.

Martin Luther said: 'This is the truth of the Gospel. It is also the principal article of all Christian doctrine. Most necessary it is, therefore, that we should know this article well, teach it unto others, and beat it into their heads continually'.

Justification is a legal declaration from God that you are innocent of sin. Instead, you are made right before Him. God the judge grants you freedom instead of a death sentence — even though your actions deserve that death sentence. The following are seven aspects of justification which I trust will help and encourage you today:

- THE GRACE OF GOD IS THE SOURCE OF OUR JUSTIFICATION: 'and are justified by his grace as a gift, through the redemption that is in Christ Jesus' Rom 3:24; 'so that being justified by his grace we might become heirs according to the hope of eternal life' Titus 3:7.
- THE BASIS ON WHICH OUR JUSTIFICATION RESTS IS OBEDIENCE TO CHRIST: 'For as by the one man's disobedience the many were made sinners, so by the one man's obedience the many will be made righteous' Rom 5:19.
- JUSTIFICATION HAS BEEN BROUGHT ABOUT BY THE BLOOD OF CHRIST: 'since, therefore, we have now been justified by his blood, much more shall we be saved by him from the wrath of God' Rom 5:9.
- The proof or confirmation of our justification is the resurrection of Christ from the dead: 'who was delivered up for our trespasses and raised for our justification' Rom 4:25.
- THE HAND THAT TAKES HOLD OF JUSTIFICATION IS FAITH: 'Therefore, since we have been justified by faith, we have peace with God through our Lord Jesus Christ' Rom 5:1; 'And the Scripture, foreseeing that God would justify the Gentiles by faith, preached the gospel beforehand to Abraham, saying, "In you shall all the nations be blessed' Gal 3:8.
- WORKS IS THE PROOF WE ARE JUSTIFIED: 'Do you want to be shown, you foolish person, that faith apart from works is useless?' James 2:20. Works doesn't save you but we are saved unto good works. They are evidence that we have been justified by faith alone.
- JUSTIFICATION IS ALL OF GOD: 'Who shall bring any charge against God's elect? It is God who justifies' Rom 8:33.

Born of the Spirit with life from above into God's family divine, Justified fully thru Calvary's love, O what a standing is mine!

And the transaction so quickly was made, when as a sinner I came, Took of the offer, of grace He did proffer, He saved me, O praise His dear name!

(John W. Peterson)

2ND MAY

SITTING AT THE FEET OF JESUS

*And she had a sister called Mary, who sat at the
Lords feet and listened to his teaching.*

Luke 10:39

The feet of the Lord Jesus are mentioned three times in connection with Mary. In our verse today Mary sat at the Lord's feet and heard His words. It was a place of learning. In John 11:32 she fell at His feet as the place of comfort in a time of sorrow: 'Now when Mary came to where Jesus was and saw him, she fell at his feet, saying to Him, Lord, if you had been here, my brother would not have died'. Then in John 12:3, Mary anointed His feet and wiped His feet with her hair as an act of worship: 'Mary therefore took a pound of expensive ointment made from pure nard, and anointed the feet of Jesus and wiped his feet with her hair. The house was filled with the fragrance of the perfume'.

Dr David Gooding commenting on Luke 10:39 & 42 said: 'amid all life's duties and necessities there is one supreme necessity which must always be given priority, and which, if circumstances compel us to choose, must be chosen at the exclusion of all others. That supreme necessity is to sit at the Lord's feet and listen to His Word. It must be so. If there is a Creator at all, and that Creator is prepared to visit us and speak to us as in His incarnation He visited and spoke to Martha and Mary, then obviously it is our first duty as His creatures, as it ought to be our highest pleasure, to sit at His feet and listen to what He says. Our prayer today can be summed up in the following words of Robert Cull's little chorus: 'Open our ears, Lord, and help us to listen. Open our eyes, Lord, we want to see Jesus

1 Sitting at the feet of Jesus,
Oh, what words I hear Him say!
Happy place! so near, so precious!
May it find me there each day;
Sitting at the feet of Jesus,
I would look upon the past;
For His love has been so gracious,
It has won my heart at last.

Sitting at the feet of Jesus,
Where can mortal be more blest?
There I lay my sins and sorrows,
And, when weary, find sweet rest;
Sitting at the feet of Jesus,
There I love to weep and pray;
While I from His fullness gather
Grace and comfort every day.

§Bless me, O my Savior, bless me,
As I sit low at Thy feet;
Oh, look down in love upon me,
Let me see Thy face so sweet;
Give me, Lord, the mind of Jesus,
Keep me holy as He is;
May I prove I've been with Jesus,
Who is all my righteousness.

(J. Lincoln Hall)

3RD MAY

FORWARD BY PRAYER

*Finally, brothers, pray for us, that the word of the Lord may
speed ahead and be honoured, as happened among you.*

2 Thessalonians 3:1

I have had the privilege of serving the Lord through a mission agency called 'One Mission Society' from 2007–2022. The following is extracts from a letter (email) sent from David Dick OMS USA in 2007 to the then UK OMS Director Mike Berkeley who in turn circulated it to the UK OMS team for encouragement:

'I am appending a recent cover article written by Dr Duewel that underscores the importance of prayer in general and prayer from OMS-UK and OMS-SA constituents in particular' David Dick:

FORWARD BY PRAYER!: As I write my autobiography, 'All For Jesus', checking back over 67 years of missionary service, the memories of spiritual battles with the powers of darkness, earnest prevailing prayer, outpourings of God's blessings come flooding back to me.

The night before we sailed for India in 1940 we were farewelled from the home of our president, Mrs Charles Cowman . . . She gave us two promises God had given her for the work in India. We were part of the initial group from OMS who began the work in India. One of the promises: 'I will do better unto you than at your beginnings: and ye shall know that I am the Lord' Ezekiel 36:11 (KJV).

Striving for souls in a Hindu-Muslim environment brought times of testing, Satan's opposition, and real spiritual warfare. After 25 years, we had averaged only one new church per year and our Bible schools and effort in three language areas had only resulted in 1500 baptized believers.

After a prayer battle nonstop for about 25 hours, God led me to ask Him for 1000 prayer partners who would promise to pray for us 15 minutes per day for one year. That year God gave me 1500 who promised. The most encouraging response was in South Africa, and Northern Ireland was next. I saw people . . . weep as they signed their commitment sheet.

Now my wife is 91 and I am 90. We are somewhat slowed down, but we can still seek to prevail in prayer. Now an average Sunday sees more than 400,000 in our churches, with a membership of 424,255 in 2136 churches. They still tell of conversions, healings, deliverance from demons, threats, persecution, but also support of their own missionaries and advances for God. They have their own India Missionary Movement, with 262 missionaries.

Dr Duewel goes on to give details of their current ministry goal. He ends by writing: 'Is that too much to ask of God? No! No! If God be God, let Him be God!!! But let us pay the price of mighty prevailing prayer and obedience until God's full answer comes as they pray and labour day by day. ALL HAIL THE POWER OF 'JESUS' NAME. Let us advance by prayer!—Wesley Duewel.

Today 'Let us advance by prayer'.

4TH MAY

HARVEST SONG

Those who sow in tears shall reap with shouts of joy!

Psalm 126:5

When I served as the OMS UK Executive Director for a two year period someone gave me old magazines of the mission. The following is an article entitled: 'Harvest Song' written by Mrs Lettie Cowman (wife of OMS founder Charles E Cowman and author of Streams in the Desert) which appeared in the Missionary Standard, November, 1948. I trust it may be a help to all who read this today:

'It seems but a few months ago when in the late spring-time we were driving in the country past a beautiful meadow. The grass was as soft and thick and fine as an immense, green, oriental rug. Several weeks later we returned, and lo!-the hand of the despoiler had been there. A ploughman in the few days had wrought a terrible havoc! How could anyone have done such a heartless thing?

And then, as if by an unseen hand, we saw a vision!-a vision of a field of ripe corn ready for harvest. We could see the giant, heavily laden stalks in the autumn sun, could almost hear the music of the wind across the golden tassels. And before we were aware of it, the brown earth took on a splendour it had not had a few days before!

When the Great Master-Ploughman comes-as He so often does-with a sharp-toothed instrument and cuts deep furrows in our souls, oh! that we could see as in a vision the abundant would-be harvest! Suffering, trial, and testing are God's ploughshares that turn the subsoil in the depths of the soul, that it may bear a richer harvest. The meadow could not save itself, it would become a harvest field. It had to surrender itself to the plough,-consent to be a furrowed field-to renounce its own life, to be stripped, despoiled, laid bare! In every life there must be grace and self-buried within, Save us, O Lord, from the follies of a fatal independence. There are blessings which cannot be obtained in any other way except through, suffering, testing, trial!

It is autumn, and Thanksgiving month is here. In fancy we stand again by the side of the road. But what a transformation from the springtime. An abundant harvest is now garnered. Methinks I hear voices of reapers. In their tones is no trace of murmuring or complaining. The atmosphere is vibrant with praise notes and songs of rejoicing. Their HARVEST DAY has come'.

Do you feel like a ploughed field in your ministry and service for the Master-Ploughman today? Hold on. Harvest day is coming.

We plough the fields and scatter
the good seed on the land,
but it is fed and watered
by God's almighty hand.

We thank you, then, Creator,
for all things bright and good,
the seed-time, and the harvest,
our life, our health, our food.

(Matthias Claudius)

5TH MAY

GO TO A WORLD THAT IS DYING

And the master said to the servant, Go out to the highways and
hedges and compel people to come in, that my house may be filled.

Luke 14:23

On various occasions I have heard preachers mention that over the inside of the entrance door of each church should be written: 'The mission field begins here'. In fact I actually saw this while in a church at which I was speaking.

The following extract from a CH Spurgeon sermon makes this point forcefully: 'Leave church, chapel, tabernacle, meeting-house at once, if the masses are not reached by you, and turn out into the public hall, the market, or the field, if there an audience can be secured. The Gospel message is not Wait Within, but Go ye Out. What saith that grand old missionary text? Go ye into all the world, and preach the Gospel to every creature. Out of your pulpit, sir; do not believe in the virtue of that cushion and tassel. Out, I say, into the public places! Nay, it is not I, but your Lord that bids you. Make the Gospel known in the highways, in the public places, bid ye as many as ye find. This is the ordained way of furnishing the wedding with guests. The old way of only bidding those to come who have been bidden many times before, has become a failure; henceforth use the generous Gospel way-seek out the strangers, the ignorant, the hitherto unbidden, and to them proclaim the acceptable year of the Lord'.

The question today is: Are you actively seeking to reach the lost by walk, witness and prayer. In today's language are we taking the Gospel to the market square, the superstores, the workplace. Can we reach people through social media platforms or give out a gospel tract. One way or other we need to reach the masses. The world population is now much higher than that of CH Spurgeon's era. At the prime of Spurgeon's preaching the world population was no more than 1.5 billion. Today it is almost 8 billion. Let us reach our generation with the Gospel. By all means win some.

His Word shall not fail you, He promised;
Believe Him and all will be well;
Then go to a world that is dying,
His perfect salvation to tell!

(Helen Howarth Lemmel)

6TH MAY

*So the Lord said to Moses, Take Joshua the son of Nun, a
man in whom is the Spirit, and lay your hand on him.*

Numbers 27:18

Succession planning in Christian life, ministry, Church and leadership just like normal family and business life is essential and biblical. Moses had Joshua, Elijah had his Elisha and Paul had Timothy. We need Sunday School Teachers, Youth Leaders, Pastors, Ministers, Elders, Deacons and Missionaries for each and every generation.

It is important to develop succession plans for the gospel. Jesus told his disciples to, 'Go, therefore, and make disciples of all nations, baptizing them in the name of the Father and of the Son and of the Holy Spirit, teaching them to observe everything I have commanded you...' Matthew 28:19–20a

Moses was a great example of this in the Old Testament. Moses kept Joshua close to him, allowing him to learn the law and experience the Lord in a much greater sense than most of the Israelites. Joshua proved his character worthy of this after he returned from spying out Canaan, proclaiming the land ready for them to take over. He was also on Mount Sinai with Moses the first time he went to receive the law. Moses also put him as the commander over Israel in the battles they fought in the wilderness, knowing Joshua would continue that kind of leadership in the Promised Land. Because Joshua was so close to Moses and the Lord, he led the Israelites well.

Elijah brought Elisha alongside him for the rest of his days as well, teaching him what he knew and offering experiences for Elisha to practice his faith and prophecy. In turn, Elisha also had a very strong prophetic ministry.

Paul and Barnabas did this well in the New Testament. Barnabas chose John Mark and Paul chose Timothy. They taught them all that they knew, had them live life and do ministry together, and encouraged them in their faith. They gave them opportunities to share with others, which in turn led them to lead churches and make disciples.

Paul summarises this in 2 Timothy 2:2: 'and what you have heard from me in the presence of many witnesses entrust to faithful men, who will be able to teach others also'.

Who are you investing in today to create succession plans for the Gospel, evangelism and Church leadership?

Sharing a word of hope with my brother
Helping to make him strong
Passin' the faith along to my brother
Passin' the faith along

The runner of a relay, finds in his baton
Countless generation of saints have come and gone
A spark ignites as an ember fades and the flames continue on
A challenge to the young, and assurance for the old
The flames burn ever brighter each time our story's told

(Jon Mohr)

7TH MAY

NEVER A MAN SPAKE LIKE THIS MAN

The officers answered, No one ever spoke like this man.

John 7:46

The words that the Lord Jesus spoke were the very words of God.

- HIS WORDS WERE GRACIOUS: 'And all spoke well of Him and marvelled at the gracious words that were coming from His mouth' Luke 4:22.
- THE WORDS SPOKEN BY JESUS WERE WITH AUTHORITY: 'for he was teaching them as one who had authority, and not as their scribes' Matthew 7:29.
- His words were not spoken from Himself but both what He should say and what He should speak were given Him from the Father. Therefore they were spirit and life to those who heard them believing: 'It is the Spirit who gives life; the flesh is no help at all. The words that I have spoken to you are spirit and life' John 6:63.
- HIS WORDS ARE LIKE SEED: 'The sower sows the word' Mark 4:14
- HIS WORDS HAVE A CLEANSING POWER: 'Already you are clean because of the word that I have spoken to you' John 15:3
- HIS WORDS ARE THE MEANS OF OUR SANCTIFICATION: 'Sanctify them in the truth; your word is truth' John 17:17
- HIS WORDS BRING US INTO LIBERTY: 'So Jesus said to the Jews who had believed him, If you abide in my word, you are truly my disciples, and you will know the truth, and the truth will set you free' John 8:31–32

- HIS WORDS BRING ETERNAL LIFE: 'Truly, truly, I say to you, whoever hears my word and believes him who sent me has eternal life' John 5:24
- THOSE WHO KEEP HIS WORDS WILL NEVER SEE DEATH: 'Truly, truly, I say to you, if anyone keeps my word, he will never see death' John 8:51
- HIS WORDS WILL JUDGE US AT THE LAST DAY: 'The one who rejects me and does not receive my words has a judge; the word that I have spoken will judge him on the last day' John 12:48
- HIS WORDS WILL NEVER PASS AWAY: 'Heaven and earth will pass away, but my words will not pass away' Matthew 24:35. Never a man spake like this man:

Jesus went to the temple
When He was only twelve
His words startled the elders
As His wisdom they beheld;
And the multitude that followed
To hear the man from Galilee
Never a man spake like this man
When He said Come follow me.

Never a man spake like this man
The glorious King of Kings
He spake to my troubled soul
And now my heart sings
He has promised in His Holy Word
Some day His face I'll see
Never a man spake like this man
When He said come follow me

(Joel Hemphill)

8TH MAY

HIS WORDS SO NATURAL, YET SO WISE

And all spoke well of him and marvelled at the
gracious words that were coming from his mouth.

Luke 4:22

All the recorded words of our Lord Jesus Christ could be printed in a sixteen page booklet. His longest address takes about fifteen minutes to read. The words of Jesus recorded in the Bible have wrought wonders in the world and revolutionised the lives of billions and brought new life, peace and rest to the living and the dying. He spoke with simplicity, directness and yet with beauty. He was a marvellous story-teller. His stories of the 'prodigal son', the 'lost sheep', the 'good Samaritan', the 'wedding feast' and the parable of 'the sower', were all easy to understand by the ordinary person. He didn't speak over people's heads: 'the great throng heard him gladly' Mark 12:37

He spoke simple, sincere, and unaffected truth based upon the scriptures. Jesus responded to the devil's temptations, attacks, and lies with the Word of God and with the Word of God only (Matthew 4:4, 7, 10). According to the Biblical record the only words Jesus spoke to the evil one were direct quotes from the Old Testament (which was the Bible at the time. There was no New Testament yet). Jesus upheld the Old Testament as the powerful, devil beating, triumphant Word of God. And although we only have these three quotes from Deuteronomy, we can responsibly conclude that He would have and could have quoted from any O. T. passage necessary to counter Satan's lies: But Jesus said, 'It is written, Man is not to live on bread only. Man is to live by every word that God speaks' Matthew 4:4. Jesus said it is written thirty times in the Gospels of Matthew, Mark, Luke and John.

There was no confusion, no uncertainty, no hesitation, and no mistakes in the words our Lord Jesus used.

Over the next days we are going to examine our Lord's references to natural objects as used in T. T. Lynch's poem:

He talked of grass, and wind, and rain,
Of Fig-trees, and fair weather;
And made it His delight to bring
Heaven and earth together.

He spake of lilies, vines, and corn,
The sparrow and raven;
And words so natural, yet so wise.
Were on men's hearts engraven.

Of yeast with bread, and flax, and cloth,
Of eggs, and fish, and candles.
See how the whole familiar world
He most divinely handles.

9TH MAY

HE TALKED OF GRASS

*But if God so clothes the grass of the field, which today
is alive and tomorrow is thrown into the oven, will he
not much more clothe you, O you of little faith?*

Matthew 6:30

Today we are commencing to look at some pictures of natural objects or from nature that our Lord Jesus Christ referred to. We need to remember that He created these in the first place. Jesus spoke in simple yet profound language so that everyone could understand. He used everyday objects and stories to achieve this objective.

Today we will look at His use of 'grass' to make His point. The key point Jesus is making in this verse is 'Don't worry'. While writing this short devotion on 'grass', I received an email correspondence from a USA ministry entitled 'America's top ten fears'. These included corrupt government officials, loved ones becoming seriously ill, Russia using nuclear weapons, loved ones dying, pollution, not having enough money for the future and economic and financial collapse. These or similar anxieties are experienced by folk all over the world resulting in fear, sleeplessness and other related conditions.

However fear and anxiety is not God's plan for you today. The only fear we should have is the godly fear or the 'Fear of God' which is a reverential fear which is healthy.

Commenting specifically about Jesus reference to 'grass' in this verse D A Carson comments: 'The Christian sees the fresh greenness of well-watered grass, and, whether or not he acknowledges the effect of chlorophyll, he certainly acknowledges the God behind the chlorophyll. God clothes the grass with a spectacular array of flowers, even though the grass is destined to be mowed down and burned up. Shall he not be even more concerned to clothe us, his children? In other words, biblical cosmology plus observant eyes engender real trust in God'.

How does Jesus respond to worrying: 'But seek first the kingdom of God and his righteousness, and all these things will be added to you. Therefore do not be anxious about tomorrow, for tomorrow will be anxious for itself. Sufficient for the day is its own trouble' Matthew 6:33–34.

You can't add a single day by worrying
You'll worry your life away
Oh don't worry your life away
You can't change a single thing by freaking out
It's just gonna close you in
Oh don't let the trouble win
You may feel alone
But you're not on your own
If He can hold the world He
can hold this moment
Not a field or flower escapes His notice
Oh even the sparrow
Knows He holds tomorrow

(Jason Gray)

10TH MAY

HE TALKED OF WIND

*The wind blows where it wishes, and you hear its sound,
but you do not know where it comes from or where it
goes. So it is with everyone who is born of the Spirit.*

John 3:8

Jesus reference to wind in this verse is in relation to the new birth or being born again. In fact Jesus said 'You must be born again'. Jesus makes it abundantly clear that the new birth is an absolutely essential spiritual experience for us individually. Those who are not born of the Spirit will never be in Heaven which only leaves one other option—Hell. Just reflecting on this thought the following words came to mind:

Born again, there's really been a change in me
Born again, just like Jesus said;
Born again, and all because of Calvary,
I'm glad so glad, that I've been born again.

(Unknown)

The late Stephen Olford commenting on the need of being born again wrote: 'The greatest message on new life ever delivered by the Lord Jesus Christ was addressed to a deeply religious man named Nicodemus. What is so significant is that this ruler of the Jews, with all his religion, was a very dissatisfied man. Something vital was missing in his life. So we find him coming to one in whom he had recognised a quality of life which transcended the religious formalism of his day. It is evident that Nicodemus longed for this new life in Christ, for he came to find out how he might possess it. In the dialogue that

followed, Jesus indicated three conditions for the start of this new life'.

The three conditions being:

- There must be the sense of need.
- There must be the step of faith.
- There must be the sign of life

Dr Olford makes the point that the Spirit must produce this new life: 'The wind blows where it wishes, and you hear its sound, but you do not know where it comes from or where it goes. So it is with everyone who is born of the Spirit' John 3:8. Humans can no more control life from above than they can govern the light breezes in the treetops. It is the sovereign power of the Holy Spirit alone to produce new life in those who are sensitive to His prompting. This is why it is so serious to resist Him when He strives with us. To refuse His offer may mean the damning of our souls'.

I trust you can say 'I'm glad so glad,
that I've been born again' today.
Never the same again,
Now I know I won't be the same again,
From the moment I met Jesus,
New life for me began,
And I won't be the same again.

(Unknown)

11TH MAY

HE TALKED OF RAIN

*For he makes his sun rise on the evil and on the good,
and sends rain on the just and on the unjust.*

Matthew 5:45

*'And the rain fell, and the floods came, and the
winds blew and beat on that house, but it did not
fall, because it had been founded on the rock'*

Matthew 7:25

As we continue to see natural objects which Jesus used to make a point we will look at how He used 'rain' to do this on two occasions in the Sermon on the Mount.

The first is in relation to loving our enemies. Jesus had enemies just as we have. He teaches that we are to love them and pray for them. This is an important part of being a son of the heavenly Father. With this in mind Jesus reminded His hearers that God: 'sends rain on the just and on the unjust'. God loved rebellious sinners, those who were at enmity with Him, so much He sent His Son to die for them: 'but God shows his love for us in that while we were still sinners, Christ died for us' Romans 5:8. If we are His sons and daughters, we too will have His character. Quite a challenge today?

The second reference today is based on a 'wise man' and a 'foolish' man and on building houses on a solid foundation. Sinclair B Ferguson commenting on this said: 'The sermon on the Mount concludes with one of Jesus' most vivid illustrations. In essence he tells us: there are two ways to respond. One is to put the sermon into practice in obedience; the other is to ignore it'.

The first man digs down until he finds rock the other just builds on the sand without any foundation or substructure. Actually when the two houses were finished they looked similar –until. Until the rains and storms come. What happens? The one on solid ground stands, the one built without foundation on the sand—crashes. What does this mean? It means obedience to Christ's word distinguishes the wise man from his foolish neighbour. When the wise man heard that there was a broad road that led to Hell and a narrow road led to Heaven he did something about it. He heard like the foolish man that 'You must be born again'. He made a choice to trust Christ. The true Christian puts into practice what he has heard from the Lord Jesus Christ in this sermon.

*My home is on the Rock,
The Everlasting Rock;
I do not fear when storms are near,
My home is on the Rock.*

*When come life's trials thick and fast,
When clouds are o'er my pathway cast,
Secure, I can withstand the blast,
My home is on the Rock.*

(Johnson Oatman, Jr.)

12TH MAY

HE TALKED OF FIG-TREES

From the fig tree learn its lesson:

Matthew 24:32

I have several books in my study written by Ernest T Wilson. I am going to let him explain the significance of the Fig Tree to us today:

'During the three years of our Lord's public ministry, there are three references to the fig tree.

Luke 13:6–4 contains the parable of the fig tree in the vineyard. For three successive years, the husbandman comes seeking fruit and finds none. He orders the caretaker to cut it down; it is only occupying space. But the caretaker intercedes: Lord, let it alone this year also, till I shall dig about it, and dung it: and if it bear fruit, well: and if not, then after that thou shalt cut it down. The application is obvious. It is a solemn warning to Israel on account of their reaction to His public ministry.

The second reference is in Matthew 21:18–22. In the last week of His ministry, returning to the city from Bethany, the Lord is hungry, and turning aside to a fig tree along the way, He looks for fruit to satisfy His hunger but He finds nothing except leaves. He curses it, and the fig tree withers. Again the lesson is plain. It is a graphic object lesson to the nation of their spiritual condition.

The third mention of the fig tree is found in Matthew 24:32–33. The application is to His teaching concerning His second coming as the Son of Man, He said: Now learn a parable of the fig tree; when his branch is yet tender, and putteth forth leaves, ye know that summer is nigh: so likewise ye, when ye shall see all these things, know that it is near, even at the doors. LUKE 21:29 adds, and all the trees. The fig tree seems to symbolize Israel as a nation in their own land, exercising all the functions of a sovereign state. If this is so, how significant is the fact that Israel is back in the land. On May 18, 1948, they became a nation once again. The fig tree has put on its green leaves. Not only Israel, but all the trees, pointing to the remarkable upsurge of nationalism all over the world'.

Some years ago I was part of a men's fellowship choir. One of the songs we sang was written by Mrs H S Lehman called 'Nothing but Leaves'. Its words challenged me then as they still do today. She applied the fig tree with only leaves to the condition of individual believers, on this side of the cross.

The Master is seeking a harvest
In lives He's redeemed by His blood;
He seeks for the fruit of the Spirit,
And works that will glorify God.

Nothing but leaves for the Master,
Oh how His loving heart grieves,
When instead of the fruit He is seeking,
We offer Him nothing but leaves.

13TH MAY

HE TALKED OF FAIR WEATHER

He answered them, When it is evening, you say,
It will be fair weather, for the sky is red.

Matthew 16:2

The Pharisees and the Sadducees were trying to trip up Jesus by asking Him to perform even more signs or miracles to prove who He said He was: 'And the Pharisees and Sadducees came, and to test Him they asked Him to show them a sign from heaven' Matthew 16:1. Jesus answered them by continuing the theme of the sky. When they saw a red sky in the evening, they forecast fair weather for the next day. They also knew that a red, threatening sky in the morning meant storms for the day. They had expertise in interpreting the appearance of the sky, but they could not interpret the signs of the times. In their day John the Baptist had heralded the advent of the Messiah. The miracles Jesus had performed in their presence prophesied of the Messiah. Yet in spite of these irrefutable evidences, they had no sense of history being made or of prophecy being fulfilled.

Today things haven't changed. We have the whole canon of Scripture, the convicting power of the Holy Spirit, the preaching of the Gospel and yet people will not believe.

However as Christians do we realise the times. Do we recognise that we should be reaching the lost right now? Jesus said: 'Do you not say, There are yet four months, then comes the harvest? Look, I tell you, lift up your eyes, and see that the fields are white for harvest'. John 4:35. Do we not see that Jesus could come back at any moment? We need to be watching, waiting and working. Today forecasters are quite good at forecasting the weather. We can pretty much go by their predictions. But can we read the signs of the times we are in?:

Let the nations awake to the signs of the times,
A voice that is mighty and strong,
Like the thunder of waters,
proclaims to the world,
Jehovah is marching along.

Then wake, let us stand with
our face to the right,
And tread 'neath our feet ev'ry wrong;
The kingdoms of darkness are
trembling with fear,
Jehovah is marching along.

Let the Christian awake to
the signs of the times,
For long at the post some have slept;
Arise, for the Master may suddenly come,
And frown at the watch you have kept.

Let the young men awake to
the signs of the times,
God calls you, because ye are strong;
You can work in the vineyard
with ardor and zeal,
For him who is marching along.

Careless sinner, awake to the signs of the times,
Give Jesus your heart while you may;
Oh, be washed in his blood—he
will make you his child,
And take your transgressions away.

(Fanny Crosby)

14TH MAY

HE SPAKE OF LILIES

Consider the lilies, how they grow: they neither toil nor spin, yet I tell you, even Solomon in all his glory was not arrayed like one of these.

Luke 12:27

When Jesus spoke of lilies what lesson did He want to teach us? He wants us to trust that God will care for us, and to accept with gratitude His provision of simple needs. We do not see the lilies at work, but we understand that they are always active, processing the sun's energy, the air around them, and the nutrients of the soil into the necessary food to continue their short lives. The birds of the air, too, are among the busiest of God's creatures. But God gave the lily its beauty, and the birds their songs. Life is about more than simple survival; and if God lavished such beauty on these simple things, how much more does He give to us-- and expect from us--who are made in His image?

We also need to remember, the fleeting life of the lily. It is here, it serves God's purpose, and then it is gone. But even this simple creation that serves God's purpose as it is intended is more beautiful than 'Solomon in all his glory'. Solomon was fabulously wealthy, but in the end his was not a happy life, and there is much to fault in his legacy. Like the lilies of the field, a humble person whom the world considers unimportant may in fact serve God with more glory than Solomon, if that person puts God's kingdom first. Today: 'Instead, seek his kingdom, and these things will be added to you' Luke 12:31.

Consider the lilies; they don't toil or spin,
But there's not a king with more
splendour than them.
Consider the sparrows; they
don't plant nor sow,
But they're fed by the Master
who watches them grow.

We have a Heavenly Father above
With eyes full of mercy and a heart full of love.
He really cares when your head is bowed low;
Consider the lilies, then you will know.

May I introduce you to this Friend of mine
Who hangs out the stars, tells
the sun when to shine.
And kisses the flowers each morning with dew,
Oh, but friend, He's not too
busy to care about you!

We have a Heavenly Father above
With eyes full of mercy and a heart full of love.
He really cares when your head is bowed low;
Consider the lilies, then you will know.

(Joel Hemphill)

Consider the lilies, how they bloom,
They toil not, neither do they spin,
Toil not nor struggle all the day
The victory of faith to win.
They toil not, they toil not,
They toil not, neither do they spin;
Then trust Him and toil not,
The victory of faith to win.

(Daniel Otis Teasley)

15TH MAY

HE SPAKE OF VINES

I am the true vine, and my Father is the vinedresser.

John 15:1

I am the True Vine in John 15:1 is the last of seven 'I am' statements of Jesus recorded only in John's Gospel. These 'I am' proclamations point to His unique divine identity and purpose.

Jesus was preparing the remaining eleven men (excluding Judas) for His pending crucifixion, His resurrection, and His subsequent departure for heaven. He had just told them that He would be leaving them. John 14:2. Knowing how disturbed they would feel, He gave them this lovely metaphor of the True Vine as one of His encouragements. Jesus wanted His friends, not only those eleven, but those of all time, to know that He was not going to desert them, even though they would no longer enjoy His physical presence. His living energy and His spiritual reality would continue to nourish and sustain them just as the roots and trunk of a grape vine produce the energy that nourishes and sustains its branches while they develop their fruit. Jesus wanted us to know that, even though we cannot see Him, we are as closely connected to Him as the branches of a vine are connected to its stem. Our desire to know and love Him and the energy to serve Him will keep flowing into and through us as long as we 'abide' in Him.

In John Jesus said that no branch can even live, let alone produce leaves and fruit, by itself. Cut off from the trunk, a branch is dead. Just as a vine's branches rely on being connected to the trunk from which they receive their energy to bear fruit, Jesus' disciples depend on being connected to Him for their spiritual life and the ability to serve Him effectively. The fruit we produce is that of the Holy Spirit: Galatians 5:22–23. Our source of life and spiritual fruit is not in ourselves; it is outside us, in Christ Jesus. We can live, live rightly, and serve Him effectively only if we are rightly connected to Him by faith in a love relationship. Jesus went on to say: 'Apart from me you can do nothing' John 15:5. No follower of Jesus can achieve anything of spiritual value independently of Him. All true branches bear fruit. Jesus is our only connection with the God who gave life and who produces in us a fruitful life of righteousness and service.

He's the vine and we're the branches,
We should e'er abide in Him,
And let Him abide within us
As the flow of life within.

In the vine, in the vine,
In the vine, in the vine,
We would know Thee, Lord,
more deeply,
E'er abiding in the vine.

(Silas Jones Vail)

16TH MAY

HE SPAKE OF CORN

Verily, verily, I say unto you, except a corn of wheat
fall into the ground and die, it abideth alone:
but if it die, it bringeth forth much fruit.

John 12:24

In our verse today Jesus is using an agricultural image to make a very important point. Jesus explains to Andrew and Philip that it wouldn't make sense for a farmer to simply keep a grain of wheat in storage or put it on his shelf to admire. The grain is completely worthless and ineffective unless planted. However, once planted, that grain of wheat dies and then becomes so much more: a field ripe for harvest. In the same way, Jesus's death, burial, and resurrection continually generates a harvest of souls. Like the single grain of wheat, His death was the path to multiplication. Having died and been buried, that single Seed of the Lord rose again, bringing many sons to glory and producing the rich harvest of a multitude of believers - a fruitful harvest that now spans over 2000 years of history.

As followers of Jesus, who have been saved by grace though faith in Christ, we have within us the life of Christ which can become abundantly fruitful, when our lives resemble His likeness. Today let us make it our goal to die to self and live for Christ - so that by God's grace, we may bring forth much fruit.

T. G. Ragland a missionary to South India in the 1840s and 50s once said: 'Of all plans of ensuring success, the most certain is Christ's own, becoming a grain of wheat, falling into the ground and dying. If we refuse to become grains of wheat we will neither sacrifice prospects, nor risk character, and property and health; nor, when we are called, relinquish home, and break family ties, for Christ's sake; then we shall abide alone. But if we wish to be fruitful, we must follow our Blessed Lord Himself, by becoming a corn of wheat, and dying, then we shall bring forth much fruit'.

There is no gain but by a loss,
You cannot save but by a cross;
The corn of wheat to multiply
Must fall into the ground and die.
Wherever you ripe fields behold,
Waving to God their sheaves of gold,
Be sure some corn of wheat has died,
Some soul there has been crucified—
Someone has wrestled, wept and prayed,
And fought hell's legions undismayed.

(Samuel Zwemer)

17TH MAY

HE TALKED OF THE SPARROW

Are not two sparrows sold for a penny? And not one of them will fall to the ground apart from your Father. But even the hairs of your head are all numbered. Fear not, therefore; you are of more value than many sparrows.

Matthew 10:29–31

If God cares for the sparrows and the robins of how much more value are we to Him as the above verses assure us.

In Matthew 10:29, Jesus said that a pair of sparrows are sold for two pennies. In Luke 12:6, Jesus said five sparrows are sold for two pennies. (You get one extra sparrow thrown in when you spend two pennies). These birds were and are so common in Israel. In fact, they are very common all over the world. Yet we read that none of them will fall to the ground without the Father's knowledge. Luke 12:6 tells us '. . . And not one of them is forgotten before God'. God will not forget you today. What a comforting thought.

In the eyes of God, no one is insignificant, especially the children of God.

In 1904, a songwriter, Mrs Civilla Martin, visited a bedridden friend and asked if the woman ever got discouraged because of her physical condition. Her friend replied: 'Mrs Martin, how can I be discouraged when my heavenly Father watches over little sparrows and I know that He loves and cares for me?' On her journey home, Mrs Martin completed composing the lyrics to her hymn, 'His Eye Is on the Sparrow', which has since been a blessing and an encouragement to so many of God's people.

Why should I feel discouraged,
Why should the shadows come,
Why should my heart be lonely,
And long for heav'n and home;
When Jesus is my portion?
My constant Friend is he;
His eye is on the sparrow,
And I know he watches me;
His eye is on the sparrow,
And I know he watches me.

Refrain:

I sing because I'm happy,
I sing because I'm free;
For his eye is on the sparrow,
And I know he watches me.

'Let not your heart be troubled,"
His tender word I hear,
And resting on his goodness,
I lose my doubts and fears;
Though by the path he leadeth,
But one step I may see;
His eye is on the sparrow,
And I know he watches me;
His eye is on the sparrow,
And I know he watches me.

Whenever I am tempted,
Whenever clouds arise;
When songs give place to sighing,
When hope within me dies,
I draw the closer to him,
From care he sets me free;
His eye is on the sparrow,
And I know he watches me;
His eye is on the sparrow,
And I know he watches me.

18TH MAY

HE SPAKE OF THE RAVEN

*Consider the ravens: they neither sow nor reap, they have
neither storehouse nor barn, and yet God feeds them.
Of how much more value are you than the birds!*

Luke 12:24

The Lord Jesus said that God provides the food for the least valued of the birds, the ravens, which are wild, roving birds, which always seem to be hungry.

God has given the raven strong wings to fly far and find plenty of food. It is only God who can supply food enough for people, and strength to get or eat it. Jesus asked the disciples: 'How much more are ye better than the fowls? Consider the lilies how they grow: they toil not, they spin not; and yet I say unto you, that Solomon in all his glory was not arrayed like one of these'.

God asks Job: 'Who provides for the raven its prey, when its young ones cry to God for help, and wander about for lack of food?' God uses this as a visual aid to Job to point out his sustaining nature, to the animals and birds He created.

Commentators believe God mentioned the raven instead of other birds as the raven was typically considered an inferior bird, which was unclean and dirty because it eats dead flesh. In addition people believed ravens didn't care well for their young in the nest, and their babies were left on their own

to find food. People also thought of them as ugly and common.

When Jesus refers to the raven in Luke 12:24, we might wonder why Jesus would choose the raven for his example. However, when we take into account how the ancients viewed the raven the reference takes on more meaning.

In the story of Elijah when he hides by the Cherith brook, he is on his own without food, yet God tells him, 'You shall drink from the brook, and I have commanded the ravens to feed you there' I Kings 17:4. God chooses the least regarded bird for the purpose of helping his prophet continue serving his creator. God entrusts the raven with the important task, not because the raven has anything to offer, but because God takes the small, weak, and ill-regarded and uses them for his purposes to show He is strong, and worthy to be glorified. His nature includes sustaining life in whatever way He desires.

The Lord Jesus wants us to know that He will sustain every single one of us because of his love. Not because we deserve it, but because God is sustaining and caring in his character.

*The raven he feedeth, then why should I fear,
To the heart of the Father his children are dear;
So, if the way darkens or storms gather o'er,
I'll simply look upward and trust him more.*

(Lewis E. Jones)

19TH MAY

HE SPAKE OF YEAST

Be careful, Jesus said to them. Be on your guard
against the yeast of the Pharisees and Sadducees.

Matthew 16:6

When the word yeast or leaven is used in the bible, it can be symbolic of sin or false teaching. Yeast is added to dough to make it rise. Yeast is a bacterium that feeds on the dough and these bacteria give off a gas that causes bread to rise. Yeast can lie dormant for many months, and then, at the first hint of moisture, it comes to life and begins its work. The yeast will completely fill the whole lump of dough.

In Matthew 16: 6, Jesus was not thinking of their food, but of His foes. In Mark 8:15 the warning also included the Herodians: 'And he cautioned them, saying, watch out; beware of the leaven of the Pharisees and the leaven of Herod'. Jesus warns the disciples and His followers to beware of the 'leaven' of the 'Pharisees' the 'Sadducees' and of 'Herod'.

As stated earlier in the Bible, leaven is a picture of sin, evil and wickedness. It is used as a picture of corruption. Believers are commanded to: 'Cleanse out the old leaven that you may be a new lump, as you really are unleavened. For Christ, our Passover lamb, has been sacrificed' 1 Cor. 5:7. We are to lay aside evil and spiritual corruption and live for the Lord. We are also warned that: 'A little leaven leavens the whole lump' 1 Cor. 5:6. The idea here is that a little sin is like yeast or leaven in our lives. When we tolerate sin, it will soon infiltrate every part of our lives.

The Pharisees were the religious conservatives of the day while the Sadducees were the religious liberals. They were worldly and secular and they joined forces with King Herod in compromising with the Romans. The leaven that infiltrated their lives and teaching was materialism, worldliness, unbelief, and compromise with the world.

Jesus is simply telling His people, regardless of the age in which they live to beware of hypocrisy, worldliness and compromise. He tells us that if we allow just a little of those things to exist in our lives, they will infiltrate every area of life, just like yeast infiltrates an entire lump of dough. It is a simple command for the people of the Lord to be clean, holy and different. Today Jesus still expects His people to live differently! Remember there is no leaven in Heaven.

Let our prayer be: Lord help me, to avoid the 'yeast' of the Pharisees, the Sadducees and Herod. Help me to trust you more deeply and consistently in all aspects of my life and living.

20TH MAY

HE SPAKE OF BREAD

Jesus said to them, I am the bread of life; whoever comes to me shall not hunger, and whoever believes in me shall never thirst.

John 6:35

The statement 'I Am' takes us back to the account in Exodus when the Holy Spirit records how Jehovah God appeared to Moses in a burning bush. When Moses asked God's name, He replied: 'I AM THAT I AM' meaning the ever present sufficient one. In John's gospel Jesus referred to Himself as the 'I AM' on seven different occasions. He employed every heavenly and earthly meaning in order to let the whole world know who He was. On this occasion Jesus describes Himself as: 'I am the bread of life'. The miracle that accompanied this statement was the feeding of five thousand men plus women and children with only five loaves and two small fishes. Interestingly this miracle is so important it is recorded in all four Gospels. Beyond this physical miraculous feeding of people Jesus is making the point that He is God and is the ultimate bread of life. Just as we need physical bread to sustain our earthly body we need eternal life and substance for our soul.

Therefore, Jesus IS THE SOURCE OF LIFE: Way back in their wilderness journey God supplied manna to the Israelites. It was a sweet mysterious daily food that fell from heaven. It provided complete nutrition for all. Since then Hebrew tradition has taught that when the Messiah comes, He will give them 'manna'. When Jesus performed the miracle of feeding the five thousand He was declaring that He was the bread sent down from heaven: Jesus then said to them, 'Truly, truly, I say to you, it was not Moses who gave you the bread from heaven, but my Father gives you the true bread from heaven' John 6:32.

Not only is Jesus the source of life; he IS THE SUSTENANCE OF LIFE. Jesus is the giver of eternal life and He also sustains that life. It is after all eternal. Jesus assured the crowd that He miraculously fed, that: 'I am the bread of life; whoever comes to me shall not hunger'. Bible scholars inform us that the original word for 'never' means 'never, never, never, no never, not ever' hunger. Jesus is always sufficient.

You are the bread of life, dear Lord, to me,
your holy word the truth that rescues me.
Give me to eat and live with you above;
teach me to love your truth, for you are love.

(Mary A. Lathbury)

For those that really know Jesus, He is also THE SATISFACTION OF LIFE. We can truly say that He saves, keeps and satisfies: 'I came that they may have life and have it abundantly' John 10:10.

21ST MAY

HE SPAKE OF FLAX

A bruised reed shall he not break, and smoking flax shall
he not quench, till he send forth judgment unto victory.

Matthew 12:20

Flax was once grown extensively in Ireland especially from the 17th century right up to the mid-20th century when there was a thriving linen industry. In Ireland flax is colloquially known as the 'wee blue blossom', given the flax flower's pale blue colour.

Flax was also a well-known plant grown in Israel. Jesus refers to 'smoking flax' in our verse for today. To better understand the statement that Jesus would not quench the smoking flax, it is helpful to go back to the original prophecy in Isaiah 42:1–4 'A bruised reed shall he not break, and the smoking flax shall he not quench'. Matthew points to the fulfilment of this passage. God had promised to bring comfort and help to Israel, and He did it through His only begotten Son, Jesus. Though God certainly had a plan for Israel in regard to their captivity in Babylon, the redemption that Isaiah spoke of was primarily spiritual rather than physical. All of Israel was under the curse of sin, and Jesus came to redeem them from sin as outlined in Luke 5:31–32.

In Matthew 12, Jesus heals a man with a shrivelled hand and later heals all who were ill among the multitude that followed Him. Those whom He healed were the 'bruised reed' and the 'smoking flax' of our verse today. The prophecy was that Jesus would not extinguish the struggling flame of those who needed Him. In His grace and mercy, He would not snuff out the dying embers of faith He encountered; rather, He was intent on fanning those flames to burn brightly for Him.

A smoking, smouldering wick is in a problematic position. It is weak; the embers are about to lose whatever heat and light they had and be darkened forever. There are many people in a similar state—they have been wounded emotionally, spiritually, or physically. They are weak and about to lose all hope. But then God steps in. The prophecy that Jesus fulfilled is that the smoking flax He would not quench. It's a prophecy that speaks of Christ's compassionate care for the frail, demoralized, and exploited. Over and over in the gospels, we see Jesus caring for the 'smoking flax' of the world.

Just as Jesus did not quench the smoking flax, as His followers we should fan the flames of flickering faith in those who struggle. In doing so, we can 'in faithfulness . . . bring forth justice' as Isaiah prophesied 2700 years ago.

Today do you feel at a low-ebb spiritually? Then take comfort from the following quote from C H Spurgeon: 'Thou art like the smoking flax: no light, no warmth, can come from thee; but He will not quench thee; He will blow with His sweet breath of mercy till He fans thee to a flame'

22ND MAY

HE SPAKE OF CLOTH

Today, I want to share two comments Jesus made about clothes and make a few remarks on how we may apply them to our daily lives and living:

1. 'Therefore I tell you, do not be anxious about your life, what you will eat or what you will drink, nor about your body, what you will put on. Is not life more than food, and the body more than clothing?' Matthew 6:25.

I am taking a thought from D A Carson on this verse which I trust will be helpful today: 'He who provides us with life, with bodies, how much more will He also provide things of lesser importance like food and clothes! Therefore, the follower of Jesus is not to worry about such needs, as basic as they are'. In Matthew 6:28–30, Jesus further expands on this point when He explains if God clothes the grass with spectacular arrays of flowers, even though the grass is destined to be mowed down and burned up shall He not be even more concerned to clothe us His children?' Be encouraged today: 'God will take care of you, through ev'ry day, o'er all the way; He will take care of you, God will take care of you' Civilla D. Martin.

2. 'Beware of false prophets, who come to you in sheep's clothing but inwardly are ravenous wolves' Matthew 7:15.

The Scripture warns us to beware of various things. Here Jesus warns us as His followers to be careful of listening to false teachers as there were many both then and now. One way of doing this is identifying good Christian leaders. Jesus explains that by their fruits we shall know them. Godly teachers will display good 'fruit' such as making disciples (Matthew 28:19), using their gifts to benefit others (Romans 12:4–8), leading lost people to Jesus (James 5:20), loving their fellow believers (1 John 3:14), and seeking humble ways to do good everywhere (Jeremiah 29:7).

O God, root out all heresy,
and of false teachers rid us
who proudly say, 'Now where is he
who shall our speech forbid us?
By right or might we shall prevail,
what we determine cannot fail;
we want no lord and master!'

(Martin Luther)

Beware, the Saviour gave command,
And watch ye unto pray'r;
That ye be wise and understand!
The teachers ye may hear.

Our Lord declares that such shall come,
Who show a pious face;
That they would come, and would presume,
To take the Saviour's place.

(Unknown)

23RD MAY

HE SPAKE OF EGGS

Or if he asks for an egg, will he give him a scorpion?

Luke 11:12

Luke chapter 11 verses 1 to 13 are instructions from Jesus teaching us about how we ought to pray. Communication with the Lord is a two way conversation. The Lord speaking to us and us speaking to the Lord are two of life's necessities for His followers. The great lesson Jesus teaches in this portion of Scripture is that God does not only hear but He answers prayer.

In Luke 11:1–4: Jesus taught His disciples a model prayer which we all know. He gives them a pattern as to how they should pray: He teaches them to pray with humility: 'Father'; with reverence: 'hallowed be your name'; with submission: 'Your kingdom come'; with dependence and trust: 'Give us each day our daily bread'; with penitence: 'and forgive us our sins, for we ourselves forgive everyone who is indebted to us' and with holy aspirations: 'And lead us not into temptation'.

Then Jesus gives us a parable teaching us about prayer Luke 11:5–8: Prayer is based on:

- A friendly relationship with God: 'What a friend we have in Jesus, all our sins and griefs to bear. What a privilege to carry everything to God in prayer'.
- Intercession for others.
- Definite and specific prayers: 'lend me three loaves'.

- Praying with earnest desperation. Holding on to God until the answer comes.
- Always be importune, meaning shameless persistence and insistence.
- Prayer is gloriously rewarded. God hears and answers prayer.

In Luke 11: 9–12, Jesus promises answers to prayer: Warren Wiersbe puts it as follows: 'Ask', makes available the Father's wealth. 'Seek', leads us to the Father's will. 'Knock', opens the door to the Father's work.

Prayer is still God's appointed way to accomplish His will on earth. Our efficiency must depend on the Lord's sufficiency. God gives good gifts to His children. If we ask for a 'fish' He will not give us 'a serpent'. If we ask for an 'egg', He will not give us a 'scorpion'. He is a God of the 'Much More'.

'Now to Him who is able to do far more abundantly than all that we ask or think, according to the power at work within us' Ephesians 3:20.

If ye ask it shall be given,
Not one will Father turn away;
Then, come and tell Him all thy longings,
For He will hear you when you pray.

Though half unspoken thy petition,
Fear not to beg far more than crumbs;
With all thy heart believe His promise,
And pray until the answer comes.

(Clara M. Brooks)

24TH MAY

HE SPAKE OF FISH

*And when they had done this, they enclosed a large
number of fish, and their nets were breaking.*

Luke 5:6

Jesus mentions fish and fishing on various occasions, mostly in relation to evangelism and discipleship.

In Matthew 4:18–22 we read: 'While walking by the Sea of Galilee, he saw two brothers, Simon (who is called Peter) and Andrew his brother, casting a net into the sea, for they were fishermen. And he said to them, Follow me, and I will make you fishers of men. Immediately they left their nets and followed him. And going on from there he saw two other brothers, James the son of Zebedee and John his brother, in the boat with Zebedee their father, mending their nets, and he called them. Immediately they left the boat and their father and followed him'. On this occasion Jesus was calling Peter, Andrew, James and John out of one career into another. From being fishers of fish, to fishers of men. Peter and Andrew were 'casting a net into the sea', representing evangelism. James and John were 'mending their nets', representing edification or discipleship.

In Luke 5:1–11 we have Jesus calling Peter and his partners James and John into full-time work. 'And when they had brought their boats to land, they left everything and followed him' Luke 5:11. (These men after their original call in Matthew 4:18–20, appeared to follow Jesus on a part-time basis, and then went back to their fishing). In this passage we see Peter's: CHALLENGE: 'Put out into the deep and let down your nets for a catch'. CALL: 'Launch out into the deep'. COMPLIANCE: 'at your word I will let down the nets'. CATCH: 'they enclosed a large number of fish'. CONFESSION: 'Depart from me, for I am a sinful man, O Lord'. CONSOLATION: 'Do not be afraid; from now on you will be catching men'. CONSECRATION: 'And when they had brought their boats to land, they left everything and followed him'. Peter now leaves all. Perhaps that is what Jesus is calling you to do today: 'Take my life and let it be, consecrated, Lord, to thee' Frances R. Havergal (1874).

*I hear the words that Jesus spake
To them of Galilee;
To fishermen beside the lake
He said: 'Come, follow Me.'*

Refrain:

*'Follow Me, Follow Me!
Fishers of men henceforth to be,
Echo the words from Galilee;
Jesus! I follow Thee!*

*I long to make Thy words my own!
O, Jesus may it be;
Thou spakest not to them alone,
But even now to me?*

*I'll follow on with all my heart,
I'll walk with Thee today;
Though vile I am, do not depart,
Forgive and cleanse, I pray!*

*Within my heart Thy love beget
A fisherman to be;
And teach me where to cast the net
As when in Galilee.*

(James M. Gray)

25TH MAY

HE SPAKE OF CANDLES

Neither do men light a candle, and put it under a bushel, but on a candlestick; and it giveth light unto all that are in the house.

Matthew 5:15 (KJV)

The word translated 'candle' refers to the oil lamps used in Israel at that time. These were usually clay containers filled with olive oil in which was placed a piece of twisted flax to serve as a wick. Since most houses had no windows, an oil lamp was necessary for the people living there to be able to see. However none of the occupants lit a lamp and then hid it under a basket. To do so would have been foolish! The lamp was lit so that the people in the house could receive the light and see other objects and people in the room.

This verse is speaking about the power of the individual follower of Jesus' witness. Just as a church has a testimony, so does each individual believer. Jesus saved us to be a light for Him. As He shines His light through us, those around us who are in darkness are helped to see their way to God.

We live in a dark, dead, deceived and doomed world. It is our responsibility to tell them about a Saviour who loves them and will save them if they will come to Him by faith. That is our mandate, (Mark 16:15) and our mission, (Acts 1:8). Are you and I fulfilling God's call to be a light for Him today?

Jesus spoke of some people who hid their candle under a bushel: People hide their light under the bushel: of fear and apathy. They don't seem to care that a lost world is going to Hell around them. We ought to be consumed with the idea that people are dying without Jesus every day! They are perishing and we hold in our hands the good news of the gospel. If we really cared, we would tell them about Jesus the mighty to save, the strong to deliver!

In Luke 8:16, Jesus adds this phrase, 'or putteth it under a bed'. The bushel speaks of the world of labour; the bed speaks of the world of leisure. Jesus seems to be saying that some people are too busy to let their lights shine and others are too lazy. I trust that neither of these apply to us today:

Let us labour for the Master from
the dawn till setting sun;
Let us talk of all his wondrous love and care

(James M. Black)

26TH MAY

IT IS NO SECRET WHAT GOD CAN DO

Now to him who is able to do far more abundantly than all that we ask or think, according to the power at work within us.

Ephesians 3:20

It is a privilege to continue visiting friends who supported me after retirement from the Mission Agency through whom I served the Lord for fifteen years. On one such visit the dear brother and I were reflecting on all the ways God has provided in miraculous ways for various ministries with which we both have been associated. He then made the comment: 'It is no secret what God can do'. After reflecting on our conversation my mind went to the truth of our scriptural text for today: 'Now to Him who is able to do far more abundantly than all that we ask or think'. God is an abundantly able God and it is no secret what He can do.

It is no secret what God can do.
What He's done for others,
He'll do for you.
With arms wide open,
He'll pardon you,
It is no secret what God can do.

(Stuart Hamblen)

The following are some of the things He does:

- HE CAN SAVE ANY SINNER: 'Consequently, he is able to save to the uttermost those who draw near to God through him, since he always lives to make intercession for them' Hebrews 7:25.

- HE CAN KEEP: 'Who are kept by the power of God through faith unto salvation ready to be revealed in the last time' 1 Peter 1:5.

- HE CAN SATISFY: 'With long life I will satisfy him and show him my salvation' Psalm 91:16. 'For he satisfies the longing soul, and the hungry soul he fills with good things'.

- HE CAN SUPPLY OUR EVERY NEED: 'And my God will supply every need of yours according to his riches in glory in Christ Jesus' Philippians 4:19.

- HE CAN REMOVE THE MOUNTAIN IN YOUR LIFE: 'Truly, I say to you, whoever says to this mountain, be taken up and thrown into the sea, and does not doubt in his heart, but believes that what he says will come to pass, it will be done for him' Mark 11:23.

God Can Do Anything, Anything,
Anything, God Can Do Anything
But Fail.
He Can Save, He Can Keep,
He Can Cleanse And He Will.
God Can Do Anything But Fail.
He's The Alpha And Omega,
The Beginning And The End.
He's The Fairest Of Ten Thousand
To My Soul. God Can Do Anything,
Anything, Anything,
God Can Do Anything But Fail.

(Unknown)

27TH MAY

THE GOOD SHEPHERD

*I am the good shepherd. The good shepherd
lays down his life for the sheep.*

John 10:11

In the Gospel of John chapter ten, John gives us at least seven ways that Jesus is the Good Shepherd for each born again child of God. That's one for each day of the week:

1. THE LORD JESUS CHRIST GAVE HIMSELF FOR EACH OF US: 'I am the good shepherd. The good shepherd lays down his life for the sheep' v. 11; and 'just as the Father knows me and I know the Father; and I lay down my life for the sheep' v. 15.

Jesus accomplished everything he had come to do for our salvation when He died for sins, was buried and rose again. Christ's sheep can say with Paul, 'The Son of God... loved me and gave himself for me' (Galatians 2:20).

2. JESUS BOUGHT US AND BROUGHT US TO HIMSELF: 'And I have other sheep that are not of this fold. I must bring them also, and they will listen to my voice. So there will be one flock, one shepherd' v. 16. The Lord Jesus called us to Himself. Not only Jews but Gentiles from every tribe, tongue and nation. He laid us on his shoulders and brought us into the fold of God.

*Then, safe within your fold,
we will exalt your name;
our thankful hearts with songs of joy
your goodness will proclaim*

(Unknown)

3. WE WERE GIVEN TO JESUS BY THE FATHER: 'My Father, who has given them to me, is greater than all, and

no one is able to snatch them out of the Father's hand' v. 29. Those who believe and follow Jesus Christ, are one of Christ's sheep. They have been given by the Father to the Son.

4. THE LORD JESUS KNOWS US THROUGH AND THROUGH: 'I am the good shepherd. I know my own and my own know me, just as the Father knows me and I know the Father; and I lay down my life for the sheep v. 14–15.

*Jesus knows all about our struggles;
He will guide 'til the day is done:
There's not a Friend like the lowly Jesus:
No, not one! no, not one!*

(Johnson Oatman)

5. WE BELONG TO JESUS: 'My sheep hear my voice, and I know them, and they follow me' v. 27.

*Following Jesus, ever day by day,
Nothing can harm me when He leads the way;
Darkness or sunshine, whate'er befall,
Jesus, the Shepherd is my All in All.*
(Unknown)

6. JESUS GIVES US ETERNAL LIFE: 'I give them eternal life v. 28.

7. JESUS KEEPS US AND GUARDS US: 'and they will never perish, and no one will snatch them out of my hand. My Father, who has given them to me, is greater than all, and no one is able to snatch them out of the Father's hand' v. 28–29. That's God's double grip.

28TH MAY

THE GREAT SHEPHERD

Now may the God of peace who brought again from the dead our Lord Jesus, the great shepherd of the sheep, by the blood of the eternal covenant, equip you with everything good that you may do his will, working in us that which is pleasing in his sight, through Jesus Christ, to whom be glory forever and ever. Amen.

Hebrews 13:20

The theme of a shepherd tending sheep is found throughout the Bible. Abraham, Jacob, Moses, and David are identified as shepherds in the Bible. The revelation of Jesus being the Shepherd of sheep, the flock of God, runs throughout the Bible: 'Know that the Lord, he is God! It is he who made us, and we are his; we are his people, and the sheep of his pasture' Psalm 100:3.

Many commentators point to Psalms 22, 23 and 24 to illustrate this. These Psalms are often collectively referred to as the Shepherd Psalms and they point us to Jesus who is the Good Shepherd, the Great Shepherd, and the Chief Shepherd.

Jesus Christ is the Good Shepherd. He is good because He sacrificed His life for the sheep. Psalm 22 tells of the Shepherd as a suffering servant. The parallel New Testament verses are found in John 10:1–18 and tell of the Good Shepherd who calls His sheep to Himself. 'I am the good shepherd. The good shepherd lays down his life for the sheep'. John 10:11.

Jesus Christ is the Great Shepherd. He is called Great because He arose from the dead and perfects His sheep: (Hebrews 13:20–21)

JESUS, great Shepherd of the sheep,
To thee for help we fly:
Thy little flock in safety keep;
For O! the wolf is nigh.

(Charles Wesley)

Jesus Christ is the Chief Shepherd. He is called Chief because He is to appear and return to earth with great glory and reward the faithful: 'And when the chief Shepherd appears, you will receive the unfading crown of glory' 1 Peter 5:4

Loving Shepherd of your sheep,
all your lambs in safety keep;
nothing can your power withstand,
none can pluck them from your hand.

May they praise you ev'ry day,
gladly all your will obey,
like your blessed ones above,
happy in your precious love.

Loving Shepherd, ever near,
teach your lambs your voice to hear;
suffer not their steps to stray
from the straight and narrow way.

Where you lead them may they go,
walking in your steps below;
then, before your Father's throne,
Savior, claim them for your own.

(Jane Eliza Leeson)

29TH MAY

A FOUR COURSE MEAL

And now I commend you to God and to the word of his grace, which is able to build you up and to give you the inheritance among all those who are sanctified.

Acts 20:32

Someone described these four verses as a spiritual four course meal: Milk, Solid food, Bread and a Sweet.

- 'Like new born infants, long for the pure spiritual MILK, that by it you may grow up into salvation' 1 Peter 2:2.
- 'I fed you with milk, not SOLID FOOD, for you were not ready for it. And even now you are not yet ready' 1 Corinthians 3:2.
- 'But he answered, it is written, Man shall not live by BREAD alone, but by every word that comes from the mouth of God' Matthew 4:4.
- 'How sweet are thy words unto my taste! yea, SWEETER than honey to my mouth!' Psalms 119:103.

One thing for sure is the fact that all of the Bible is the written Word of God.

I must accept its authority, assimilate its truth and accept its principles: 'All Scripture is breathed out by God and profitable for teaching, for reproof, for correction, and for training in righteousness, that the man of God may be complete, equipped for every good work' 2 Timothy 3:16–17.

WE SHOULD:

- RECEIVE IT: 'Therefore put away all filthiness and rampant wickedness and receive with meekness the implanted word, which is able to save your souls' James 1:21.
- READ IT: 'Blessed is the one who reads aloud the words of this prophecy, and blessed are those who hear, and who keep what is written in it, for the time is near' Rev 1:3.
- RESEARCH IT: 'Now these Jews were more noble than those in Thessalonica; they received the word with all eagerness, examining the Scriptures daily to see if these things were so.' Acts 17:11.
- REMEMBER IT: 'I have stored up your word in my heart, that I might not sin against you' Psalm 119:11.
- REFLECT ON IT: 'Blessed is the man who walks not in the counsel of the wicked, nor stands in the way of sinners, nor sits in the seat of scoffers; but his delight is in the law of the Lord, and on his law he meditates day and night' Psalm 1:1–2. 'But be ye doers of the word, and not hearers only, deceiving your own selves' James 1:22.

The B-I-B-L-E, Yes that's the book for me;
I stand alone on the Word of God,
The B-I-B-L-E

The B-I-B-L-E I'll take it along with me,
I'll read and pray, and then obey,
the B-I-B-L-E.

By F-A-I-T-H, I'm S-A-V-E-D,
I'll stand alone on the word of God,
The B-I-B-L-E.

The B-L-O-O-D That Jesus shed for me
Cleansed me from sin, I belong to him,
The B-L-O-O-D

(Unknown)

30TH MAY

FULLY RELYING ON GOD

*Behold, God is my salvation; I will trust, and will
not be afraid; for the Lord God is my strength and
my song, and he has become my salvation.*

Isaiah 12:2

I recently came across notes which I used while giving a closing epilogue at a youth fellowship back in September 2004. I was conveying a message to the young folk that they could fully rely on God.

The following are some of the thoughts I shared with the young people on that evening which I trust will be helpful to us today:

Sadly there are those who don't believe that there is a God: 'The fool says in his heart, there is no God' Psalm 14:1. However we are told in God's Word by the prophet Amos to: 'prepare to meet your God' Amos 4:12.

There is a God and we can fully rely on Him:

We see Him in the SKY: 'The heavens declare the glory of God, and the sky above proclaims his handiwork' Psalm 19:1.

We see Him in the SCRIPTURES: 'In the beginning, God created the heavens and the earth' Genesis 1:1.

We see Him in the SAVIOUR: 'No one has ever seen God; the only God, who is at the Father's side, He has made Him known' John 1:18. Therefore we can fully rely on God.

The Bible declares God to be a Spirit. God is infinite, eternal and unchanging. Because God has no limitations He can be everywhere at once, He can hear all, see all, and know all.

This speaks of His: divine omniscience meaning: the state of knowing everything, divine omnipresence meaning: the presence of God everywhere at the same time, divine omnipotence meaning: the quality of having unlimited power. There is no limit to His wisdom, power, love and mercy. Therefore we can fully rely on God.

The Bible also declares that God is a person. Everything we attribute to a person is attributed to God. He feels, thinks, loves, forgives and sympathises with the problems and sorrows that we face. Therefore we can fully rely on God.

The Bible also states that God is holy and righteous: 'Behold, the Lord's hand is not shortened, that it cannot save, or his ear dull, that it cannot hear; but your iniquities have made a separation between you and your God, and your sins have hidden His face from you so that He does not hear' Isaiah 59:1–2. However because of God's love, grace and mercy He has provided a remedy for sin through the Lord Jesus Christ John 3:16, Romans 5:8. All those who repent of their sin and put their faith and trust in Christ alone for salvation become the sons and daughters of God: 'But to all who did receive Him, who believed in His name, He gave the right to become children of God' John 1:12.

God is our heavenly Father if we are saved and we can fully rely on Him.

31ST MAY

HIS HARVEST

The Lord of the harvest.

Matthew 9:38

The following are notes about 'His Harvest' I have from March 2007. Just one month after hearing God calling me out of my job as an animal feed sales director to become a missionary representative. The Lord took me from earthly harvest fields which produced grains for animal feed to His harvest fields for souls, the souls of people. One was temporal the other eternal. At that time I noted that the Church has two legitimate programmes, 1. The edification of saints and 2. The evangelism of sinners. I then recorded a remark I had either heard or read, that generally speaking, 90% of time, talent and treasure edifies the saints while 10% evangelises the sinners. Then we ask 'what went wrong with the harvest?' Two important traits characterise the harvest: urgency and importance. Ripened harvests do not wait. A golden harvest soon perishes. Why would a farmer permit his harvest to perish? Only two reasons can be given; lack of labourers or laziness of labourers! A whitened harvest cries for urgent measures. The harvest leaps out of the gospels. One of Charles T Studd's reasons for going to be a missionary to China was the following statement of an atheist:

'Did I firmly believe, as millions say they do, that the knowledge and practice of religion in this life influences destiny in another, religion would mean to me everything. I would cast away earthly enjoyment as dross, earthly cares as follies, and earthly thoughts and feelings as vanity. Religion would be my first waking thought, and my last image before sleep sank me into unconsciousness. I would labour in its cause alone. I would take thought for the morrow of eternity only. I would esteem one soul gained for Heaven worth a life of suffering. Earthly consequences should never stay my hand, nor seal my lips. Earth, its joys and griefs, would occupy no moment in my thoughts. I would strive to look upon eternity alone, and on the immortal souls around me, soon to be everlastingly happy or everlastingly miserable. I would go forth to the world and preach in season and out of season, and my text would be, 'What shall it profit a man, if he gain the whole world and lose his own soul?''.

Jesus wept over the harvest. He died for the harvest. He rose for the harvest. He intercedes for the harvest. One glad day He will return for the harvest.

The question today is: 'How do you and I view His harvest? How are we spending our talents, treasure and time in His harvest in this our day and generation?

1ST JUNE

BMW: BE MY WITNESS

You will be my witnesses.

Acts 1:8

Just before Jesus returned to heaven, He explained to his disciples what they were to do after his departure. What he said to them, he also says to us. He left us on the earth that we might be his witnesses. Jesus promised that we would be given power to witness: 'But you will receive power when the Holy Spirit has come upon you, and you will be my witnesses' Acts 1:8. David Platt commenting on Acts 1:8 said: 'That is a potent verse. Jesus promising His disciples, to me, you, every follower of Christ, that He is going to put His Holy Spirit in us with all of His Power. Man, think about that, the Holy Spirit of God. This is the God who is reigning sovereign right now over 7.2 billion people in the world. He is in control of everything in all the universe, he's upholding Mars right now. His power is on display in all of creation…… The power of God's Spirit living in us and the purpose is clear. He's given us His power so we'll be His witnesses, so that we will testify to who He is to make Him known in the world around us, not just around us, but everywhere, to the end of the Earth, so that every follower of Christ has been given the power of the Spirit, for the display and declaration of the Gospel to the ends of the Earth.'

Some years ago I visited David McCammond one of the prayer warriors for the mission I served with at that time, who was in a convalescing home recovering after a serious operation. In our conversation David told me that he gave a hearty 'praise the Lord' when the surgeon told him that the operation was successful. In response I said to David 'you are not ashamed to own your Lord, no matter the situation'. He replied, 'Why wouldn't I? Because I was there when it happened and I ought to know' (speaking of his conversion). David went on to share how the Lord saved him and his wife on the last night of a mission held at Tullygarley Mission Hall near Ballymena many years earlier. David giving his thanks to God publically in hospital is an example of witnessing in a real life situation.

The following little hymn written by Jonny Cash gives a flavour of what a witness is:

There are some people who say we cannot tell
Whether we are saved or whether all is well
They say we only can hope and trust that it is so
Well, I was there when it happened
and so I guess I ought to know

Yes, I know when Jesus saved me, saved my soul
The very moment He forgave me, made me whole
He took away my heavy burdens
Lord, He gave me peace within

Today look out for an opportunity to witness for and about Jesus.

2ND JUNE

BMW: YOU ARE WITNESSES

You are witnesses of these things.

Luke 24:48

On this occasion Jesus was speaking to the disciples after His resurrection. He was giving to them another aspect of the great commission: 'and said to them, thus it is written, that the Christ should suffer and on the third day rise from the dead, and that repentance for the forgiveness of sins should be proclaimed in his name to all nations, beginning at Jerusalem. You are witnesses of these things'. Jesus was outlining the gospel message: repentance towards God and faith in Him and Him alone for salvation.

We weren't with the disciples on that occasion. We were not 'witnesses to these things' in the same way. We didn't get to see the risen Jesus, to touch him, and to have him open our minds to the Scriptures. But those first disciples were obedient and shared what they learned. In so doing, by the power of the Holy Spirit they opened the minds of others. And what they learned was eventually written down. And we are blessed to be able to read their inspired words, and to have our minds opened, too. We are invited again today to turn from whatever we are placing our ultimate hope and trust in, and to place it in our crucified and risen Lord Jesus. When we do we are invited to go and bear witness to these things. To proclaim the good news message that Christ died, for all. That Christ was raised again, for all. And that Christ will come again, for all.

While walking down Royal Avenue in Belfast I saw John a member of the church I attend walking across the street with a tea and sandwich carryout. He was heading towards a homeless man covered with a blanket sitting in a doorway. The carryout was for this dear man. John witnesses on Royal Avenue each Tuesday, Thursday and Saturday. He has various tracts for various situations. For the homeless he has one called: 'HOMELESS!' John witnesses by word and deed. He also hands out a sweet with each tract. As he does he says to the recipient: 'taste and see that the Lord is good'. By the way John is 87 years old. This is yet another example of a follower of Jesus being obedient to Christ's command to 'be a witness' for Him.

How I praise Thee, precious Savior,
That Thy love laid hold of me;
Thou hast saved and cleansed and filled me
That I might Thy channel be.

Channels only, blessed Master,
But with all Thy wondrous pow'r
Flowing through us, Thou canst use us
Every day and every hour.

Just a channel full of blessing,
To the thirsty hearts around;
To tell out Thy full salvation,
All Thy loving message sound.

(Mary E. Maxwell)

How might we find ways to reach the lost with the gospel today?

3RD JUNE

BMW: YOU WILL BE A WITNESS

For you will be a witness for him to everyone
of what you have seen and heard.

Acts 22:15

Witness (Greek = martus/martys) basically means one who remembers something and testifies concerning what they remember. According to biblical scholars 'martus' has two meanings 1. It describes one who has seen and/or experienced something or someone and 2. One who testifies to what he or she saw. The testimony could be in a legal setting or in the general sense of recounting first-hand knowledge.

A 'martus' or 'witness' is one who attests to a fact or event, one who gives evidence, one who has seen or has personal knowledge of something or someone, especially as an 'eye witness'. A witness is one who furnishes evidence or proof, confirming the truth by verbal testimony.

Greek Word Studies describes 'a witness' as follows: 'gives testimony in a court trial. Scripture repeatedly refers to the Old Testament 'formula' of witnesses to some event using the phrase 'two or three witnesses' (Matt 18:16, 2 Cor 13:1, 1 Tim 5:19, Heb 10:28) the witnesses of Hebrews 11 are those whose lives speak of the reality of their faith in God (Heb 12:1)'.

The point today is: 'Are we witnesses in and to our generation'. C. H. Spurgeon in his devotional 'And ye shall be witnesses unto me' comments:

'In order to learn how to discharge your duty as a witness for Christ, look at His example. He is always witnessing: by the well of Samaria, or in the Temple of Jerusalem: by the lake of Gennesaret, or on the mountain's brow. He is witnessing night and day; His mighty prayers are as vocal to God as His daily services. He witnesses under all circumstances; Scribes and Pharisees cannot shut His mouth; even before Pilate He witnesses a good confession. He witnesses so clearly, and distinctly that there is no mistake in Him - Christian, make your life a clear testimony.

Never, for fear of feeble man, restrain your witness. Your lips have been warmed with a coal from off the altar; let them speak as like heaven-touched lips should do - In the morning sow thy seed, and in the evening withhold not thine hand.

Watch not the clouds, consult not the wind-in season and out of season witness for the Saviour, and if it shall come to pass that for Christ's sake and the Gospel's you shall endure suffering in any shape, shrink not, but rejoice in the honour thus conferred upon you, that you are counted worthy to suffer with your Lord; and joy also in this-that your sufferings, your losses, and persecutions shall make you a platform, from which the more vigorously and with greater power you shall witness for Christ Jesus - Study your great Exemplar, and be filled with his Spirit'.

Let us always be witnessing today whether by life or lip or both.

4TH JUNE

GOD ANSWERS PRAYER

When he calls to me, I will answer him.

Psalm 91:15

Recently while visiting Ballymoney, the town I lived in for fifteen years, I was browsing in a Christian Charity Shop. While there I purchased a little book on the life of Dr Bill Holley entitled 'More than a doctor'. I first heard about Dr Holley when Speedy Moore was giving his testimony at Ballymoney Elim Church. Speedy was an alcoholic. On one of his visits to Dr Holley in relation to his alcoholism he communicated to Speedy that he couldn't do anything more for him but he could tell him about one who could. That being the Lord Jesus Christ. As a result in time Speedy came to know Jesus and was totally transformed by His grace. Speedy went on to witness, sing and play gospel songs using various instruments.

Dr Holley was a medical missionary in Nigeria for many years. Here is a lovely story from the book I purchased demonstrating that God hears and answers prayer: 'One of the most harrowing experiences of the Holley's term at Etinan was the serious illness of Margaret Currie, the eleven year old daughter of Mr and Mrs Donald Currie, then living at Ikot Idong. At first her symptoms seemed to indicate a bad dose of malaria. Soon it became all too clear that she was suffering from the dreaded blackwater fever. Horrified at what he saw and realising his own inexperience, Dr Holley sent an urgent appeal for help from the Church of Scotland Leprosy Settlement, over thirty miles away at Itu. Dr McDonald responded immediately but there was little anyone could do apart from praying. Dr Holley's diary recorded his deepest fears and also his faith in the power of God: 'Outlook very grave—but GOD. There is nothing too hard for the Lord—our eyes are towards Thee'.

A meeting of the Field Executive had been arranged for that Saturday but, instead, the missionaries gave themselves to prayer. Next day the regular church services were abandoned so that hundreds of believers could spend the time in intercession. The little girl, struggling for life, was surrounded by a great wave of faith and love. By 12 noon the bleeding had ceased and she began a slow but sure return to health. Her mother recalls: 'Bill stayed with us for a week and it was such a comfort and joy to have him'. She herself, a nurse, had first recognised the illness and, turning in anguish to her Daily Light, had read 'This sickness is not unto death, but to the glory of God'. So indeed it proved to be. Marion Holley remembers: 'What a boost this was to the Nigerian Christians and missionaries alike! There was a great rejoicing at the gracious answer from the Lord in sparing this young life. A renewed confidence in prayer and in a wonder-working God was given to all".

5TH JUNE

GOD ANSWERS PRAYER, O DO NOT DOUBT HIM

O you who hear prayer, to you shall all flesh come.

Psalm 65:2

Today I want to share another story about answered prayer recorded in a book which I purchased in a Christian Charity Shop written about Dr Bill Holley a missionary to Nigeria 1948–1961.

This story is about a twelve year old boy. Dr Holley recalled: 'His body was thin, his legs completely paralysed and his face emaciated. But his sunken eyes were bright with expectant hope that he would be healed. He was suffering from advanced tuberculosis of the spine for many months'.

Someone told his family of the missionary dispensary and his brother carried him about twelve miles to Ochadamu.

Dr Holley continues the story: 'Humanly speaking, it seemed hopeless, but we felt we couldn't turn the boy away. After all, many folk were praying that God would manifest His power in cases just like this, so he was brought into one of the little mud huts. His brother agreed to stay and supply his food, while we treated his sickness. That evening we explained that this disease was very advanced, but that God in whom we trusted was a Great Physician. We knelt in prayer, asking God to guide us in the treatment so that he might walk again. Then something very wonderful happened. Within forty-eight hours we had a visit from the chemist who had been supplying our drugs. He had travelled almost three hundred miles and this was the first and only time he visited Ochadamu during our two and a half years there. He spent about an hour with us. Just as he was leaving, he offered us samples of a new drug which was being used in the treatment of tuberculosis—a drug which, until that time, had not been used in Nigeria. We told him about our young patient and he gave us all the samples he possessed, so treatment began that very evening'.

Three months later the boy walked down the road with his brother perfectly well. Better still over those three months the boys had heard the gospel and had trusted the Saviour. As Dr Holley put it: 'both realised that Jesus was not only the Great Physician, but also their Saviour'.

God answers prayer, O do not doubt Him;
God answers prayer, believe His Word:
God answers prayer, now venture on Him,
His Word the test of time has stood.

God answers prayer, O soul, believe Him;
God answers prayer, I've proved Him true!
God answers prayer, now venture on Him;
He answered me, He'll answer you.

God answers prayer, fear not to trust Him;
God answers prayer, He longs to save:
God answers prayer, look up believing,
For this His only Son He gave.

(George Bennard)

Truly God answers prayer. Be encouraged. Keep on praying and believing today.

6TH JUNE

THIS BOOK IS ALIVE

*The grass withers, the flower fades, but the
word of our God will stand forever.*

Isaiah 40:8

Over the past two days I have used examples from the life and ministry of the late Dr Bill Holley to demonstrate that God hears and answers prayer. Today I am going to draw some thoughts from Dr Holley regarding the Word of God the Bible. Dr Holley made a return visit to Nigeria twenty years after he served as a missionary there. One of his first speaking engagements was at the annual prize day at the Samuel Bill Theological College. The following is what he shared with students: 'I can think of no better introduction to our Nigerian visit than this Bible College Prize-giving, for surely it is the Bible and its message which unites us in Christ Jesus'

He went on to speak about 'that transforming book as the Word of God in which He reveals His will to man; as the Bread of Life to nourish our spiritual lives; as the Sword of the Spirit by which we conquer Satan; as the Hammer which breaks down resistance in sinful hearts; as the Light which penetrates darkness. This Book is alive. It is different from every other book in the world. Know it in your head, stow it in your heart, show it in your life, sow it in the world; and may you know the anointing and enabling of the Holy Spirit'.

I trust all who read this treasures the grand old book. Let us daily read, meditate upon and study God's Word.

- READING: 'Until I come, devote yourself to the public reading of Scripture, to exhortation, to teaching' 1 Timothy 4:13.

- EXAMINING: 'Now these Jews were more noble than those in Thessalonica; they received the word with all eagerness, examining the Scriptures daily to see if these things were so' Acts 17:11.

- FINDING: 'I rejoice at your word like one who finds great spoil' Psalm 119:162.

- MEDITATING: 'Your words were found, and I ate them, and your words became to me a joy and the delight of my heart, for I am called by your name, O Lord, God of hosts' Jeremiah 15:16.

- PRACTISING: 'But be doers of the word, and not hearers only, deceiving yourselves. For if anyone is a hearer of the word and not a doer, he is like a man who looks intently at his natural face in a mirror. For he looks at himself and goes away and at once forgets what he was like. But the one who looks into the perfect law, the law of liberty, and perseveres, being no hearer who forgets but a doer who acts, he will be blessed in his doing' James 1:22–25.

*The Grand Old Book
You Find The Words Of Comfort
Wherever You May Look
In Sorrow Or In Pain
His Promises Are Plain
So Keep On Believing
In The Grand Old Book*

(Unknown)

7TH JUNE

10 REASONS WHY THE BIBLE IS GOD'S WORD

*For the word of the Lord is upright, and all
his work is done in faithfulness.*

Psalm 33:4

Reuben Archer Torrey (1856–1928) was an American evangelist, pastor, educator, and writer. The following is an article in which RA Torrey gives 10 reasons why he believes the Bible is God's Word:

- From the testimony of Jesus Christ. Mark 7:13; Luke 24, 44; John 14:26.
- The fulfilled prophecies concerning the Jews, the heathen nations, and the Messiah.
- The unity of the Book. The Bible consists, as you know, of sixty-six books, written by more than thirty different men, extending—in period of composition—over more than fifteen hundred years, and by men on every plane of social life, from herdsman and fisherman, and politician, to the king on his throne. Yet in all this wonderful conglomeration we find an absolute unity of thought.
- The immeasurable superiority of the teachings of the Bible to those of any other and all other books. This is not a large Book. I carry a copy in my waistcoat pocket, and yet in this one Book there is more truth than in all of history.
- The history of the Book, from its victory over attack.
- The character of those who accept compared with those who reject the Book.
- The influence of the Book. There is more power in that Book to save men, and purify, gladden and beautify their lives, than in all other literature put together.
- The inexhaustible depth of the Book. George Muller read it through 100 times, and said it was fresher every time he read it.
- The fact that as we grow in knowledge and holiness we grow towards the Bible.
- The direct testimony of the Holy Spirit. A great Bible expositor said: 'I believe the Bible is the inspired Word of God, because it inspires me'.

In the year of writing this devotion I read the following disturbing article in the press regarding the Bible: 'Great Britain's main prosecution service says it is 'no longer appropriate' to read parts of the Bible aloud. The Crown Prosecution Service said it contains references 'which are simply no longer appropriate in modern society and which would be deemed offensive if stated in public''.

Today remember that: 'All Scripture is breathed out by God and profitable for teaching, for reproof, for correction, and for training in righteousness, that the man of God may be complete, equipped for every good work' 2 Timothy 3:16–17.

*Ev'ry promise in the book is mine,
Ev'ry chapter, ev'ry verse, ev'ry line;
All are blessings of His love divine,
Ev'ry promise in the book is mine.*

(Unknown)

8TH JUNE

PROGRESSIVENESS

Beloved, although I was very eager to write to you about our common salvation, I found it necessary to write appealing to you to contend for the faith that was once for all delivered to the saints.

Jude 3

A dangerous movement called 'Progressive Christianity' began in 2006. Alisa Childers the author of 'Another Gospel' describes it as follows: 'Since then they have been infiltrating and influencing the Evangelical church. This movement seeks to re-interpret the Bible, re-assess historic doctrines, and re-define core tenets of the faith. While claiming the title 'Christian,' and boasting a high view of the Bible, it is sweeping up many unsuspecting Christians into a false view of who God is and how he saves people'.

So in these days we need to be on our guard and stick to the truth of God's Word. However as Christians we should be making progress in our Christian life and walk all the time. The following are Biblical truths regarding progressiveness as seen in Christians:

1. As Christians we need the 'go on' to perfection: 'Therefore let us leave the elementary doctrine of Christ and 'GO ON' to maturity, not laying again a foundation of repentance from dead works and of faith toward God' Hebrews 6:1. As Christians we are to forsake immaturity. Herman A Hoyt puts it as follows: 'progress should characterise the believer's life. This is true, first of all, in the teaching which the believer receives'. To grow in grace, to 'go on' with God we need to study

His Word and sit under Biblical teaching in a Bible believing Church.

2. As Christians we need to 'press toward' for the prize: 'I PRESS ON TOWARD the goal for the prize of the upward call of God in Christ Jesus' Philippians 3:14. Paul was pressing toward the goal. Press denotes an athlete who runs without swerving off course. Paul's idea was that he had started out with Jesus and he was going through:

Many they are who start in the race;
But with the light they refuse to keep pace;
Others accept it because it is new,
But not very many expect to go through

I'm going through, yes, I'm going through;
I'll pay the price, whatever others do;
I'll take the way with the Lord's despised few,
I'm going through, Jesus, I'm going through.

(Herbert Buffum)

As Christians we need the 'more and more' of love: 'Now concerning brotherly love you have no need for anyone to write to you, for you yourselves have been taught by God to love one another, for that indeed is what you are doing to all the brothers throughout Macedonia. But we urge you, brothers, to do this MORE AND MORE' 1 Thessalonians 4:9–10

9TH JUNE

REAL CHRISTIAN PROGRESS

For certain people have crept in unnoticed who long ago were designated for this condemnation, ungodly people, who pervert the grace of our God into sensuality and deny our only Master and Lord, Jesus Christ

Jude 4

Yesterday we warned against so called 'Progressive Christianity'. Anything that moves away from the teachings of the Bible is anything but progressive. However it is necessary to make progress in our Christian life and living. In that sense we can look at progressiveness as seen in Bible believing Christians. Yesterday we looked at three ways in which this is seen. Today we will consider another 4 more ways to progress in our walk with God:

1. As Christians we need the 'abound' of hope: 'May the God of hope fill you with all joy and peace in believing, so that by the power of the Holy Spirit you may ABOUND IN HOPE' Romans 15:13. In these days as Christians we should be, yes, must be people of hope:

Now I've a hope that will surely
endure after the passing of time;
I have a future in heaven for sure,
there in those mansions sublime.

And it's because of that wonderful
day when at the cross I believed;
Riches eternal and blessings supernal
from His precious hand I received

(John W. Peterson)

2. As Christians we need the 'increase' of knowledge: 'so as to walk in a manner worthy of the Lord, fully pleasing to him: bearing fruit in every good work and INCREASING in the knowledge of God' Colossians 1:10.

As we do the will and work of God, we increase in the knowledge of Him. This is true progress.

3. As Christians we need the 'growth' of faith: 'We ought always to give thanks to God for you, brothers, as is right, because your faith is GROWING abundantly, and the love of every one of you for one another is increasing' 2 Thessalonians 1:3. Paul writing to the believers at Thessalonica mentions how he is encouraged about their faith. In spite of the persecution they were enduring, their faith was growing and spreading. These Christians were not just holding their own in the face of persecution; they were growing, moving ahead, making progress. Are you making progress in your faith today no matter in which circumstances you find yourself.

4. As Christians we need to 'abide' in the Word: 'So Jesus said to the Jews who had believed him, If you ABIDE in my word, you are truly my disciples' John 8:31. In other words continue in the Word of God. We cannot progress if we do not feed on the Word of God, the Bible.

To be like Jesus, to be like Jesus!
My desire - to be like Him!
All thru life's journey from earth to glory,
My desire - to be like Him.

I trust that day by day this year we are making progress in our faith and walk with God.

10TH JUNE

PRAYER RALLY

Be constant in prayer.

Romans 12:12

One of the great joys I had as a missionary representative was to inform, encourage, speak at and hold special events for our mission's 'Prayer Groups'. One such event was the annual get together of our 'Prayer Group' leaders. Dr Wesley Duewel who served with OMS for many years in India and then as our President had written two books on prayer. One called was 'Touch the World through Prayer', which sold over 1 million copies. Dr Duewel, was not only well known within our Mission, but throughout missionary circles. I asked him if he would record a short devotional DVD to play at our 'Prayer Group' leaders' meeting in November 2008, which he did. In addition to his recorded message he sent me a written copy as well. I am sharing its contents today and tomorrow. I trust you will be encouraged and challenged by its contents:

'What a privilege and joy it is to me to greet my long-term friends and prayer partners in Britain and Ulster. Oswald Chambers was so impressed with our OMS work in Japan that in 1905 he brought the Cowmans to Britain, and they returned for ministry in 1907, 1912, and 1913. It was my privilege to spend several weeks and up to two months in Britain and Ulster seven times from 1948 ton 1996. Most of those times I spent precious weeks in Ulster. On September 4, 1958, while riding in a bus from Belfast to Killinchy, I was feeling how desperately we needed more prayer for our work in India. I felt we just had to get more prayer for a breakthrough and harvest in India. As I sat on the back seat praying, I wrote the words of my poem 'Pray On!' I suddenly realised a woman had gotten up from her seat in the front of the bus and was now standing in front of me. She said, 'Brother Duewel, I just happened to turn around and saw you sitting here. I just want you to know that for the past 18 years I have been praying for you every day'. Tears filled my eyes and I said, 'Sister, I was just sitting here feeling so strongly my need of prayer and was writing a poem, "Pray On!' Here are the words:

PRAY ON! (Verses 1&2)

How often do you bear a burden
In intercession for the lost?
How deeply do you feel compassion?
Or do you shun to pay the cost?
Is prayer for you mere relaxation,
A passing pleasure now and then?
Or do you pray in intercession
With burdened heart for souls of men?

How often do you feel the hunger
That cannot rest unsatisfied?
That keeps you praying ever longer
Until the answer is supplied?
How often are you lost in praying
Until, forgotten, pass the hours,
Until you wrestle, not delaying,
And seize the vict'ry from hell's powers.

11TH JUNE

PRAY ON!

You do not have, because you do not ask.

James 4:2

Yesterday I shared with you part of a message Dr Wesley Duewel sent to be shared with our 'Prayer Group' leaders at our annual get together in 2008. Dr Duewel continues:

'After 25 years of earnest work and much prayer, days of prayer and fasting, I was called to the United States to report on the India work, where by that time I was the director. I was so burdened by the comparative fruitlessness that I prayed all the way to the States as we flew from Delphi to Los Angeles. 'Lord, where is the harvest, the souls You sent us to reach?' Somewhere between Honolulu and Los Angeles, I felt led to ask God for 1,000 people to pray 15 minutes a day for India. God gave 1,500—especially in Britain and South Africa. Within one or two years we began to see the difference. It was like a spiritual 'jump start.'

Today, there are 403,495 members and over 2,500 organised churches. God has answered prayer. We have no missionary left in India. But we have three Seminaries and 13 Bible Schools. Our Indian leaders, meeting without any missionary presence, have set as a prayer goal 10,000 churches and 2,000,000 believers by 2020. Is that too much? No! One fifth of the world is now in India—most of whom are on the way to hell—without Christ and without hope. Let us pray and, at times, fast for miracle harvest before our Lord returns.

PRAY ON! (Verses 3&4)

How often do the tears unbidden,
Hot burning tears, course down your cheek
As on you pray and bear the burden
And for God's promised answer seek?
'Tis then you go into the garden
And share with Christ the sweat of blood;
'Tis then you lead lost souls to pardon
And bring joy to the heart of God.

O saint of God, keep praying, pleading;
Pray on, weep on, believer, and fast.
Faint not nor fear, keep interceding;
God's hour of pow'r will come at last –
His perfect answer long awaited,
Souls saved and Satan's full defeat,
Your long desire, with blessings freighted,
And trophies to lay at His feet.

I trust these messages from Dr Duewel will spur us to 'Pray On!' in this our day and generation praying for a harvest of precious souls at home and abroad.

12TH JUNE

MENTAL HEALTH

You keep him in perfect peace whose mind is
stayed on you, because he trusts in you.

Isaiah 26:3

During the time of writing this devotion Dr Sarah Hughes the Chief Executive in England and Wales of the mental health charity Mind said 'We are really worried. This feels like a perfect storm that we need to take hold of. We have got the recovery from the pandemic, the cost of living crisis and the impact of the war in Ukraine and global instability. All of these contribute greatly to the vulnerability that we are experiencing to a greater or lesser extent. The mental health of the nation is probably worse than it has ever been.

At the Church of which I am a member we had a mental health specialist give a talk to our seniors group. Permission was given by 'Teen Challenge' to give to the attendees at the meeting a copy of a leaflet they produced entitled: '9 Ways to Improve Your Mental Health'. Today I am going to share extracts from the leaflet with you:

1. TELL YOURSELF SOMETHING POSITIVE: 'For God so loved the world, that he gave his only Son, that whoever believes in Him should not perish but have eternal life' John 3:16; 'I praise you, for I am fearfully and wonderfully made' Psalm 139:14; 'For I know the plans I have for you, ... to give you a future and a hope' Jeremiah 29:11. So, God says you are loved, you are wonderfully made and He has a plan for your life! Now that's positive.

2. WRITE DOWN SOMETHING YOU ARE GRATEFUL FOR: 'Give thanks to the Lord, for he is good, for his steadfast love endures forever' Psalm 136:1.

3. Focus on one thing (In the moment): 'Looking to Jesus, the founder and perfecter of our faith, who for the joy that was set before Him endured the cross, despising the shame, and is seated at the right hand of the throne of God. Consider Him who endured from sinners such hostility against himself, so that you may not grow weary or fainthearted' Hebrews 12:2–3.

4. EXERCISE: Exercise is a powerful antidote to stress, anxiety, and depression.

5. EAT A GOOD MEAL: 'Oh, taste and see that the Lord is good!' Psalm 34:8.

6. OPEN UP TO SOMEONE: 'Come to me, all who labour and are heavy laden, and I will give you rest' Matthew 11:28.

7. DO SOMETHING FOR SOMEONE ELSE: 'Therefore encourage one another and build one another up, just as you are doing' 1 Thessalonians 5:11.

8. TAKE A BREAK: 'Be still, and know that I am God' Psalm 46:10.

9. GO TO BED ON TIME: 'In peace I will both lie down and sleep; for you alone, O Lord, make me dwell in safety' Psalm 4:8.

13TH APRIL

THE STEADFAST LOVE OF THE LORD

Your steadfast love, O Lord, extends to the heavens, your faithfulness to the clouds . . . How precious is your steadfast love, O God! . . . Oh, continue your steadfast love to those who know you.

Psalm 36:5, 7, 10

The following are some aspects of the Lord's steadfast love for us to consider today:

- IT IS UNPARALLELED LOVE: 'For one will scarcely die for a righteous person—though perhaps for a good person one would dare even to die' Rom 5:7.
- IT IS UNMERITED LOVE: 'but God shows his love for us in that while we were still sinners, Christ died for us' Rom 5:8.
- IT IS UNMISTAKABLE LOVE: 'For God so loved the world, that he gave his only Son, that whoever believes in Him should not perish but have eternal life' John 3:16.
- IT IS UNENDING LOVE: 'I have loved you with an everlasting love; therefore I have continued my faithfulness to you' Jer 31:3.

His love has no limit, His grace has no measure,
His power no boundary known unto men,
For out of His infinite riches in Jesus,
He giveth and giveth and giveth again

(Annie Johnson Flint)

The steadfast love of the Lord never ceases;
God's mercies never come to an end.
They are new every morning,
new every morning;
great is your faithfulness, O Lord,
great is your faithfulness.

(Edith McNeill)

We see the Lord's steadfast love demonstrated to Mary, Martha and Lazarus in John 11. 'Now Jesus loved Martha and her sister and Lazarus' John 11:5.

- IT WAS A PERSONAL LOVE: It was concentrated on each of the three.
- IT WAS A PERFECT LOVE: Christ's love is always unselfish, self-denying and self-sacrificing: 'Greater love has no one than this, that someone lay down his life for his friends' John 15:13; 'For the love of Christ controls us, because we have concluded this: that one has died for all, therefore all have died' 2 Cor 5:14; 'I have been crucified with Christ. It is no longer I who live, but Christ who lives in me. And the life I now live in the flesh I live by faith in the Son of God, who loved me and gave himself for me' Gal 2:20.
- IT WAS A PERSISTENT LOVE: 'Now before the Feast of the Passover, when Jesus knew that his hour had come to depart out of this world to the Father, having loved his own who were in the world, he loved them to the end' John 13:1.
- IT WAS A POWERFUL LOVE: 'No, in all these things we are more than conquerors through him who loved us' Rom 8:37.
- IT WAS A PERMANENT LOVE: 'Who shall separate us from the love of Christ? Shall tribulation, or distress, or persecution, or famine, or nakedness, or danger, or sword?' Rom 8:35.

Praise God today: His steadfast love NEVER ceases.

14TH JUNE

'HALLELUJAH'

Praise the Lord! Praise the Lord, O my soul!

Psalm 146:1

On Wednesday 24th October, 2012 I was invited to bring the opening prayer and greetings at the 100th birthday service for Mr James McCullough. (Jim was able to touch his toes on the evening of the service). I shared with the gathering that evening that: 'I first met Jim in the year 2000 when he was just a young man of 88 years, at this very Mission Hall: Ballyrobert Mission Hall. It did not take long to see by his lip and life that Jim was a man of God and a godly man who loves his Saviour. I soon learned that by some he was affectionately known as 'Hallelujah Jim', and I soon learned by experience as well. If Jim was in agreement with the words of a hymn or with something the preacher was bringing from God's Word he shouted out a hearty "HALLELUJAH", which by the way is quite biblical and in order when done appropriately and prompted by the Holy Spirit'.

The last 5 Psalms 146–150 start and finish with the words 'Praise the Lord'. They are known as the 'Hallelujah' Psalms. So in reality 'Hallelujah means 'Praise the Lord'.

IN PSALM 146 WE HAVE:

- THE CHALLENGE TO PRAISE: 'Praise the Lord!' v. 1;
- THE CALL TO PRAISE: 'Praise the Lord, O my soul!' v. 1;
- THE COMMITMENT TO PRAISE: 'I will praise the Lord as long as I live; I will sing praises to my God while I have my being' v. 2. It is an earthly commitment: 'Nevertheless, do not rejoice in this, that the spirits are subject to you, but rejoice that your names are written in heaven' Luke 10:20. It is an eternal commitment: 'And whenever the living creatures give glory and honour and thanks to Him who is seated on the throne, who lives forever and ever, the twenty-four elders fall down before Him who is seated on the throne and worship Him who lives forever and ever. They cast their crowns before the throne, saying, Worthy are you, our Lord and God, to receive glory and honour and power, for you created all things, and by your will they existed and were created' Revelation 4:9–11.

- THE CAUTION OF PRAISE: 'Put not your trust in princes, in a son of man, in whom there is no salvation. When his breath departs, he returns to the earth; on that very day his plans perish v. 3–4.

- THE CAUSES OF PRAISE: v. 6–10: The greatness of God v. 6 and the grace of God v. 7–10.

Praise ye the Lord! Hallelujah!
Praise ye the Lord!
O praise ye the Lord! Praise Him upon earth,
In tuneful accord, ye sons of new birth;
Praise Him who hath brought
you His grace from above,
Praise Him who hath taught
you to sing of His love.

(Henry W. Baker)

15TH JUNE

REVIVAL IN SOUTH WALES

Will you not revive us again?

Psalm 85:6

While serving the Lord as the OMS UK leader I had the privilege of visiting each region of the UK. One of these was South Wales. While there I visited Moriah Chapel. It was here that under God Evan Roberts led the 1904 Welsh Revival. The following is an extract from a leaflet given to me while there called: A Short History of Moriah Chapel and the 1904 Welsh Revival: 'Evan Roberts, the devoted son of Henry and Hannah Roberts, Island House, Bwlchymynydd, Loughor, a miner by profession, preached his first sermon at Moriah on Sunday morning, the 18th December 1903, on the text from St Luke, chapter 9, verse 23; 'And he said to all, If anyone would come after me, let him deny himself and take up his cross daily and follow me'. At the age of 26, his heart was set on going into ministry. On the 13th September 1904, he went to Newcastle Emyln to attend a Grammar School. This was to obtain a basic qualification so that he could then enter Theological College at Trefecca.

During the service at Bethel Newcastle Emlyn on Sunday evening 30th October, Evan Roberts felt the presence of the Holy Spirit urging him to return the following day to work with the young people at Moriah. His arrival at Island House at mid-day on Monday was totally unexpected and his mother presumed he was ill or that he was preaching somewhere in the area. The next fortnight

has been rightly called 'The Dawn of the Revival in Loughor'. Wales had never witnessed such a fortnight in its history since the exciting days of 1859. Commencing on Monday night, 31st October 1904, a series of meetings was held at Moriah in which Evan Roberts made urgent appeals to the people to rise and confess Christ publicly. At first, the reception he received was one of indifference, due to his unorthodox ways of conducting services, the failure to realise that what he prophesied could come about and more than anything, the cold reception given to anyone who aspires to great things in his own locality. However, this local prejudice soon gave way to the firm reality that Evan Roberts was under the complete guidance of the Holy Spirit. On Sunday night, the 6th November 1904, the Holy Spirit descended with great fire upon the people present and they prayed until the early hours of the morning. This religious fervour spread rapidly and there was a genuine upheaval. Night after night Moriah was crowded to capacity and the services continued until 4 and 5am. People of all denominations took part and made their way to the scene of this great Pentecost from many different countries'.

God has not changed; what He did in 1904 He is able to do again

16TH JUNE

EARTHQUAKES

And behold, there was a great earthquake

Matthew 28:2

On the occasion of writing this article the death toll from the recent Turkey-Syria earthquakes is nearing 44,000.

The Bible mentions earthquakes on quite a number of occasions. Today we will look at what these earthquakes teach us.

THE EARTHQUAKE ASSOCIATED WITH RULES: 'Now Mount Sinai was wrapped in smoke because the Lord had descended on it in fire. The smoke of it went up like the smoke of a kiln, and the whole mountain trembled greatly' Exodus 19:18. On this occasion the entire scene was so terrifying that Moses himself was trembling. It speaks of the nature and ministry of the Law. It is a picture of God's righteous requirements and wrath against sin. The law was given to produce a knowledge of sin. 'So then, the law was our guardian until Christ came, in order that we might be justified by faith' Galatians 3:24

THE EARTHQUAKE ASSOCIATED WITH REDEMPTION: 'And behold, the curtain of the temple was torn in two, from top to bottom. And the earth shook, and the rocks were split'. 'When the centurion and those who were with him, keeping watch over Jesus, saw the earthquake and what took place, they were filled with awe and said, Truly this was the Son of God!'. Matthew 27:51'54. Here Christ is the mediator of the New Covenant. Before God could righteously make this Covenant, the Lord Jesus had to die. He had to seal the Covenant with His own blood and give Himself a ransom for many. He secured the blessing of the New Covenant for His people by His death. He ensures the blessings for them by His endless life. He preserves His people to enjoy the blessings in a hostile world by His present ministry at God's right hand.

The terrors of law and of God
With me can have nothing to do;
My Saviour's obedience and blood
Hide all my transgressions from view

(Augustus Montague Toplady)

Now we are free, there's no condemnation,
Jesus provides a perfect salvation;
'Come unto Me,' O hear His sweet call,
Come, and He saves us once for all

(P. P. Bliss)

THE EARTHQUAKE ASSOCIATED WITH THE RESURRECTION: 'Now after the Sabbath, toward the dawn of the first day of the week, Mary Magdalene and the other Mary went to see the tomb. And behold, there was a great earthquake, for an angel of the Lord descended from heaven and came and rolled back the stone and sat on it. His appearance was like lightning, and his clothing white as snow. And for fear of him the guards trembled and became like dead men' Matthew 28:1–4. The resurrection proved that Jesus was the Son of God and that He had defeated death for the believer. Because He lives we shall live also.

17TH JUNE

A GREAT EARTHQUAKE

And there will be famines and earthquakes in various places.

Matthew 24:7

On average, there are about 15 large earthquakes in the world every year with magnitudes greater than 7.0. The most recent one at the writing of this devotional was in Turkey and Syria causing death and destruction. Yesterday we commenced looking at some references to earthquakes in the Bible. We will conclude this study today:

THE EARTHQUAKE ASSOCIATED WITH REGENERATION: 'About midnight Paul and Silas were praying and singing hymns to God, and the prisoners were listening to them, and suddenly there was a great earthquake, so that the foundations of the prison were shaken. And immediately all the doors were opened, and everyone's bonds were unfastened. When the jailer woke and saw that the prison doors were open, he drew his sword and was about to kill himself, supposing that the prisoners had escaped' Acts 16:25–27.

However you know the sequel: 'The frightening sounds and disturbing effects of the earthquake awakened every member of the jailor's household and staff, and as they stood watching they were amazed to see prisoners being led by their master into the courtyard' (John Phillips). This earthquake led to the entire household coming to Christ.

THE EARTHQUAKE ASSOCIATED WITH RETURNING: 'There will be great earthquakes, and in various places famines and pestilences. And there will be terrors and great signs from heaven' Luke 21:11.

Earthquakes will increase as we approach the return of Jesus for the Church. In these days as believers we need to be watching, waiting and working as our redemption draws nigh.

THE EARTHQUAKE ASSOCIATED WITH RETRIBUTION: 'The seventh angel poured out his bowl into the air, and a loud voice came out of the temple, from the throne, saying, It is done! And there were flashes of lightning, rumblings, peals of thunder, and a great earthquake such as there had never been since man was on the earth, so great was that earthquake. The great city was split into three parts, and the cities of the nations fell, and God remembered Babylon the great, to make her drain the cup of the wine of the fury of his wrath. And every island fled away, and no mountains were to be found. And great hailstones, about one hundred pounds each, fell from heaven on people; and they cursed God for the plague of the hail, because the plague was so severe' Revelation 16:17–21.

This unbelieving world has yet to experience its greatest ever earthquake as God finally pours out His wrath on a world who has rejected Him, His truth and His ways.

Let earth's inmost centre quake,
And shattered nature mourn,
Let the unwieldy mountains shake,
And fall by storms up torn,
Fall with all their trembling load
Far into the ocean hurled,
Lo! We stand secure in God,
Amidst a ruined world.

(Charles Wesley)

18TH JUNE

A RELAY TEAM

*And what you have heard from me in the
presence of many witnesses entrust to faithful
men, who will be able to teach others also.*

2 Timothy 2:2

In April 2009 I had the privilege of visiting the missionaries from N Ireland in Ecuador who were serving with One Mission Society. I spent a number of days with Julia Henry in the area called El Oriente. El Oriente, which means 'the east' is a vast area that stretches from the eastern slopes of the Andes to the border with Peru. Julia was working with others in the OMS 'Chaski Ministry'.

The Chaskis were the messengers of the Inca Empire. Agile, highly trained and physically fit, they were in charge of carrying the quipus, messages and gifts, up to 240 km per day through the Chaskis relay system. Chaskis were not just messengers; they were trained to be able to read and translate the quipus to each other and higher authorities. Not only were they used to transport oral messages, but they also helped the inspector general, the Sapa Inca's brother, keep track of the people in the empire. Chaski were dispatched along thousands of kilometres of the Andes in Ecuador and Peru. The acted as a relay team. So messages were passed on quickly throughout the Kingdom.

And so it is in Christian service. We must pass on the message of our King to others who in turn will pass it on to others. This can be applied in a family setting. We need to pass the message on to our children. We need to disciple, train and mentor new believers so they too can pass the message on to others. It involves succession planning in local churches at all levels as it does in para-church organisations. The question today is: who are we passing the message on to. Who are we equipping and mentoring. Who are we sending out prayerfully and financially?

It was amazing spending some days in the Ecuadorian Jungle experiencing a young woman from N Ireland passing on the message of King Jesus and training others to pass His message on in the jungle region of Ecuador, South America.

*The runner of a relay, finds in his baton
Purpose for the running and strength to carry on
We hold within our grasp the faith that makes us strong
And like the relay runner, we seek to pass it on*

*Passin' the faith along to my brother
Passin' the faith along
Helping to build the faith of another
Passin' the faith along*

(Unknown)

19TH JUNE

HOPE IN TIMES OF TROUBLE

Whoever follows me will not walk in darkness,
but will have the light of life.

John 8:12

In 1995 Luis Palau came to N Ireland to speak at a mission in Londonderry from the 17th-21 May. The Church of which I was a member of along with other evangelical Churches in that town distributed the invitation leaflet for the mission and organised a bus to bring folk to the mission. The following is part of the message entitled 'Hope in times of trouble' that Dr Palau had on the invitation leaflet: 'For a moment we sat in stunned silence, trying to block out the doctor's words: The tumour is malignant and radical surgery must be performed immediately. Surgery was planned for the following Monday. Pat, my wife, had cancer. We can't delay. When we arrived home, I headed for my basement office. I had to come to grips with this terrible news. A hundred emotions welled up inside me and I started to cry. This was the sort of thing that happened to other people. But not to my wife. Not Pat. My thoughts were suddenly interrupted by the strains of a familiar old song. Where was it coming from? No one was at home except Pat and me. Slowly it dawned on me—Pat was playing the piano and singing 'How firm a foundation'. While the bottom seemed to be falling out of our lives, my wife found strength and security in the firm foundation of her relationship with Jesus Christ. Because Jesus Christ died for our sins and rose again, He is the only sure foundation on which we can build our life'.

How firm a foundation, ye saints of the Lord,
Is laid for your faith in His excellent word!
What more can He say than to you He hath said,
To you who for refuge to Jesus have fled?

Fear not, I am with thee, O be not dismayed,
For I am thy God, and will still give thee aid;
I'll strengthen thee, help thee, and cause thee to stand,
Upheld by My righteous, omnipotent hand.

When through the deep waters I call thee to go,
The rivers of sorrow shall not overflow;
For I will be with thee, thy troubles to bless,
And sanctify to thee thy deepest distress.

When through fiery trials thy pathway shall lie,
My grace, all sufficient, shall be thy supply;
The flame shall not hurt thee; I only design
Thy dross to consume, and thy gold to refine.

E'en down to old age all My people shall prove
My sovereign, eternal, unchangeable love;
And then, when grey hairs shall their temples adorn,
Like lambs they shall still in My bosom be borne.

The soul that on Jesus hath leaned for repose,
I will not, I will not desert to his foes;
That soul, though all hell should endeavour to shake,
I'll never, no, never, no, never forsake!

20TH JUNE

MOT

Examine yourselves, to see whether you are in the faith. Test yourselves. Or do you not realize this about yourselves, that Jesus Christ is in you?—unless indeed you fail to meet the test!

2 Corinthians 13:5

Once a car is four years old in Northern Ireland it must be tested each year to check that it meets road safety and environmental standards. This Ministry of Transport test is commonly known as an 'MOT'. MOT tests are carried out at driving and vehicle test centres around the country. An MOT involves dozens of checks on your car, ranging from the brakes and fuel system to lights, mirrors, seatbelts, windscreen wipers and exhaust system. Before I brought my car for the test, I booked it in with my mechanic to give it a check over to see if was compliant with the requirements of the test. In fact some minor things needed to be done.

Just as our cars get an MOT check-up, our spiritual lives also need a check-up.

While sitting in the waiting area of at the MOT centre as my car was going through its annual test my attention was drawn to the biblical principle of regularly carrying out a spiritual check on myself to see if I meet God's requirements as a Christian or are there areas that would need attention.

The following are some areas that should form a spiritual check-up:

- Is there a growing awareness of God's presence in your life?
- Am I spending appropriate time praying?
- Are you reading and meditating on the Bible and applying its teachings to your life and living?

- Are you pursuing God's plan for your life and how do you fit into God's global purpose?
- Are you growing in love for God and others including those who have been difficult for you to love?
- Is your thirst to know God greater today than it was this time last year?
- Is spiritual growth a priority?
- Are you actively involved in a local church?
- Is your lifestyle noticeably different from your peers who do not know Jesus?
- Are you grateful because of what God has done for you?
- Are we living, learning, obeying, serving and praying like the Lord whom we claim to follow:

To be like Jesus, to be like Jesus!
My desire - to be like Him!
All thru life's journey from earth to glory,
My desire - to be like Him.

(Unknown)

- Are you loving, waiting for and expecting the Lord's return?

These are but a few thoughts regarding a spiritual check-up. I praise God that He's still working on me. There is a day coming that I shall be like Him: 'Beloved, we are God's children now, and what we will be has not yet appeared; but we know that when he appears we shall be like him, because we shall see Him as He is' 1 John 3:2.

21ST JUNE

ENLARGE THE PLACE OF THY TENT

Then after fasting and praying they laid their hands on them and sent them off. So, being sent out by the Holy Spirit, they went down to Seleucia, and from there they sailed to Cyprus.

Acts 13:3–4

In 1792 William Carey published a book called: 'An Enquiry into the Obligations of Christians, to use means for the Conversion of the Heathens in which the Religious State of the Different Nations of the World, the Success of Former Undertakings, and the Practicability of Further Undertakings, are Considered'. The rather long title, typical for the day, accurately conveyed the contents. In it he forcefully answered the objections of those who raised practical obstacles to missions.

At a Baptist ministers' meeting in June 1792, Carey brought his book's arguments to bear in a sermon, based on Isaiah 54:2, 3—'Enlarge the place of thy tent'. He concluded with an unforgettable call: 'Expect great things! Attempt great things!'

However these ministers still hesitated to form a mission's society as Carey was recommending.

In the end Carey's passion prevailed. Within five months, on October 2, 1792, twelve ministers formed a society 'for the propagation of the Gospel among the heathen, according to the recommendations of Carey. In his book he elaborated on the necessity to pray, plod, plan and pay for missions.

Section 5 of his book is entitled: 'An Enquiry into the Duty of Christians in general, and what Means ought to be used, in order to promote this Work'.

He pointed out that: 'One of the first, and most important of those duties which are incumbent upon us, is fervent and united prayer'. He also pointed out the need of wholly relying on the leading and guidance of God the Holy Spirit. He said without the power of the Holy Spirit the work 'will be ineffectual. If a temple is raised for God in the heathen world, it will not be by might, nor by power, nor by the authority of the magistrate, or the eloquence of the orator; but by my Spirit, saith the Lord of Hosts. We must therefore be in real earnest in supplicating his blessing upon our labours.

The most glorious works of grace that have ever taken place, have been in answer to prayer; and it is in this way, we have the greatest reason to suppose, that the glorious out-pouring of the Spirit, which we expect at last, will be bestowed'.

He then added: 'we must not be content however with praying, without exerting ourselves in the use of means for the obtaining of those things we pray for'. Those means included sending workers by planning, by proxy (In other words you are sending people on your behalf) and by paying. I trust like Carey we too are involved in mission at home and abroad. The starting point being that of praying intentionally for mission and missionaries.

22ND JUNE

A PLODDER

When he came and saw the grace of God, he was glad, and he exhorted them all to remain faithful to the Lord with steadfast purpose

Acts 11:23

In 1792, Carey published an eighty-seven page manuscript, popularly known as his '*Enquiry*' The book contains an introduction, and five sections or chapters. In part as a result of this book, the *Baptist Missionary Society* was formed.

In the Introduction of the *Enquiry*, Carey sets forth the question of whether Jesus' teaching recorded in Matthew 28:18–20 remains as an obligation on Christians after the apostles.

Chapter I includes Carey's treatment of Matthew 28:18–20 in relation to Christians of the late eighteenth century.

In Chapter II, Carey reviews former attempts to convert various peoples of the world to Christianity; included in this chapter is Carey's rehearsal of Christian missionary history, including an exposition of *Paul's four missionary journeys* as recorded in the New Testament book, the Acts of the Apostles.

Chapter III contains a survey of the world's countries, those countries' land size, populations, and religious preferences. Carey presents twenty-three tables of detailed statistical information, followed by a discussion of the information in the tables.

In Chapter IV, Carey offers a defence in support of sending Christian missionaries to the peoples of the world who had not heard the Christian message.

Lastly, in Chapter V, Carey presents an argument in support of Christians' duty to promote missionary efforts to peoples who had not heard the Christian message.

It is therefore no wonder that William Carey has been described as the 'Father of modern Protestant missions'. Ultimately he became a missionary to India at great cost. The results of his work are still being felt today. When I visited a ministry called 'Good News India' in Vijayawada, Andhra Pradesh State, South India the Bible version they read in Telugu was Carey's translation.

When Carey was asked later in life how someone might describe his ministry and service he said: 'If he gives me credit for being a plodder he will describe me justly. Anything beyond that will be too much. I can plod. I can persevere in any definite pursuit. To this I owe everything'.

It behoves us all to be 'plodders' in God's service. Keep on keeping on. Unfortunately on some occasions when the going got tough for me in certain areas of service I stepped away. Many of these I now regret. However the Lord is gracious and redirected me to other areas of service.

Plodders are people of: DEDICATION: 'And let us not grow weary of doing good, for in due season we will reap, if we do not give up' Galatians 6:9; DIRECTION: They know where they are going; DISCIPLINE: Plodders have their eyes on the goal; they resist every effort to get them on detour; DUTY: 'Jesus said to them, "My food is to do the will of him who sent me and to accomplish his work' John 4:34.

23RD JUNE

A GIVING PORTFOLIO

And you Philippians yourselves know that in the beginning of the gospel, when I left Macedonia, no church entered into partnership with me in giving and receiving, except you only.

Philippians 4:15

In his 'Enquiry' William Carey lays out means involved with promoting mission and reaching the lost with the gospel. One of those means is 'giving' or 'paying' towards making mission happen. This is what Carey said: 'We are exhorted to lay up treasure in heaven, where neither moth nor rust doth corrupt, nor thieves break through and steal. It is also declared that whatsoever a man soweth, that shall he also reap. These scriptures teach us that the enjoyments of the life to come, bear a near relation to that which now is; a relation similar to that of the harvest, and the seed. It is true all the reward is of mere grace, but it is nevertheless encouraging; what a treasure, what a harvest must await such characters as PAUL, and ELLIOT, and BRAINERD, and others, who have given themselves wholly to the work of the Lord. What a heaven it will be to see the many myriads of poor heathen people, of Britons amongst the rest, who by their labours have been brought to the knowledge of God. Surely a crown of rejoicing like this is worth aspiring to. Surely it is worthwhile to strive with all our might, in promoting the cause, and kingdom of Christ'.

This 'Paying' can be done at a Church or individual level. However it is as important as praying and going. It was Amy Carmichael another missionary to India who said: 'You can give without loving. But you cannot love without giving'.

The Bible teaches: 'Each one must give as he has decided in his heart, not reluctantly or under compulsion, for God loves a cheerful giver' 2 Corinthians 9:7. The question today to consider is: Do I have a giving portfolio towards the Lord's work and mission that is in alignment with God's will? If we are clear on the teaching on giving to the Lord's work and have given intentional prayerful thought on giving, we can start to build a giving portfolio that has both breadth and depth. This will certainly involve giving to your local church and then ministries, missions and missionaries God has put on your heart.

I trust we can say a warm amen to the words of Frances Ridley Havergal's hymn: 'Take my silver and my gold; Not a mite would I withhold', when it comes to support the Lord's work and the missionary cause.

24TH JUNE

ARE THE LOST REALLY LOST?

For the Son of Man came to seek and to save the lost.

Luke 19:10

Dr David Long when holding the office of the President of the Mission I had the privilege of serving the Lord with (OMS)wrote an article in the OMS Outreach Magazine entitled Are the Lost Really Lost?: 'This issue of OMS Outreach presents answers to the question, 'Where are the lost?' Foundational to that question, 'Are the lost really lost?' The political correctness of the pluralistic world in which we live may make the answer more uncertain for some, but for more than a century, One Mission Society has remained called by and committed to the proclamation of the Gospel to the lost, those who have not accepted salvation by grace through faith in Jesus Christ.

In 1919, OMS cofounder Charles Cowman wrote in The Oriental Missionary Standard, 'Let us lift our eyes and look upon the fields and thus give Him every chance to speak to us in His great loving desire to reach every lost soul with the knowledge of salvation through the blood atonement of His beloved Son, in whom He is well pleased'. Later that same year, the questions were posed 'Do the heathen really need the Gospel? Is their own religion not good enough for them and more suitable for them?' We may appropriately avoid the term 'heathen' as duly offensive today, but the scriptural answer given then remains the same.

'And there is salvation in no one else, for there is no other name under heaven given among men by which we must be saved' Acts 4:12. Luke 19:10. 'Indeed, under the law almost everything is purified with blood, and without the shedding of blood there is no forgiveness of sins' Hebrews 9:22.

A few years later, OMS cofounder E A Kilbourne wrote, '. . . from the throne of the universe has gone forth the command, Go into all the world and preach the Gospel to every creature. Thus is the divine plan revealed for the evangelisation of world'.

Dr Long concludes by stating: 'God's unchanging plan is known to us. We dare not ignore the pre-eminence Jesus gave to the command by uttering it no less than 5 times in the 40 days between His resurrection and ascension. Yes, the lost really are lost'.

He concludes by making the point that the value of our Mission 'is still measured by the commitment to take the Gospel to those who are lost'.

Am I, are you committed to reaching the lost with the glorious Gospel today?

God loved the world of sinners lost
And ruined by the fall;
Salvation full, at highest cost,
He offers free to all

(Martha M. Stockton)

25TH JUNE

THE MISSIONARY MODEL

Jesus said to them again, Peace be with you. As the
Father has sent me, even so I am sending you.

John 20:21

'What is the missiological signifi-cance of missions in the Johannine writings?' was one of the questions I was set to write about whilst I was studying for my masters in theol-ogy. (The Johannine writings being: John's Gospel' 1st, 2nd, 3rd John and Revelation).

The whole idea of sending mis-sionaries and being sent by God is significant in John's writings as it is throughout the Bible. A missionary is not someone who goes; it is some-one who is sent on a mission: 'And I heard the voice of the Lord saying, whom shall I send, and who will go for us? Then I said, here I am! Send me' Isaiah 6:8.

David Brainerd (1718 -1747) was a missionary to the native Indians on the border of New York, New Jersey, and Pennsylvania. He really got what it meant to be sent when he said: 'Here am I, send me; send me to the ends of the earth; send me to the rough, the savage lost of the wilder-ness; send me from all that is called comfort on earth; send me even to death itself, if it be but in your service, and to promote your kingdom'.

The Lord Jesus Christ is the mis-sionary model. The descent of Christ into our midst illustrates outreach in its truest sense: 'As you sent me into the world, so I have sent them into the world' John 17:18. Jesus refers 32 times in John's Gospel alone to God the Father sending Him into the world. Christ sent out the twelve then the seventy on missionary ser-vice. He did not stop sending when He ascended back to heaven. Today He continues to send men and women to the nations with the Gospel. I had the privilege of serving with a missions sending agency for 15 years. You will note the question in Isaiah 6:8: 'who will go for us?' The three persons of the trinity are involved as should be the local church and therefore every believer should be involved in being sent or being a sender. John Piper put it as follows: 'Go, send or disobey'. I trust the Great Commission is central to our Christian life, walk and witness.

Call me forth to active service.
And my prompt response shall be,
'Here am I! send me;'
I am ready to report for orders,
Master, summon me,
And I'll go on any errand of love for Thee.

(E. A. Hoffman)

26TH JUNE

Shall your brothers go to the war while you sit here?

Numbers 32:6

The question asked by Moses to the children of Gad and Rueben reminds me of a similar situation in Judges. In the time that Deborah judged Israel Jabin king of Canaan oppressed the children of Israel for 20 years. God used Deborah along with Barak and a number of the tribes of Israel to destroy Jabin. In chapter 5 of Judges Deborah identifies a number of tribes that went into battle with her: 'That the leaders took the lead in Israel, that the people offered themselves willingly, bless the Lord!' v. 2; 'From Ephraim their root they marched down into the valley, following you, Benjamin, with your kinsmen; from Machir marched down the commanders, and from Zebulun those who bear the lieutenant's staff; the princes of Issachar came with Deborah, and Issachar faithful to Barak; into the valley they rushed at his heels.' v. 14–15; 'Zebulun is a people who risked their lives to the death; Naphtali, too, on the heights of the field' v. 18.

However in the same chapter she also identifies those who didn't go to battle: 'Among the clans of Reuben there were great searching's of heart. Why did you sit still among the sheepfolds, to hear the whistling for the flocks? Among the clans of Reuben there were great searching's of heart' v. 15–16; 'Gilead stayed beyond the Jordan; and Dan, why did he stay with the ships? Asher sat still at the coast of the sea, staying by his landings' v. 17.

Judges 5 reveals praise and blame in the day of battle: There was: The willing, The uncertain: 'great searching of heart', The slackers: who did not respond, The daring: who hazarded their lives, and sadly the cursed: 'Curse Meroz, says the angel of the Lord, curse its inhabitants thoroughly, because they did not come to the help of the Lord, to the help of the Lord against the mighty' v. 23.

The challenge for today is this: Life brings to each believer its opportunity. The battle is real. What part do we play in it? To which do we belong? Those that are involved or with those who refuse to get involved. Can I suggest neutral you cannot be?

Your brethren—shall they go to war,
And bear the toil and pain,
While idly you remain at home,
Engrossed in selfish gain?
Perish the thought! Let all respond,
And war with might and main.

Is there no part that you can play
In this unceasing fight,
While all around you soldiers die
With never help in sight?
Each one can intercede that they
Will triumph in God's might.

(TS Rendall)

27TH JUNE

He put a new song in my mouth, a song of praise to our God.

Psalm 40:3

There is just something about singing praise to God that can really lift our hearts and spirits. The following are some references to songs and singing in the Bible:

A SONG ABOUT THE PIT: 'I waited patiently for the Lord; he inclined to me and heard my cry. He drew me up from the pit of destruction, out of the miry bog, and set my feet upon a rock, making my steps secure. He put a new song in my mouth, a song of praise to our God. Many will see and fear, and put their trust in the Lord' Psalm 40:1–3. This is really a song to do with David's salvation and testimony. David's mud slide was a moral one. Yet David could testify that the Lord heard him and helped him. Up from the miry clay and safe on the Rock. One has said that the Lord took David 'out of the mire and put him in the choir'. Today let us sing praises to our God for His great salvation.

A SONG ABOUT THE PRESERVED: 'Then Moses and the people of Israel sang this song to the Lord, saying, I will sing to the Lord, for he has triumphed gloriously; the horse and his rider he has thrown into the sea. The Lord is my strength and my song, and he has become my salvation; this is my God, and I will praise him, my father's God, and I will exalt him' Exodus 15:1–2.

Just as the Lord preserved the first born in each home of the Israelites that were under the blood, just as the Lord preserved Israel at the Red Sea, so will He preserve each truly born again, blood bought child of God. What a reason to sing praises to our God.

A SONG ABOUT THE PRISON: 'About midnight Paul and Silas were praying and singing hymns to God, and the prisoners were listening to them' Acts 16:25. Beside this verse in the margin of my Bible is written: 'A revival meeting in a prison cell: A time of prayer 'Paul and Silas were praying'; A Time of praising: 'and singing hymns to God'; A time of power (God's) Acts 16: 25–40. This included being released and pointing the prison warden, his family and household to Christ. What cause for singing praise to our God.

A SONG ABOUT THE PERSON: 'And they sang a new song, saying, Worthy are you . . . for you were slain, and by your blood you ransomed people for God from every tribe and language and people and nation' Revelation 5:6.

Praise him, praise him!
Jesus, our blessed redeemer!
Sing, O earth, his wonderful love proclaim!

(Fanny Crosby)

28TH JUNE

SIMPLE YET PROFOUND

William Cowper the great songwriter of the 18th Century said: it is my labour, and my principal one, to be as clear as possible. The following are some simple yet profound words that make the Gospel and its effects clear:

NO good: 'For I know that in me (that is, in my flesh,) dwelleth no good thing: for to will is present with me; but how to perform that which is good I find not' Romans 7:18 (KJV). This verse outlines our state by nature. This is further explained by Paul in Romans 3:10–12: 'as it is written: None is righteous, no, not one; no one understands; no one seeks for God. All have turned aside; together they have become worthless; no one does good, not even one'. By birth, nature and practice we are sinners without exception, excuse and escape. However, praise God we move from 'NO good' to 'SO loved'. God has made an escape for us:

SO loved: 'For God so loved the world, that he gave his only Son, that whoever believes in him should not perish but have eternal life' John 3:16. This speaks of God's grace. God not only loves us, He so loves us. What matchless grace. In John 3:16 we have a love that is pre-eminent: 'For God so loved'; a gift that is provided: 'that he gave'; an offer presented: 'that whoever believes in him'; a danger that is present: 'should not perish'; and a treasure that is permanent: 'eternal life'. And the good news is that the invitation is for everyone: 'HO everyone':

HO, everyone: 'Ho, every one that thirsteth, come ye to the waters, and he that hath no money; come ye, buy, and eat; yea, come, buy wine and milk without money and without price' Isaiah 55:1 (KJV). To my understanding this is like someone in the market place shouting 'Hi you there come'! This speaks of God's call of mercy. George F Root in his hymn put it this way: 'Come to the Savior, make no delay; Here in His word He's shown us the way; Here in our midst He's standing today, Tenderly saying, Come!'. For those that do, we hear those lovely words of Jesus say: 'GO in peace'

GO in peace: 'And he said to the woman, your faith has saved you; go in peace' Luke 7:50. This speaks of the peace of God. For those who have come to Jesus in repentance and faith in Him alone for salvation He sends away with a peace that passes all understanding.

Oh how unlike the complex works of man,
Heaven's easy, artless, unencumbered plan!
Inscribed above the portal, from afar
Conspicuous as the brightness of a star,
Legible only by the light they give,
Stand the soul-quickening words-BELIEVE AND LIVE.
Too many, shocked at what should charm them most,
Despise the plain direction and are lost.

W. Cowper

29TH JUNE

TESTIMONY OF A CHANGED LIFE

A woman from Samaria came to draw water.
Jesus said to her, Give me a drink.

John 4:7

John chapter 4 is one of my favourite chapters in the Bible. This chapter contains the testimony of the Woman of Samaria. If you were talking to this lady after her encounter with Jesus she would concur with the lovely words of the hymn of Rufus H. McDaniel:

What a wonderful change in
my life has been wrought
Since Jesus came into my heart!
I have light in my soul for which
long I have sought,
Since Jesus came into my heart!

In this story John 4: 5–42; we have the SAMARITAN WOMAN: 'A woman from Samaria came to draw water' v. 7; the SAVIOUR OF THE WORLD: 'and we know that this is indeed the Saviour of the world' v. 42 and SYCHAR'S WELL: 'So he came to a town of Samaria called Sychar, near the field that Jacob had given to his son Joseph. Jacob's well was there' v. 5–6. Isn't it wonderful where we can have an encounter with Christ? I trust you can look to a point in your life when you had an encounter with Christ—and how it changed everything. In this lady's testimony we see that she was A SINFUL WOMAN v. 17–18. However that is true of us all. We may not be into the deep sins of this woman, nevertheless we are all sinners. Then we see how Jesus gave her

SATISFYING WATER: 'but whoever drinks of the water that I will give him will never be thirsty again. The water that I will give him will become in him a spring of water welling up to eternal life' v. 14:

Drinking at the springs of living water,
Happy now am I,
My heart they satisfy;
Drinking at the springs of living water,
O wonderful and bountiful supply!

(John W. Peterson)

Then she became a SPIRITUAL WORSHIPPER: 'God is spirit, and those who worship him must worship in spirit and truth' v. 24. However her testimony didn't end there. She also became A SAVED WITNESS: 'They said to the woman, it is no longer because of WHAT YOU SAID that we believe' v. 42. This lady that is now saved starts witnessing to the people of her town. She also became A SOUL-WINNER: 'Many Samaritans from that town believed in Him because of the woman's testimony' v. 39.

Why not reflect on your story of your encounter with Christ. Are you now worshipping and witnessing for Jesus. Are you a soul-winner by life and lip? And praise God for a changed life.

30TH JUNE

TIED UP WITH THREAD

The iniquities of the wicked ensnare him, and
he is held fast in the cords of his sin.

Proverbs 5:22

One of my colleagues with whom I worked with many years ago was the Superintendent of the Sunday school of the Church of which he was a member and elder. He also ran a very successful children's work in the villages and hamlets around the area where the church was based. He once told me of a visual aid he used with children to demonstrate the power of sin to bind. Trevor would invite a child to come and take a seat at the front of the meeting. He would then put one piece of thread around the child and then tell him he was a prisoner. Of course the child could easily break the one thread and go free. He would then do it a second time with two threads, and the same would happen. The child could break free. This caused laughter and fun for the child. They were not made a prisoner. However in the course of the demonstration Trevor would wind the thread around the child one hundred times. At this point the child was bound. He could not break free, he was a prisoner!!! All his efforts to wriggle his way out of the situation were in vain. The lesson was simple. Sin binds us, at first weak, but daily growing stronger with constant indulgence until Satan has us bound. Then Trevor would take a pair of scissors and release the child, thus showing that only someone else can free us from sin. That one being Jesus:

Once I was bound by sin's galling fetters,
Chained like a slave I struggled in vain;
But I received a glorious freedom,
When Jesus broke my fetters in twain.

Glorious freedom, wonderful freedom,
No more in chains of sin I repine!
Jesus the glorious Emancipator,
Now and forever He shall be mine.

(Haldor Lillenas)

Today I will leave you with three verses of Scripture to meditate upon. They are relevant to believers and unbelievers: 'In him we have redemption through his blood, the forgiveness of our trespasses, according to the riches of his grace' Ephesians 1:7; 'But if we walk in the light, as he is in the light, we have fellowship with one another, and the blood of Jesus his Son cleanses us from all sin' 1 John 1:7; and 'My little children, I am writing these things to you so that you may not sin. But if anyone does sin, we have an advocate with the Father, Jesus Christ the righteous' 1 John 2:1

1ST JULY

JESUS IS PASSING THIS WAY

And they came to Jericho. And as he was leaving Jericho with his disciples and a great crowd, Bartimaeus, a blind beggar, the son of Timaeus, was sitting by the roadside. And when he heard that it was Jesus of Nazareth, he began to cry out and say, Jesus, Son of David, have mercy on me

Mark 10:46–47.

It is a wonderful thing when a church, individual or a group of churches or individuals are exercised to hold a mission or outreach in their area. This was how my father and mother were both saved. A mission was held in their locality. They were invited along, the Holy Spirit convicted them, and they repented from their sin and put their faith in Christ. For them Jesus passed by and in doing so saved them. I feel wherever an effort is made to reach people with the Gospel: Jesus is passing that way.

This reminds me of the story of 'Blind Bartimaeus'. As I write this I am praying for a mission that is going to be held in the locality where I live in a few months' time. My prayer is that many in my locality will recognise that during the time of mission 'Jesus is passing this way'.

Bartimaeus seized the opportunity as Jesus passed by his locality (Mark 10:46–52):

He CRIED out: 'he began to cry out' v. 47. Paul writing to the Romans said: 'For everyone who calls on the name of the Lord will be saved' Rom 10:13.

He was CHARGED to be silent: 'And many rebuked him, telling him to be silent' v. 48. Satan and the world would want to stop people meeting Jesus by discouraging them or trying various methods not to call out to Him for salvation.

Bartimaeus CRIED the more: 'But he cried out all the more' v. 48. This is a picture of a true desire. Bartimaeus was persistent. He was genuine.

Jesus COMMANDED for him to be called: 'And Jesus stopped and said, Call him.' v 49. Where there is a seeking sinner, there is a seeking Saviour. The invitation is to all.

Jesus COMFORTED HIM: 'Take heart' v. 49. When Jesus passes by there is good news for the sinner.

He CAST away his garments: 'And throwing off his cloak, he sprang up and came to Jesus' v. 50. All hindrances were removed: Bartimaeus could say: 'I gave Him my old dirty garment, He gave me a robe of pure white'.

He CAME to Jesus: 'he sprang up and came to Jesus' v. 50. And what was the result: 'he recovered his sight and followed him on the way' v. 52.

Is there a heart that is waiting,
Longing for pardon today?
Hear the glad message proclaiming
Jesus is passing this way.

Is there a heart that has wandered?
Come with thy burden today;
Mercy is tenderly pleading,
Jesus is passing this way.

(Fanny Crosby)

2ND JULY

SAVIOUR OF THE WORLD

Father has sent his Son to be the Saviour of the world

1 John 4:14.

William Young Fullerton the writer of the hymn 'Saviour of the World' was born in Belfast in 1857. As a boy William had often heard the Gospel, and long desired to be good. However William did not grasp the reality of saving grace until a new minister arrived at his Church when he was thirteen. I will let William take up his testimony story: 'the new minister gave his first address to the Sunday School. He said many things, but I can only remember one sentence, and that was the living word for me: 'All you have to do to be saved is to take God's gift, and say Thank-you'. Here was a new and great light. Hitherto I had been trying to get God to take my gift, and trying to make it great enough to be worthy of His acceptance; and lo! It was I who had to take, and it was His to give. Simply and quietly that Sunday afternoon my heart turned to God, and I took the gift for which I have been trying to say 'Thank-You' ever since'. Four years later he was greatly impacted by the ministry of D L Moody when he visited Belfast. William was called into Christian ministry. He became a Baptist preacher, administrator, and writer. As a young man he was influenced by the preaching of evangelist, Charles Spurgeon, who became his friend and mentor. He became pastor of the Melbourne Hall Baptist Church. Thousands of people came to Christ under his ministry.

I cannot tell why he, whom angels worship,
should set his love upon the sons of men,
or why, as Shepherd, he should seek the wanderers,
to bring them back, they know not how or when.
But this I know, that he was born of Mary
when Bethl'em's manger was his only home,
and that he lived at Nazareth and laboured,
and so the Saviour, Saviour of the world, is come.

I cannot tell how silently he suffered,
as with his peace he graced this place of tears,
or how his heart upon the cross was broken,
the crown of pain to three and thirty years.
But this I know, he heals the broken-hearted
and stays our sin and calms our lurking fear
and lifts the burden from the heavy laden;
for still the Saviour, Saviour of the world is here.

I cannot tell how he will win the nations,
how he will claim his earthly heritage,
how satisfy the needs and aspirations
of east and west, of sinner and of sage.
But this I know, all flesh shall see his glory,
and he shall reap the harvest he has sown,
and some glad day his sun will shine in splendour
when he the Saviour, Saviour of the world, is known.

3RD JULY

Will you not revive us again?

Psalm 85:6

I have the privilege of serving the Lord as a volunteer with a ministry called Coaching for Christ based in a village called Ahoghill in Co Antrim, N Ireland. Ahoghill means 'Ford of the Yew Tree'. In recent years it won the title 'Best Small Town' nine years in a row in the 'Ulster in Bloom' competition. Ahoghill was one of the key centres in the 1859 Ulster revival.

In the 1850s many churches in Ireland had fallen into a state of apostasy and luke-warmness. Many young people had immigrated to America as a result of the great famine. However news reached Ireland of revival blessing in America. A deep desire among some believers that heard of this caused them to pray that the Spirit of God would move in the same way in Ulster. As a result James McQuilkin, Jeremiah Meneely, Robert Carlisle and John Wallace commenced a weekly prayer meeting in the old National School House in Kells. Soon the burden for the Land became so great that more people started attending the prayer meeting. J H Moore the local Presbyterian Minister and his congregation in nearby Connor Presbyterian Church encouraged further opportunities for prayer. Leading up to the revival approximately 100 prayer meetings each week were linked to their Church. In early 1859 the Connor Congregation was spiritually awakened with a Godly fear gripping their hearts. There was a very real sense of the Lord's presence in the midst.

Very shortly the revival spirit spread to Ahoghill, ten miles away. On the 14th March 1859 James McQuilkin addressed a meeting at 1st Ahoghill Presbyterian Church. So many people attended that the meeting had to be dismissed. The crowd moved to the town's main square where they were addressed by James Bankhead, a convert of the Connor awakening. At this meeting hundreds fell on their knees in the mud, calling to God to save them. Reporting on this later the Rev Fred Buick minister of 1st Ahoghill Presbyterian Church said: 'The open field and the public roadside, even in the cold evenings were scenes over which angels hovered with joy: for when the buildings were too small to hold people, meetings were held everywhere. They assembled anywhere they could to hear their brethren talk plainly about the things of God. These meetings were characterised by the burning prayers that were lifted up to God; a deep conviction of sin that was felt by all who attended and by the sobs and crying that only got louder as the meetings progressed'.

The Rev Buick prayed: 'Lord send more plenteous rain still'. The Lord answered his prayer, the revival continued and spread. It is reported that over 100,000 people came to Christ throughout Ulster in the year 1859.

Our prayer today is.: 'Lord do it again in our day and generation in our locality and Land'.

4TH JULY

ALL YOU CAN

Be faithful unto death.

Revelation 2:10

It was John Wesley who said: 'Do all the good you can, by all the means you can, in all the ways you can, in all the places you can, at all the times you can, To all the people you can, as long as ever you can'. In a similar vein of thought my good friend Dick Keogh, founder of Cherith Gospel Outreach has a saying which goes as follows: 'Let us do WHAT we can, to reach AS MANY as we can, AS SOON as we can'. These quotes and sayings have a Biblical basis, which I trust will be beneficial to you as we consider them today:

DO ALL THE GOOD YOU CAN: 'Whatever your hand finds to do, do it with your might.' Ecclesiastes 9:10.

IN ALL THE WAYS YOU CAN: 'In the same way, let your light shine before others, so that they may see your good works and give glory to your Father who is in heaven'. Matthew 5:16.

TO ALL THE PEOPLE YOU CAN: 'So then, as we have opportunity, let us do good to everyone, and especially to those who are of the household of faith.' Galatians 6:10.

IN EVERY PLACE YOU CAN: 'how God anointed Jesus of Nazareth with the Holy Spirit and with power. He went about doing good and healing all who were oppressed by the devil, for God was with him'. Acts 10:38.

AT ALL THE TIMES YOU CAN: 'how God anointed Jesus of Nazareth with the Holy Spirit and with power. He went about doing good and healing all who were oppressed by the devil, for God was with him'. 1 Corinthians 15:58.

AS LONG AS EVER YOU CAN: 'Be faithful unto death, and I will give you the crown of life'. Revelation 2:10.

O Jesus, I have promised
To serve thee to the end;
Be thou forever near me,
My Master and my friend;
I shall not fear the battle
If thou art by my side,
Nor wander from the pathway
If thou wilt be my guide.

(John Ernest Bode)

There are lives that may be brighten'd
by a word of hope and cheer,
There are souls with whom life's
blessings I should share;
There are hearts that may be lightened
of the burdens which they bear;
Let me take the blessed hope of the gospel there.

(E. A. Hoffman)

5TH JULY

NOW I BELONG TO JESUS

My beloved is mine, and I am his.

Song of Solomon 2:16

I love the chorus of the song 'Jesus my Lord will love me forever', written in 1943 by Norman J. Clayton: 'Now I belong to Jesus, Jesus belongs to me, Not for the years of time alone, but for eternity'. And here is the reason why: the words are biblical and bring great assurance to the child of God.

Our verse today brings this out in a lovely way:

'My beloved': A PRESENT POSSESSION: 'For it stands in Scripture: Behold, I am laying in Zion a stone, a cornerstone chosen and precious, and whoever believes in him will not be put to shame. So the honour is for you who believe, but for those who do not believe, the stone that the builders rejected has become the cornerstone'. 1 Peter 2:6–7. 'Whom have I in heaven but you? And there is nothing on earth that I desire beside you' Psalm 73:25

'Is': PRESENT POSSESSION: 'The Lord is my chosen portion and my cup; you hold my lot' Psalm 16:5. 'So we can confidently say, The Lord is my helper; I will not fear; what can man do to me?' Hebrews 13:6.

'Mine': PERSONAL POSSESSION: 'Thomas answered him, My Lord and my God!' John 20:28. 'And my spirit rejoices in God my Saviour' Luke 1:47.

'I': PRIZED POSSESSION: 'Because you are precious in my eyes, and honoured, and I love you, I give men in return for you, peoples in exchange for your life' Isaiah 43:4. 'As Christ loved the church and gave himself up for her' Ephesians 5:25.

'Am': PERMANENT POSSESSION: 'I give them eternal life, and they will never perish, and no one will snatch them out of my hand' John 10:28. 'And this is the will of him who sent me, that I should lose nothing of all that he has given me, but raise it up on the last day' John 6:39.

'His': PURCHASED POSSESSION: 'for you were bought with a price. So glorify God in your body' 1 Corinthians 6:20. 'Who gave himself for us to redeem us from all lawlessness and to purify for himself a people for his own possession who are zealous for good works' Titus 2:14.

Jesus, my Lord will love me forever,
From Him no pow'r of evil can sever,
He gave His life to ransom my soul;
Now I belong to Him;

Chorus

Now I belong to Jesus,
Jesus belongs to me,
Not for the years of time alone,
But for eternity.

Once I was lost in sin's degradation,
Jesus came down to bring me salvation,
Lifted me up from sorrow and shame,
Now I belong to Him;

Joy floods my soul for Jesus has saved me,
Freed me from sin that long had enslaved me
His precious blood, He came to redeem,
Now I belong to Him;

6TH JULY

HE LEADETH ME

He leads me beside still waters.

Psalm 23:2

Today we will consider some thoughts from the Psalms about discipleship. A disciple is a follower: someone who wants to be led. The psalmist requests to be led:

1. IN HIS RIGHTEOUSNESS: 'Lead me, O Lord, in your righteousness because of my enemies; make your way straight before me' Psalm 5:8.

2. IN HIS TRUTH AND TO BE TAUGHT BY HIM: 'Lead me in your truth and teach me, for you are the God of my salvation; for you I wait all the day long' Psalm 25:5.

3. IN A LEVEL OR PLAIN PATH: 'Teach me your way, O Lord, and lead me on a level path because of my enemies' Psalm 27:11.

4. FOR THE LORD'S NAME SAKE: 'For you are my rock and my fortress; and for your name's sake you lead me and guide me' Psalm 31:3. In other words it is all about you Lord:

Jesus, Lover Of My Soul
All Consuming Fire Is In Your Gaze
Jesus, I Want You To Know
I Will Follow You All Of My Days
For No One Else In History Is Like You
And History Itself Belongs To You
Alpha And Omega, You Have Loved Me
And I Will Share Eternity With You
It's All About You, Jesus

(Michael W. Smith)

When mountains of doubt
hem me in on each side,
And waves of affliction roll in like a tide;
When vainly I seek some new pathway to try,
Oh, lead me to the Rock that is higher than I.

Refrain:

Oh, lead me to the Rock, Oh, lead me to the Rock,
Oh, lead me to the Rock that is higher than I.
Oh, lead me to the Rock, Oh, lead me
to the Rock that is higher than I.

(R. A. Searles)

5. TO THE ROCK THAT IS HIGHER THAN I: 'from the end of the earth I call to you when my heart is faint. Lead me to the rock that is higher than I' Psalm 61:2.

6. IN THE WAY EVERLASTING: 'And see if there be any grievous way in me, and lead me in the way everlasting!' Psalm 139:24.

7. IN HIS WILL BY THE SPIRIT OF GOD: 'Teach me to do your will, for you are my God! Let your good Spirit lead me on level ground!' Psalm 143:10.

He leadeth me: O blessed thought!
O words with heavenly comfort fraught!
Whate'er I do, where'er I be,
Still 'tis God's hand that leadeth me.

He leadeth me, he leadeth me;
by his own hand he leadeth me:
his faithful follower I would be,
for by his hand he leadeth me.

(Joseph H. Gilmore)

7TH JULY

We must obey God rather than men.

Acts 5:29

While visiting farms in the Czech Republic with some others to study calf rearing production systems we spent some time sight-seeing in Prague. One of my highlights there was to go to see the monument of Jan Hus (John Huss) at the Prague Old Town Square.

John Huss (1369–1415) was a Roman Catholic priest in Bohemia who became a pre-Protestant Reformation reformer of the church. Huss earned a doctorate and became the preacher at the Bethlehem Chapel in Prague. The more he studied the Bible, the more he noticed a significant difference between what the Bible teaches and what the Roman Catholic Church practiced. Reading the writings of John Wycliffe further influenced John Huss in an anti-Catholic direction.

Ignoring church directives, John Huss began to preach his sermons at Bethlehem Chapel in the Czech language instead of Latin. He also began teaching against Roman Catholic abuses at the University of Prague. These actions led to a conflict with Huss and his followers on one side and the Roman Catholic Church and Holy Roman Empire on the other. However, due to the fact that the Bohemian king supported Huss, he suffered no significant consequences.

The conflict between Huss and the Roman Catholic Church greatly intensified when antipope John XXIII authorized the selling of indulgences to raise money for a military conflict against a rival pope claimant. Huss began preaching against the papacy itself, emphasizing the authority of the Bible and the fact that Christ alone is the head of the church. Due to political pressure from Rome, the king of Bohemia could no longer protect Huss, resulting in him being officially excommunicated.

In 1414, John Hus was commanded by Holy Roman Emperor Sigismund to come to Constance, Germany, and appear before the Council of Constance. Huss was guaranteed safe passage, but, when he arrived, he was arrested and imprisoned. A mock trial occurred, and, when Huss refused to recant his teachings, he was burned at the stake a martyr on the 6th July 1415. His last words recorded were, 'Lord Jesus, I am willing patiently and publicly to endure this dreadful, shameful and cruel death for the sake of thy gospel and the preaching of the Word'.

Huss would become a hero to Luther and many other Reformers. His courage inspired Luther, and his writings taught Luther to bind his conscience to the Word alone. Luther taught that to the world, and, as bible believing Christians, we live and stand in that truth today. It is said that Wycliffe struck the spark, Huss kindled the coal and Luther blew the Reformation into a flame.

After his death his followers became the foundation for the Moravian Brethren, who would play an influential role in the conversion of the Wesley brothers, among others.

O glorious King of martyr hosts,
Thou crown that each confessor boasts,
Who leadest to celestial day
The saints who cast earth's joys away
(Unknown)

8TH JULY

CLEANED AND SEALED

Jesus said to him, the one who has bathed does not need to wash, except for his feet, but is completely clean. And you are clean, but not every one of you

John 13:10

Between 'Lockdowns' during the corona virus pandemic period I was able to make a ministry visit to the ROI. While there I stayed overnight in a Maldron Hotel. At that stage there were still many regulations and protocols. When I reached the door of my room there was a seal on my door which said, 'Cleaned & Sealed'. On the other side of the sticker it said, 'Maldron Hotels—Caring For Your Well-Being'.

AS I reflected on this the Lord directed my thoughts to the fact that as believers we are cleaned and sealed. When we come as sinners to Jesus in true repentance and faith and trust Him as Saviour and Lord He cleanses all our sins away by His precious blood. In addition to this we are sealed by the Spirit of God. God not only cares for our earthly well-being but also for our eternal well-being. Today we will look at the truth that we are clean. It doesn't matter what your past has been Jesus has promised to all those that come to Him He will make them clean:

Would you be free from your passion and pride?
There's pow'r in the blood, pow'r in the blood;
Come for a cleansing to Calvary's tide;
There's wonderful pow'r in the blood.

(Lewis E. Jones)

It will never lose its pow'r,
It will never lose its pow'r;
The blood that cleanses from all sin
Will never lose its power.

(Civilla D. Martin)

Paul writing to the Church at Corinth regarding some of their membership said: 'Or do you not know that the unrighteous will not inherit the kingdom of God? Do not be deceived: neither the sexually immoral, nor idolaters, nor adulterers, nor men who practice homosexuality, nor thieves, nor the greedy, nor drunkards, nor revilers, nor swindlers will inherit the kingdom of God. And such were some of you. But you were washed, you were sanctified, you were justified in the name of the Lord Jesus Christ and by the Spirit of our God' 1 Corinthians 6:9–11. These dear folk were made clean. One commentator said: 'It was no promising material that confronted the early preachers, but people whose values were the very opposite of Christ. It required the mighty power of the Spirit of God to turn people like that away from their sins, and to make them members of Christ's Church'.

I praise thee, Lord, for cleansing me from sin;
Fulfill thy Word, and make me pure within.
Fill me with fire where once I burned with shame;
Grant my desire to magnify thy name.

(J. Edwin Orr)

9TH JULY

*And do not grieve the Holy Spirit of God, by whom
you were sealed for the day of redemption.*

Ephesians 4:30

Yesterday I shared about staying in a Hotel in the Republic of Ireland between the 'Lockdown' periods in the Covid-19 pandemic period. When I went to the door of my room it had a sticker on it which said: 'Cleaned and Sealed'. This led me to think on the truth that as born again Christians we too have been cleaned by the Holy Spirit and cleaned by the precious blood of our Lord Jesus Christ. Today we will reflect on the fact that we are 'Sealed'. Paul writing to the Church at Ephesus said: 'And you also were included in Christ when you heard the message of truth, the gospel of your salvation. When you believed, you were marked in Him with a seal, the promised Holy Spirit' Ephesians 1:13. God marks us as His very own by sending the Holy Spirit, to indwell us according to the promise He Himself had given. God seals every redeemed person as His purchased possession, and the Spirit Himself is the seal. Not only that, we are promised that we are sealed unto the day of redemption: 'And do not grieve the Holy Spirit of God, by whom you were sealed for the day of redemption' Ephesians 4:30. This day of redemption is when Jesus comes back for His own. We are His forever. The seal, the mark is a sign of genuineness, ownership and security. Lehman Strauss comments: 'The seal of the Spirit is the stamp of divine likeness upon the heart of the believer and

is, thereby, the mark of ownership and security. We can sing with confidence:

*Now I Belong To Jesus
Jesus Belongs To Me,
Not For The Years Of Time Alone,
But For Eternity.*

(Norman J. Clayton)

*Wash'd in the blood, by the Spirit sealed,
Christ in His word is to me revealed;
Glory to God! in my soul doth shine
God, my salvation, and His life is mine!*

*Washed in the blood, washed in the blood!
Washed in the blood, in the soul-cleansing blood!
Washed in the blood, washed in the blood!
Sealed in the Spirit true, and washed in the blood!*

(Charles Price Jones)

*Blessed assurance, Jesus is mine!
Oh, what a foretaste of glory divine!
Heir of salvation, purchase of God,
Born of his Spirit, washed in his blood.*

(Fanny Crosby)

John Phillips comments: 'Sealed! What a comforting word. It suggests a finished transaction, absolute assurance, eternal security'.

- We are saved by grace: Ephesians 2:8;
- Sealed with the Spirit: Ephesians 1:13;
- Seated with Christ: Ephesians 2:6.

10TH JULY

HOW CAN I BLASPHEME MY SAVIOUR

The blood of the martyrs of Jesus.

Revelation 17:6

It is believed that the Apostle John, who was the youngest of the Apostles, died around the year 100 A.D. With his death, the last physical connection the church had with Christ was gone. Thereafter the next best thing was speaking to those who had been actually taught by the Apostles themselves. Polycarp of Smyrna was one such person. It is thought he came to Christ under the ministry of the Apostle John. John became his mentor. His ministry was a bridge of truth for the second century Christians who would be seeking to know the true apostolic message.

Polycarp was ordained probably in his early twenties in the mid to late 90s. He died around 155 A. D. Irenaeus one of the early Church Fathers comments: 'But Polycarp also was not only instructed by the apostles, and acquainted with many that had seen Christ, but was also appointed by apostles in Asia bishop of the church of Smyrna. We too saw him in our early youth; for he lived a long time, and died, when a very old man, a glorious and most illustrious martyr's death, having always taught the things which he had learned from the apostles'.

It is how Polycarp faced his death as a Martyr that really caught my attention while studying church history. John Foxe comments: 'Polycarp, hearing that he was in great danger, escaped, but his hiding place was discovered by a child. From this circumstance, and having dreamed that his bed suddenly became a fire, and was consumed in a moment, he concluded it was God's will he should suffer martyrdom. He therefore did not attempt to make a second escape when he had the opportunity of doing so, and those who took him were amazed at his serene and cheerful countenance. After feasting with them, he desired an hour for prayer, which being allowed, he prayed with such fervency that his guards repented that they had come for him'.

During his time standing before the Roman official, Polycarp was given the chance to offer allegiance to Caesar. It would have been a simple thing, but he would not. He answered with one of the most powerful statements known within Christian history: 'Eighty and six years have I served Him, and He never did me any injury: how can I blaspheme my King and my Savior?'

Finally he was condemned to be burned at the stake. Christians later came and gathered up his bones and gave them a proper burial.

'Over 360 million Christians suffer persecution and discrimination. They follow Jesus, no matter the cost' (Open Doors 2023).

'Every day, 13 Christians worldwide are killed because of their faith, 12 churches or Christian buildings are attacked, 12 Christians are unjustly arrested or imprisoned and another five are abducted' (Cru 2023).

Today make a point of praying for the persecuted Church.

11TH JULY

FRESH, FLOURISHING AND FRUITFUL IN TIMES OF ATTACK

*But I am like a green olive tree in the house of God. I
trust in the steadfast love of God forever and ever.*

Psalm 52:8

In Psalm 52, David confronts the wicked (verses 1–7). And he states his confidences in the Lord (verses 8–9).

Earlier in Psalm 52 David described his enemy as a plant which will be completely uprooted (v 5). Unlike this boastful enemy, David is like an olive tree in the House of the Lord (8). While the enemy will be uprooted and destroyed, David's roots are like a well-watered olive tree, fruitful and abundant.

In verse 8 David is making the point that he is safe and happy. This is against the backdrop that Doeg his enemy, the informer, was making every effort to secure his destruction. However, David had been kept unharmed, like a green and flourishing tree—a tree protected in the very courts of the sanctuary—safe under the care and the eye of God. No matter what the enemy was doing to him, David remained in the house of God, full of spiritual vigour, bringing forth evergreen leaves and annual fruit, as the olive does when planted in proper soil and good situation.

Perhaps you are going through difficulties today, opposed by your enemies. Stay at your post in the house of God. Not only will you be protected there but you will produce and prosper spiritually. When Doeg and his brethren had withered and perished, David, who had made God his refuge, would be established and flourish.

One commentator expressed how David reacted to his enemy as follows: 'Thus, when Doeg blasted David, David blessed himself. Let him flourish in the court, I shall much more in the house of God. My name shall be precious among the saints when he stinketh above ground; he shall wither when I shall be FRESH, FLOURISHING, AND FRUITFUL' (Hawker's Poor Man's Commentary).

As you stick with God through the opposition and obstacles of the enemy I trust you find the following comments in Dr Constable expository notes helpful: 'He repudiated the confidence of the wicked and reaffirmed his trust in the Lord. He pictured himself as a flourishing olive tree, in contrast to his uprooted enemy (Psalm 52:5; 1:3; Hosea 14:6). Olive trees live unusually long, and they are productive and attractive. They were and are very numerous in Israel. The tree David saw was in the tabernacle courtyard, symbolic of his nearness to God'.

What are the trials, troubles, and tribulations you are facing? No matter what is going on in your life or in the world around you, you can face them like a green olive tree in the house of God. Through faith in the Lord Jesus Christ, focus on God and not your circumstances. Live with assurance that God is obviously present, actively in-charge, and dynamically at-work.

12TH JULY

GOD WANTS SPIRITUAL FRUITS NOT RELIGIOUS NUTS

And the surviving remnant of the house of Judah shall
again take root downward and bear fruit upward.

Isaiah 37:31

I stayed regularly overnight in Manchester in the period I as served as the Executive Director of OMS UK. In the evenings I would go out for a walk, and when the occasion to witness presented itself I would do so. On one occasion I had opportunity to speak to a man who was slightly intoxicated. In the midst of the conversation he said: 'God wants spiritual fruits not religious nuts'. I found out later that this indeed is a well-known expression. And it's true. God wants us to produce spiritual fruits.

The production of 'fruit unto God' is wholly dependent on the existence of spiritual life in the soul: there can be no fruit whatever without it. Even where that life does exist, the fruit varies. In John 15 we learn of 'Fruit', 'More Fruit', and 'Much Fruit'. In Matthew 13:23 we learn of those who yield 'thirtyfold, sixtyfold and one hundredfold'.

The question today is: am I a fruit yielding Christian?. A B Simpson known as a missionary statesman commenting on bearing fruit as outlined in John 15 said: 'Let us observe that the vine consists not only of the stem, but of branches; so Christ identifies Himself with all His members and counts them part of Himself. We are the very same substance of our living Head, partake of His own personal life. The fruit is not borne by the stem, but by the branches. So the Lord Jesus did not, in His own personal ministry, bring many souls to God, but left the most glorious fruit of the gospel to be gathered by His disciples. He still honours His most feeble members by permitting us to bring forth much fruit'.

To be a fruit bearing Christian John points out three essentials in John 15:4–5: 'Abide in me, and I in you. As the branch cannot bear fruit by itself, unless it abides in the vine, neither can you, unless you abide in me. I am the vine; you are the branches. Whoever abides in me and I in him, he it is that bears much fruit, for apart from me you can do nothing'.

Jesus says 'Abide in me, and I in you'. These are two essentials. In other words we are saved, and walking in fellowship with Christ. The third essential is recognising that without Jesus we can do nothing.

We are dwelling in the Spirit,
By our Father's blest design;
Through His grace we're made partakers
Of His nature, pure, divine.

By His faith alone I'm living,
For with Christ to sin I died;
I will bear abundant fruitage,
That His name be glorified.

I am the Vine, I am the Vine,
Ye are the fruitful branches.

(Clara McAlister Brooks)

13TH JULY

THE WORD OF GOD

*For the word of God is living and active, sharper than
any two-edged sword, piercing to the division of soul
and of spirit, of joints and of marrow, and discerning
the thoughts and intentions of the heart.*

Hebrews 4:12

God has placed a lot of importance upon His words. In fact Jesus said: 'Heaven and earth will pass away, but my words will not pass away' Matthew 24:35. The Psalmist said in Psalm 138:2: 'I bow down toward your holy temple and give thanks to your name for your steadfast love and your faithfulness, for you have exalted above all things your name and your word'; and in Psalm 119:89: 'Forever, O Lord, your word is firmly fixed in the heavens'.

The spiritual life-blood of the human race is the word of God. It brings salvation: 'since you have been born again, not of perishable seed but of imperishable, through the living and abiding word of God' 1 Peter 1:23. The word of God produces faith: 'So faith comes from hearing, and hearing through the word of Christ' Romans 10:17. It produces spiritual growth: 'Like new born infants, long for the pure spiritual milk, that by it you may grow up into salvation' 1 Peter 2:2.

Truly, we can say today:' I have a precious book. It is the Word of God':

*I Have A Precious Book, It's
The Word Of God.
It's The Only Book That God Has Given.
As I Read, God Speaks To Me,
I See Christ And Calvary.*

*The Wonderful Word Of God.
Forever It Will Stand As The Ages Roll,
It's The Living And Eternal Word.
It's My Guiding Light Each Day,*

*And Without It I Would Stray;
The Wonderful Word Of God.
Dear Lord May I Each Day
Read Thy Precious Word.*

*May I Love It And Obey It Too.
May I Grow To Be Like Thee.
May My Friends See Christ In Me.
In Jesus' Name, Amen.*

(Unknown)

14TH JULY

A HARVEST IN DUE TIME

*And let us not grow weary of doing good, for in
due season we will reap, if we do not give up.*

Galatians 6:9

I had the privilege of serving the Lord as a 'homeland' missionary for OMS UK for a number of years. One of the privileges of the role was meeting missionary 'retirees'. One such couple was Joe and Ruby Black. I have in my possession various articles they wrote while on the field. The following is a sample: 'Let me thrill your hearts with accounts of transformed lives' writes Joe. He continues: 'Palmoo, wife of Gyan Das, from a remote mountain village but now working in Simla, became possessed by evil spirits after the death of their first baby. Desperation and despair drove them near and far, to one Hindu priest after another, in a futile effort to have the demons exorcised. With hope and money gone, they related their experiences to Rup Hans, one our young converts. Without hesitation he convinced them Jesus Christ alone could give complete deliverance. He persuaded them to come and meet his Pastor. Next day the Christians were called to prayer and on coming into their midst, Palmo was immediately stricken by the tormentor. In an agony of distress, distortion, and exhaustion she fell prostrate on the floor—as dead. While the Christians cried unto God, claiming deliverance in the name of Jesus Christ, the miracle happened. Palmo sat up, her face aglow with awe, wonder, and a beautiful radiance. She was set free! Both husband and wife embraced Jesus Christ as Lord. Now after many months and never another attack, Gyan and Palmo are among our most radiant witnesses in the Simia Church'.

On another occasion he wrote: 'One of Satan's major tools for hindering God's work is discouragement over lack of results. And nowhere can he use it more effectively than in the Ganges River Valley across Northern India'. He goes on to relate the following encouragement: 'So the question keeps recurring: How many days can we expect our faithful national brother to continue in a lonely location, cut off from regular fellowship with other Christians, where the seed of the Gospel seems to find no root at all? When offered a new appointment after several years of barrenness, one of the faithful national couples requested to remain. Had not God promised a harvest in due time? So they stayed on. Just a few months later a well-educated young man responded to the claims of Christ and was baptized'.

Joe and Ruby are now with the Lord. The question today is, who will replace them to go, pray and give to reach the lost in difficult places:

Far, far away, in heathen darkness dwelling,
Millions of souls forever may be lost;
Who, who will go, salvation's storytelling,
Looking to Jesus, minding not the cost?

(James McGranahan)

15TH JULY

HOW BLESSED

His master said to him, well done, good and faithful servant. You have been faithful over a little; I will set you over much. Enter into the joy of your master

Matthew 25:21

Joe and Ruby Black were two retired missionaries when I first met them. They faithfully served the Lord in India for many years. In their retirement they prayerfully and financially continued to support national workers in India.

While serving in India Joe wrote the following article asking for prayer for an outreach he was involved in: 'This January the annual Hindu 'mela' (festival) will take place in the same area. More than two million pilgrims will bathe in the sacred waters to wash sin according to their Hindu belief. Each year we make a special effort to reach as many as possible with the Gospel message. For thousands this will be their ONE and ONLY chance of receiving the true message of salvation. Put yourself in their place. Only ONE OPPORTUNITY to receive Christ. With minds darkened by centuries of heathenism can they believe? Only if there is vital intercession which can 'open their eyes, and turn them from darkness to light, and from the power of Satan unto God'.

These dear missionaries have heard the 'Well done' of God. They have been 'promoted to glory'.

At the time of Joe's death Dr Wesley Duewel, President Emeritus of One Mission Society, and who was the OMS India Field Director when Joe and Ruby were there sent the following tribute to Joe Black which was read at his funeral: 'The arrival of Joe and Ruby Black in North India brought much blessing to OMS over the years. They played a vital role in the organisation and growth of the work in various sections of India: Simla, Allahabad and Delhi (the capital) in the north, and Madras in the south. God used Joe's typical Irish determination, and persistent, unceasing zeal and joyful service to bless us all. What glory Joe is experiencing in heaven now. All praise to Jesus. Dr Duewel concludes with one of his poems entitled 'How Blessed!':

How blessed are the dead
Who served God mid earth's strife!
Now only glory lies ahead
And everlasting life.

How blessed there to stay
On heaven's glory shore,
To live in never-ending day
Where night and sin are o'er!

How blessed there to live
Where God's plans are fulfilled,
Where each can perfect service give
And do all God has willed!

How blessed to behold
The Saviour's love-crowned face,
While God's eternal days unfold
More love and joy and grace!

How blessed, but not dead—
All live on heaven's shore—
Eternal blessings lie ahead
And life forevermore!

(Dr Duewel since then has also heard the 'Well done' of God. And has experienced just 'How blessed are the dead who served God mid earth's strife!)

16TH JULY

GOD LOVES GIVERS

Give, and it will be given to you. Good measure, pressed down,
shaken together, running over, will be put into your lap. For
with the measure you use it will be measured back to you.

Luke 6:38

Paul writing to the Church at Corinth expresses the point that God has a special love for those who give to His cause: 'Each one must give as he has decided in his heart, not reluctantly or under compulsion, for God loves a cheerful giver' 2 Corinthians 9:7. At the end of the day it is only His cause that really matters. His cause is eternal. God loves those that give decidedly. Not haphazardly, but those who have decided to give and decided what to give towards and have done so from the heart. Not reluctantly, but eagerly. Not under compulsion but constantly and joyfully.

Dr Wesley Duewel one of the past presidents of One Mission Society expressed giving as follows: 'If you want to sense God's special love, prove your love by great gifts to Him. Jesus, at the temple, watched to see how people gave. He paid eternal honour to a widow who gave beyond her means. He praised a repentant, sinful woman who lavishly proved her love. Jesus watches today to see how largely, how joyously, and how sacrificially you give. He knows what amount is sacrificial for you. Have you ever given a costly gift for the cause so close to Christ's heart—missions?'

Before going back to Heaven, Jesus gave us the great commission to complete the missionary task. When completed He will come again. Amongst others, one of the hindrances to mission work, evangelism and outreach is the lack of funds.

Dr Duewel in his article on giving to OMS continues as follows: 'We are not materialistically minded. We know that more gifts of time, love and life are more costly than money. We believe prayer is our greatest need. We depend on God—not on money. Yet, God has commanded us to give money. And unless God's people give more money, we will deny many requests—for evangelism, for literature, for new churches. Your gift is a 'Yes' to some request for advance. Your failure to give means 'No' to some need'.

Today let God speak to your heart as to how you can support His cause, and through which channel in the context you are in.

Take my silver and my gold;
Not a mite would I withhold

(Frances R. Havergal)

17TH JULY

ARISE LET US BE GOING

'Oh, that I had wings like a dove! I would fly away and be at rest'

Psalm 55:6

Reading the thoughts of missionaries and mission leaders from the past can motivate us to Christian service today. The following is an article written by Mrs Lettie Cowman the wife of Charles Cowman co-founder of OMS which I trust will speak to us today:

'The shepherd lad David, was listening one day to the voice of the tempter. The Master Musician had placed him in the heart of a storm to teach him how to sing, but, listen to this moaning cry: 'Oh, that I had wings like a dove! I would fly away and be at rest!' Our all-wise loving God was too loving to answer his prayer. No, the sweetest songs were born in a storm, out of the tempest rose loud notes of praise to God on high, and we have the beautiful 23rd and 91st Psalms. What would David have gained had God granted his prayer and given to him a pair of doves' wings? How far could he have flown away from trouble on such frail pinions? And what would the world have lost? Let us be watchful of our prayers in times of temptation and physical weariness!

Today Satan is seeking to thwart the fulfilment of the Great Commission—to every creature. To all mission boards he has sent an advance notice, 'the day of missionary service is ended'. To the youth of the world, Satan has given counsel: "Don't waste your lives in preparation for missionary service; your wonderful talents will be needed in the homelands—build for business; help make a new world; do not bury your lives among the wild, uneducated heathen people!

And to that long line of invisible helpers, unsung heroes—the men and women in the homelands whose sacrificial gifts have made possible the almost miraculous spread of the gospel in heathen lands—has he shown a deep interest and concern. To them Satan has said: 'lay up your treasures on earth'.

Shall we eavesdrop and listen to the replies? 'Some fields may seem to be closed just now, but there is the Hand of Another on the gateway to the seas. He said, "Behold I have set before thee an open door that no man can shut'. Mission boards answer, 'God's tomorrow, the greatest day of all days, is lying before us'. The youth respond wholeheartedly, 'We have seen a pierced Hand pointing to the farthest shore where human hands outstretched are begging for the Christ who conquered, and, lo, it is enough. WE GO!' From the lips of those who have so loyally stood by, we hear these words: 'Nothing lasts but God; we build no earthly nests, our home lies yonder within the gates of pearl in the land of Beulah'.

Silence thou lying tempter: We believe God! Arise let us be going'

18TH JULY

A WITNESS!

It is these who follow the Lamb wherever he goes.

Revelation 14:4

'What is life for? Is it a brief span in which to eat, drink, and be merry, for tomorrow we might die? Nay! It is a sacred TRUST. 'As my father hath sent me, even so send I you!' We who have been drawn by the cords of His love, and found in Him a resting place, and know by experience the meaning of having been delivered from the power of darkness and translated into the Kingdom of His dear Son, have a debt to pay! And to pay it means the yielding up of our lives as a living sacrifice to our God. We are His purchased possession, and are NOT our own! Unto us He has committed the ministry of reconciliation!'

The previous paragraph was written by Lettie Cowman in 1946. However its contents are just as relevant today.

Mrs Cowman continues: 'What is a Christian? A WITNESS! A follower of the Lamb whithersoever He goeth! Shall we search ourselves to see whether we be in the faith? Search as we shall be searched in that day when everyone will render up an account to God? What a solemn day that will be, when we stand before the Throne with the multitudes who have gathered there, when the Book of Life will be opened and our record read! My record and yours! To those of us who have lived in lands where the gospel light shines so brightly, the searching question is ARE WE SHARING THAT LIGHT WITH OUR HEATHEN BROTHERS. Have we eaten our morsel alone while they have starved for the Bread of Life? What does our Lord say today as He looks down on earth's lost billions? A cry enters His ears'. She then goes on to mention various regions from where the cry is coming: 'China, India and Rome-controlled lands'. She continues: 'A CRY! As of pain, for liberation pierces through the heavens and reaches God's ear! I . . . have heard their cry . . . 'I know their sorrows; and I am come down to deliver them', spake our Lord so long ago, when He beheld the cruel bondage of His people. And He CAME down to deliver them! He left on record the WAY He came down in the ancient day. He came through Moses! He came through personalities and led His people out through the impassable Red Sea, while Pharaoh followed them in pursuit!'

Today we can think of many lands, countries, regions and groups which CRY out. The question today is: As followers of the Lamb what are we going to do about it? I will finish with Mrs Cowman's challenge: 'Rise up . . . ye careless ones who are at ease, shake yourselves! Out! Out of this lethargy! The harvest time is here'.

19TH JULY

SEND US THE FUNDS WE NEED

*And he sat down opposite the treasury and watched the
people putting money into the offering box. Many rich
people put in large sums. And a poor widow came and
put in two small copper coins, which make a penny.*

*And he called his disciples to him and said to them, Truly,
I say to you, this poor widow has put in more than all
those who are contributing to the offering box. For they all
contributed out of their abundance, but she out of her poverty
has put in everything she had, all she had to live on.*

Mark 12:41–44

I believe Hudson Taylor's quotation: 'God's work done in God's way will never lack God's supply',

Regarding resourcing Christian work, service and missions is very Biblical. I have seen this happen time and time again while serving the Lord in various capacities over the years. That said God resources His work financially through His people. In my experience this means teaching, reminding and sharing this truth with His people.

The following are some extracts from an article I read in a mission magazine written in the 1960s which is just as relevant today: 'Money can be filthy lucre. It can also be a sacred love-gift. Given from holy hands and a loving heart it can be spiritual worship of God. . . . You cannot love without giving something. If you love God, if you love the souls of men, you will long to give'.

On way of expressing this is giving to missionary causes. You can reflect on this today as you read through the following poem written by Dr Wesley Duewel and published in an edition of the 'Missionary Standard' in the 1960s regarding giving to missions:

*Stretching our empty hands to Thee,
Longing with prayerful agony,
Wait we the miracle to see-
Lord, send the funds we need*

*Why are our funds still short? We cry.
Why are we hungered, Saviour, why?
Surely Thou wilt our need supply-
Lord, send the funds we need.*

*How can we face the unmet need?
Where are the funds for which we plead?
Wilt Thou not tears and fasting heed?
Lord, hear our urgent cry!*

*Dost Thou not our condition see?
Wilt thou reject our long-urged plea?
Lord, for the sake of Calvary
Send us the funds we need.*

*Surely some saint Thy voice can hear!
Speak to them now, Lord, make it clear.
Speed Thou their gifts, oh speed the here!
Lord, speed the funds we need.*

*Earnestly, Lord again we cry;
Lord, Thou wilt not our need deny!
Out from Thy infinite supply
Send us the funds we need.*

20TH JULY

HOPE IN GOD.

*Why are you cast down, O my soul, and why are
you in turmoil within me? Hope in God; for I shall
again praise him, my salvation and my God.*

Psalm 42:11

We live in a world of war and rumours of wars. We live in a climate of secularism, materialism and immorality at every level. While as Christians we are not of this world, yet as God's dear children we must live in the midst of these hopeless conditions and situations.

However, God is the solver of our difficulties. He can make out of the most hopeless conditions and impossible situations the background for fresh revelations of His grace and power. It is in such situations that we prove Him, and He proves us. Our God is the God who is able.

I trust you find the following comments by George Mueller who has been described as the apostle of faith helpful today:

'There is never a time when we may not hope in God! Whatever the necessities, however great our difficulties, and though to all appearances help is impossible, yet our business is to hope in God, and it will be found that it is not in vain. In the Lord's own time help will come. Oh, the hundreds, yea, thousands of times I have found it thus within the past seventy years and four months. When it seemed impossible that help would come, help did come; for God has His own resources, He is not confined. In ten thousand different ways, and at ten thousand different times, God may help us. Our business is to spread our cases before the Lord; in child-like simplicity to pour out all our heart before God, saying, 'I do not deserve that Thou shouldst hear me and answer my requests, but for the sake of my precious Lord; for His sake answer my prayer. For I believe Thou wilt do it in Thine own time and way'. More prayer, more exercise of faith, more patient waiting, and the result will be blessing—abundant blessing. Thus I have found it many hundreds of times, and therefore I continually say to myself. 'Hope thou in God''.

All my hope on God is founded:
He doth still my trust renew.
Me thro' change and chance He guideth,
Only good and only true.
God unknown, He alone
Calls my heart to be His own.

(Joachim Neander)

21ST JULY

A SACRED TASK

What shall I do, Lord?

Acts 22:10

Throughout this devotional I am sharing thoughts from leaders of yesteryear within the mission I served the Lord through for fifteen years which will be helpful in our walk with God in this present generation. The following are thoughts from Mrs Lettie Cowman wife of the co-founder of our mission and author of the devotion 'Streams in the Desert', on our 'sacred tasks' as followers of Jesus:

'A vision of God's plan for our lives and obedience to the same is the most significant thing that can possibly come to us, at some time or other, visions of tasks which are ours to perform; contributions we can make to the whole of life. We are called to be workers together with God, where tears fall, where breaking hearts are, and where sorrows gush like streams from mountains. Blessed are they who follow the visions that God sends them! The obedient child of God often completes certain tasks, and it is well for him to know, when his work is done in a certain place, that if he continues on he will unfit himself for the task that lies ahead. When the Lord makes it known that our present task is finished, we will find that just around the bend in the road are new tasks awaiting us, the scroll unrolls and we are told what to do on the next step of our journey. Oh, the radiance of a revelation.

Today is the day of intense missionary activity, and the whole wide world is waiting for the coming of the messengers of peace. To the children of God a tremendous responsibility has been given. A sacred task—and no longer can we plead ignorance, evade or neglect our responsibility to get the gospel to the whole wide world, calling the situation an impossibility'.

God's plan and commission is still the same today 'Go' to every person and preach the Gospel. As a follower of Jesus are you fulfilling the sacred task God has given you? Has your current task come to or is coming to an end? Then seek the Lord on what your next one is.

The task your wisdom has assigned,
O let me cheerfully fulfil;
In all my works your presence find,
And prove your good and perfect will.

(Charles Wesley)

To love someone more dearly ev'ry day,
To help a wand'ring child to find his way,
To ponder o'er a noble tho't and pray,
And smile when evening falls,
And smile when evening falls,
This is my task.

(Maude Louise Ray)

22ND JULY

WHY I AM A MISSIONARY?

Hitherto hath the LORD helped us.

1 Samuel 7:12

Getting to know missionaries and missionary couples in retirement who had served the Lord for many years from various fields was one of my privileges as a homeland missionary representative. Of course you soon learned that they were not in retirement, rather they were in a new phase of service back home. This included being involved in their home churches again, active in prayer groups, missionary conferences, encouragement and keeping in contact with nationals and missionaries on the field where they served the Lord. One such couple was Tommy and Margaret Scott. Today for your encouragement I am going to share Margaret's testimony from an article she wrote many years ago:

'To parents who feared and honoured God it was my privilege to be born. God's servants who frequented our home in Northern Ireland influenced me greatly. At the age of nine I opened my heart to Jesus—a very real and definite experience. From that time on the Lord quietly but continuously worked in my life. Very patiently and step by step He put me where He wanted me. Many, many times I heard that the Lord had a plan for my life. So I began to pray that He would direct my paths. At times I wanted to obey and yet there was something inside which rebelled. But a message preached on a life completely and fully surrendered to God brought me face to face with myself and I took the following hymn as my prayer:

Thou sweet, beloved will of God,
My anchor ground, my fortress hill,
My spirit's silent, fair abode,
In Thee I hide me and am still.

O Will, that willest good alone,
Lead Thou the way, Thou guidest best;
A little child, I follow on,
And, trusting, lean upon Thy breast.

Within this place of certain good
Love evermore expands her wings,
Or nestling in Thy perfect choice,
Abides content with what it brings.

Oh, lightest burden, sweetest yoke;
It lifts, it bears my happy soul,
It giveth wings to this poor heart;
My freedom is Thy grand control.

Upon God's will I lay me down,
As child upon its mother's breast;
No silken couch, nor softest bed,
Could ever give me such deep rest.

(M Guyon)

As God took control, what a difference. Through nurse's training and Bible school, His guidance never failed. Now my husband and I, with our two girls, are serving a second term in Brazil. I am a missionary because I know this is God's plan. And I rejoice that hitherto He has led me'.

Tommy and Margaret still call their home 'hitherto'. Have you surrendered your life, yes, your all to Jesus? If not why not today.

23RD JULY

THE RIGHT CONNECTIONS

Finally, brothers, pray for us, that the word of the Lord may speed ahead and be honoured, as happened among you, and that we may be delivered from wicked and evil men. For not all have faith. But the Lord is faithful. He will establish you and guard you against the evil one

2 Thessalonians 3:1–3

Yesterday I shared about one half of a wonderful retired missionary couple, Tommy and Margaret Scott. Like many missionary couples I have the privilege of knowing, they remind me of 'Aquilla and Priscilla', fellow missionaries with Paul in the early Church. The following is an interesting article Tommy wrote in 1974 (50 years ago) while serving in Brazil:

'A cold fog shrouded Sao Paulo as Oscar, our crusader, and I began to work out problems delaying the evangelistic campaign in one of the city's suburbs. Before erecting our tent a license must be obtained from the city council. And we needed permission from the police department to use the public address system. As we went from department to department trying to contact the person in charge, we met only with attitudes and responses that matched the weather. How easy it would have been to give up in discouragement. But somehow we seemed upheld and strengthened to plod on in spite of the obstacles. Finally, after four difficult days, we realised the results we had set to obtain.

Why had we not been defeated? The answer is that a few days before, on August 24, through inter-cesso-Gram many people were praying for us. God had answered those prayers by giving strength, when the going was hard and patience essential. Prayer is a privilege. May we never take it for granted. May we never neglect it. God gives powerful promises to those who pray. And He does powerful things for those who pray.

Prayer is also a gift. It is free to us, but cost Jesus a great deal. Because of Him we can speak directly to our Father in heaven—the most wonderful and far-reaching communication in the world. Through radio, television, telegraph, and telephone men can talk to men. But through prayer men can converse with God at any time, in any place, in any circumstance. How glad we are that many made connections with God on our behalf'.

I can testify to the faithful prayer life of Tommy and Margaret over many years. How is your prayer life today? Are you making connections with God on behalf of harvest workers today?

24TH JULY

DANGER: HARD HEART AREA

To one a fragrance from death to death, to the other a fragrance from life to life.

2 Corinthians 2:16

Today I am sharing another story from Brazil which Tommy Scott wrote for a missionary magazine in the 1970s while serving the Lord there, to encourage us today.

'Our crusade ministry included an evangelistic thrust in the great city of Sao Paulo this year. Oscar, our leader there, writes: 'The campaign brought us into one of the most dangerous and criminal districts of Sao Paulo. Right from the beginning we had several teenagers whose main purpose was to cause disturbance. We faced them with much prayer and courage. On occasions shots were fired nearby and once a bullet hit the fence surrounding our tent. But one evening during the invitation, the ring leader of the gang came forward for prayer and asked forgiveness. Only a miracle could have transformed this life. Salvation, yes, but also judgement. A man who lived near the tent spent much time in a nearby bar ridiculing and attempting to hinder our work. One morning when he went to catch the bus, he was crushed between it and a pole and died. Since that day we have been free from disturbance in the meetings. After two months of services, however, we suffered the loss of the tent in a hurricane. But many, including some who never entered the tent, are requesting we continue the campaign because of the change evident in the community. Many of the teenagers who formerly roamed the streets have given up vandalism and sought employment'

Another example of faithful missionaries sharing Christ and seeing lives and communities changed through the power of the Gospel.

The power of the Gospel continues today from the seed sown under difficult and dangerous conditions by faithful missionaries like Tommy and Margaret: A 2020 survey by the private institute Datafolha showed that the percentage of Catholics in Brazil is on the decline (around 51 percent of the total population) while the percentage of evangelicals is rapidly growing (around 31 percent). This signals a major transformation in a country where more than 90 percent of the population identified as Catholic in 1970. (Source: Raphael Tsavkko Garcia Brazilian journalist and researcher).

Tommy and Margaret could be described as being like Aquilla and Priscilla. Aquilla and Priscilla were love partners in ministry.

- THEY WERE IN HARMONY. (See their story in Acts 18:2–3, 18 & 26; Rom 16:3–5; 1 Cor 16:19 and 2 Cor 4:19).
- THEY WERE HOSPITABLE, they gave Paul accommodation, and they received Apollos. At least two churches met in their house.
- THEY WERE HELPFUL: They helped protect Paul, instructed Apollos and nourished at least two church plants.

In summary they were faithful, available and surrendered to all the will of God. Please pray and support missionary couples like Tommy and Margaret as they reach the nations in this our day and generation.

25TH JULY

THE BIBLE A MISSIONARY BOOK

*Ask of me, and I will make the nations your heritage,
and the ends of the earth your possession.*

Psalm 2:8

The Bible has been described as a missionary book. In his book: The Bible Basis of Missions, Robert Hall Glover comments that: 'From cover to cover the Bible is a missionary book'. George W. Peters in his book: A Biblical Theology of Missions, writes: 'The Bible is not a book about theology as such, but rather, a record of theology in mission—God in action on behalf of the salvation of mankind'. And Graham Cheesman writing about mission, makes the point that: 'Mission is biblical. It is woven into scripture as a whole'.

A number of years ago I had the privilege of giving a number of talks on 'Missions' to a group of young Christian workers. I shared with them as I do with you today the following George W. Peters quote on missions: 'God is a God of missions. He wills missions. He commands missions. He demands missions. He made missions possible through His Son. He made missions actual in sending the Holy Spirit'.

Therefore 'missions' is a vital and integral part of our Christian life. In endeavour to get a better understanding of missions we looked at it from three aspects: I. What is Mission: Biblical mission brings the message of salvation in Christ alone to all ethnic groups so that they have the undisputed opportunity to become new persons in Christ (2 Corinthians 5:17). 2. What are Missions?: 'Missions are a specialized term. By it I mean the sending forth

of authorized persons beyond the borders of the New Testament church and her immediate gospel influence to proclaim the gospel of Jesus Christ in gospel-destitute areas, to win converts from other faiths or non-faiths to Jesus Christ, and to establish functioning, multiplying local congregations who bear the fruit of Christianity in that community and to that country' (George W Peters). 3. What is a Missionary?: A missionary is one who is commissioned and sent out by his or her local church to cross cultural boundaries in order to be a witness for Jesus Christ. These boundaries may be those of language, geography, or society. He or she would also intentionally: introduce people to Christ by his or her life, attitudes, actions and words - Seek to introduce those who come to Christ to join with others in the fellowship of a church. A church will need to be planted, if it doesn't exist.

This is just a very basic and limited definition of missions. However it should allow you today to assess if 'missions' are an integral part of your Christian life and experience. If the Bible is a missionary book, and it is, then missions should be a priority for us today.

*All the world for Jesus!
Be this our earnest aim;
To spread the blessèd tidings
Of Him who once was slain.*

(Grace Weiser Davis)

26TH JULY

THE MISSION COMMAND

And this gospel of the kingdom will be proclaimed throughout the whole world as a testimony to all nations, and then the end will come

Matthew 24:14

What is the mandate for missions? When we use the word mandate we mean: who gives an authoritative command or instruction. A command or an authorization. An official order or commission to do something. Scripture is clear on this—God does. We engage in mission because God told us to. The Great Commission given by Jesus at the end of His earthly ministry commanded God's people for all time the duty of taking the gospel to all the peoples of the world. This said the subject of world mission does not begin with the New Testament. It begins at the very opening of the scriptures and is woven into the whole of God's word. The whole Bible is the story of world mission. It is the revelation of God's heart for this entire world through the pages of scripture. Robert E Coleman writing about missions said: 'there are no loopholes. The mandate simply underscores a life-style incumbent upon the whole church. There are no escape clauses, no substitute options. As we might say in the academic world, the Great Commission is not an elective course; it is part of the required curriculum'.

So what does this mean for us today: According to John Piper the author of 'Let the nations be Glad' commenting on mission as found in the Great Commission Mandate in Matthew 28:18–20 wrote: 'This passage is often called the Great Commission. The first thing to make clear about it is that it is still binding on the present day church. It was not merely given to the apostles for their ministry, but was given to the church for its ministry as long as this age lasts'. Stephen Gaukroger in his book: Why Bother with Mission? said: 'So the command (and the comfort) is not time-limited. This is not a specific command to a particular group of 1st century Jewish men! It is a command to disciples of Jesus in every age, to be obeyed until the final age dawns. The church has its marching orders from the commander- in- chief. Our role as individual believers may vary depending on our gifts and calling, but no disciple of Jesus can evade the thrust of His command. Only the King's return will remove the obligation of obeying the King's command'. No doubt this is why Hudson Taylor's remark that: 'The great commission is not an option to be considered; it is a command to be obeyed', is often quoted.

Facing a task unfinished
that drives us to our knees,
a need that, undiminished,
rebukes our slothful ease,
we who rejoice to know you
renew before your throne
the solemn pledge we owe you
to go and make you known.

(Frank Houghton)

27TH JULY

You shall teach them diligently to your children, and shall talk of them when you sit in your house, and when you walk by the way, and when you lie down, and when you rise.

Deuteronomy 6:7

According to its official website: 'The Ulster Folk Museum puts the past in dialogue with the present in order to inspire and shape the future. Discover how reconnecting with the past can help us grow and thrive in the world today'.

My wife and I had a wonderful day out with some of our grandchildren at the Ulster Folk Museum as it re-opened after the covid-19 lockdown. It was just wonderful revisiting homes of the early 20th century. One of the things that caught my attention was that every home from a protestant background had pictures with verses of scripture or hymns displayed on their walls. This was a God fearing generation. Over the next few days we will consider some bible verses and thoughts from the walls of these homes.

In one of the homes is displayed: 'Give us this day our daily bread'. This of course is taken from the disciples' prayer as outlined by Jesus in His sermon on the mount: 'after this manner therefore pray ye: Our Father which art in heaven, Hallowed be thy name. Thy kingdom come, Thy will be done in earth, as it is in heaven. Give us this day our daily bread. And forgive us our debts, as we forgive our debtors. And lead us not into temptation, but deliver us from evil: For thine is the kingdom, and the power, and the glory, for ever. Amen' Matthew 6:9–16 (KJV). This prayer was prayed each morning in our home as I was a boy growing up in the 1960s. People in the early 20th Century in Ulster relied on God's daily provision. Do we? And are we thankful for God's daily provision of our physical needs?.

In another home a framed picture with the following words were on display: 'Nothing in my hand I bring'. This is a line of Augustus Toplady's well-known hymn 'Rock of ages', written in 1776:

> *Nothing in my hand I bring,*
> *simply to the cross I cling;*
> *naked, come to thee for dress;*
> *helpless, look to thee for grace;*
> *foul, I to the fountain fly;*
> *wash me, Savior, or I die.*

This again indicated to me that the dear folk in this home were relying totally on Christ alone and His finished work on Calvary for their eternal salvation.

The fact that we need to rely on God for 'our daily bread' and we cannot earn our salvation by the works of our hands are two great lessons we can learn from Christian homes of yesteryear in Ulster.

28TH JULY

*Who, when he came, and had seen the grace of God,
was glad, and exhorted them all, that with purpose
of heart they would cleave unto the Lord.*

Acts 11:23

We continue to view scriptural verses and Christian hymns and poems on plaques on the walls of Christian homes in the early 20th Century as displayed at the Ulster Folk Museum at Cultra, Holywood, N Ireland. I trust that we will be encouraged, challenged, learn from, and be blessed by their messages in the 21st Century

In one home a picture displayed the text: 'Cleave unto the Lord'. When the early Church was persecuted in Jerusalem they moved out and lived in other regions. As they went they preached the Gospel. As a result the first Gentile Church was established at Antioch. When the Jerusalem Church learned about this they sent Barnabas to check out that it was 'sound'. When Barnabas arrived he was delighted to find that the Antioch Church was indeed genuine, steadfast in godliness and in faithfulness. It had been established by the grace of God.

He then exhorted them: 'that with purpose of heart they would cleave unto the Lord'. The word 'cleave' means to adhere, to persist, to hold on, even under great pressure to not to let go; to continue in communion and attachment. Barnabas was constantly urging them, time after time telling them as he ministered to them to Cleave, adhere to the Lord. The Lord, the One to whom you belong, the One who owns you now by virtue of His death upon the cross, by virtue of His mighty power in saving you. Cleave to this Lord Jesus Christ. And do this, he said, with purpose of heart. That means: intelligently, sincerely, deliberately, and persistently. They were to cleave to the Lord with purpose of heart, that is, with a deep and abiding commitment of the heart.

When Barnabas says to them, 'Cleave to the Lord', he is telling them to draw their courage, their strength, their wisdom, their moderation, their zeal from the Lord. Barnabas was calling them to a necessary and total dependency upon the Lord.

In this materialistic and self-serving age are we totally depending upon the Lord? The Christians in the early Church like the Christians in early 20th Century Ulster had very little of earthly possessions. Therefore they 'Cleave to the Lord'. Today let us do likewise:

*Cleave to the Saviour day by day
Tempted by sin, go seek Him in pray'r,
Duty perform, and courage display,
Cleave to the Saviour every—where.*

(JH. Martin)

29TH JULY

THE FAMILY BIBLE

This Book of the Law shall not depart from your mouth, but you shall meditate on it day and night, so that you may be careful to do according to all that is written in it. For then you will make your way prosperous, and then you will have good success.

Joshua 1:8

We continue our walk around Christian homes in the early 20th Century as displayed at the Ulster Folk Museum. Today we will note the place of prominence in which the Bible was held in such homes. In this case we visit the Kennedy home. In it the museum displays the 'Kennedy Family Bible'. On the display they make the following remarks: 'The Family Bible in Ulster: Use of the King James Bible extended beyond the Established Church in Ireland and was adopted by all the main Protestant denominations for use in worship. As literacy and the availability of bibles became more widespread between 1800 and 1900, the tradition of families owning their own bible became embedded in Ulster Protestant culture.

As a treasured and indeed sacred object, family bibles had a sense of permanence which other household possessions did not, and were frequently used to record important family events such as births, marriages and deaths.

This practice extended right through society, from the great landowners like the Kennedys down to poor tenant farmers. The majority of these bibles are still in existence today and provide a rich source of family and cultural history'.

How important is the Bible is in your home? And more importantly do you read it, study it and obey it?

Remember it is God's Word therefore submit your ways unhesitatingly to it. Bank on its promises and obey it exactly and immediately.

There's a family Bible on the table
Each page is worn and hard to read
But the family Bible on the table
Will ever be my key to memories

At the end of day when work was over
And when the evenin' meal was done
Dad would read to us from the family Bible
And we'd count our many blessings, one by one

I can see us sittin' round the table
When from the family Bible dad would read
I can hear my mother softly singing
Rock of ages
Rock of ages cleft for me

Now this old world
Of ours is filled with troubles
This old world would also better be
If we'd found more Bibles on the tables
And mothers singin' rock of ages, cleft for me

I can see us sittin' round the table
When from the family Bible dad would read
And I can hear my mother softly singin'
Rock of ages
Rock of ages cleft for me

Rock of ages
Rock of ages cleft for me

(Willie Nelson)

30TH JULY

FEAR GOD AND KEEP HIS COMMANDMENTS

The end of the matter; all has been heard. Fear God and keep his commandments, for this is the whole duty of man.

Ecclesiastes 12:13

From the picture on this wall in an early 20th century home as depicted at the Ulster Folk Museum we are exhorted to 'Fear God and keep His commandments'.

Believers in a bygone age knew what the 'whole duty of man' was. For the believer, to fear God and keep His commands begins with recognizing Jesus as Saviour and Lord and receiving the free gift of salvation. As believers today, Solomon presents two strong reasons to what our duty or purpose is. We should live in reverential awe of God and obedience to Him. This is for all men in all ages, therefore includes you and me. Reverence and obedience are the duty of everyone. Fearing God puts Him front and centre of our lives. To fear God recognises that all of this life under the sun has its end in Him and so do we.

When you fear God it means you recognise his awesome power, his perfect wisdom and justice, his goodness, his mercy, his beauty. You see it, and you see your own sinfulness and frailty. And you're so dazzled by his strength and his beauty that you're in awe of him. It's not a fear that sends you running away from God. It's a holy fear that sends you running to God.

The Westminster Catechism tells us our purpose in life is to glorify God and enjoy Him forever. And that's actually not very different from what Ecclesiastes has told us. It's just saying it a little differently.

When you know the fear of God that sends you running to him, instead of away from him, you're going to glorify God. This leads to you wanting to keep His commandments and finding joy when you obey Him.

The Psalmist says in Ps 119:14: 'I rejoice in following your statutes as one rejoices in great riches'. He rejoices when he keeps God's commands. It brings him joy, like he'd just found a buried treasure.

The point is, Ecclesiastes 12:13 points us away from ourselves and toward honouring God, serving God, and ultimately finding our deepest joy in God. That's our purpose, that's our whole duty.

I want a principle within of
watchful, godly fear,
A sensibility of sin, a pain to feel it near.
I want the first approach to feel
of pride or wrong desire,
To catch the wandering of my will,
and quench the kindling fire.

(Charles Wesley)

Trust and obey, for there's no other way
to be happy in Jesus, but to trust and obey.

(John H. Sammis)

31ST JULY

TRUST IN HIM AT ALL TIMES

*Trust in him at all times, O people; pour out your
heart before him; God is a refuge for us.*

Psalm 62:8

Today we continue to view verses of Scriptures found on the walls of homes in Ulster in the early 1900s as presented at the Ulster Folk Museum at Holywood, N Ireland:

It is thought that David wrote Psalm 62 at the time of Absalom's rebellion. At a very difficult time in David's life and experience.

Having spoken of his personal trust in God in verses 6–7, David then encourages his subjects to do the same, saying, 'Trust in Him at all times, O people; pour out your heart before Him; God is a refuge for us Selah' Psalm 62:8. David's wise counsel to others is to 'Trust in Him at all times'. To have trust expresses that sense of well-being and security which results from having something or someone in whom to place confidence. There is no greater trust one can have than in the Lord Himself, and this trust should be in Him at all times and in all situations.

In contrast to God who is able to save those who trust in Him, David advises his subjects not to place ultimate confidence in men, might or money in verses 9–10. Wiersbe notes, 'David's enemies had acquired their power and wealth by oppressing and abusing others, and David warned his own people not to adopt their philosophy of life. How tragic when God's people today put their trust in their wealth, positions, and human abilities and not in the God who alone can give blessing'.

Just like Christians living through hard times throughout history we to can trust the Lord at all times and rest in His divine promises. God is with us: 'Keep your life free from love of money, and be content with what you have, for he has said, I will never leave you nor forsake you. So we can confidently say, The Lord is my helper; I will not fear; what can man do to me?' Hebrews 13:5–6. God is for us: 'What then shall we say to these things? If God is for us, who can be against us?' Romans 8:31. God will guard our hearts and minds when we live by faith: 'do not be anxious about anything, but in everything by prayer and supplication with thanksgiving let your requests be made known to God. And the peace of God, which surpasses all understanding, will guard your hearts and your minds in Christ Jesus' Philippians 4:6–7.

Simply trusting every day;
Trusting through a stormy way;
Even when my faith is small,
Trusting Jesus, that is all.

Trusting as the moments fly,
Trusting as the days go by,
Trusting Him, whate'er befall,
Trusting Jesus, that is all.

(Edgar Page Stites)

1ST AUGUST

SHEW ME THY WAYS O LORD

Make me to know your ways, O Lord; teach me your paths.

Psalm 25:4

The verses of Scriptures displayed on early 20th century homes at the Ulster Folk Museum can give us a window to look through to see the way Christians in that era lived their lives, and as a result challenges us in this our generation.

In the Authorised version of the Bible Psalm 25:4 reads:' Shew me thy ways, O Lord; teach me thy paths'. According to the verse on the wall the people in the home we are visiting today sought the Lord to show, lead, direct and guide them in their daily walk with Him.

In Psalm 25:4–14, David wrote, 'Shew me thy ways. . . teach me thy paths. . . lead me in thy truth'. This is the progression that you find in your spiritual growth. First, the Lord shows you his ways, then he teaches you his paths, then he leads you in his truth. His truth, of course, is found in your Bible. God doesn't shew you, teach you and lead you without the reading of His Manual the Bible.

In Psalm 25 God reveals who He shows His ways to:

- THOSE WHO ARE SAVED: Psalm 25:5, 7: God has to be the God of your salvation for him to not remember the sins of your youth. Once you are saved, then he will teach you. Psalm 25:8 says, 'therefore he instructs sinners in the way'

- THOSE WHO WAIT ON GOD: Psalm 25:5: We must wait on the Lord if we are going to be able to follow his lead. We must wait for him to shew us, teach us and lead us.

- THOSE WHO OBEY GOD'S WORDS: Psalm 25:9–10—the meek are submissively obedient; they keep the Lord's covenant and testimonies. The Lord won't teach you and lead you if you aren't going to obey what he is showing you to do.

- THOSE WHO CONFESS THEIR SINS: Psalm 25:11: David said, 'pardon my guilt, for it is great'. When you get saved, there are some sins you deal with immediately. But after you get saved, the Lord will show you some sins in your life of which you weren't initially aware, as in Psalm 19:12–13. When he shows you, you should confess those sins to him and then change from your ways to his ways. Holiness and sanctification are a necessary part of your spiritual growth.

- THOSE WHO FEAR THE LORD: the fear of the Lord is wonderful because it leads you to obey the Lord at all times, whether you are aware that he is looking or not. When the Lord knows you fear him, he will shew you, teach you and lead you (Psalm 25:12–14).

2ND AUGUST

WHATSOEVER HE SAITH UNTO YOU DO IT

His mother said to the servants, do whatever he tells you.

John 2:5

Over these past days we have looked at verses of Scriptures that were displayed on the walls of homes in Ulster in the early 20th Century. Today we look at another 'Whatsoever He saith unto you do it':

Mary made this statement at a wedding in Cana of Galilee where Jesus performed His first miracle.

The following is what the late Adrian Rodgers said about this statement which I trust we will find helpful today: The first thing he encourages us to do is: Ponder it: 'we must obey whether we can understand or not. When Jesus was at the wedding in Cana, the servants had no way of knowing what Jesus was going to do. It must have seemed silly to be filling pots with water. But Jesus' mother gave them some very wise advice we would do well to heed: 'Whatever He says to you, do it.' It wasn't a matter of whether they understood it or not, just that He told them to do it. The same Jesus who turned water into wine can transform your home, can transform your life, can transform your family, and can transform your future. That same Jesus is still in the miracle-working business. His business is the business of transformation. Someone has well said that nature forms us, sin deforms us, the penitentiary reforms us, education informs us, the world conforms us, but only Jesus transforms us'. Then Adrian admonishes us to Practice it: 'Many times your mind is going to say,

'Well, that's old-fashioned,' or 'That doesn't make sense.' Never come to the Bible that way. Never parade the Bible across the judgment bar of your reason. Whatever He says to you, do it'.

Mary gave two very useful pieces of information from this incident:

1. IN TIMES OF TROUBLE, DIFFICULT OR IMPOSSIBLE SITUATIONS: Flee to the Lord: When the problem arose, Mary took it to the Lord. This is what we need to do:

> *Take your burden to the Lord*
> *and leave it there.*
> *If you trust and never doubt, He*
> *will surely bring you out,*
> *Take your burden to the Lord*
> *and leave it there.*

(Charles Albert Tindley)

2. IN TIMES OF DIFFICULTIES: Follow His Commands This is the only command ever issued by Mary in the entire Bible. For those who feel that Mary is to be reverenced, adored, worshipped and obeyed, this is excellent advice! Just do as the Lord says!

> *Whatever he says to you—Do it*
> *Whatever he says to you—Do it*
> *And the water will turn into wine*
> *Sight will come to the blind*
> *So, whatever he says to you—Do it*

(Unknown)

3RD AUGUST

GOD IS LOVE

Beloved, let us love one another, for love is from God, and whoever loves has been born of God and knows God. Anyone who does not love does not know God, because God is love.

1 John 4:7–8

How reassuring for families being brought up in difficult times in early 1900s and read on a picture on the wall of their living room that 'God is love'. Such a verse is depicted in such a home at the Ulster Folk Museum. And things haven't changed. God is still love in the truest and purest sense. John in his first epistle makes it clear that 'love is from God' and 'God is love'. One has said that Christianity is a religion of love. Love has its origin in God: 'but God shows his love for us in that while we were still sinners, Christ died for us' Romans 5:8. No wonder Gloria Gaither wrote:

Redeeming love, a love that knows no limit;
Redeeming love, a love that never dies;
My soul shall sing throughout the endless ages,
The adoration of this great love on high.

So we see love proclaimed: 'God is love'. But then we see love proved: 'In this the love of God was made manifest among us, that God sent his only Son into the world, so that we might live through him' 1 John 4:9. The word 'manifested' means 'made visible'. God wanted to prove beyond doubt that He loved us. God loved us so much that He sent His Son into the world to be our Saviour.

What wondrous love is this,
O my soul, O my soul!
What wondrous love is this, O my soul!
What wondrous love is this that

caused the Lord of bliss
to bear the dreadful curse for
my soul, for my soul,
to bear the dreadful curse for my soul!

(Anonymous)

Not only do we see love proclaimed and proved but God wants to see His love practised through us His children: 'So we have come to know and to believe the love that God has for us. God is love, and whoever abides in love abides in God, and God abides in him' 1 John 4:16. 'We love because he first loved us' 1 John 4:19.

Come, ye that know and fear the Lord,
And raise your thoughts above:
Let every heart and voice accord,
To sing that God is love.

This precious truth His Word declares,
And all His mercies prove;
Jesus, the gift of gifts, appears,
To show that God is love.

Behold His patience, bearing long
With those who from Him rove;
'Till mighty grace their heart subdues,
To teach them—God is love.

Oh, may we all, while here below,
This best of blessings prove;
Till warmer hearts, in brighter worlds,
Proclaim that God is love.

(George Burder)

4TH AUGUST

THINE EYES SHALL SEE THE KING IN HIS BEAUTY

Your eyes will behold the king in his beauty;
they will see a land that stretches afar.

Isaiah 33:17

It was just wonderful to walk around the Ulster Folk Museum and see how people who lived in Christian homes lived by reading the verses of Scripture they displayed on the walls of their homes. One thing is for sure they had a high view of Jesus and His word. While times were hard they reminded themselves of what they had in Christ now and hereafter. They stood on the promises of God. One such promise displayed was: 'Thine eyes shall see the king in his beauty'.

In the most immediate sense, this referred to Hezekiah; but in the ultimate sense, to our Beautiful Saviour Jesus Christ.

Augustine of Hippo, commenting on 'the King in His beauty' wrote: 'He then is beautiful in heaven, beautiful on earth; beautiful in the womb, beautiful in his parents' arms; beautiful in his miracles; beautiful under the scourge; beautiful when inviting to life ... beautiful in laying down his life; beautiful in taking it up again; beautiful on the cross; beautiful in the sepulchre; beautiful in heaven'.

CH Spurgeon made the following comments regarding believers in respect of leaving this world to be with Jesus: 'Saints show how precious Christ is to them, in that He is their heaven. Have you never heard them, when dying, talk about their joy in the prospect of being with Christ?

They have not so much rejoiced because they were escaping the woes of this mortal life, nor even because they would rest from their toils, but because they would behold the Lord. Often have we seen the eye sparkle, as the dying believer said, 'I shall see the King in His beauty before many hours have passed.' When saints quit the world, their last thought is that they shall be with their Redeemer; and when they enter heaven, their first thought is to behold His glory'.

What a prospect every blood bought child of God has. Their eyes will see the King in His beauty: The LORD will bless His righteous ones. They will have a place of defence, a fortress, and bread and water will not fail them. But far above these material blessings, they will see the King in His beauty. Beyond all the material glory, splendour, and comfort of heaven, this is the greatest glory of heaven: not to be personally glorified, but to see the King in His beauty. We see Jesus now only in a dim, unclear way, but one day we will see Him with perfect clarity.

I shall see the King in His beauty,
In the land that is far away,
When the shadows at length have lifted,
And the darkness has turned to day.

(Adoniram J. Gordon)

5TH AUGUST

RECTOR OF KNOCKNAMUCKLEY

*And there was much weeping on the part of all; they embraced
Paul and kissed him, being sorrowful most of all because of the
word he had spoken, that they would not see his face again.*

Acts 20:37–38

The following is a poem written by a
member of the Church mourning the
loss of their godly Minister Richard
Oakes in 1896:

Rest and peace and pure delight,
Is in that land where there is no night;
Christ is the light, with his bright face
He fills all Heaven with happiness.

Angels are singing through the air
Rich Songs of praise with accents rare,
Death and sin cannot enter there.
Only they who are cleansed from sin,

And sanctified can dwell therein;
Thousands of every tribe and nation,
Evermore free'd from tribulation,
Sing songs of praise and adoration

My pen, once more, I take in hand
As my heart doth o'erflow,
With sorrow now to write of one
Who is through death laid low.

But death, to him hath brought no sting,
Since Christ his Saviour rose,
And broke the bonds of death and Hell
In triumph o'er His foes.

Amongst the congregation all
Great is the sympathy;
The counsel that he gave to them
Shall long remembered be.

He did much reprove the people
Hypocrisy to avoid,
And taught them that they must upon
Christ's finished work abide.

The Bible's precious truths he made
His study here below,
And pondered the truth in meekness
More of its precepts know.

But now the work is finished, here
He can no longer stay;
Bright angels bear his spirit home
To realms of endless day.

To sing the song with saints above,
Still new but ever old,
To angels playing with delight
On harps of purest gold.

There death can never enter,
There grief can never stay,
For troubles all are vanquished,
And sorrows passed away.

In that land where all are happy,
Where all is joy and peace;
For God shall wipe all tears away,
And bid all crying cease.

With heartfelt strains of deepest grief
All hearts should now o'erflow,
For the bereaved who mourn his loss
Our sympathies to show.

6TH AUGUST

O THOU THAT CHANGEST NOT

Like a robe you will roll them up, like a garment they will be changed. But you are the same, and your years will have no end.

Hebrews 1:12

We live in a world of change. In this 21st century the pace of change is mind boggling. We all know that the only constant in life is change. For thousands of years, the pace of change for humans was fairly steady and to some degree, predictable. Until it wasn't. Now, change is accelerating at an unprecedented speed. The pace of life is also accelerating. However as Christians we have some constants. We have unchanging things to hold on to.

- We have AN UNCHANGEABLE GOD: 'For I the Lord do not change' Malachi 3:6.
- We have an UNCHANGEABLE SAVIOUR: 'Jesus Christ is the same yesterday and today and forever' Hebrews 13:8. Yesterday He bore our sins on the Cross; today He bears our cares on the throne; tomorrow ourselves into Glory.

Change and decay in all around I see.
O thou who changest not, abide with me.

(Henry Francis Lyte)

Yesterday, today, forever, Jesus is the same,
All may change, but Jesus never glory to His name!
Glory to His name! Glory to His name!

(Albert B. Simpson)

- We have AN UNCHANGEABLE SPIRIT: 'And I will ask the Father, and he will give you another Helper, to be with you forever' John 14:16. Forever. One has said that's a long time. We may grieve Him, quench Him but never banish Him.
- We have AN UNCHANGEABLE WORD: 'but the word of the Lord remains forever' 1 Peter 1:25.

UNCHANGEABLE almighty Lord,
Our souls upon thy truth we stay;
Accomplish now thy faithful word,
And give, O give us all one way!

(Charles Wesley)

Spirit of the Living God,
Fall afresh on me,
Spirit of the Living God,
Fall afresh on me.
Break me, melt me, mould me, fill me.
Spirit of the Living God,
Fall afresh on me.

(Daniel Iverson)

- We have AN UNCHANGEABLE INHERITANCE: 'that is imperishable, undefiled, and unfading, kept in heaven for you' 1 Pet 1:4.

This unchangeable inheritance is:

'Imperishable' therefore not subject to death.
'Undefiled' therefore not subject to defect.
'Unfading' therefore not subject to decay.
'Kept in Heaven' therefore not subject to dissolution.

Time is filled with swift transition,
Naught of earth unmoved can stand,
Build your hopes on things eternal,
Hold to God's unchanging hand.

(Jennie B. Wilson)

7TH AUGUST

BEWARE!

Even Satan disguises himself as an angel of light.

2 Corinthians 11:14

In the 1980s and 90s there was a very popular TV programme called 'Beadle's About'. The main aspect of the show involved Jeremy Beadle carrying out some brilliant practical jokes on members of the unsuspecting public.

Today I want to share about one who deceives, plays tricks and tells lies to unsuspecting folk. However his tricks are real. His name is called the 'Devil' or 'Satan'. He too, wears disguises: 'even Satan disguises himself as an angel of light' 2 Corinthians 11:14.

Vile tempter, quick be gone,
Thy snares are spread in vain;
Thy fiery darts, to wound my soul,
Retort on thee again.

Though in an angel's form,
Through the disguise I see;
Thou art an enemy to God,
A cruel foe to me.

(Benjamin Beddome)

Here are some things we need to watch out for as Christians and as non Christians:

BEWARE OF FORGETTING GOD: 'then take care lest you forget the Lord, who brought you out of the land of Egypt, out of the house of slavery . . .. Take care lest you forget the Lord your God by not keeping his commandments and his rules and his statutes, which I command you today' Deuteronomy 6:12; 8:11.

BEWARE OF EVIL AND UNCHARITABLE THOUGHTS: 'Take care lest there be an unworthy thought in your heart and you say, The seventh year, the year of release is near,' and your eye look grudgingly on your poor brother, and you give him nothing, and he cry to the Lord against you, and you be guilty of sin' Deuteronomy 15:9. Beware of dangers foretold: 'Beware lest wrath entice you into scoffing, and let not the greatness of the ransom turn you aside' Job 36:18. This is a warning to none Christians.

BEWARE OF THE WRATH OF GOD: 'Beware, therefore, lest what is said in the Prophets should come about' Acts 13:40. This warning was given after the glorious gospel message.

BEWARE OF FALSE TEACHERS: 'Beware of false prophets, who come to you in sheep's clothing but inwardly are ravenous wolves' Matthew 7:15.

BEWARE OF MEN: 'Beware of men' Matthew 10:17. The fear of men can be our great snare. Men may laugh you into hell but they cannot laugh you out of it.

BEWARE OF THE ERROR OF THE WICKED: 'You therefore, beloved, knowing this beforehand, take care that you are not carried away with the error of lawless people and lose your own stability' 2 Peter 3:17. This warning is given in connection with the dangers of the last days being evil.

8TH AUGUST

WATCH OUT SATAN'S ABOUT

The god of this world has blinded the minds of the unbelievers, to keep them from seeing the light of the gospel of the glory of Christ, who is the image of God

2 Corinthians 4:4

There was a very popular TV programme in the 1980s and 90s called 'Beadle's About'. It's theme was called 'Watch out Beadle's about'. The main aspect of the show involved Jeremy Beadle carrying out some brilliant practical jokes on members of the unsuspecting public. One of the most memorable pranks the show carried out was when they convinced a lady called Janet Elford that an alien had actually landed in her back garden. However, when Jeremy removed his disguise he would normally be instantly recognisable to the members of the public who were being set up! Sadly Jeremy Beadle died of pneumonia on 30th January 2008 after a long illness. He was 59 years old.

Today we need to watch out for the enemy of our souls that old serpent the devil. In other words we need to watch out Satan's about. In the Bible we are warned: 'Be sober-minded; be watchful. Your adversary the devil prowls around like a roaring lion, seeking someone to devour' 1 Peter 5:8.

Here are some reasons outlined by John Piper as to why we need to 'Watch out Satan's about':

- 'Satan lies, and is the father of lies. (John 8:44)
- He blinds the minds of unbelievers. (2 Cor 4:4)
- He masquerades in costumes of light and righteousness. (2 Cor 11:13–15)
- Satan does signs and wonders. (2 Thess 2:9)
- Satan tempts people to sin. (Matt 4:1–11; 2 Cor 11:3)
- Satan plucks the word of God out of people's hearts and chokes faith. (Mark 4:1–9, 15; 1 Thess 3:5)
- Satan causes some sickness and disease. (Luke 13:16; Acts 10:38)
- Satan is a murderer. (John 8:44)
- Satan fights against the plans of missionaries. (1 Thess 2:17–18)
- Satan accuses Christians before God. (Rev 12:10)'

And yet we praise God that Satan is indeed a defeated foe. God's Word instructs us to: 'Submit yourselves therefore to God. Resist the devil, and he will flee from you'.

Thou artful stratagems
Shall teach me to beware;
Great is thy cruelty and rage,
And great shall be my care.

Or should I feeble prove,
Know, Jesus is my friend;
Through him thy base attempts shall fail,
And in confusion end.

He conquered on the cross,
And will new conquests gain;
Begone, seducer vile, be gone,
Thy snares are spread in vain.

(Benjamin Beddome)

In the name of Jesus, in the name
of Jesus, we have the victory.
In the name of Jesus, in the name of
Jesus, Satan, you have to flee.

Oh, Tell me, who can stand before us
when we call on that great name?
Jesus, Jesus, precious Jesus, we have the victory.

(Unknown)

9TH AUGUST

EXPENDABLE

I will most gladly spend and be spent for your souls.
If I love you more, am I to be loved less?

2 Corinthians 12:15

Jim Smyth served the Lord through OMS in Colombia for 34 years. He is now retired and resides with his wife Grace in Pennsylvania USA. While in retirement Jim made a visit home to N Ireland in 2009. On this visit he gave a report of his work over the years while in Colombia, at a meeting I attended run by Men for Missions, a ministry of OMS. Jim took us back to the days he lived here in N Ireland. He told us how he attended a mission conducted by Frank Marshall (Irish Evangelist Band Evangelist) at Ballyrobert Mission Hall which had a major impact on his life and calling to be a missionary. Jim served the Lord in very difficult and dangerous times in Colombia. However he saw God at work in the salvation of precious souls, the planting of various churches and the discipleship of national workers who went on to be key Church leaders and Pastors in Colombia.

Jim outlined three principles at work in his service for Jesus in Colombia, he was expendable, he became a mentor, and then backed off and let those he had mentored get on with the work.

It is the idea of being 'expendable' I want to think about today. Jim said that a Rev David McKee taught him about the word 'expendable' and all it entailed before going to Colombia.

Clearly this had a great impact on Jim because he made himself 'expendable' with his resources, time and love for the people of Colombia.

2 Corinthians 12:15 summarises what it means to be 'expendable'. David Platt commenting on this verse writes: 'what a simple statement here in 2 Corinthians 12:15 that reflects a sombre commitment to say to other people, 'I will gladly, most gladly, spend my life for your soul'. Be spent like, 'God use my life however you want for the good of these other souls'. What a picture of commitment to say, 'My life is not ultimately about me. I am living for the glory of God and specifically for the glory of God and others. I want to spend my life for the good of others, for the eternal good of others. I want my life to be spent by God for that purpose.' Are you spending your life for the good of the souls of others? God, give us a desire to spend our lives for the good of others like 2 Corinthians 12:15 describes'.

Patrick speaking about the people of Ireland said: 'I still spend, and will spend more. The Lord is powerful, and he can grant me still to spend my very self for the sake of your souls'.

Are you and I 'expendable' in the service of the Master and the good of souls?

10TH AUGUST

THE WAY OF LOVE

If I speak in the tongues of men and of angels, but have not love, I am a noisy gong or a clanging cymbal.

And if I have prophetic powers, and understand all mysteries and all knowledge, and if I have all faith, so as to remove mountains, but have not love, I am nothing.

If I give away all I have, and if I deliver up my body to be burned, but have not love, I gain nothing.

Love is patient and kind; love does not envy or boast; it is not arrogant or rude. It does not insist on its own way; it is not irritable or resentful; it does not rejoice at wrongdoing, but rejoices with the truth. Love bears all things, believes all things, hopes all things, endures all things. Love never ends.

As for prophecies, they will pass away; as for tongues, they will cease; as for knowledge, it will pass away. For we know in part and we prophesy in part, but when the perfect comes, the partial will pass away.

When I was a child, I spoke like a child, I thought like a child, I reasoned like a child. When I became a man, I gave up childish ways.

For now we see in a mirror dimly, but then face to face. Now I know in part; then I shall know fully, even as I have been fully known.

So now faith, hope, and love abide, these three; but the greatest of these is love

1 Corinthians 13

I had the privilege of speaking about mission at Ebenezer Baptist Church, Hendersonville, NC, USA in 2011. It was while there that I first heard of the late Pastor Adrian Rodgers from Tony Hall, the Pastor of Ebenezer. Since then I have read and listened to some of his sermons. I also get information from a ministry called 'Love worth Finding' (LWF), which he established in 1987.

Today I felt it would be beneficial to share comments made by Gary E. Vaughn of LWF on 1 Corinthians 13 for us to consider and apply to our lives: 'Do I really love God? How do I know that I really love God?'

Reflecting on this question Cary came up with the following self-checks to ask himself:

- How is my worship? Is it me-centred or Jesus-centred?
- How is my fellowship? Am I demonstrating God's love to those around me?
- How is my generosity? Is God leading me to give more to the advancement of His kingdom?
- How is my service? What have I done in the past 30 days to serve the Lord beyond just church attendance?
- How is my witness? Have I shared the love of Jesus with anyone in the past month?

Gary then closes with an Adrian Rodgers quote: 'If the greatest commandment is to love God with all of your heart, the greatest sin is not to do it'

11TH AUGUST

BRANDED

From now on let no one cause me trouble, for
I bear on my body the marks of Jesus.

Galatians 6:17

The Rev Stanley Banks was the Principal of Emmanuel Bible College in Birkenhead Cheshire, England. The Emmanuel College united with the Nazarene Theological College, Manchester in 1997. A number of OMS missionaries attended the college over the years, including Mabel Callendar (nee Kelly), who went on to serve the Lord in Ecuador and Mozambique. The Rev Banks wrote articles for OMS and for a period was their 'Minister at Large'.

The following is an article written by the Rev Banks in the 1960s for 'The Missionary Standard', an OMS publication entitled 'branded': 'The Christian life to many is nothing more than a pleasant picnic. But to the Apostle Paul it was a conflict. He knew nothing of the cheap, easy-going religion so prevalent today. While many rock themselves to sleep in evangelical chairs, the devil has a jubilee and the world hastens to destruction.

The Apostle Paul would certainly have endorsed the sentiments of General Booth, who, on being complimented by an outstanding national figure on the number of converts the Army was gaining, retorted: 'Converts? We don't want converts; we want soldiers'. The apostle was a soldier; he had been in the heat of the battle for a number of years when he wrote his letter to the churches in Galatia. For Paul, the answer was apparent. 'Here are my credentials', he wrote. 'I bear in my body the marks of Jesus. I am branded. I carry the scars of the conflict. I have not been a spectator on the side-lines or a critic in the press box. I have been in the arena fighting the powers of hell and darkness, seeking to rescue lost men and women".

Perhaps this is a good place to stop and pose the question: Am I, are you soldier a or a spectator?

Am I a soldier of the cross,
A foll'wer of the Lamb?
And shall I fear to own His cause
Or blush to speak His name?

Must I be carried to the skies
On flow'ry beds of ease,
While others fought to win the prize
And sailed through bloody seas?

Are there no foes for me to face?
Must I not stem the flood?
Is this vile world a friend to grace,
To help me on to God?

Sure I must fight if I would reign:
Increase my courage, Lord;
I'll bear the toil, endure the pain,
Supported by Thy word.

(Isaac Watts)

12TH AUGUST

From henceforth let no man trouble me: for I bear in my body the marks of the Lord Jesus. Brethren, the grace of our Lord Jesus Christ be with your spirit. Amen.

Galatians 6:16–18 (KJV)

Yesterday I shared part of an article called 'branded' written by the late Rev Stanley Banks, one time Minister at Large with OMS. Today we will glean some more thoughts on the second part of the article: 'In Paul's day it was common for people to be branded. Slaves were branded as a mark of ownership; soldiers were branded as a mark of allegiance; devotees were branded as a mark of devotion; and the abhorred as a mark of reproach. But the apostle's brand signified all of these. Christ was not only his owner but it was to Him he gave his allegiance and devotion. It was also for Christ that he suffered reproach. No chocolate soldier, he.

Qualifications have their place; training is essential; authorization is necessary. But what are these if there are no evidences of the conflict, no brand marks?

After the battle of Marengo, Napoleon prepared a medal for his soldiers. On one side it stated the name of the battle; on the other inscribed, 'I was there'. Where was David when his armies marched out to battle? This man who had slain Goliath and composed spiritual songs was with another man's wife. Where was Peter when Christ was on trial? Warming himself at the fireside of Christ's enemies. Where was Paul when missionaries were needed in Philippi, Ephesus, Corinth . . .?

Joyfully he could say, 'I was there'. He bore the marks of the conflict.

When the record of the battle for souls is assessed at the judgement seat of Christ, will we be able to report, 'I was there'? Dear Christian friend, what is the Christian life to you—a picnic or a conflict? ARE YOU BRANDED?'

Billy Graham preaching a message called: 'Do you bear the marks of Christ?' to USA soldiers in and to the people of South Korea in 1952, summarised his message as follows: 'What Marks Will You Have?

- When this life of perils and conflict and suffering is over, what marks will you have?
- Did you bear in your body the brand of the Lord Jesus?
- Did the whole world know that you belonged to Him—body, soul and spirit?
- Did you bear His reproach?
- Did you commit and surrender your life to Him?
- Are you a Christian and proud of it? You should be able to say with Paul, 'I am not ashamed of the gospel of Christ, for it is the power of God to salvation for everyone who believes' (Romans 1:16, NKJV)'.

How about you and I today?

13TH AUGUST

WITHOUT A DOUBT

And Jesus answered them, Have faith in God.

Mark 11:22

Daniel in the den of lions, and the three Hebrew children in the midst of the fiery furnace have ever been a challenge to our faith! How steady they were! How unwavering. Take courage, tested and tried one, and you, shall come forth with a shout of triumph and will be able to say with the Psalmist, 'We went through fire and through water, but thou broughtest us into a wealthy place'. Why doubt? One falling leaf is not a sign of winter. One rainless day is not a sign of drought!

Our Master said, Have the faith of God' (Mark 11:22). The faith of God is inwrought within our hearts by the Holy Ghost! And that faith is the faith which will say to the mountains, 'Be removed!'—And will melt like wax at His spoken Word through us.

'Let patience have her perfect work, that ye may be perfect and entire, wanting nothing'. Throughout testing time, wait!—In faith; in patience! God's time of deliverance is never late!—Even when Pharaoh's host is on Israel's heels, a path through the waters will suddenly be opened. And when the bed of the brook is dry Elijah shall hear the guiding voice. Wait! God never is late! Remember, tempted one, that God 'standeth in the shadow keeping watch above His own'.

In the pathway of faith we come to learn that the Lord's thoughts, nor His ways are our ways. Both in the physical and spiritual realm, great pressure means more power! Although circumstances may bring us into the place of death, that need not spell disaster—for if we trust in the Lord and wait patiently, that simply provides the occasion for the display of His almighty power, 'Remember His marvellous works that He has done; his wonders, and the judgements of His mouth' (Psalm 105:5).

Do you remember how your way was blocked,
And coming to the gate you knocked and knocked?
Till God's time came and then opened wide
A way thine eyes ne'er saw, thy foot ne'er tried.

(The above is an excerpt from an editorial written by Lettie Cowman in the 1940s which I trust you will find helpful and encouraging today. Mrs Cowman was the wife of Charles Cowman the founder of the Mission through which I served the Lord for 15 years).

Have faith in God, the sun will shine,
Though dark the clouds may be today;
His heart has planned your path and mine;
Have faith in God, have faith always

(May Agnew Stephens)

14TH AUGUST

YOU WILL DO

I was not disobedient to the heavenly vision.

Acts 26:19

Today we will consider another article written by Lettie Cowman in 1947 which is just as relevant today:

'The same vision that came to St Paul came to Livingstone—a child of poverty in a small village in Scotland. At daybreak his little fingers were found guiding the thread in the factory, and when darkness fell he was still standing beside the loom. Days, weeks, months went by; and then manhood reached. He heard the cry of dwellers in darkness and said, 'Lord, here am I; send me!' To others in the same factory no vision was given. It came to just one man! And one man with God makes a majority! When a man knows he is called to do a certain work he is invincible. He is not unconscious of his own deficiencies, whether they are natural or intellectual. He was God's co-partner. Livingstone and God! The blood of his sacrifice gets into our veins like hallowed fire, and it is through such sacrifices that the race renews its youth.

The same vision came to William Carey as he worked away at his shoemaker's bench, and immediately he rose up, claimed a new continent for Christ! William Carey became a true Knight of the cross. We cannot measure the preciousness of just one life given away in lavish surrender to a noble cause, or measure the results of the influence of such a life! William Carey and God! Burma and Carey's God!

> *Bring to God your gift my brother,*
> *He'll not need to call another*
> *You will do.*

> *He will add His blessing to it,*
> *And the two of you will do it,*
> *God and you.*

His completeness will flow around your incompleteness. Leadership will come when you lose your life. To an outstanding businessman, more than 46 years ago, a vision came. He, too, heard a voice saying, 'come over and help us'. When this was known among his friends they thought him mad; beside himself; but, 'in spite of the stares of the wise and the world's derision', he rose up, left all, followed through—and OMS is today the glorious answer.

> *What will be your response to the vision?*
> *Dare to follow the star-blazed road!*
> *Dare to follow the vision!*

15TH AUGUST

YES, YOU

*And a vision appeared to Paul in the night: a man
of Macedonia was standing there, urging him and
saying, Come over to Macedonia and help us.*

Acts 16:9

Today I want to share another article written in the past (by Mrs Cowman in June 1947) to inform us in God's ways today:

'A vision with amazing accuracy was given to St Paul! It was not something mystical, uncertain, mis-understand-able—and it blazed in his soul in lines of fire. There stood a man of Macedonia beside him, saying, 'Come over and help us'. Ever since his experience on the Damascus road, he kept to the appointed path, with vigilant fidelity and an utter abandonment to the will of God. He was in the rightful place to receive a further revelation, a vision of God; to hear His voice; and never missed his guidance, and never lost it. After this fresh illumination and enlarged vision came for his lifework, what did he do? Begin to reason things out? Allow his mind to be filled with all kinds of suggestions?—Which if once he followed would multiply like a mountain! Did he reply to the Lord, 'Let my answer be postponed while I think it through?' No! There was no hesitation on his part. Indifference and inertia ill becomes those who are entrusted with a great concern. There is no time for dalliance in the camp when the Captain of the Lord's host has issued orders, 'forward into the battle!' Instant obedience is the only kind of obedience. Delayed obedience is complacent obedience. Paul never did things coldly. All issues of his life were burning with passionate devotion. After he had seen the vision, 'Immediately he endeavoured to go'. We may triumphantly go forward with our Master amid the burning splendour of a vision of God; and when He says, Go today, let no man answer, tomorrow!

The direction now given to Paul was clear and definite. 'Into Macedonia'. He was called to a place, to a people, to a work planned for him from eternity. No other person in the world could have done that work or filled that place at that time.

Were visions given only to first-century saints? No, a long line has since followed, and Christ binds the ages together. He steps into each era. God's territory is boundless, and He wants us to rise up, go in, and take possession—because it is Christ's promised inheritance. Let us listen for His voice, His divine revelation to our hearts, and be ready to act.

God will entrust you with a vision. Yes, you! You are God's opportunity in your day. He has waited for a person just like you. If you refuse Him, then God loses His opportunity which He saw through you—and He never will have another, for there never will be another person on earth just like you'.

*Give Me A Vision, Lord, I Plead,
Vision Of Souls And A World In Need:*

(John W. Peterson)

16TH AUGUST

THE OPPORTUNITY TO HEAR, UNDERSTAND, AND BELIEVE THE GOOD NEWS OF JESUS CHRIST

So faith comes from hearing, and hearing through the word of Christ.

Romans 10:17

While serving with One Mission Society the then Global President Dr Bob Fetherlin cast a vision for the mission, our missionaries, and national workers and partners to reach one billion people with the Gospel over a ten year period. It was called: 'The One Billion-One opportunity Vision'. Bob expressed the vision in the following way: 'We are asking God, by His power and grace, and for His glory alone, to enable OMS and our partners to give one billion people the opportunity to hear, understand, and believe the Good News of Jesus Christ over the next ten years'. Quite a vision! But one God would be well pleased with. It reminded me of Oswald Smith's famous quote: 'No one has the right to hear the gospel twice, while there remains someone who has not heard it once'.

Against the background of this vision along with other leadings I was exercised to send a piece with the approval of OMS UK of Gospel literature into every home in N Ireland. Three pieces of Gospel literature were selected deemed suitable for the various regions it was sent into. To the glory of God this was achieved over a period of four years.

This was backed by folk praying for the initiative as the literature went out. The following are extracts from the monthly prayer letters sent out at that time: 'Prayer is the only adequate way to multiply our efforts fast enough to reap the harvest God desires' (Dr Wesley Duewel).

'What breaks God's heart should break ours. In Exodus 3, God explained to Moses, I have heard my people crying out because of their slave drivers, and I am concerned about their suffering. So I have come down to rescue them (v 7–8). God loved people then, and He loves them now. He is deeply concerned for lost people and has come down in the person of Jesus to rescue them and provide a way to restore them into a loving relationship with Him. If God is deeply concerned about lost people, we should be as well . . . to the point of all-out obedience in carrying out His mission, the ministry of reconciliation he has entrusted to us, even if it costs us much'. (Dr Bob Fetherlin).

Rescue the perishing, Care for the dying,
Snatch them in pity from sin and the grave;
Weep o'er the erring one, lift up the fallen,
Tell them of Jesus the mighty to save.

(Fanny Crosby)

17TH AUGUST

STUDYING YOUR BIBLE

Do your best to present yourself to God as one approved, a worker who has no need to be ashamed, rightly handling the word of truth.

2 Timothy 2:15

Studying God's Word is essential in being a follower of the Lord Jesus. When we pray we talk to God, when we read and study God's Word He talks to us.

The golden rule of Bible reading and study as laid down by Wilbur Chapman is helpful:

- STUDY IT THROUGH: Never begin a day without mastering a verse.
- PRAY IT IN: Never leave your Bible until the verse or passage you have studied is part of your being.
- PUT IT DOWN: The thoughts that God gives you, put in the margin of your Bible, or in a notebook.
- WORK IT OUT: Live the truth you get in the morning through all the hours of the day.
- PASS IT ON: Seek to tell someone else what you have learned.

Still on Thy holy Word,
We'd live and feed and grow.
Go on to know the Lord,
And practice what we know.

(Joseph Hart)

Pastor Adrian Rodgers suggested five simple steps for studying the Bible:

- PRAY OVER IT: Begin with prayer. Ask for God's cleansing and the ability to receive what He wants to teach you.

- PONDER IT: What did it mean? What does it mean now? What does it mean to me?
- PUT IT DOWN IN WRITING: Write down what the Holy Spirit is revealing to you.
- PRACTICE IT: Find ways you can incorporate the truths you've been shown into your own life.
- PROCLAIM IT: Contemplate ways to share the knowledge God has given you.

Here are further questions to ask yourself while reading the Bible:

- Is there a promise to claim?
- Is there a lesson to learn?
- Is there a blessing to enjoy?
- Is there a command to obey?
- Is there a sin to avoid?
- Is there a new thought to carry with me?

Reading the Bible—I love the Word of God!

Every verse reveals Yourself to me,
Every line conveys reality.
When I pray the words that You breathed out
You become so real to me.

As I read, I pray, as I pray, I read,
Mingling both as one spontaneously.
You respond within with words so sweet,
I repeat these words to Thee.

(Unknown)

18TH AUGUST

THE SAVIOUR'S RETURN

For yet a little while, and the coming one
will come and will not delay.

Hebrews 10:37

THE PROMISE OF THE SAVIOUR'S RETURN is repeated time and time again in the New Testament. This promise should stir the spirits of every believer with daily renewed freshness of hope in these closing days. In His own words, directed to His disciples shortly before His death on Calvary's Cross, Jesus intended to encourage them in view of His leaving them for a season. He must return to the Father so that the Holy Spirit would come and baptise believers into one body, thus forming the Church (1 Corinthians 12: 12–13). However He assures them in John 14:3: 'And if I go and prepare a place for you, I will come again and will take you to myself, that where I am you may be also'. Present conditions in the world today indicate that the fulfilment of this promise can be expected at any moment! When the hour appointed by the Father arrives, He 'will come and will not delay'.

When the trump of the great archangel
Its mighty tones shall sound,
And, the end of the age proclaiming,
Shall pierce the depths profound;
When the Son of Man shall come in His glory
To take the saints on high,
What a shouting in the skies
From the multitudes that rise,
Changed in the twinkling of an eye.

(Fanny Crosby)

THE PROCEDURE OF THE SAVIOUR'S RETURN is outlined for us in the Scriptures: 'For the Lord himself will descend from heaven with a cry of command, with the voice of an archangel, and with the sound of the trumpet of God. And the dead in Christ will rise first. Then we who are alive, who are left, will be caught up together with them in the clouds to meet the Lord in the air, and so we will always be with the Lord' 1 Thessalonians 4:16–17. The Lord will be the Bridegroom coming for the Bride.

When He comes in the clouds descending,
And they who loved Him here,
From their graves shall awake and praise Him
With joy and not with fear;
When the body and the soul are united,
And clothed no more to die,
What a shouting there will be
When each other's face we see,
Changed in the twinkling of an eye.

(Fanny Crosby)

THE PROSPECT OF THE SAVIOUR'S RETURN has been set before the believer from the beginning of the proclamation of the Gospel: 'For they themselves report concerning us the kind of reception we had among you, and how you turned to God from idols to serve the living and true God, and to wait for his Son from heaven, whom he raised from the dead, Jesus who delivers us from the wrath to come' 1 Thessalonians 1:9–10.

19TH AUGUST

THOU WHO CHANGEST NOT

For I the LORD do not change.

Malachi 3:6

We live in a world of changing scenes, changing circumstances and changing people. Yet as believers we can rest in the assurance we belong to and serve an unchanging Christ and His unchanging presence. In Hebrews we have:

HIS UNCHANGING PERSON: 'And, You, Lord, laid the foundation of the earth in the beginning, and the heavens are the work of your hands; they will perish, but you remain; they will all wear out like a garment like a robe you will roll them up, like a garment they will be changed. But you are the same, and your years will have no end.' Hebrews 1:10–12. A billion, billion, billion years from now and thereafter in timeless eternity, Jesus Christ will still be on the throne. He will be the same and will still love and care for us.

Swift to its close ebbs out life's little day;
earth's joys grow dim, its glories pass away.
Change and decay in all around I see.
O thou who changest not, abide with me.

(Henry Francis Lyte)

HIS UNCHANGING PRIESTHOOD: 'but he holds his priesthood permanently, because he continues forever' Hebrews 7:24. Jesus never dies. He is always there to represent: Consequently he is able to save to the uttermost those who draw near to God through him, since he always lives to make intercession for them' v. 25.

HIS UNCHANGING POSITION: 'But when Christ had offered for all time a single sacrifice for sins, he sat down at the right hand of God' Hebrews 10:12. The one sacrifice that Jesus made paid not only for all our past sins and present sins; it also paid for all future sins. That work of Christ is eternal in its ramifications.

HIS UNCHANGING PURPOSE: 'FOR, Yet a little while, and the coming one will come and will not delay' Hebrews 10:37.

HIS UNCHANGING PRESENCE: 'Keep your life free from love of money, and be content with what you have, for he has said, I will never leave you nor forsake you'. Hebrews 13:5. We can be content because in Christ we have everything we need, and He will never leave us or forsake us. We can put our trust in Him.

Faithful One, So Unchanging
Ageless One, You're My Rock Of Peace
Lord Of All I Depend On You
I Call Out To You, Again And Again
I Call Out To You, Again And Again

You Are My Rock In Times Of Trouble
You Lift Me Up When I Fall Down
All Through The Storm
Your Love Is The Anchor
My Hope Is In You Alone

(Brian Doerksen)

20TH AUGUST

SEVEN INVITATIONS OF THE LORD JESUS CHRIST

The Spirit and the Bride say, 'Come.' And let the one who hears say, 'Come.' And let the one who is thirsty come; let the one who desires take the water of life without price.

Revelation 22:17

AN INVITATION OF SALVATION: 'Come unto me, all ye that labour and are heavy laden, and I will give you rest'. Matthew 11:28

I have the following notes written in the margin of my Bible beside this verse: Bound and burdened by the guilt and power of sin, the sinner hears the sweet and tender invitation of Christ: 'Come'.

AN INVITATION OF SANCTIFICATION: 'In the last day, that great day of the feast, Jesus stood and cried, saying, If any man thirst, let him come unto me, and drink'. John 7:37.

Jesus doesn't just save us and leave us. He changes us day by day by the power of His Spirit. This is known as progressive sanctification. Jesus is inviting us to live in and by the power of the Holy Spirit.

AN INVITATION OF SERVICE: 'And Jesus said unto them, Come ye after me, and I will make you to become fishers of men'. Mark 1:17. No one can make themselves a soul-winner. They must come to Christ, who will equip and fit them to catch men.

AN INVITATION OF SIGHT: He saith unto them, Come and see. They came and saw where he dwelt, and abode with him that day: for it was about the tenth hour. John 1:39.

This invite extends to all. We are blind spiritually until we come to Him, and ask Him as blind Bartimeus did to receive his sight. And Jesus answered: 'Receive your sight'.

AN INVITATION OF SEPARATION: And he said unto them, Come ye yourselves apart into a desert place, and rest a while: for there were many coming and going, and they had no leisure so much as to eat. Mark 6:31. Here the Lord calls His servants to separate from the rush, turmoil and weariness of service for a time for rest and refreshment with Him. As we do we are renewed and refreshed for further service.

AN INVITATION OF SATISFACTION: Jesus saith unto them, Come and dine. And none of the disciples durst ask him, Who art thou? knowing that it was the Lord. John 21:12.

All of His children are invited to sit down and sup with Him: Revelation 3:20.

AN INVITATION OF SUFFERING: Come, take up the cross, and follow me. Mark 10:21.

The believer is called not only to believe on His name but to suffer for His sake. We suffer now that we may reign hereafter.

Let us consider and apply each of these invitations to our lives today.

21ST AUGUST

PRECIOUS LORD, TAKE MY HAND

Nevertheless, I am continually with you; you hold my right hand.

Psalm 73:23

In the months after 'Lockdown', in many Countries due to the Covid-19 Pandemic in 2020 the well-known Gospel singers Bill and Gloria Gaither posted various short devotional videos on their Facebook account. On one occasion they featured the song 'Precious Lord, take my hand'. Gloria Gaither made the point that during times of difficulty 'prayer songs', such as 'Precious Lord' are very helpful. The song was written by Thomas A Dorsey. Known as the 'Father of Black Gospel Music', Dorsey (1899–1993) became a Christian in 1928. In 1932, Dorsey's wife, Nettie, was in her last month of pregnancy. Dorsey was scheduled to be the soloist at a large evangelistic meeting in St. Louis around the time of her due date. While he was playing on stage at the meeting, a messenger boy ran up with a Western Union telegram informing Dorsey that his wife had died. Upon his return to Chicago, Dorsey learned that Nettie had given birth to a boy, but shortly after her death, their son also died. Dorsey buried both Nettie and their child in the same casket. The loss and grief dealt a major blow to Dorsey's faith. Caught up in his bereavement, he questioned God's character and no longer had a desire to serve Him. In the days after the funeral, a friend took him to a nearby music school, letting him sit down at the piano, and this song is the result.

The song expresses the sorrow and reaching out to Jesus in the midst of their tragedy. The first verse uses the image of a stormy night; the second refers to a dark path; the third verse depicts the worshiper standing at a river at night. In each verse, the worshiper petitions, 'Take my hand, precious Lord, lead me home'. It's an expression of hope and of trusting God's nearness and guidance, even in our darkest moments. It recognizes that God alone can sustain us when our 'way grows drear' and when the 'life is almost gone'.

Precious Lord, take my hand,
Lead me on, let me stand.
I am tired, I am weak, I am worn,
Through the storm, through the night,
Lead me on to the light,
Take my hand precious Lord, lead me home.

When my way grows drear
Precious Lord linger near.
When my life is almost gone
Hear my cry, hear my call,
Hold my hand lest I fall,
Take my hand precious Lord, lead me home.

When the darkness appears
And the night draws near,
And the day is past and gone.
At the river I stand,
Guide my feet, hold my hand,
Take my hand precious Lord, lead me home.

22ND AUGUST

GUIDE ME, O THOU GREAT JEHOVAH

And the Lord will guide you continually and satisfy your desire in scorched places and make your bones strong; and you shall be like a watered garden, like a spring of water, whose waters do not fail.

Isaiah 58:11

Over and over again we find the subject of God's guidance brought before us in the Word of God. In the Old and New Testaments we have wonderful promises of guidance and examples of those who sought and found the Lord's will for their lives. We also have a number of very clear statements which show us our need of guidance; for example, Jeremiah 10:23: 'I know, O Lord, that the way of man is not in himself, that it is not in man who walks to direct his steps'. In Psalm 25 the psalmist assumes the need for guidance, and of course not one of us would question the fact that God's people do need guiding. They need to pray: 'Make me to know your ways, O Lord; teach me your paths' Psalm 25:4. 'Lead me in your truth and teach me, for you are the God of my salvation; for you I wait all the day long' Psalm 25:5. 'He leads the humble in what is right, and teaches the humble his way' Psalm 25:9.

Commenting on Isaiah 58:11 Alan Redpath said: What a picture of the blessedness of Christian experience: It is a guided life: The Lord will guide you. It is a satisfied life: He shall satisfy you. It is a fragrant life, like a watered garden. It is a freshly sustained life, like a spring of water'. Praise God for a guided life. My late father often quoted the first verse of 'Guide me, O thou great Jehovah' in his prayers. Likewise we all need to be guided by God:

Guide me, O Thou great Jehovah,
pilgrim through this barren land;
I am weak, but Thou art mighty;
hold me with Thy powerful hand.
Bread of heaven, bread of heaven,
feed me till I want no more,
feed me till I want no more..

Open now the crystal fountain,
Whence the healing stream doth flow.
Let the fire and cloudy pillar
lead me all my journey thru.
Strong Deliverer, strong Deliverer,
Be Thou still my strength and shield,
Be Thou still my strength and shield.

When I reach the river Jordan,
Bid my anxious fears subside;
Bear me thru the swelling current,
land me safe on Canaan>s side.
Songs of praises, songs of praises
I will ever give to Thee,
I will ever give to Thee.

(William Williams)

23RD AUGUST

MISSION MINDED PEOPLE

Epaphras, who is one of you, a servant of Christ Jesus, greets you, always struggling on your behalf in his prayers.

Colossians 4:12

A number of years ago I was asked to say a few words at the 97th birthday party of a dear brother called Jim McCullough, who had a heart for mission. He used the occasion of his birthday to raise funds for Mission. I also had the privilege along with others to say a few words at his 100th birthday. He went on to live to the good old age of 102.

I have notes of some of the things I said at his 97th birthday which were certainly true of Jim. Let them also be true of us today:

His Passion for Mission was lived out in:

HIS PRAYER LIFE: Having had the privilege of meeting with Jim and others on a Friday night for prayer, I just knew how fervent in prayer he was for mission, Christian workers, revival and for the lost. He believed in the primacy of prayer and he practiced prayer. He prayed much in private and in public at the prayer meetings he attended. He was a man of faith and power in prayer. Today we need a new generation of prayer warriors to replace the Jims of this world. Jim belonged to the Wesleyan background. He whole heartedly believed the following words of Charles Wesley:

Faith, mighty faith, the promise sees
And looks to that alone;
Laughs at impossibilities
And cries: It shall be done!

HIS PERSON: Jim gave his person to mission in what I am going to call the three Ls: Life, Lip and Literature. Jim lived out his Christian life for all to see. He shared his faith, especially in one to one evangelism and he distributed many gospel tracts all over the country. Jim gave his person to mission. He was all in:

Lord, speak to me that I may speak
In living echoes of your tone.
As you have sought, so let me seek
Your erring children, lost and lone

(Frances R. Havergal)

HIS PURSE: Jim was a great supporter of the Lord's work, especially that of mission. He gave graciously, gladly and genuinely. Genuinely in the sense not to be seen or praised of men. Because he basically gave in secret. He gave so that the work of God would move forward. He gave that labourers could be sent into the harvest fields:

Take my silver and my gold;
not a mite would I withhold.
Take my intellect and use
every power as thou shalt choose,

(Frances R. Havergal)

24TH AUGUST

SEVEN

*And on the seventh day God finished his work
that he had done, and he rested on the seventh
day from all his work that he had done.*

Genesis 2:2

After retiring my wife and I sold our house and downsized to a bungalow. This gave us an opportunity to purchase a used static mobile home on a site on the North Coast of County Londonderry, N Ireland. Interestingly the number of our pitch is number 7. The previous owner served the Lord as a Pastor, Bible College lecturer and principal and after retiring he and his wife started a Christian Ministry supporting God's work in Romania. They displayed the number of the site 7 on a beautifully painted large stone with the verse Isaiah 58:11, also painted on the stone below the number. Of course the mobile home is still identified in this way. I trust it continues to be a witness to all who see it.

This led me to reflect on the Biblical significance of Bible numbers and the number 7 in particular.

In Genesis 2:2 we read that on the seventh day, God rested. He had finished creation and declared it to be complete and perfect. The number 7 refers to rest, completion, and perfection.

So, from the beginning, we see that numbers are significant. Dr A. T. Pierson comments: 'A mathematical mind is manifest in the universe, in the planetary and stellar worlds, their distances and dimensions, densities, proportions, orbits, and periods of revolution'.

The number seven appears over 700 times in the Bible. The following are some examples: On the seventh day, he rested after creating the heavens and the earth. Before blowing their horns, the Israelites walked around the wall seven times. Following Jesus' feeding of the multitude of 4,000, the disciples gathered seven baskets of leftovers. The number 'seven' appears frequently throughout the book of Revelation, including references to the seven churches, seven bowls, seven seals, seven trumpets, seven thunders, seven Spirits of God, seven stars, seven lampstands, seven eyes and horns of the Lamb of God, seven heads and diadems of the dragon, and so on. The number seven frequently represents the completion of divine fulfilment.

It is worth mentioning that not every seven mentioned in the Bible is significant. When it comes to biblical symbolism, we should always proceed with caution and compare everything to Scripture and the original context.

However as I looked at and reflected on the Bible meaning of the number 7 on my new holiday home it reminded me of richness of Scripture, even in its numbers. Why not take time to study the arithmetic of heaven. You will find that numbers in the Word of God are significant and instrumental for understanding biblical truths. Biblical numbers do not merely hold numerical value, they also convey important spiritual concepts.

25TH AUGUST

NO LONGER I

And he died for all, that those who live might no longer live for themselves but for him who for their sake died and was raised.

2 Corinthians 5:15

Becoming a Christian is the most momentous event in the life of anyone. The hymn writer Hugh Bourne put it as follows:

> *My soul is now united to*
> *Christ, the living vine;*
> *His grace I long have slighted,*
> *but now I feel him mine;*
> *I was to God a stranger till Jesus took me in,*
> *He freed my soul from danger*
> *and pardoned all my sin.*

From that moment on born again Christians should 'live no longer for themselves but for him who for their sake died and was raised'. In fact Paul in 2 Corinthians 5:17 writes: 'Therefore, if anyone is in Christ, he is a new creation. The old has passed away; behold, the new has come'. True disciples of Jesus follow him, learn from Him and live for Him. William Henry Temple Gairdner who was a British Christian missionary with the Church Missionary Society in Cairo, Egypt, described the new birth as follows: 'That sense of newness is simply delicious. It makes new the Bible, and friends, and all mankind, and love, and spiritual things, and Sunday, and church and God Himself. So I've found'. A Christian can be defined as one who has been intellectually convinced that the Lord Jesus Christ is the Son of God and that He died for the sons of men on the cross, and therefore them individually and personally. They also have been morally convicted of their own need of a Saviour as Jesus, who alone can deal with the problem of their sin. A Christian is one who has been spiritually converted from a life of self-interest to a life lived in allegiance to the One who died and rose again for them. As a result as followers of Jesus we live no longer unto ourselves but unto the one who saved us and redeemed us by His own precious blood.

C T Studd the cricketer turned missionary founded WEC in 1913. Studd was one of the Cambridge Band also called the Cambridge Seven—seven members of Cambridge University who offered themselves for service under the China Inland Mission as a result of a visit by the American evangelist D. L. Moody to the campus in 1884. Studd's motto was 'If Jesus Christ be God and died for me, then no sacrifice can be too great for me to make for Him'.

> *It's no longer I that liveth,*
> *But Christ that liveth in me.*
> *He lives, He lives, Jesus is alive in me!*
> *It's no longer I that liveth,*
> *But Christ that liveth in me.*

(Unknown)

26TH AUGUST

NO RESERVE, NO RETREAT, NO REGRETS

*If anyone would come after me, let him deny himself
and take up his cross daily and follow me.*

Luke 9:23

Salvation is free to the sinner, however it cost Christ His life to purchase our Salvation. While salvation is free, becoming a follower of Jesus costs us everything. It is well, at the outset of our Christian life, to understand how hard a thing it is to follow Jesus. Jesus told his followers that they were, in fact, to follow him by taking up their cross. They do this, by fully identifying with him, whatever that would cost them and wherever that would take them. Suffering for the sake of the gospel is a way in which we identify with Christ's sufferings—and he, in turn, identifies with the sufferings of His people. Around the world, many Christians are persecuted by imprisonment, even killed for their faith. Currently, there are over 300 million people facing persecution daily. We in the West don't really appreciate what it means to be a Christian in many countries. From the outset the Lord Jesus left His contemporaries under no delusions on the subject. Indeed it was the vision of what Calvary had cost their Master that was the inspiration of the early Christian witness.

While at Yale University William Borden was left a fortune. At about the same time he had begun seriously to consider his duty as a disciple of Jesus Christ. With more of life's comforts than he could do with, and with little serious care for the future, he heard Christ's call 'take up his cross daily and follow me'. He did just that. He gave away his fortune, and handed his life and his fortune into the keeping of His Master. Within seven years he had died in Egypt at the age of twenty four while studying two difficult languages, Arabic and Chinese, with a view to evangelising the hardest people in distant China, and the Moslems of Kansu Province. His biographer discloses the secret of William Borden's life in these words, 'No reserve, no retreat, no regrets'.

Quite a challenge for us today. To follow Christ without reserve, retreat or regrets does not necessarily mean that we, like Borden become missionaries. But it does mean that we must become willing to do anything for Christ.

I will follow where He leadeth,
I will pasture where He feedeth,
I will follow all the way, Lord,
I will follow Jesus ev'ry day.

(Charles F. Weigle)

Let me die, let me die;
Unto the world and its applause,
To all the customs, fashions, laws,
Of those who hate the humbling cross

(Janette Palmiter)

27TH AUGUST

ILLUMINATE

*To open their eyes, so that they may turn from
darkness to light and from the power of Satan to God,
that they may receive forgiveness of sins and a place
among those who are sanctified by faith in me.*

Acts 26:18

It is a privilege to serve the Lord in Ireland through various outreach ministries over the years. One of the things I developed was to use the acrostic 'IRELAND' as an aid to get people to pray for that land. I = Illuminate, R = Revival, E = Evangelism, L = Leadership, A = Assemble, N = Nurture, D = Discipleship. Of course an acrostic could be used for almost any country or region of the world. Today we will look at the first letter of the acrostic 'I' = 'illuminate'. According to the dictionary illuminate means: 'make (something) visible or bright by shining light on it; light up, to put light in or on something'.

When you look at light you think of: God:

- THE LORD IS DEFINED AS LIGHT: 'This is the message we have heard from him and proclaim to you, that God is light, and in him is no darkness at all' 1 John 1:5
- THE LORD DWELLS IN LIGHT: 'He who is the blessed and only Sovereign, the King of kings and Lord of lords, who alone has immortality, who dwells in unapproachable light, whom no one has ever seen or can see. To him be honour and eternal dominion. Amen' 1 Timothy 6:15–16
- THE LORD DISTRIBUTES LIGHT: 'And night will be no more. They will need no light of lamp or sun, for the Lord God will be their

light, and they will reign for ever and ever' Revelation 22:5
- THE LORD DIVIDES LIGHT FROM DARKNESS: ' And God saw that the light was good. And God separated the light from the darkness' Genesis 1:4.
- THE SON OF GOD IS LIGHT: 'Again Jesus spoke to them, saying, "I am the light of the world. Whoever follows me will not walk in darkness, but will have the light of life' John 8:12.
- THE SCRIPTURES OF GOD ARE LIGHT: 'Your word is a lamp to my feet and a light to my path' Psalm 119:105.
- THE SAINTS OF GOD ARE LIGHT: 'In the same way, let your light shine before others, so that they may see your good works and give glory to your Father who is in heaven' Matthew 5:16.

Let our prayer today be: Lord Send the light:

*There's a call comes ringing
o'er the restless wave,
'Send the light! Send the light'
There are souls to rescue, there are souls to save,
Send the light! Send the light!*

*Send the light, the blessed gospel light;
Let it shine from shore to shore!
Send the light the blessed gospel light;
Let it shine for evermore!*

(Chas. H. Gabriel)

28TH AUGUST

REVIVAL

Will you not revive us again, that your people may rejoice in you?

Psalm 85:6

Yesterday I shared about the acrostic Ireland that can be used as an aid for praying for that land. The first letter I = Illuminate. Today we come to the second letter R = Revival.

The Revivalist, Duncan Campbell came to the Faith Mission Bible College in Scotland and spoke to the students while the Lewis Revival was still going on. He told of a midwife having a vision of Ireland all in darkness but then a light breaking out in the South filled the whole land. In 1964 while preaching at a conference in N Ireland Mr Campbell prophesied, 'Ireland will have riots and revival'. In the light of this he came to seek the face of God during which he received a vision of revival coming to Ireland, He described how God would visit the island through small bands of praying people in the country districts. That evening after preaching his last message of the convention, God took over. The people were gripped with awe and no-one could move for the next half-an-hour during this divine stillness and quietness. At least four people heard indescribable sounds from heaven. Then the people began to weep and pray. (Source: posted on Sermon Index: 27/02/2007).

Ireland has indeed seen the riots. Our sincere prayer is that we will soon see the revival.

Prayer as in all revivals was prominent in the 1859 revival in Ulster. The following are extracts from an article in the spring addition of 'The Congregationist' in 2009, that makes this very point: 'The spiritual awakening which rendered the year 1859 forever famous in the annals of Ulster, also furnishes one of the most remarkable illustrations in all history, of Christianity suddenly and potently revived and exercising a transforming influence, swift in its action and wide in its sphere, upon all classes of society . . . No world-famous name is associated with the Revival. Nevertheless, beginning in the prayer meetings and wayside conversations of a few humble work-people, it speedily attained proportions of a national movement. . . Jeremiah McQuilken, Jeremiah Meneely, John Wallace and Robert Carlisle commenced in a little schoolhouse at Kells, Antrim, a Believers' Fellowship Meeting. Month after month passed and kindred spirits joined them in intercession, as they wrestled and prevailed. McQuilken had been carefully studying the Bible and was also much helped by a record of the life of George Muller. In 1858, there were remarkable conversions. Steadily converts multiplied, and the Rev JH Moore, minister of the Presbyterian congregation at Connor, gave every encouragement, conducting countless services . . . Within the bounds of Connor congregation a hundred prayer meetings were held every week'.

And finally in 1859 God moved by His Spirit in a marvellous way when it is recorded that over 100,000 people trusted Christ as Saviour and Lord in that year alone. Our prayer today is: 'Lord do it again'.

29TH AUGUST

Now those who were scattered went about preaching the word.

Acts 8:4

Yesterday I shared about the acrostic Ireland that can be used as an aid for praying for that land. The first letter I = Illuminate, the second letter R = Revival and today we will consider the third letter E = Evangelise.

Today we will ask some questions in regards to evangelise which I trust will challenge, encourage and motivate us to be more effective in reaching the lost for Jesus.

Q.1. WHO SHOULD EVANGELISE? 'All this is from God, who through Christ reconciled us to himself and gave us the ministry of reconciliation; that is, in Christ God was reconciling the world to himself, not counting their trespasses against them, and entrusting to us the message of reconciliation. Therefore, we are ambassadors for Christ, God making his appeal through us. We implore you on behalf of Christ, be reconciled to God' 2 Corinthians 5:18–20.

Answer: All Christians.

Q.2. WHY DO WE EVANGELISE? 'Go therefore and make disciples of all nations, baptizing them in the name of the Father and of the Son and of the Holy Spirit' Matthew 28:19.

Answer: Out of obedience and inner passion. Because it is God's chosen means. It gives personal reward which draws us closer to God and glorifies our Saviour the Lord Jesus Christ.

Q.3. WHEN SHOULD WE EVANGELISE? 'But in your hearts honour Christ the Lord as holy, always being prepared to make a defence to anyone who asks you for a reason for the hope that is in you; yet do it with gentleness and respect' 1 Peter 3:15.

Answer: Always be prepared.

Chares Finney said: 'It is the great business of every Christian to save souls. People often complain that they do not know how to take hold of this matter; why the reason is plain enough—they have never studied it. They have never taken the proper pains to qualify themselves for the work. If you do not make it a matter of study on how you may successfully act in building the Kingdom of Christ, you are acting a very wicked and absurd part as a Christian'. Today let us take pains to reach the lost for Jesus. It was Oswald W Smith that said 'Oh, my friends we are loaded down with countless activities, while the real work of the Church, that of evangelising and winning the lost, is almost entirely neglected. The body of Christ is not a pleasure cruiser on its way to heaven, but a battle ship stationed at the gate of Hell'.

To encourage you the following is God's perspective on evangelism: 'How beautiful upon the mountains are the feet of him who brings good news, who publishes peace, who brings good news of happiness, who publishes salvation, who says to Zion, 'Your God reigns.''.

Let us all get involved in the soul winning business wherever we live today.

30TH AUGUST

LEADERSHIP

*And when they had appointed elders for them in
every church, with prayer and fasting they committed
them to the Lord in whom they had believed.*

Acts 14:23

Over these past days we are looking at the acrostic Ireland that can be used as an aid for praying for that land. We have considered the letter I = Illuminate, R = Revival, and E = Evangelise. Today we will meditate on the letter L = Leadership. The Church in every country and region needs Godly leaders at every level, Godly: Pastors/Ministers, Elders, Deacons, Sunday School teachers, Youth workers, Para-church leaders, missionaries and the list goes on.

I think it is true to say that one of the church's greatest needs is sound and faithful leadership. Biblical leadership is a Divine Appointment: 'Pay careful attention to yourselves and to all the flock, in which the Holy Spirit has made you overseers, to care for the church of God, which he obtained with his own blood' Acts 20:28. It is a Divine Assignment: 'care for the church of God'. The assignments may be varied. However it comes down to winning the lost, making disciples which ultimately leads to caring for the Church of God. What an assignment, what a privilege. Leaders also have a: Divine Assurance: 'And now I commend you to God and to the word of his grace, which is able to build you up and to give you the inheritance among all those who are sanctified' Acts 20:32.

Paul commended the leaders to God and to the word of His grace. We know that if God is for us who then can be against us.

Perhaps God is calling you into a place of leadership. Will you step up to the plate? Today we need to pray for our leaders, and where leaders are required pray that God will raise up leaders to fill the vacancies. It is said that God doesn't call the equipped, he equips the called.

When God wanted a new King for Israel David was the most likely of Jesse's sons, but he was God's man. Why: 'I have found in David the son of Jesse a man after my heart, who will do all my will' Acts 13:22. When Moses died, Joshua had big shoes to fill, but what did God tell him: 'Moses my servant is dead. Now therefore arise, go over this Jordan, you and all this people, into the land that I am giving to them, to the people of Israel. Every place that the sole of your foot will tread upon I have given to you, just as I promised to Moses' Joshua 1:2–3.

Let us really pray for our leaders in every area of our Churches today. Pray for their ministries, homes, families, quiet time, purity and faithfulness. They need our prayers not our criticisms. Pray that God will raise up leaders wherever they are needed.

31ST AUGUST

ASSEMBLE

And let us consider how to stir up one another to love and good works, not neglecting to meet together, (Not forsaking the assembling of ourselves together AV) as is the habit of some, but encouraging one another, and all the more as you see the Day drawing near.

Hebrews 10:24–25

Some years ago I developed a book-marker using the acrostic Ireland to be an aid for praying for that land. We have considered the letter I = Illuminate, R = Revival, and E = Evangelise, L = Leadership.

Today we will consider the letter A = Assemble or Assembling, which in its context is speaking of the local church. On the little bookmarker against A –Assemble, I wrote; Pray that those that come to know the Lord will become part of the fellowship of a Bible believing Church and where none exists churches will be strategically planted. Then I referenced these comments with Hebrews; 24–25 and Acts 2:47; 'praising God and having favour with all the people. And the Lord added to their number day by day those who were being saved'.

The local church is vital. Indeed Jesus said: 'And I tell you, you are Peter, and on this rock I will build my church, and the gates of hell shall not prevail against it' Matthew 16:18. Today let us pray for our local churches, other bible based local churches and the planting of biblical churches where they are required.

The Church shall never perish.
Her dear Lord to defend,
to guide, sustain, and cherish,
is with her to the end.

Tho' there be those that hate her
and strive to see her fail,
against both foe and traitor
she ever shall prevail.

(S. J. Stone)

Stephen Olford comments: 'The priority programme on heaven's agenda is the calling out and completion of the church, the body of Christ. When Jesus declared 'I will build my church, and the gates of hell shall not prevail against it', He launched a movement no devil in hell or angel in heaven can ever thwart. Notwithstanding its many failures and factions, the true church of redeemed and regenerated souls will prevail. One day soon she will be raptured and presented before the presence of the Saviour Himself 'so that he might present the church to himself in splendour, without spot or wrinkle or any such thing, that she might be holy and without blemish' Ephesians 5:27. It follows, therefore, that our main task as pastors, teachers, and leaders is 'warning everyone and teaching everyone with all wisdom, that we may present everyone mature in Christ' Colossians 1:28. To this end we need to give ourselves to a church-family ministry.

1ST SEPTEMBER

NUTURE

Like new born infants, long for the pure spiritual milk, that by it you may grow up into salvation.

1 Peter 2:2

'But grow in the grace and knowledge of our Lord and Savior Jesus Christ. To him be the glory both now and to the day of eternity. Amen

2 Peter 3:18

In the last number of devotions I have used the acrostic Ireland to demonstrate key prayer areas for that land. We have considered the letter I = Illuminate, R = Revival, and E = Evangelise, L = Leadership, and A = Assemble.

Today we will look at the letter N = Nurture. Beside this Letter I have put: Pray that God will provide teachers and Bible courses and that Bible study groups will be formed to feed young believers in the faith.

The evangelical church is growing in the Republic of Ireland. However many of the believers are 1st generation Christians with very little knowledge of Scripture, therefore the need of being nurtured in the things of God is immense. A lovely Irish couple who came to know Christ while at university identified this need and have started an on-line Bible course to address this issue, called 'The open Bible academy'. The mission of The academy according to their website is undergirded by the following core values:

- MAKING DISCIPLES: Matt 28:18–20
- TRAINING TO LIVE GODLY: 2 Tim 3:16–17

- EXCEPTIONAL TEACHING: James 3:1
- COMMITTED TO EXCELLENCE: 1 Tim 4:16
- BRINGING PRAISE TO GOD: Rom 15:7
- ENCOURAGING ONE ANOTHER: 1 Thess 5:11.

Of course the need for nurturing young believers and indeed not so young is vital to all believers. Jesus said: 'It is written, 'Man shall not live by bread alone, but by every word that comes from the mouth of God.''

- THE WORD OF GOD SAVES: 'receive with meekness the implanted word, which is able to save your souls' James 1:21.
- THE WORD OF GOD STABLISHES: 'rooted and built up in him and established in the faith, just as you were taught, abounding in thanksgiving' Colossians 2:7.
- THE WORD OF GOD SATISFIES: 'The water that I will give him will become in him a spring of water welling up to eternal life' John 4:14.
- THE WORD OF GOD SANCTIFIES: 'Sanctify them in the truth; your word is truth' John 17:17.
- THE WORD OF GOD STRENGTHENS: 'but he grew strong in his faith as he gave glory to God' Romans 4:20.
- THE WORD OF GOD SHINES: 'Your word is a lamp to my feet and a light to my path' Psalm 119:105.
- THE WORD OF GOD SPEAKS: 'You shall teach them diligently to your children, and shall talk of them when you sit in your house, and when you walk by the way, and when you lie down, and when you rise' Deuteronomy 6:7.

2ND SEPTEMBER

DISCIPLESHIP

Then Jesus told his disciples, If anyone would come after me,
let him deny himself and take up his cross and follow me.

Matthew 16:24

Today we conclude our thoughts where we have used the acrostic Ireland to demonstrate key prayer areas for that land. We have considered the letter I = Illuminate, R = Revival, and E = Evangelise, L = Leadership, and A = Assemble, and N = Nurture. Today we will reflect on the letter D = Discipleship. Of course we can apply these letters to many countries, regions, areas and situations.

The term disciple is used constantly throughout the four Gospels. It describes the relationship between the Lord Jesus Christ and His followers. This terminology continued following the day of Pentecost. The word runs throughout the book of Acts. The members of the early Church were known as disciples before they were called 'Christians' at Antioch Acts 11:26. The word signifies 'a taught or trained one'. Jesus is the teacher and we are the learners. Every day for the believer should be a school day. William MacDonald makes the point that 'true discipleship begins when a person is born again and when the following things take place in his or her life:

- They must understand that they stand before God as a sinner, lost, naked and blind.
- They must admit that neither their good character nor good works can change this situation in any way.
- They must believe that the Lord Jesus Christ died on the cross for them.
- They must (I would add: repent of their sin) freely decide to put their complete trust in Jesus Christ alone, and recognise Him as their Lord and Master'.

From that point on you are a disciple, a follower of the Lord Jesus Christ as your Lord and Saviour. MacDonald then gives seven terms for Christian Discipleship:

- A SUPREME LOVE FOR JESUS CHRIST: Luke 14:26.
- A DENIAL OF SELF: Matt 16:24.
- A DELIBERATE CHOOSING OF THE CROSS: Matt 16:24.
- A LIFE SPENT IN FOLLOWING CHRIST: Matt 16:24.
- A FERVENT LOVE FOR ALL WHO BELONG TO CHRIST: John 13:35.
- AN UNSWERVING CONTINUANCE IN HIS WORD: John 8:31.
- A FORSAKING OF ALL TO FOLLOW HIM: Luke 14:33.

No matter who we are, as believers we are called to be disciples and make disciples. We will mature in our faith only as we daily bring our lives under the Master-ship of His personal tuition:

At the feet of Jesus, Listening to His word;
At the feet of Jesus is the place for me,
There a humble learner would I choose to be

(Philip P. Bliss)

To be like Jesus, to be like Jesus!
My desire - to be like Him!
All thru life's journey from earth to glory,
My desire - to be like Him.

(Unknown)

3RD AUGUST

HE LEADETH ME

I will instruct you and teach you in the way you should go.

Psalm 32:8

One of the things I love doing is browsing through the Christian book section of charity shops on the look-out for a good book at a bargain price! On such an occasion I purchased along with some other books a little booklet called 'When God Guides' written by the late Colin Peckham. Over the years I had the privilege of sitting under his ministry at various 'Faith Mission' events. In the book-let Mr Peckham pointed out the cer-tainty of divine guidance. Over the next few days we will look at a sum-mary of the points he made which I found beneficial. I trust they are to you as well.

God through His Word has prom-ised to guide us: 'And the Lord will guide you continually' Isaiah 58:11; 'Again Jesus spoke to them, saying, 'I am the light of the world. Whoever follows me will not walk in dark-ness, but will have the light of life" John 8:12.

God guides us in spite of our ABJECT IGNORANCE: 'And I will lead the blind in a way that they do not know, in paths that they have not known I will guide them' Isaiah 42:16.

Even though we may be ignorant and inexperienced of God's truth and ways, His promise is sure—He will guide.

Though we may be slow to under-stand His leading and may not rate ourselves as pillars in the church—He will guide.

Though we are so earnest that by our intense desire to do the will of God we actually blur the vision and confuse the issue still further—He will guide.

Though we feel puzzled and per-plexed, dull and distressed, weary and worn—He will guide.

He leadeth me, O blessed thought!
O words with heav'nly comfort fraught!
Whate'er I do, where'er I be
Still 'tis God's hand that leadeth me.

He leadeth me, He leadeth me,
By His own hand He leadeth me;
His faithful foll'wer I would be,
For by His hand He leadeth me.

Sometimes 'mid scenes of deepest gloom,
Sometimes where Eden's bowers bloom,
By waters still, o'er troubled sea,
Still 'tis His hand that leadeth me.

Lord, I would place my hand in Thine,
Nor ever murmur nor repine;
Content, whatever lot I see,
Since 'tis my God that leadeth me.

And when my task on earth is done,
When by Thy grace the vict'ry's won,
E'en death's cold wave I will not flee,
Since God through Jordan leadeth me.

(Joseph H. Gilmore)

4TH SEPTEMBER

WHEN GOD GUIDES

And I will lead the blind in a way that they do not know, in paths that they have not known I will guide them. I will turn the darkness before them into light

Isaiah 42:16

Yesterday we observed that God guides in spite of our abject Ignorance. As we continue to study the subject of guidance as outlined in Colin Peckham's booklet 'When God Guides' we find that:

God guides in spite of Apparent Darkness: 'I will turn the darkness before them into light' Isaiah 42:16. It would seem at times that no light shines upon our pathway and we are in complete darkness. No doors open and there seems to be no way ahead. We are saddened, confused and depressed. Yet God promises to shine through it all, 'I will turn the darkness before them into light'. Oh, trust Him in the darkness. Keep on trusting Him and His light will begin to glimmer. Soon it will come streaming through and will banish the darkness. God will usher in a day of light and joy in Himself and in His leading. This reminded me of the following song written by Don Moen:

God will make a way
Where there seems to be no way
He works in ways we cannot see
He will make a way for me

He will be my guide
Hold me closely to His side
With love and strength for each new day
He will make a way, He will make a way

By a roadway in the wilderness, He'll lead me
And rivers in the desert will I see
Heaven and Earth will fade but
His word will still remain
And He will do something new today

Oh, God will make a way
Where there seems to be no way
He works in ways we cannot see
He will make a way for me

He will be my guide
Hold me closely to His side
With love and strength for each new day
He will make a way, He will make a way

By a roadway in the wilderness, He'll lead me
And rivers in the desert will I see
Heaven and Earth will fade but
His word will still remain
And He will do something new today

Oh, God will make a way
Where there seems to be no way
He works in ways we cannot see
He will make a way for me

He will be my guide
Hold me closely to His side
With love and strength for each new day
He will make a way, He will make a way

With love and strength for each new day
He will make a way, He will make a way

5TH SEPTEMBER

LEAD ME ON

I will turn . . . the rough places into level ground. These are the things I do, and I do not forsake them.

Isaiah 42:16

Today we continue our thoughts on 'When God Guides'. Already we have considered that God guides in spite of our ABJECT IGNORANCE and of APPARENT DARKNESS.

Today we are going to learn that God guides in spite of AWKWARD OBSTACLES: 'I will turn . . . the rough places into level ground'. Obstacles sometimes crowd the pathway, obstructing the vision and seeming at times to be quite impenetrable. In his booklet Mr Peckham goes on to point out various obstacles such as:

- Physical weakness or sickness would appear to be a barrier to some aspects of God's service. Timothy, however, did not allow his 'frequent illnesses' to deter him from God's will for him. CT Studd, whose body was described as 'a museum of diseases' nevertheless plunged into the heart of Africa to establish a world-wide missionary society. Sickness and weakness could well be the instrument in God's hand to guide you into another form of service, yet it must be well tested to find out whether or not it is being used by Satan to divert you from God's highest will.
- Personalities differ and whilst one might fit the youth scene another might be used amongst the sick . . .
- To some their age is an obstacle. Either they are too young (Jeremiah's complaint) or too old. I am always reminded at what

Caleb said at the age of eighty five: 'So now give me this hill country of which the LORD spoke on that day . . . and I shall drive them out just as the LORD said' Joshua 14:12.

- The lack of finance has ever been and will ever be a stumbling block. It would seem, however, that if we are walking in the perfect plan of God, we need not be concerned about this aspect of things. Hudson Taylor's maxim still holds true: 'God's work done in God's way will never lack God's supplies'. I have found this to be true on many occasions over the years.
- The ordering of circumstances may seem to be a barrier. However, wherever you are, in whatever circumstances you will find yourself to be, God's promises hold true— He will be your guide.

Precious Lord, take my hand,
Lead me on, let me stand,
I am tired, I am weak, I am worn;
Through the storm, through the night,
Lead me on to the light:

(Thomas A. Dorsey)

Give me this mountain
I will not be turning back
Give me this mountain
For Your glory
Give me this mountain
Jesus' blood has overcome
So I'm not quitting till it's done

(Graham Kendrick)

6TH SEPTEMBER

LEAD US

Lead me, O Lord, in your righteousness because of my enemies; make your way straight before me.

Psalm 5:8

Today we conclude our thoughts on guidance taken from chapter 1 of Colin Peckham's little booklet called 'When God Guides' entitled 'The Certainty of God's Guidance'. We have reflected on the truths that God guides in spite of our ABJECT IGNORANCE, APPARENT DARKNESS and of AWKWARD OBSTACLES.

God also guides in spite of ACTIVE OPPOSITION: 'Lead me, O Lord, in your righteousness because of my enemies'. Satanic opposition is constant and relentless. From this we will never be free. Satan hates God's light and always seeks to sow confusion and bring darkness, using every means at his disposal. Our deliverance is constant recourse to the Blood of Jesus, to the trysting place (the practice of meeting in private) with God, to the place of quiet rest in Him. A more subtle from of opposition comes from uncrucified flesh, jealously, envying, and pride in the lives of fellow believers which may bring discouragement and a deviation from God's plan for you. An attack from without can be withstood in the name of the Lord, but subtle forms of backbiting, sly insinuations, hurtful attitudes and sometimes open confrontations with Christians when motives and actions are questioned, can cast us into a dungeon of despair and succeed in diverting us from God's perfect will. But worse still is our own unsanctified heart. Unless we are fully yielded, wholly cleansed, and completely controlled by the Lord, we can become our own enemy. Another source of opposition is the strong ideas of spiritual men or women whom we hold in high regard. They might be wholly wrong in their assessment of things because of their background, teaching, or grasp of the situation. In the strong attitudes they may adopt they could well turn us from what God would reveal of His plan and purpose. Finally God guides in spite of ATTEMPTED FLIGHT: 'If I take the wings of the morning and dwell in the uttermost parts of the sea, even there your hand shall lead me, and your right hand shall hold me' Psalm 139:9–10. When burdens become too great, you might want to run away—yes, even from God—and give it all up. But you cannot. You cannot separate yourself from the One who lives in you. Run from circumstances as you will, flee from God as you may, He will lead you. You cannot hide from God. Cast yourself upon His love and grace and allow Him to lead you.

I trust these thoughts about guidance based on thoughts from Colin Peckham's booklet: 'When God Guides', have been a help, encouragement and blessing to you.

Lead us, heavenly Father, lead us
o'er the world's tempestuous sea;
guard us, guide us, keep us, feed us,
for we have no help but thee;
yet possessing every blessing,
if our God our Father be.

(James Edmeston)

7TH SEPTEMBER

I ONCE WAS FAR FROM THE SAVIOUR

Therefore, if anyone is in Christ, he is a new creation.
The old has passed away; behold, the new has come.

2 Corinthians 5:17

This is the verse that Maureen Mateer used in the introduction to the book she wrote about her father Herbie Mateer called 'Stir Me'. Mr Mateer was the founder of the 'Bangor Worldwide Convention' held each year to inform and promote mission. From the age of eighteen months Herbie grew up in an hotel and bar environment in an Hotel in Ballyclare. As a result Herbie heard little of the gospel as a young boy and early teenager. However, his next door neighbour who was a drunkard came to know Christ as Lord and Saviour. Herbie saw a wonderful change in this life man's life, and wanted to know more about what happened to make such a change. In November 1925 a man by the name of Alex Kerr held a gospel mission in the town. God marvellously moved in the salvation of many mill workers in the town of Ballyclare at that time. Herbie decided to attend the meetings. His daughter writes that: 'When he listened that night to Alex Kerr, his response to the Lord was definite; he made a clear choice, a serious commitment to follow the Lord as He guided him through life'. And God did exactly that. Herbie went on to be used greatly of God. It is no wonder that one of Herbert J. Mateer's favourite songs was: 'I was once far away from the Saviour, And as vile as a sinner could be', written by Charles J. Butler.

I was once far away from the Saviour,
And as vile as a sinner could be;
I wondered if Christ, the Redeemer,
Could save a poor sinner like me.

I wandered on in the darkness,
Not a ray of light could I see,
And the tho't filled my heart with sadness,
There's no help for a sinner like me.

And then in that dark, lonely hour,
A voice sweetly whispered to me,
Saying Christ, the Redeemer, has power
To save a poor sinner like me.

I listened, and lo! 'twas the Saviour
Who was speaking so kindly to me;
I cried, I'm the chief of sinners,
Oh, save a poor sinner like me.

I then fully trusted in Jesus,
And, oh, what a joy came to me!
My heart was filled with his praises,
For saving a sinner like me.

No longer in darkness I'm walking,
For the light is now shining on me,
And now unto others I'm telling
How he saved a poor sinner like me.

And when life's journey is over,
And I the dear Saviour shall see,
I'll praise him for ever and ever,
For saving a sinner like me.

8TH SEPTEMBER

THE LAND OF SAINTS AND SCHOLARS

Look, I tell you, lift up your eyes, and see that the fields are white for harvest

John 4:35

I had the privilege of attending and manning a mission's stand in the 'Global Village' at the Bangor Worldwide Missions Convention' over a ten year period. Bangor is a seaside resort, in Co Down, Northern Ireland. The history of Bangor goes back to the fifth century. When Christianity was being threatened with extinction Bangor was sending missionaries to carry the Gospel to Britain and Europe. A thoroughly evangelical Church had been established in Bangor by St Patrick some years earlier. The fruit of his work was a Church sending out foreign missionaries. Comgall was one of Patrick's followers. The ancient Abbey of Bangor, which was founded in 588 A.D by Comgall, quickly became one of the most famous monastic settlements and missionary schools of Western Christendom. So many young men wanted to follow Comgall's teaching and that resulted in it not being able to house them all in one place. As a result many cell groups were formed and other monasteries were built throughout the whole Island of Ireland. The students were taught the Christian faith and how to share it with others. For almost three hundred years these missionaries' schools were famous all over Europe. As a result Ireland became known as 'The land of Saints and Scholars'. It is estimated that some three thousand missionaries left its shores to go to Scotland, England and on to mainland Europe.

It is easy to see how God would continue to use Bangor as a place to promote the Great Commission. The following are the first and last verses and chorus of a hymn written in 1937 by James E Simpson for the first Bangor Worldwide Convention:

Ancient seat of Christian learning, from your shores have sped
Saints and Scholars, with the Gospel, So divinely led.
To those shores from other nations, seeking truth they came;
Learned the truth of God's salvation, Forth they went again.

Who from ancient seat of learning,
Scorning dangers, perils, daring,
Will go forth to hearts still yearning,
With the light again?

Hearken, all ye men and maidens seeking honour, name;
Hear the call for more disciples, Must it sound in vain?
Thrill with pride at holy mem'ries, Town of ancient fame,
Answer, 'Glory is reviving'. We'll go forth again.

Since 1937 God has used the Bangor Worldwide Convention to showcase the missionary cause. Many have heard the call to go, other to pray and others to give or indeed a combination of all three.

9TH SEPTEMBER

Pray without ceasing.

1 Thessalonians 5:17

During the year of writing this devotional book the BBC reported that Gracehill village near Ballymena Co Antrim Northern Ireland, has moved a step closer to securing World Heritage Site status. Gracehill was founded by the Moravian Church in 1759 and is the only complete Moravian settlement in Ireland.

The Moravian Church was founded by Jan Hus in the early 15th-century. The eighteenth century saw the renewal of the Moravian Church through the patronage of Count Nicholas Ludwig von Zinzendorf. The Moravians were passionate about prayer and missions. Count Zinzendorf said, 'I have but one passion — it is He, it is He alone. The world is the field and the field is the world; and henceforth that country shall be my home where I can be most used in winning souls for Christ'.

When Zinzendorf was 27 years old, he took into his home a single Moravian refugee. Before long, Zinzendorf had 300 Moravian refugees living on his estate and he became their spiritual leader. They lived in a village called Hernnhut, Germany. Under Zinzendorf's leadership, they prayed together, studied God's Word together, and grew spiritually together.

There on August 12, 1727, a great revival started. According to Oswald Smith, 'They made the discovery that the Church could not save them, that there was no salvation in its creeds, doctrines or dogmas; that good works, moral living, commandment-keeping, praying and Bible reading, could not avail, much less culture, character or conduct. They found that Christ alone could save, that He was willing and able to receive sinners at a moment's notice, that justification, the forgiveness of sins, the new birth, etc. were instantaneous experiences received the very moment a sinner believed on Christ, that salvation was through grace and by faith, apart from the deeds of the law, that when a man is saved he has peace with God, and that he receives the assurance of salvation by the witness of the Holy Spirit in his heart'

On August 12, 1727, the Moravians conducted an all-night prayer meeting. The group decided to start a prayer vigil. They designated a place of prayer in the village, and they prayed in groups of two or three for one-hour increments.

There are 168 one-hour time slots in a week. The Moravians filled all 168-hour time slots with two to three people per hour. For 24 hours a day, seven days a week, two to three people were always praying in the place of prayer. This around the clock prayer meeting went on for 110 years.

By 1791, 65 years after commencement of those prayer meetings, the small Moravian community had sent 300 missionaries to the ends of the earth.

O that today the Holy Spirit may ignite in us a passion for prayer and a fearless ambition for the gospel and the Great Commission.

10TH SEPTEMBER

THE BIBLICAL THRESHOLD

The years of our life are seventy, or even by reason of strength eighty; yet their span is but toil and trouble; they are soon gone, and we fly away.

Psalm 90:10

The coronation of King Charles III aged 74 years took place on May 6th 2023. On his 70th birthday he was invited by the Editor of Country Life to take over the editorship of the November edition. In it speaking about the Editor's invitation to do so he said: 'However, he told me the intention was to mark my 70th birthday, which, of course, is extremely kind of him, but is nevertheless associated with the alarming realisation that I have reached the biblical threshold of three score years and ten, with all the scars that go with it'.

It is good to know that King Charles 111 is aware of his mortality. However, with that knowledge comes a responsibility. In verse 12 of Psalm 90 we further read: 'So teach us to number our days that we may get a heart of wisdom'.

In this verse we have:

1. THE TEACHER: The Lord Himself is the teacher of this truth: 'So teach us to number our days'. In His life on earth He taught us this all important truth. He taught us to prepare in this life for eternity. In fact He asked the question: 'For what does it profit a man to gain the whole world and forfeit his soul?' Mark 8:36. Jesus came into the world to die. The hour that shadowed all His life was the hour of His death. His eye was ever towards His finished work on the Cross.

For this very purpose He came into the world.

2. THE TEACHING: 'to number our days'. We need always to be doing a sum. That of adding up our days on earth. And yet only God can teach us the true answer. We do know however, that our days are short, uncertain and swift. The hymn writer put it as follows:

Time is gliding swiftly by,
Death and judgment draweth nigh,
To the arms of Jesus fly,
Be in time.

Oh, I pray you count the cost,
Ere the fatal line be crossed,
And your soul in hell be lost,
Be in time.

Thomas Carlyle often said: 'Prepare us for those solemn events, death, judgment, and eternity'

3. THE TAUGHT: 'that we may get a heart of wisdom'. Those who are really taught have heart wisdom. Therefore the most important thing people can do in life is to prepare for death by repenting of their sins and putting their faith in the Lord Jesus Christ as Saviour and Lord. That is heart wisdom. For believers true wisdom is to do His will, walk in His ways, and work for Him until He calls us home or until He comes again.

11TH SEPTEMBER

HOUSEBOUND

And Paul dwelt two whole years in his own hired
house, and received all that came in unto him.

Acts 28:30

One of the prayer points on most Church Prayer Bulletins is to pray for those who can no longer come to the Church meetings due to old age or illness. Paul knew what it was like to be housebound for two years while he was detained in Rome. Most of us experienced what it was like to be housebound through the various 'Lockdowns' due to the coronavirus pandemic in 2020 and 2021. It was just wonderful to get back to Church and to get out and about thereafter again. Therefore today let us give prayerful thought to those who are housebound, to their carers and to those who visit and minister to them. The following is a little poem called 'Housebound' which I kept from a Church bulletin I received many years ago:

LORD—today I need a little help for I'm feeling rather low,
I know I'm getting older Lord and I've become a little slow.
This pain is hard to bear sometimes so forgive my falling tears,
I'm here alone most every day and my heart is full of fears.

I know that you are with me Lord and we have a little talk each day,
But I need a little company still for this I humbly pray.
Your church is only down the road, how I wish I could get there,
I'd love again to worship and find fellowship in prayer.

Your people are so busy Lord there's lots to do,
But I'd love to have them visit me and tell me more of you,
I miss the lovely hymns I sang when first you touched my heart,
I often close my eyes in prayer and once more take a part.

With those who really love you Lord I can see them in my mind,
And though I can't be really there true fellowship I find.
For you are with them, my Lord, yet I know you're also here with me,
I thank you for this hour of prayer, your love and company.

I'm feeling so much better Lord For this time I've spent with you.
Forgive self-pity, discontent, Your love will see me through.

(Unknown)

Dr Sandy Rodgers speaking at a missionary conference I attended made the following remarks on the ministry of confinement based on Acts 28:30: though restricted in movement by being chained in his hired house Paul used his pen, said his prayers and talked to people. Basically. Paul was saying I am restricted in movement. I am chained but the Word of the Lord is not bound. Perhaps due to unseen circumstances you are restricted in movement and now housebound. God can still use you in ministry and to minister from there.

12TH SEPTEMBER

DEFENDER OF THE FAITH - NOT DEFENDER OF FAITH

*Beloved . . . contend for the faith that was
once for all delivered to the saints.*

Jude 3

King Charles 111 has always shown an interest in being an interfaith monarch. In the 1990s he said he would like to be 'Defender of Faith'. The question to be considered today is: what does the Bible say on this matter?

Paul Young commenting on Jude 3 wrote: 'The faith here actually means: what is believed or the contents of belief. It is essentially the things which are believed in, especially about the Lord Jesus. This body of truth, namely the Holy Bible, was finally given once for all'.

Dr Sam Gordon comments in a similar vein of thought: 'There is a distinction in the New Testament between 'faith' and 'the faith'. 'Faith' refers to act of believing; 'the faith' speaks of things believed. It is the sum total of revealed truth; the final and full revelation of God as we have in the scriptures. It is the body of doctrine unfolded from Genesis to Revelation. The Faith is the Word of God'.

In the light of this we can conclude that if the Christian faith is not the only true religion, it is not true at all. Christ said 'I am the way, and the truth, and the life. No one comes to the Father except through me' John 14:6. The first disciples preached the same message: 'And there is salvation in no one else, for there is no other name under heaven given among men by which we must be saved' Acts 4:12. Not only does the Bible claim Jesus Christ as the only Saviour, it also declares 'the God and Father of our Lord Jesus Christ' to be the only true God: 2 Corinthians 1:3. He is the true and living God.

Let us in our day and generation: 'contend for the faith that was once for all delivered to the saints'

*Thy hand, O God, has guided
thy flock, from age to age;
the wondrous tale is written,
full clear on every page;
our fathers owned thy goodness,
and we their deeds record;
and both of these bear witness:
one Church, one Faith, one Lord.*

*Thy heralds brought glad tidings
to greatest as to least;
they bade men rise and hasten
to share the great King's feast;
and this was all their teaching
in every deed and word;
to all alike proclaiming:
one Church, one Faith, one Lord.*

*Through many a day of darkness,
through many a scene of strife,
the faithful few fought bravely
to guard the nation's life.
Their gospel of redemption,
sin pardoned, man restored,
was all in this enfolded:
one Church, one Faith, one Lord.*

(Edward Hayes Plumptre)

13TH SEPTEMBER

HOW TO USE THE BIBLE

Until I come, devote yourself to the public reading
of Scripture, to exhortation, to teaching.

1 Timothy 4:13

The following is a list of recommended portions of scripture to read for various situations you may find yourself in which I have in my study for many years from an unknown source. I trust you find God speaking into various situations you might find yourself in through them

- When in sorrow, read John 14.
- When men fail you, read Psalm 27.
- When you have sinned, read Psalm 51.
- When you worry, read Matthew 6:19–34.
- When you are in danger, read Psalm 91.
- When you are depressed, read Psalm 34.
- When God seems far away, read Psalm 139.
- When you are discouraged, read Isaiah 40.
- When doubts come upon you, try John 7.17.
- When you are lonely or fearful, read Psalm 23.
- When you forget your blessings, read Psalm 103.
- When your faith needs stirring, read Hebrews 11.
- When you feel down and out, read Romans 8: 31–39.
- When you want courage for your task, read Joshua 1.
- When the world seems bigger than God, read Psalm 90.
- When you want peace and rest, read Matthew 11:25–30.
- When you want Christian assurance, read Romans 8:1–30.
- When you leave home, read Psalm 121.
- When you grow critical or bitter, read 1 Corinthians 13.
- When your prayers grow selfish, read Psalm 67.
- When you think of investments, read Mark 10:17–31.
- If you want to be fruitful, read John 15. (And we all should).
- For Paul's secret of happiness, read Colossians 3:12–17.
- For Paul's idea of Christianity, read 2 Corinthians 5:15–19.
- For Paul's rule of daily life, read Romans 12.
- For a great invitation and opportunity, read Isaiah 55.
- For Jesus' idea of a Christian, read Matthew 5.
- For James' idea of religion, read James 1:19–27.
- For Jesus idea' of prayer, read Luke 11:1–13.
- For a picture of worship, read Isaiah 58:1–12.
- For the Prophet's idea of religion, read Isaiah 1:10–18.
- Why not follow Psalm 119:11, and hide some of these in your memory?

Reading the Bible—
I love the Word of God!
Reading the Bible—
I love the Word of God!

Every verse reveals Yourself to me,
Every line conveys reality.
When I pray the words that You breathed out
You become so real to me.

14TH SEPTEMBER

PRAYING FOR MISSIONARIES

Whenever Moses held up his hand, Israel prevailed, and whenever he lowered his hand, Amalek prevailed. But Moses hands grew weary, so they took a stone and put it under him, and he sat on it, while Aaron and Hur held up his hands, one on one side, and the other on the other side. So his hands were steady until the going down of the sun. And Joshua overwhelmed Amalek and his people with the sword

Exodus 17:11–13

The Aarons and Hurs who hold up the hands of missionaries, ministers and frontline Christian workers by earnest prayer may be the ones who decide the victory. Victory or defeat will crown their service in the Lord's harvest fields! The following is a list of ways which show how you might pray for missionaries: PRAY FOR:

PROTECTION: Pray that the Lord would protect and provide the missionary and his family with safety on and off the field. Unfamiliar areas of the world present unique and different conditions from those in the home country of the missionary.

PENETRATION: Pray that the Lord will provide help for the missionary in completing the necessary paperwork and securing the visa required for entering the country of service. I spoke recently to a missionary family who moved from N Ireland to the Republic of Ireland. The amount of paperwork concerning getting the children into schools, registering with doctors, driving licences and the list goes on, was massive. Yet God gave them grace and help to work their way through it.

PRIORITY: Pray that the missionaries would stay focused on their primary task of spreading the Gospel.

PLANTING OF CHURCHES: Pray for the salvation of souls and that the missionary would be successful in establishing New Testament Churches.

PURITY: Pray that the missionary would be delivered from temptations and remain pure and upright as they serve the Lord Jesus.

PHYSICAL HEALTH; Pray for their overall health and any specific health needs they have made known.

PROVISION: Pray that the Lord would provide for their financial, physical, social and spiritual needs.

PREPARATION: Pray that the Lord would provide them quality study and prayer time to prepare for preaching, teaching and for meaningful family worship.

POWER: Pray that the missionary would be filled with the Holy Spirit, have the mind of Christ, and bear fruit.

The work of Aaron and Hur was apparently more important than the work of Moses and Joshua. The battle for or against God's people went, not according to the faithfulness and intercession of Moses or the courage and strength of Joshua, but according to the undergirding support of Aaron and Hur. Our faithfulness in prayer is more important than we can possibly realise: 'And whatever you ask in prayer, you will receive, if you have faith' Matthew 21:22.

15TH SEPTEMBER

FREEDOM

And wherever he enters, say to the master of the house, The Teacher says, where is my guest room, where I may eat the Passover with my disciples?

Mark 14:14

I had the privilege of making a short-term mission trip to Haiti in 2008 as regional director of OMS in N Ireland to spend time with some of our missionaries and visit the various ministries our mission was involved in. One of those was a radio ministry.

While there I spent a day on outreach with Emmanuel Felix who at that time was the Extension Director of Missionary Activities of 4VEH in Haiti. Here is an outline of his testimony for your encouragement today:

'In 1969, as the Chief Civil Court Judge for my hometown, I did all I thought could lead me to happiness and freedom—participated in worldly pleasures with the crowd and worked to fulfil an ambition to become a member of the Haitian Parliament. Suddenly, without warning, I was arrested and thrown into a filthy prison. I was a victim of politics and jealous men. Later I was transferred to a Cap-Haitian prison. There I heard a voice in the darkness, 'Lord, have pity on these. They are goats, some sheep. Remind the sheep of Your pasture'... I prayed, 'Lord, if I am a goat, make me a sheep of Your pasture. Cleanse my soul and change my heart'. This was my very first prayer of repentance. Later, in my distress, I prayed, 'Lord, I have not yet had the privilege of reading Your Word, give me Your Word'. But where was I to find a copy of God's Word in the filth of a prison? Ten days later a prisoner loaned me his New Testament until he was freed. 'Lord, send me a New Testament of my own so I can read its entirety'. What a miracle—a New Testament arrived at dawn the next day!

My conversion to Jesus Christ came through reading Mark 14:12–15. The word 'disciple' puzzled me. I asked myself 'what is a disciple? Am I a disciple?' A voice responded, 'The Holy Spirit convicted you so you could become a disciple, now it's time for you to decide'. I made my decision, 'Lord save me and make me Your disciple'. On the afternoon of August 26, 1969, I was granted my physical freedom. My true freedom came the next afternoon as I confessed Jesus as Lord before those who had been steadfast in prayer for me. Jesus Christ made me a new man, a worker in His Kingdom, an ambassador for God—His disciple!'

'So if the Son sets you free, you will be free indeed' John 8:36.

16TH SEPTEMBER

A LIGHT AND BANNER

Little children, you are from God and have overcome them,
for he who is in you is greater than he who is in the world.

1 John 4:4

While in Haiti in 2008 I read the following article written by an unknown author, which I feel will encourage you and make you aware of real spiritual warfare in various parts of the world:

'The Bible tells us of God's awesome power, how He astonished the nations with wonders. We rarely, if ever, see events like that. Some try to explain that these things just don't happen anymore. People in the western world place faith in science—that which can be sensed, measured, quantified. Haiti is one country that recognises the power of the spiritual realm and is a nation gripped by the power of voodoo. Historically, witchcraft came to the island with the slaves. The people of Haiti made a contract with Satan that if he delivered them from Napoleon's armies they would dedicate their nation to him for 200 years. In 1804 the island was freed from the French, and darkness has reigned ever since. But even in desperate darkness, the light shines. One U. S. pastor recently returned from a trip to Haiti. During this trip he had an opportunity to talk with a couple of witchdoctors. From inside a cockfighting ring they discussed different aspects of the spiritual world. The witchdoctors said they could control the lives of the people, even cast spells on each other, but they could not put a spell on an 'authentic Christian'. They said that their spells or incantations had no power over a 'genuine Christian'. Who is a 'genuine Christian?' Years ago a missionary felt guided to focus his evangelism on one Haitian witch, who was in charge of over 600 other witches and witchdoctors throughout Haiti. Eventually this lady was won to Christ. Since most witchcraft takes place at night the missionary asked how she knew who Christians were in the dark. She said that in the dark true Christians had a light coming from their forehead. This enabled her to see a banner on their chest. She added that some of the people the missionary thought would have a light, didn't have a light. This is real, folks!'

In 1997, many Haitians sought to renew the contract with Satan. Because Christians prayed, a torrential down pour and bolts of lightning kept the people from the renewal ceremony. Attempts were also made to renew the contract in 2004. It also failed. The sacred tree where the original ceremony took place is dying. Prayer is a powerful weapon. Keep on praying.

Jesus is stronger than Satan and sin,
Satan to Jesus must bow;
Therefore I triumph without and within:
Jesus saves me now.

(Arthur Cleveland Downer)

17TH SEPTEMBER

NO FREEDOM FOR HAITI WITHOUT JESUS

*For you were called to freedom, brothers. Only
do not use your freedom as an opportunity for the
flesh, but through love serve one another.*

Galatians 5:13

Two years after my visit to Haiti in 2008, it had a devastating earthquake on the 12th January 2010, when it is estimated 200,000 people lost their lives and 300,000 were injured. Just weeks before the earthquake one of our young OMS missionaries a physiotherapist by profession returned to that land. As the news of the earthquake spread many churches throughout the UK but particularly in N Ireland gave thousands of pounds to the Christian relief effort through OMS. In times of great need it is just wonderful to experience the generosity of God's people. At that time one newspaper described Haiti as follows: 'Until Tuesday afternoon a cataclysmic earthquake was the only disaster that had not befallen Haiti in the 205 years since a slave revolt won independence from Napoleonic France. Bankrupt, barren, misruled and ravaged by nature and human violence, the country on the western end of Hispaniola island serves as a text-book example of a dysfunctional nation'.

Can God work in such a situation? Does God honour the prayers and giving of His people at such a time? I will endeavour to answer these questions from two snippets of information sent to me later that year from two of our workers there. The first is a response from Julie Briggs a young missionary from N Ireland to a request I made that she send me a short report to share at a Sunday service I was taking: 'I am sure everyone wants to know what OMS Haiti is doing right now post the earthquake. First we ran 4 weeks of mobile clinics in Diquini, Port-Au-Prince where thousands of people were given medical treatment and over 700 people came to know the Lord. As a result OMS planted a church right there in the middle of tent city. One of our seminary students has been leading the church until August when he returns to the seminary. We have had two trips back to Port-Au-Prince, one in April and one in October to continue with evangelism and to encourage the church. The church is growing and doing well'. The second is an extract from a report from Storly Michel one of our national OMS workers: 'I don't know how any other nation on earth would react to such a tragedy, such a poor response from our own government and so forth. I still don't know what will happen in Haiti long term but all secular journalists, missionaries, the church in Haiti and myself have witnessed something extraordinary in the midst of all this suffering: people are praising God for His faithfulness'.

Remember the prayers, love and giving of God's people makes a massive difference no matter the circumstances, to the people affected and to missionaries and national believers living there.

18TH SEPTEMBER

LET THE LOWER LIGHTS BE BURNING

*For at one time you were darkness, but now you are
light in the Lord. Walk as children of light.*

Ephesians 5:8

One morning I went to get my daily newspaper. However on that particular day they were all gone, so I purchased the 'Daily Express' instead. In it there was a little column called 'Forgotten Verse'. They promote the column as follows: 'If you can't remember the words to a favourite verse or song from yesteryear, send a snippet and we'll do our best to find all the wonderful words'. On this occasion a lady remembers her Royal Marine grandfather owning a Pianola with one roll featuring a line about a struggling seaman. The song is identified as 'Let the lower lights be burning'. They then go on to print the song and give the following explanation about it: 'The work is by 19th century American composer and hymn writer Philip Bliss, who was inspired by a sermon on a ship being wrecked near Cleveland harbour, because the lower beams of a lighthouse were not shining:

*Brightly beams our Father's mercy
From His lighthouse evermore;
But to us He gives the keeping
Of the lights along the shore.*

Refrain:

*Let the lower lights be burning!
Send a gleam across the wave!
Some poor fainting, struggling seaman
You may rescue, you may save.*

*Dark the night of sin has settled,
Loud the angry billows roar;
Eager eyes are watching, longing,
For the lights along the shore.*

*Trim your feeble lamp, my brother!
Some poor seaman, tempest-tossed,
Trying now to make the harbour,
In the darkness may be lost.*

On further investigation I found out that Bliss was in a meeting where DL Moody was preaching. He related the story of a shipwreck on a dark and tempestuous night, when not even a star was visible. A ship was approaching the harbour of Cleveland, with a pilot on board. The captain, noticing only one light as they drew near — that from the lighthouse —asked the pilot if he was quite sure that it was Cleveland harbour, as other lights should have been burning at the harbour mouth. The pilot assured him it was. However, in the darkness of the harbour mouth he missed the channel, the ship struck many rocks, and in the stormy waters many lives were lost. Moody concluded by saying, 'Brethren, the Master will take care of the great lighthouse; let us keep the lower lights burning'. This inspired Bliss to write this challenging song. Bliss likens the main lighthouse to the mercy of God and the Lord's gracious provision for the salvation of sinners. And he uses the channel lights to picture our witness to what Christ has done. If we do not shine with the light of the gospel, who knows how many will fail to make the safe harbour of God's salvation?

I trust our lower lights are burning today.

19TH SEPTEMBER

THE LORD'S HOUSE

Even the sparrow finds a home, and the swallow a nest for herself, where she may lay her young, at your altars, O Lord of hosts, my King and my God

Psalm 84:3

It is thought that Psalm 84 was written by King David while he was an exile from Jerusalem during the rebellion of his son Absalom. He was a man who loved the House of the Lord. To David, there was no place on this earth as special as that one place where the Lord had chosen to place His Name and demonstrate His presence. For David, the Tabernacle was the place where he desired to be. In this New Testament era this equates to the local bible believing church. One bible commentator said: 'It is at church that we get a glimpse, a foretaste, an appetizer for heaven. If you are looking forward to heaven, then you should also look forward to attending church, because church is the practice ground for heaven.'

As David thought about the Lord's House and about how far away from it he was, he began to reflect on the little birds that made their homes in the Lord's tabernacle. He mentions, the sparrow and the swallow. The sparrow could be described as a worthless bird and the swallow as a wandering bird. However, David tells us that both the sparrow and the swallow found exactly what they needed at the House of God.

How lovely is thy dwelling place,
O Lord of hosts, to me!
The tabernacles of thy grace,
how pleasant, Lord, they be!

My thirsty soul longs vehemently;
it faints thy courts to see:
my very heart and flesh cry out,
O living God, for thee.

Behold the sparrow findeth out
a house wherein to rest;
the swallow also for her young
hath built herself a nest,

Thine altars, where she might bring forth
her young in safe abode,
O thou Almighty Lord of hosts,
my Sovereign and my God.

How blest are they that in thy house
forever give thee praise.
Blest are all those whose strength thou art,
in whose heart are thy ways. (Unknown)

How lovely is your dwelling-place,
O Lord of hosts, to me;
my thirsting soul longs eagerly
within your courts to be.

Beside your altars, Lord of all,
the swallows find a nest;
happy are those who dwell with you
and praise you without rest;

And happy those whose hearts are set
upon the pilgrim ways:
you are the water when they thirst,
their guide towards your face.

How blest are they that in your house
for ever give you praise:
one day with you is better spent
than thousands in dark ways.

The Lord will hold back no good thing
from those who justly live;
to all who trust, the Lord of hosts
will all his blessings give.

(Scottish Psalter, 1650)

20TH SEPTEMBER

HOW GOD ANSWERS PRAYER

O you who hear prayer, to you shall all flesh come.

Psalm 65:2

Every time I read verse two of Psalm 65 my heart rejoices. One of the reasons being I have proved it to be true. God does listen to our prayers, but more importantly He also answers our prayers according to His will. The following is a lovely story I read which makes the point clearly:

'One Sunday morning, Dr George W. Truett took the following verse as his text for his message: 'If two of you shall agree on earth as touching anything that they shall ask, it shall be done for them of My Father which is in heaven.' (Matthew 18:19). Having quoted his text, Dr Truett asked: 'Do you believe it?'

Of course he did not expect an answer, but he paused for a moment that his question might be understood. A very poor member of the congregation rose to her feet and said, 'I believe it, pastor, and I want you to claim that promise with me.'

'It staggered me, "said Dr Truett'. I knew I did not have the faith to claim the promise, but before I had time to answer, a big, burly blacksmith in the congregation rose to his feet; 'I'll claim that promise with you, Auntie', he said, and together the two, the poor washer-woman and the blacksmith, dropped to their knees in the aisle and poured out their hearts in prayer for the salvation of the woman's husband."

Now it happened that this man was a riverboat captain on the Rio Grande, a swearing, foul-mouthed drunken sot, and he was at that moment sleeping off a drink at home. That night, for the first time in many years at least, the old riverboat captain was in the church and while the pastor preached the woman prayed, not for the salvation of her husband, rather she was thanking God for it, for she seemed to know it would happen that night. And of course, when the invitation was given, this old foul-mouthed captain came to give his heart to the Lord, and he became one of the most dependable and faithful workers in that church.

Hear our prayer, O LORD,
hear our prayer, O LORD;
incline thine ear to us,
and grant us thy peace.

(Unknown)

When my way groweth drear
Precious Lord, linger near
When my light is almost gone
Hear my cry, hear my call
Hold my hand lest I fall
Take my hand, precious Lord
Lead me on

(Thomas A. Dorsey)

21ST SEPTEMBER

INSPIRED OBEDIENCE

And Samuel said, "Has the Lord as great delight in burnt offerings and sacrifices, as in obeying the voice of the Lord? Behold, to obey is better than sacrifice, and to listen than the fat of rams

1 Samuel 15:22

One of our retired missionaries Jim Smyth now in his 89th year residing in the USA, sent me a number of magazines published in the 1960s and 70s by 'The Oriental Missionary Society'. The following is part of an article on 'Inspired Obedience' in one of its issues that I trust you find helpful and challenging: 'Obedience to God is one of the essential factors of the Christian life. But this obedience is not the laborious and painful task of following a system of laws, regulations and standards in our own strength; rather, it is the obedience inspired by love to God, obedience which is spontaneous and normal because of the presence and power of the Holy Spirit in the heart. This inspired obedience is real, it is 'in order that the righteous requirement of the law might be fulfilled in us, who walk not according to the flesh but according to the Spirit' Romans 8:4. It is the obedience of love 'Love does no wrong to a neighbour; therefore love is the fulfilling of the law' Romans 13:10.

The new covenant is the basis of such inspired obedience, for in this new covenant, God said, 'For this is the covenant that I will make with the house of Israel after those days, declares the Lord: I will put my laws into their minds, and write them on their hearts, and I will be their God, and they shall be my people' Hebrews 8:10. Hence, the living of a life of obedience to God is not a burden and struggle to a devoted Christian. Obedience is the delightful response of a surrendered heart; the inspiration of an inner devotedness to God. (Selected).

Can you be obedient
To the Lord of all,
Though the earth should totter,
Though the heav'ns should fall?
Face e'en a disaster
With a faith-filled heart,
Knowing naught can harm him
Who with Christ will start?

Can you be obedient
To the Lord you serve,
Never even flinch, friend,
Never even swerve;
Though your next step onward
Seems to lead to death?
Can you then obey Him
Without bated breath?

Can you trust your Leader
When He bids you go
Right into a battle
With a mighty foe?
Can you step up briskly
And with joy obey?
Can you fight the battle,
Till the end of day?

Can you? Then beloved,
Christ just waits for you;
Listen for His orders,
Glad His will to do;
Then when soldiers muster
At the set of sun,
And your name is mentioned,
Christ will say, 'Well done.'

(Margaret E. Barber)

22ND SEPTEMBER

NO BOOK LIKE IT

Your word is a lamp to my feet and a light to my path.

Psalm 119:105

On a recent visit at my daughter's home she showed me three new copies of the Bible she had purchased for her three children. In the front of her son's she referenced Psalm 119:105. You can give no better gift to your children than the Word of God.

I was also blessed by the following heading referring to the Bible in the 'News Letter' newspaper: 'Bible still most read book', the article went on to say that The Global United Bible Societies network (UBS) has confirmed that a record number of 57 new translations of the Bible or its parts were completed in 2022. Of these 14, were full translations such as those for Nigerian or Ethiopian languages, five were New Testament, and 38 were for specific parts of the Bible. This means 100 million individuals worldwide can read and access scripture in their native language for the first time. What a blessing.

Samuel Chadwick (1860–1932) was an English Methodist preacher. He was born in Burnley into a strong Methodist home, he signed the pledge when he was eight, worked in a cotton mill 12 hours per day as a youth, and was minimally educated. He was converted at the age of ten, and immediately began praying three times a day.

He began preaching at the age of 16. He went on to be a Methodist Minister and was President of the Methodist Conference 1918–1919. Chadwick was known as a man of prayer but also had a high regard for the Word of God. Speaking of the Bible he said: 'I have guided my life by the Bible for more than sixty years, and I tell you there is no book like it. It is a miracle of literature, a perennial spring of wisdom, a wonder of surprises, a revelation of mystery, an infallible guide of conduct, and an unspeakable source of comfort. Pay no attention to people who discredit it, for I tell you that they speak without knowledge. It is the Word of God itself. Study it according to its own direction. Live by its principles. Believe its message. Follow its precepts. No man is uneducated who knows the Bible, and no one is wise who is ignorant of its teachings'.

The Grand Old Book
You Find The Words Of Comfort
Wherever You May Look
In Sorrow Or In Pain
His Promises Are Plain
So Keep On Believing
In The Grand Old Book

(Unknown)

23RD SEPTEMBER

POSTBOX TO HEAVEN

*About midnight Paul and Silas were
praying and singing hymns to God.*

My attention was drawn to an article in the press regarding installing 'postboxes to heaven' in graveyards. Apparently 'The Postbox to Heaven' idea has been developed in England and it was given particular comfort to children who have lost a grandparent helping them deal with the loss. The whole idea is fraught with various logistical problems. But more importantly it has no Biblical support.

However we as Christians reverently speaking have a post-box to Heaven. That 'post-box' being that of prayer. Not only can we send messages to Heaven through the avenue of prayer but we also get a response back. God does hear and answer prayer.

Prayer is possible at all times, prayer is profitable at all times, and prayer is powerful at all times. The following are a few scriptural references making this point in the book of James: 'If any of you lacks wisdom, let him ask God, who gives generously to all without reproach, and it will be given him. But let him ask in faith, with no doubting, for the one who doubts is like a wave of the sea that is driven and tossed by the wind' James 1:5–6; 'Is anyone among you suffering? Let him pray. Is anyone cheerful? Let him sing praise. Is anyone among you sick? Let him call for the elders of the church, and let them pray over him, anointing him with oil in the name of the Lord. And the prayer of faith will save the one who is sick, and the Lord will raise him up' James 5:13–15; 'Elijah was a man with a nature like ours, and he prayed fervently that it might not rain, and for three years and six months it did not rain on the earth. Then he prayed again, and heaven gave rain, and the earth bore its fruit' James 5:17–18. Yes prayer does change things.

Come, my soul, thy suit prepare:
Jesus loves to answer prayer;
He Himself has bid thee pray,
Therefore will not say thee nay;
Therefore will not say thee nay.

(John Newton)

Approach, my soul, the mercy seat
Where Jesus answers prayer;
There humbly fall before his feet,
For none can perish there.

(John Newton)

I believe God answers prayer,
Answers always, everywhere
I may cast my anxious care,
Burdens I could never bear,
On the God who heareth prayer.

Never need my soul despair
Since He bids me boldly dare
To the secret place repair,
There to prove He answers prayer.

(George Mueller)

24TH SEPTEMBER

ETERNAL DESTINY

Today, if you hear his voice, do not harden your hearts.

Hebrews 3:15

While writing this devotional I read an article in one of the daily papers about procrastination. The following is an extract from the article: 'Procrastination is the thief of time, so the saying goes—and a new study seems to support it. It is found that those with a tendency to dither and delay not only waste time but are more likely to be unhealthy, financially worse off and depressed'. Not a good advertisement for putting things off, suggesting negative outcomes in this life.

However it led me to think that it is much more serious to procrastinate about spiritual matters. They have serious consequences regarding our eternal destiny and welfare. The following is a warning regarding this, written in 1837 by Joseph A Alexander:

There is a time, we know not when,
A place, we know not where,
That marks the destiny of men
In glory or despair

There is a line by us unseen,
That crosses every path;
The hidden boundary between
God's patience and His wrath

O what is that mysterious bourn,
By which man's path is crossed,
Beyond which, God Himself has sworn,
The soul that goes is lost.

How long might I go on in sin?
How long will God forbear?
Where does hope end, and where begin
The confines of despair?

The answer from the skies is sent:
Ye who from God depart
While it is called today repent,
And harden not your heart.

How wonderful it is having your eternal destiny settled. What peace and joy it brings in this life and then bliss in heaven throughout eternity. However for those who know not Jesus, who perhaps put off the most important decision they can ever make, eternity will be that of eternal despair.

Don't let it be said, too late; but come,
There's naught to win by delay;
Prepare then thy soul for its heav'nly home,
And enter the fold today.

Don't let it be said, too late, too late,
Or, vain will thy pleadings be;
Be ready to enter the golden gate
While open it stands for thee

(Ida L. Reed)

25TH SEPTEMBER

SIMPLE EFFECTIVE PERSONAL PRAYERS

Lord, teach us to pray.

Luke 11:1

James Montgomery got it right when he wrote the following verse of his lovely hymn: 'Prayer is the soul's sincere desire '

*Prayer is the simplest form of speech
that infant lips can try,
prayer the sublimest strains that reach
the Majesty on high.*

Today I want to look at four simple personal prayers of four well known Bible characters which God answered:

- PETER: Save ME: 'But when he saw the wind, he was afraid, and beginning to sink he cried out, LORD, SAVE ME' Matthew 14:30
- DAVID: Teach ME: 'TEACH ME your way, O Lord, and lead me on a level path because of my enemies' Psalm 27:11.
- ISAIAH: Send ME: 'And I heard the voice of the Lord saying, Whom shall I send, and who will go for us? Then I said, Here I am! SEND ME' Isaiah 6:8.
- JABEZ: Keep ME: ' Jabez called upon the God of Israel, saying, Oh that you would bless me and enlarge my border, and that your hand might be with me, and that you would KEEP ME from harm so that it might not bring me pain! And God granted what he asked' 1 Chronicles 4:10.

You can bring your individual needs to Jesus. You can tell it to Jesus. A dear ninety year old brother in the church of which I am a member wept as he quoted the following hymn in his prayer which perhaps will speak into your situation today:

*Are you weary, are you heavy-hearted?
Tell it to Jesus, Tell it to Jesus;
Are you grieving over joys departed?
Tell it to Jesus alone.*

Refrain:

*Tell it to Jesus, tell it to Jesus,
He is a friend that's well-known;
You've no other such a friend or brother,
Tell it to Jesus alone.*

*Do the tears flow down your cheeks unbidden?
Tell it to Jesus, Tell it to Jesus;
Have you sins that to men's eyes are hidden?
Tell it to Jesus alone.*

*Do you fear the gath'ring clouds of sorrow?
Tell it to Jesus, Tell it to Jesus;
Are you anxious what shall be tomorrow?
Tell it to Jesus alone.*

*Are you troubled at the thought of dying?
Tell it to Jesus, Tell it to Jesus;
For Christ's coming kingdom are you sighing?
Tell it to Jesus alone.*

(Edmund S. Lorenz)

26TH SEPTEMBER

IN LO-DE-BAR

*Jonathan, the son of Saul, had a son who was crippled
in his feet. He was five years old when the news about
Saul and Jonathan came from Jezreel, and his nurse took
him up and fled, and as she fled in her haste, he fell and
became lame. And his name was Mephibosheth.*

2 Samuel 4:4

I had the privilege of leading an outreach team from the UK to Mexico City in 2011. While there we were introduced to a ministry called MEFI. MEFI is a ministry reaching out to Mexico City's homeless children and young people. MEFI plays off the name 'Mephibosheth' from 2nd Samuel 9. It is a ministry aimed at saving street children from a life of drugs, prostitution and abuse.

Mephibosheth was the son of Jonathan, who was the son of King Saul. Earlier Saul tried to kill David because he was jealous of him. Jonathan had been a special friend of David and helped him escape from his father. Later Jonathan was killed in a battle. After David had been King he remembered that he promised to never forget Jonathan's kindness to him. Once David was King he sent his servants to find anyone from the house of Saul that he might bless them. The one person they found was Jonathan's son, Mephibosheth, who had been injured in both legs when he was just five years old. Mephibosheth had been taken to the land of Gilead, where he was kept in the house of Machir at Lo-de-bar. Lo-de-bar means a place of 'no bread' or 'no pasture'. Mephibosheth's life was a real mess. His toe nails had not been trimmed in years and he was dirty and unkempt. (Very much like the dear street children who are seen as the last, the least and the lost).

When Mephibosheth was brought to King David he said: 'What is your servant that you should look upon such a dead dog as I?' While David understood all that Mephibosheth's had said and felt, nevertheless he immediately ordered his servants to care for him. From then on Mephibosheth was kept from harm and given a home for his entire life. He sat at the King's table.

The story of David's kindness and love toward Mephibosheth reminds us of God's love for us in that while we were yet sinners, Christ died for our sins. That is what King Jesus does for all who come to Him in repentance, humility and faith, including the 'street children' in Mexico City.

In Lo-debar, I was just lame there,
So crippled, so sad, and so poor.
In fear of my life with no answers,
My future so bleak and unsure.

Where are you, came the sweetest voice
I love you, I'll care for your need!
Come, enjoy this feast at My table here.
I have covered your poor crippled feet.

(Unknown)

27TH SEPTEMBER

A CHRISTIAN

And when he had found him, he brought him to Antioch. For a whole year they met with the church and taught a great many people. And in Antioch the disciples were first called Christians.

Acts 11:26

I love to purchase Christian books in charity shops. They usually are quite cheap and very often dated but many contain jewels of truth which are most helpful. The following are some thoughts from one such book written by George Goodman away back in 1939 (but just as relevant today) regarding answering the question: 'What is a Christian?' Today we will look at some aspects of what a Christian is and I trust they apply to our own lives. A Christian is:

- A NEW CREATURE BECAUSE OF THE SECOND BIRTH: 'Therefore, if anyone is in Christ, he is a new creation. The old has passed away; behold, the new has come'. 2 Cor 5:17.

I Am a New Creation,
No more in Condemnation,
Here in the Grace of God I stand.

(Dave Bilbrough)

- A CHILD OF GOD BY ADOPTION: 'The Spirit himself bears witness with our spirit that we are children of God' Rom 8:16.

I once was an outcast stranger on earth,
A sinner by choice, and an alien by birth,
But I've been adopted, my name's written down,
An heir to a mansion, a robe and a crown.

(Harriet E. Buell)

- A SON OF GOD BY SEPARATION: 'and I will be a father to you, and you shall be sons and daughters to me, says the Lord Almighty'. 2 Cor 6:18.
- AN HEIR OF GOD BY INHERITANCE: 'and if children, then heirs—heirs of God and fellow heirs with Christ, provided we suffer with him in order that we may also be glorified with him' Rom 8:17
- A SAINT BECAUSE OF HIS HOLINESS: 'To all those in Rome who are loved by God and called to be saints:' Rom 1:7
- A BELIEVER BECAUSE OF HIS FAITH: 'And more than ever believers were added to the Lord, multitudes of both men and women' Acts 5:14.
- A BROTHER BECAUSE OF HIS LOVE: 'no longer as a bondservant but more than a bondservant, as a beloved brother' Philemon 16.
- A SERVANT BECAUSE OF HIS LABOUR: 'But now that you have been set free from sin and have become slaves of God, the fruit you get leads to sanctification and its end, eternal life' Rom 6:22.

In the harvest field there is work to do,
For the grain is ripe, and the reapers few;
And the Master's voice bids the workers true
Heed the call that He gives today.

Labour on, labour on,
Keep the bright reward in view,
For the Master has said
He will strength renew;
Labour on till the close of day.

(C. R. Blackall)

28TH SEPTEMBER

WHAT IS A CHRISTIAN?

*And Agrippa said to Paul, In a short time would
you persuade me to be a Christian?*

Acts 26:28

Yesterday we started to outline some truths regarding what a Christian is, and if you are a Christian blessed by just what we are in Christ. If you are not a Christian then I trust you will be persuaded today to become one. We will continue to outline today further aspects of what it means to be a Christian. They are:

- A FRIEND BECAUSE OF HIS OBE-DIENCE: 'You are my friends if you do what I command you' John 15:14
- A WITNESS BECAUSE OF TES-TIMONY: 'But you will receive power when the Holy Spirit has come upon you, and you will be my witnesses in Jerusalem and in all Judea and Samaria, and to the end of the earth' Acts 1:8.
- A BRANCH BECAUSE OF HIS TES-TIMONY: 'I am the vine; you are the branches. Whoever abides in me and I in him, he it is that bears much fruit, for apart from me you can do nothing' John 15:5
- A TEMPLE BECAUSE OF THE INDWELLING SPIRIT: 'What agreement has the temple of God with idols? For we are the temple of the living God; as God said, I will make my dwelling among them and walk among them, and I will be their God, and they shall be my people' 2 Corinthians 6:16
- A PILGRIM BECAUSE YOU ARE NOT OF THIS WORLD: 'Beloved, I urge you as sojourners and exiles to abstain from the passions of the flesh, which wage war against your soul' 1 Peter 2:11
- A STEWARD BECAUSE YOU PUT ON TRUST: 'As each has received a gift, use it to serve one another, as good stewards of God's varied grace' 1 Peter 4:10
- A LIVING STONE BECAUSE YOU ARE ON THE ROCK: 'you yourselves like living stones are being built up as a spiritual house, to be a holy priesthood, to offer spiritual sacrifices acceptable to God through Jesus Christ' 1 Peter 2:5.
- A PRIEST BECAUSE OF HIS WOR-SHIP:' But you are a chosen race, a royal priesthood, a holy nation, a people for his own possession, that you may proclaim the excellencies of him who called you out of darkness into his marvellous light' 1 Peter 2:9.
- A CHRISTIAN BECAUSE OF HIS CONFESSION: 'For this is why the gospel was preached even to those who are dead, that though judged in the flesh the way people are, they might live in the spirit the way God does' 1 Peter 4:6.

I trust we are blessed and encouraged as we looked at what a Christian is over these last two days. If you are not yet a Christian 'come, come today':

Almost persuaded, come, come today;
Almost persuaded, turn not away;
Jesus invites you here,
Angels are lingering near,
Prayers rise from hearts so dear;
O wanderer, come.

29TH SEPTEMBER

YOU'RE SPECIAL

I praise you, for I am fearfully and wonderfully made.

Psalm 139:14

While in Co Fermanagh with my wife visiting her aged parents I had an opportunity to take a walk in Enniskillen while the ladies were doing some shopping. On passing one of the well-known clothing shops I noticed they had a 'Sale Rail' with the price of gents' jackets reduced dramatically. Anyhow this led to me making a purchase. Afterwards while wearing the Jacket I put my hand in the side pocket and felt a leaflet which I thought might be an information leaflet about the jacket. However when taking it out I found it to be a gospel tract entitled: 'You're Special'. Obviously someone had 'slipped' these tracts into the pockets of the jackets on the rail. I still haven't worked out if this could be described as creative evangelism or perhaps someone taking a little bit too much liberty. However we are by all means to win some.

Anyhow back to the 'Tract'. The following are some extracts from it that we can reflect on today: 'Believe it or not—no one is just like you. Your physical appearance, your voice and personality traits—your habits, intelligence, personal tastes—all these make you one of a kind. Even your fingerprints distinguish you from every other human being—past, present or future. You are not a product of some cosmic assembly line'.

The author of the tract went on to say: 'but the most important facet of your identity is that God made you in His own image (Genesis 1:27)', and that: 'The Bible reveals God's total interest in you as an individual'. He then makes the reader aware of the fact we are sinners due to the fall and because of this: 'God's design for our lives are then blocked; His mercies do not come to the unwilling. But even here we are precious to God . . . He loves us so much He gave His only Son to die for our sins. . . . He wants to forgive us and give us a full, meaningful life. When we trust in Jesus Christ and let Him put our lives together, the Bible says we become God's masterpiece' Ephesians 2:10. The writer of the 'Tract' then asks the question: 'Can anyone be more special than that?'

As I reflected on all this the words of 'I'm Special' written by Graham Kendrick came to mind:

I'm special because God has loved me,
For He gave the best thing that
He had to save me;
His own Son Jesus, crucified to take the blame
For all the bad things I have done.
Thank You Jesus, thank You Lord,
For loving me so much.
I know I don't deserve anything.
Help me feel Your love right now,
To know deep in my heart
That I'm Your special friend.

30TH SEPTEMBER

THE PHYSICIAN OF THE SOUL

But when he heard it, he said, Those who are well have no need of a physician, but those who are sick. Go and learn what this means: I desire mercy, and not sacrifice. For I came not to call the righteous, but sinners.

Matthew 9:12–13

Sin is likened to a disease. The good news is that the Lord Jesus Christ is the good physician of the soul. While I believe Jesus can and does heal people today this was not the reason He came to earth. Disease and death are still with us today. As believers our bodies are still waiting for their redemption: 'And not only the creation, but we ourselves, who have the first fruits of the Spirit, groan inwardly as we wait eagerly for adoption as sons, the redemption of our bodies'.

Praise God one day we will have a body like unto His glorious body: 'who will transform our lowly body to be like his glorious body, by the power that enables him even to subject all things to himself' Philippians 3:21. For this to happen we need the sin problem dealt with first.

The gospel can be explained in the following way:

1. DISEASE: All of us are infected with the disease known as sin: 'for all have sinned and fall short of the glory of God' Romans 3:23.

2. DEATH: Sin leads to death which is the penalty of sin: 'Therefore, just as sin came into the world through one man, and death through sin, and so death spread to all men because all sinned' Romans 5:12.

3. DECREE: Because God is righteous and holy, He cannot overlook sin. Someone has to pay for it: 'And just as it is appointed for man to die once, and after that comes judgment' Hebrews 9:27.

4. DELIVERER: Someone else has paid for our sin and is our deliverer from sin and its penalty. The penalty has been already paid by Jesus Christ on the cross of Calvary: 'but God shows his love for us in that while we were still sinners, Christ died for us' Romans 5:8.

5. DECLARATION: The Bible declares that this salvation cannot be earned. It is a free gift from God to those who accept it by faith. Ephesians 2:8–9.

6. DELIVERANCE: Our deliverance comes when we receive Jesus Christ into our lives by a prayer of true repentance and faith: 'But to all who did receive him, who believed in his name, he gave the right to become children of God' John 1:12.

The worst of all diseases
Is light, compared with sin;
On ev'ry part it seizes,
But rages most within.

There is a balm in Gilead,
To make the wounded whole,
There's pow'r enough in Jesus,
To cure a sin-sick soul.

'Tis palsy, plague, and fever,
And madness all combined,
And none but a believer,
The least relief can find.

(John Newton)

1ST OCTOBER

THE BELIEVERS' BLESSED HOPE

Waiting for our blessed hope, the appearing of the glory of our great God and Savior Jesus Christ.

Titus 2:13

When thinking of the blessed hope of the believer the words of a verse of John W Peterson's hymn 'Heaven Came Down and Glory Filled My Soul' came to my mind:

Now I've a hope that will surely endure
After the passing of time
I have a future in heaven for sure
There in those mansions sublime
And it's because of that wonderful day
When at the cross I believed
Riches eternal and blessings supernal
From His precious hand I received

The following are some well-known scriptures concerning the blessed hope of the believer which I trust will encourage us on our earthly journey towards heaven:

- WE WILL BE CAUGHT UP TO MEET JESUS: 'Then we who are alive, who are left, will be caught up together with them in the clouds to meet the Lord in the air' 1 Thess 4:17.
- THEREAFTER WE WILL BE FOREVER WITH HIM: 'and so we will always be with the Lord'. 1 Thess 4:17.
- WE WILL REIGN WITH HIM: 'if we endure, we will also reign with him; if we deny him, he also will deny us' 2 Tim 2:12.
- WE WILL SEE HIS FACE: 'They will see his face, and his name will be on their foreheads' Revelation 22:4.
- WE WILL SERVE HIM: 'No longer will there be anything accursed, but the throne of God and of the Lamb will be in it, and his servants will worship him' Revelation 22:3.
- WE SHALL BE LIKE HIM: 'We know that when he appears we shall be like him, because we shall see him as he is' 1 John 3:2.

O shout aloud the tidings,
Repeat the joyful strain;
Let all the waiting nations
This message hear again;
The spotless Lamb of glory,
Who once for man was slain,
Soon o'er all the earth shall reign.

Looking for that blessed hope,
Looking for that blessed hope;
We know the hour is nearing,
The hour of His appearing,
We're looking for that blessed hope.

Signs in the Heav'n above us,
In sun and moon and sky,
Proclaim to all the faithful
Redemption draweth nigh;
The hearts of men are quaking,
And failing them for fear;
Jesus' coming draweth near.

We'll watch for His returning
With lamps well-trimmed and bright;
He cometh to the careless
As thieves break thro' at night;
Well done, thou good and faithful,
O may we hear the word,
'Share the joy of Christ thy Lord.'

(Thoro Harris)

2ND OCTOBER

DOUBLE RAINBOW

*I have set my bow in the cloud, and it shall be a sign
of the covenant between me and the earth.*

Genesis 9:13

In the period of writing this devotional Queen Elizabeth 11 died. She was the longest reigning monarch in the history of the UK. She reigned throughout my entire lifetime up to that point. For me like many others she was always there and therefore we sensed a great loss. Many momentous things happened during the days and weeks after her passing. One of those was a double rainbow which appeared over Buckingham Palace. One of the daily newspapers described this as follows: 'Poignant moment a DOUBLE RAINBOW appeared above Buckingham Palace and another at Windsor Castle as crowds broke into the national anthem after the Queen's death was announced'.

From a biblical perspective rainbows remind us of God's promises. The rainbow for me is one of earth's loveliest sights. The rainbow was chosen by God as a token of a covenant of grace made with Noah after the terrible judgement of the flood. It is a guarantee to us of the regular order of seedtime and harvest, summer and winter, day and night, and that not again will the earth be destroyed with a flood. It is a beautiful illustration of the New Covenant of grace in the Lord Jesus Christ.

Immediately after my own mother's death, I was driving up the MI Motorway towards my home. Just about where the turn off for Portadown is a lovely double rainbow appeared in the sky. The Lord reminded me again through His Word of the tremendous hope and promise that every born again Christian has: 'For we know that if the tent that is our earthly home is destroyed, we have a building from God, a house not made with hands, eternal in the heavens. For in this tent we groan, longing to put on our heavenly dwelling, if indeed by putting it on we may not be found naked. For while we are still in this tent, we groan, being burdened—not that we would be unclothed, but that we would be further clothed, so that what is mortal may be swallowed up by life. He who has prepared us for this very thing is God, who has given us the Spirit as a guarantee' 2 Corinthians 5:1–5

God has set His sign, a rainbow,
Midst the rainy clouds above;
'Tis the token of His cov'nant
With the man and earth He loves;
Ne'er again to send a deluge,
Hence His faithfulness is told!
He is true to every promise,
And His changeless word we hold!

(Franz Joseph Haydn)

3RD OCTOBER

FIVE RAINBOWS

And around the throne was a rainbow that
had the appearance of an emerald.

Revelation 4:3

Queen Elizabeth at age 96 years died at Balmoral, her beloved Scottish estate. At Windsor Castle, an incredible rainbow arched over the grounds just as the Union Jack flag began to be lowered in honour of the monarch's death.

On a walk about after the Queen's burial on September 19th 2022, Prince William said the Royal Family had seen 'five rainbows' above Balmoral Castle in the Scottish Highlands since his beloved grandmother, the Queen, died on September 8. Prince William made the comments while chatting with a group of people. Prince William said in conversation: 'You hardly ever see rainbows up there, but there were five'.

The first rainbow on earth was just after the flood at the time of Noah as recorded in Genesis 6–8. After this when rain appeared it would cause fear of another flood. However God made a covenant or promise with Noah that He would not destroy the earth by a flood ever again. He gave the rainbow as a token of that promise. When dark threatening clouds gathered the folk would quiet their hearts by faith in the promise, and when the rainbow appeared, welcome it as a token of that promise. The rainbow gave promise of temporal blessings as outlined in Genesis 8:21- 22: 'And when the Lord smelled the pleasing aroma, the Lord said in his heart, I will never again curse the ground because of man, . . .

While the earth remains, seedtime and harvest, cold and heat, summer and winter, day and night, shall not cease'. God promised that there would not be a universal flood ever again.

The covenant with Noah also helps us as believers to understand the new covenant we have in Christ: It comes from God. It was because God loved us that He gave us His only begotten Son to mediate the New Covenant by His own blood, that salvation and eternal life might come to us. It was based on sacrifice just as Noah offered burnt offerings: Genesis 8:20. Christ offered Himself without spot to God, an offering of sweet smelling savour: Ephesians 5:2. It is on the basis of the precious blood of our Lord Jesus Christ that the promises are given. The once for all, never to be repeated flood, was a figure of the judgement of God that fell upon Jesus (the Ark) when at Calvary He offered the once for all, never to be repeated Sacrifice for sin, by which His saints are perfected for ever: 'For by a single offering he has perfected for all time those who are being sanctified' Hebrews 10:14.

May the meaning of the rainbow
Be our full reality;
In the church and in our living,
God expressed for all to see.

(Franz Joseph Haydn)

4TH OCTOBER

A PRAYER FOR OPENED THINGS

O Lord, open the eyes of these men, that they may see.

2 Kings 6:20

The following are things for you to pray for God to open in your life and walk as you follow Him today:

OPEN MY EYES THAT I MAY SEE: 'Open my eyes, that I may behold, wondrous things out of your law' Psalm 119:18.

OPEN MY LIPS TO SPEAK OF THE LORD: 'O Lord, open my lips, and my mouth will declare your praise' Psalm 51:15.

OPEN TO ME THE WORD OF GOD: 'They said to each other, did not our hearts burn within us while he talked to us on the road, while he opened to us the Scriptures?' Luke 24:32.

OPEN MY UNDERSTANDING LORD: 'Then he opened their minds to understand the Scriptures' Luke 24:45.

OPEN THE DOOR OF FAITH TO ME: 'And when they arrived and gathered the church together, they declared all that God had done with them, and how he had opened a door of faith to the Gentiles' Acts 14:27.

OPEN MY HEART WITH LOVE TO HEAR WHAT THE LORD IS SAYING TO ME: 'One who heard us was a woman named Lydia, from the city of Thyatira, a seller of purple goods, who was a worshiper of God. The Lord opened her heart to pay attention to what was said by Paul' Acts 16:14.

OPEN NEW DOORS OF SERVICE FOR ME: 'for a wide door for effective work has opened to me, and there are many adversaries' 1 Corinthians 16:9.

OPEN MY MOUTH TO SHARE THE GOSPEL: 'And also for me, that words may be given to me in opening my mouth boldly to proclaim the mystery of the gospel' Ephesians 6:19.

Open my eyes that I may see
glimpses of truth thou hast for me.
Place in my hands the wonderful key
that shall unclasp and set me free.
Silently now I wait for thee,
ready, my God, thy will to see.
Open my eyes, illumine me,
Spirit divine!

Open my ears that I may hear
voices of truth thou sendest clear,
and while the wave notes fall on my ear,
ev'rything false will disappear.
Silently now I wait for thee,
ready, my God, thy will to see.
Open my ears, illumine me,
Spirit divine!

Open my mouth and let me bear
gladly the warm truth ev'rywhere.
Open my heart and let me prepare
love with thy children thus to share.
Silently now I wait for thee,
ready, my God, thy will to see.
Open my mouth, illumine me,
Spirit divine!

(Clara H. Scott)

5TH OCTOBER

THE NEED FOR SUITABLE PLACEMENTS

*Therefore I tell you, whatever you ask in prayer, believe
that you have received it, and it will be yours.*

Mark 11:24

While serving as the UK Executive Director of One Mission Society I travelled to various parts of the UK. One of the airports I flew into was at Bristol. On one of my visits I made time to visit George Muller's grave and the Museum at Muller House. I was greatly blessed by visiting the George Muller Museum and learning of the tremendous things God achieved through this man of faith and prayer, especially through the children and orphan homes he built in the 19th century.

The following is an example George Muller gave regarding the power of prayer: 'In the early part of the summer 1862, it was found that several boys were ready to be apprenticed; but there had been no applications made by masters for apprentices. As all the boys were invariably sent out as apprentices, this was no small difficulty, for we not only look for Christian masters, but consider their business, and examine their position to see whether they are suitable. The master must also be willing to receive the apprentice into his own family. Under these circumstances, we again gave ourselves to prayer, as we had done for more than twenty years before, concerning this thing. Instead of advertising, which in all probability would only bring before us masters who desire apprentices for the sake of the premium, we remembered how good the Lord had been to us, in having helped us hundreds of times before in this very matter. Some weeks passed, but difficulty remained. We continued, however in prayer, and then one application was made, and then another; and since we first began to pray about this matter, last summer, we have been able to send out altogether 18 boys up to May 26, 1863; the difficulty was thus again entirely overcome by prayer, as every one of the boys, whom it was desirable to send out, had been sent'.

Is there a matter in your life, you are struggling with. Take it to the Lord in prayer. George Muller lifted all his needs to God in prayer relying on Him alone for answers.

*I believe God answers prayer;
I am sure God answers prayer;
I have proved God answers prayer:
Glory to His Name.*

(Bessie Porter Head)

6TH OCTOBER

PRAYING FOR UNBELIEVING FRIENDS

I call upon you, for you will answer me, O God;
incline your ear to me; hear my words.

Psalm 17:6

George Muller was a tremendous man of prayer. Over the years he prayed for the salvation of his five friends. The following is the story: In November 1844 George Muller began to pray for the conversion of five individuals. He prayed every day without one single intermission, whether sick or in health, on land or on the sea, and whatever the pressure of his engagements might have been. 18 months elapsed before the first was converted. He thanked God, and prayed on for the others. Five years elapsed, and then the second was converted. He thanked God, and prayed on for the other three. Day by day he continued to pray for them and six more years passed before the third was converted. He thanked God for the three, and went on praying for the other two. These two remained unconverted. The man to whom God in the riches of His grace had given tens of thousands of answers to prayer, in the same day or hour in which they were offered, went on praying day by day for nearly 36 years for the conversion of these two individuals, and yet they remained unconverted. George Muller put his hope in God, prayed on and continued to seek the answer. He encouraged others to go on waiting upon God to go on praying, only being sure that they are asking for things that are according to the mind of God: 'Go on praying, expect an answer, look for it, and in the end you will have to praise God for it'. Of the two individuals still unconverted when George Muller gave this illustration in a sermon, both became Christians in the following years.

Are you praying for the conversion of an unsaved loved one, pray on? God hears and answers prayer. Recently I was speaking to a godly lady. She and her late husband prayed about a situation that seemed impossible to resolve for 18 years, and then came a wonderful answer to their prayers. Also an 88 year old man shared with a men's fellowship group that he has prayed for his son's conversion for the past 62 years and will continue to do so until his son is converted or until the Lord calls him home. So keep on persevering in the place of prayer. The answer will come in God's way at God's time.

Tho' the foes of right oppress,
Keep on praying;
Christ, the Lord, is near to bless,
All prevailing.

Let not fear your heart appall,
Naught of evil can befall,
Stronger is your God than all;
Keep on praying.

Keep on praying,
Keep on praying,
Thro' the Saviour's blessed name,
All prevailing.

(Robert O. Smith)

7TH OCTOBER

HE DID—HE CAN—HE WILL

Now to him who is able to do far more abundantly than all that we ask or think, according to the power at work within us.

Ephesians 3:20

The God of yesterday is the same today. What happened in the past can happen again.

A boy gave his lunch and 5,000 men beside women and children were fed: 'There is a boy here who has five barley loaves and two fish, but what are they for so many?' John 6:9.

A slave girl spoke to her mistress about God—and her master, healed of his leprosy, became a devout believer: 'Now the Syrians on one of their raids had carried off a little girl from the land of Israel, and she worked in the service of Naaman's wife. She said to her mistress, would that my lord were with the prophet who is in Samaria! He would cure him of his leprosy. Naaman went in and told his lord, thus and so spoke the girl from the land of Israel.... Then he returned to the man of God, he and all his company, and he came and stood before him. And he said, behold, I know that there is no God in all the earth, but in Israel' 2 Kings 5:2–4'15.

An aged Monk counselled Martin Luther to trust God's forgiveness of his sins—and Luther, finding peace with God, became the pioneer of biblical Protestantism. Luther was attributed with writing the following poem sometime after his conversion:

The God that stopped the sun on high,
And sent the manna from the sky,
Laid flat the walls of Jericho,
And put to flight old Israel's foe,
Why can't He answer prayer today,
And drive each stormy cloud away?

Who turned the water into wine,
And healed a helpless cripple's spine –
Commanded tempests, 'Peace, be still',
And hungry multitudes did fill,
His power is just the same today,
So why not labour, watch, and pray?

He conquered in the lions' den,
Brought Lazarus back to life again.
He heard Elijah's cry for rain,
And freed the sufferers from pain.
If He could do those wonders then,
Let's prove our mighty God again.

Why can't the God who raised the dead,
Gave little David Goliath's head,
Cast out the demons with a word,
Yet sees the fall of one wee bird,
Do signs and miracles today,
In that same good old-fashioned way?
He can-He's just the same today.

8TH OCTOBER

THIS OLD HOUSE

*For we know that if the tent that is our earthly home
is destroyed, we have a building from God, a house
not made with hands, eternal in the heavens.*

2 Corinthians 5:1

Martin Ralph DeHaan (1891—1965) was an American Bible teacher, the founder of Radio Bible Class, and the co-editor of the monthly devotional guide Our Daily Bread, which is still widely read by Christians all over the world today. Shortly before his death Dr DeHaan wrote: 'The owner of the 'house' I have occupied here on earth has served notice that I must soon move out. He will not make any more repairs—since I am going to vacate it anyway. The foundation is crumbling, the roof leaks, the heating system is failing, and the windows are getting dim. The steps are getting shaky and the hinges are getting rusty and squeaky. I have been overwhelmed by the innumerable advantages of the new Home over the old one; so much so that now instead of dreading it, I am beginning to get anxious to move. If it were not for a few things I still have to do, I would want to move pronto. 'So we do not lose heart. Though our outer self is wasting away, our inner self is being renewed day by day'.

Stewart Hamblen, caught the idea of moving out of the earthly and temporal home of our body to our eternal new home in Heaven in his song 'This Old House':

This old house once knew my children
This old house once knew my life
This old house was home and comfort
As we fought the storms of strife
This old house once rang with laughter
This old house heard many shouts
Now she trembles in the darkness

When the lightning walks about
Ain't gonna need this house no longer
Ain't gonna need this house no more
Ain't got time to fix the shingles
Ain't got time to fix the floor
Ain't got time to oil the hinges
Nor to mend the window pane
Ain't gonna need this house no longer
I'm getting ready to meet the saints

This old house is gettin' shaky
This old house is gettin' old
This old house lets in the rain
This old house lets in the cold
On my knees I'm gettin' chilly
But I feel no fear or pain
'Cause I see an angel peekin'
Through a broken window pane

This old house is afraid of thunder
This old house is afraid of storms
This old house just groans and trembles
When the night wind flings its arms
This old house is gettin' feeble
This old house is needin' paint
Just like me it's tuckered out
But I'm getting' ready to meet the saints

9TH OCTOBER

JESUS WILL DO IT

Heaven and earth will pass away, but my words will not pass away.

Matthew 24:35

If you ask anything in my name, I will do it.

John 14:14

While serving the Lord in a UK missionary role I had the privilege of visiting Moriah Calvinistic Methodist Chapel, Loughor, where Evan Roberts is buried in South Wales. One of the greatest revivals in the UK was undoubtedly the Welsh revival, which had its greatest instrument in Evan Roberts. This revival which was birthed by God through young people was led by Evan Roberts who at the time of the revival was only 26 years old. In the year 1904/05 100,000 souls were reached for Christ. While visiting the Chapel, I picked up an A4 sheet which had the following message written by Evan Roberts IN 1928:

JESUS WILL DO IT:

As long as sun doth show that distant hill;
And moon benign protect this darkened path;
And man and woman each the other need;
And hunger, weary, seek the bread of life;
And fire reveal the majesty of heat;
And water cleft by sword return and kiss;
And clouds with weeping ease the aching soil;
And Saints believing ask with righteous faith;
So long will Jesus do what you desire.

So long will Jesus answer when you call;
And open every door at which you knock;
And give you rightly what, you, needing, ask;
And honour faith which cometh godly way;

And silence terror in the erstwhile mute;
And make the Bible ever rock of hope;
And by His blood prevail for sinner's plea;
And through His light dispel a world of woe;
And with His rest release each burdened mind;
And in Saint's joy a newer song create;
So long shall all you ask be heard. So long?
His spoken word shall never pass away.

Since this be true, be dead a thousand cares!
Be buried! And let not doubt forget your graves!
Petition, weeping, heart, on faithful knee,
For greater bonds than blood shall asking forge:
Love's precious deed shall follow sacred lips.

You having Him, shall have His gifts as well.
Go, seek a temple; kneel, and tell thy Lord
All you need done. Let Jesus do it all.

Henceforth, all goodness in His name beseech;
With simple heart profoundly call on Christ;
For whosoever asketh, goeth home
In harvest time, each 'whatsoever' done!

Ask on undoubting, daily, need by need;
Believe with fullness of God-armoured faith;
Expecting answers at appointed times;
Expecting answers at appointed times;
AND, JESUS THANK WHILE HOPE
AWAITS THESE DEEDS.

This is the Bible message, Friend, to YOU;
ASK IN HIS NAME. THAT,
JESUS, THEN WILL DO.

10TH OCTOBER

HOURS IN THE PRESENCE OF GOD

*And Elijah said, 'As the Lord of hosts lives, before whom
I stand, I will surely show myself to him today'*

1 Kings 18:15

To be a follower of Jesus, you need to spend time in His presence. While attending the South West England and South Wales OMS Conference in Gorseinon I visited the Church Evan Roberts was brought up in and where the 1904 Welsh revival commenced. While there I was given an outline Bible study that Evan Roberts had prepared many years ago entitled 'Hours in the Presence of God 'Before whom I stand' I Kings 18:15'. Over the next few days we will share and develop some thoughts on this study:

- Answers to prayer are 'all in all' of your asking. Do not forget them: 'If you abide in me, and my words abide in you, ask whatever you wish, and it will be done for you' John 15:7.
- Burdens of prayer should be heeded, sensed, discerned, expressed and valued: 'Moreover, as for me, far be it from me that I should sin against the Lord by ceasing to pray for you, and I will instruct you in the good and the right way' 1 Samuel 12:23.
- Calls to prayer should be obeyed. Watch for prayer. Listen to God's voice and fulfil: 'Praying at all times in the Spirit, with all prayer and supplication. To that end, keep alert with all perseverance, making supplication for all the saints' Ephesians 6:18.
- Devotions are highly important. They create an essential prayer atmosphere: 'But when you pray,

go into your room and shut the door and pray to your Father who is in secret. And your Father who sees in secret will reward you' Matthew 6:6.
- Energy has to be sacrificed if the Kingdom of God is to succeed: 'Epaphras, who is one of you, a servant of Christ Jesus, greets you, always struggling on your behalf in his prayers, that you may stand mature and fully assured in all the will of God' Colossians 4:12.; 'Therefore, brothers, pick out from among you seven men of good repute, full of the Spirit and of wisdom, whom we will appoint to this duty. But we will devote ourselves to prayer and to the ministry of the word' Acts 6:3–4.

From the study so far we can see from Evan Roberts' thought process the high cost of being used mightily of God. Are we constantly asking God for His will to be done in the salvation of precious souls in our families and sphere of influence? Are we burdened enough to be constant in the place of prayer reading the scriptures. How is our devotional life? Are we praying for fellow believers, our ministers and pastors and missionaries?

*Almighty God, in humble prayer
To Thee our souls we lift:
Do Thou our waiting minds prepare
For Thy most needful gift.*

(James Montgomery)

11TH OCTOBER

SPENDING TIME WITH GOD

And he told them a parable to the effect that they
ought always to pray and not lose heart.

Luke 18:1

Today we continue to glean thoughts from an outline study of the late Evan Roberts who was greatly used in the 1904 Welsh revival entitled 'Hours in the presence of God'.

- God is the centre around which all prayer activities revolve. Remember God always: Heb 5:12–14.
- The heavenlies are full of enemies. War with them: Eph 6:10–18.
- Be above principalities Eph 2:6:
- Jesus Christ's cross and blood and death and name make prayer possible: 'I am the vine; you are the branches. Whoever abides in me and I in him, he it is that bears much fruit, for apart from me you can do nothing' John 15:5. 'Therefore, brothers, since we have confidence to enter the holy places by the blood of Jesus, by the new and living way that he opened for us through the curtain, that is, through his flesh, and since we have a great priest over the house of God, let us draw near with a true heart in full assurance of faith, with our hearts sprinkled clean from an evil conscience and our bodies washed with pure water. Let us hold fast the confession of our hope without wavering, for he who promised is faithful. And let us consider how to stir up one another to love and good works' Hebrews 10:19–24.
- Know the will of God about each thing you pray over: 'And so, from the day we heard, we have not ceased to pray for you, asking that you may be filled with the knowledge of his will in all spiritual wisdom and understanding' Colossians 1:9. One of the greatest things we can do is know the will of God and do it.
- In Psalm 142:10 we read: 'Teach me to do your will, for you are my God! Let your good Spirit lead me on level ground!' Here we have the heart-cry of the psalmist for grace to know and to do God's will 'Teach me to do your will'. There is only one thing that really matters in the life of the Christian; it is to know and to do the will of God. This being the case knowing and doing the will of God is of vital importance. To know and to do God's will was the supreme thing in the life of our Lord Himself.

Keep on praying, keep on praying,
You shall have your reward sometime, somewhere;
Trust Him, believe, and thy reward receive;
Keep on praying, God will answer your prayer.

(Chas. H. Gabriel)

12TH OCTOBER

KEYS TO REVIVAL

The prayer of a righteous person has great power as it is working.

James 5:16

According to an article on the Bible College of Wales' website the story of Evan Roberts and the Welsh Revival are intertwined and almost synonymous. Evan Roberts was a man marked by the Lord as His catalyst for the revival. While visiting Moriah chapel, Loughor, where the 1904 Welsh revival commenced I was given a Bible study outline written by Evan Roberts called 'Hours in the Presence of God'. Over the last two days we have looked at some of the points Evan Roberts made. Today we will conclude by looking at the following points from this study.

- Salvation is the big thing to pray out into the world. 'Never forget sin, sinner, Saviour: The saying is trustworthy and deserving of full acceptance, that Christ Jesus came into the world to save sinners, of whom I am the foremost' 1 Timothy 1:15.
- Universal prayer is expected of you. Pray for all saints and all nations: 'He is the propitiation for our sins, and not for ours only but also for the sins of the whole world' 1 John 2:2. 'That they may all be one, just as you, Father, are in me, and I in you, that they also may be in us, so that the world may believe that you have sent me' John 17:21.
- These are two key points and certainly cause for spending 'Hours in the Presence of God'. Praying for the salvation of the lost both locally and globally. Praying for unity amongst all truly born again believers. Roberts realised that is where God commands the blessing. That is when you get revival.
- Victory in prayer guarantees that prayer wins each time. Be violent in asking: 'From the days of John the Baptist until now the kingdom of heaven has suffered violence, and the violent take it by force' Matthew 11:12.
- Expect answers to all your prayers. Fan the fire of your hope: Hebrews 11:1–40.
- Zeal is wrestling with God. Burn while you pray: 'Pray without ceasing' 1 Thessalonians 5:17.
- Words for prayer should be sought, studied, uttered and remembered: James 5:16–18.

The following are keys to the Welsh Revival through Evan Roberts:

- He developed a passion for Revival through reading revival histories and biographies.
- He prayed intensely and continually for revival to come.
- He was totally submissive, consecrated and yielded to the Lord Jesus.
- A passionate love for Jesus Christ and his will to be done.
- A deep repentance of sins, including 'doubtful things.'
- A total surrender to God.
- Being filled with the Holy Spirit and obedient to his prompting.
- Corporate prayer
- Specific and continual prayer for an immediate visitation of the Holy Spirit

13TH OCTOBER

*And thus I make it my ambition to preach the
gospel, not where Christ has already been named,
lest I build on someone elses foundation.*

Romans 15:20

In August 2012 one of our prayer group leaders sent me the following email: 'I would be grateful if you would have a special word for our special friends as they go forward in the will of God'. The leader was referring to a young couple who with their young daughter were going to a 'closed' country to serve the Lord. Previous to this they had to take any reference to their names being connected with any Church or Missionary Agency down from any social media sites. The following are some of the points the Lord led on my heart to share:

The first thing I did was to share the Lord's PROMISE He gave in Matthew 28:19–20; 'Go therefore and make disciples of all nations, baptizing them in the name of the Father and of the Son and of the Holy Spirit, teaching them to observe all that I have commanded you. AND BEHOLD, I AM WITH YOU ALWAYS, to the end of the age'. The Amplified Bible translates as follows: 'and lo, I am with you always [remaining with you perpetually—regardless of circumstance, and on every occasion], even to the end of the age'. What a promise. The Lord was going to be with them each step of the way.

This also speaks of the Lord's PRESENCE: 'remaining with you perpetually—regardless of circumstance'.

Moses was given a similar answer in response to his questions and fears: 'Therefore, come now, and I will send you to Pharaoh, and then bring My people, the children of Israel, out of Egypt." But Moses said to God, 'Who am I, that I should go to Pharaoh, and that I should bring the children of Israel out of Egypt?' And God said, 'CERTAINLY I WILL BE WITH YOU".

I also shared about the Lord's PARTNERSHIP: 'For we are God's fellow workers' 1 Corinthians 3:9. Of course this would include those of God's people at home partnering in prayer and resources.

It was wonderful to also share about the Lord's PEACE which He had given them: 'And the peace of God, which surpasses all understanding, will guard your hearts and your minds in Christ Jesus' Philippians 4:7.

In conclusion I used the following quote of John Henry Jowett: 'There need be no 'buts' in our relationship to God's will. Nothing will take the Lord by surprise. The entire field has been surveyed and the preparations are complete. When the Lord says 'I will send you' every PROVISION has been made for the appointed task. 'I will not fail you'. He who gives the command will also give the equipment'.

14TH OCTOBER

THE BIBLICAL MODEL OF MISSIONS

And what you have heard from me in the presence of many witnesses entrust to faithful men, who will be able to teach others also.

2 Timothy 2:2

As a missionary rep and worker, I had to give various talks at Churches, Mission Halls, Conferences, and Missionary Reports at Missionary Meetings and the list goes on. Very often I shared points that I had gleaned from others along with those of my own. According to 2 Timothy 2:2 this approach is quite biblical. The following is one such example given on 'The Biblical Model of Missions':

IN MATTHEW 28:19–20, THE EMPHASIS IS ON THE PURPOSE OF MISSIONS: 'Go therefore and make disciples of all nations, baptizing them in the name of the Father and of the Son and of the Holy Spirit, teaching them to observe all that I have commanded you. And behold, I am with you always, to the end of the age'. Here we have instruction to; Win them, Wet them, and Work them. Put another way: Evangelise, Baptise, Exercise.

IN MARK 16:15 & 20, THE EMPHASIS IS ON THE PREACHING OF MISSIONS: 'And He said to them, Go into all the world and preach the gospel to all creation . . . And they went out and preached everywhere, while the Lord was working with them and confirming the word by the signs that followed'. Here we have the command, commission and consolation of missions.

IN LUKE 24:47, THE EMPHASIS IS ON THE PROCLAMATION OF MISSIONS: 'and that repentance [necessary] for forgiveness of sins would be preached in His name to all the nations, beginning from Jerusalem'. Here we find that we must preach the need of repentance of and remission of sins.

IN JOHN 20:21, THE EMPHASIS IS ON THE POWER OF MISSIONS: 'Jesus said to them again, 'Peace be with you. As the Father has sent me, even so I am sending you'. Here we have the model of the Father sending the Son, and the model of the Son sending us.

IN ACTS 1:8, THE EMPHASIS IS ON THE PLACES OF MISSION: 'But you will receive power when the Holy Spirit has come upon you, and you will be my witnesses in Jerusalem and in all Judea and Samaria, and to the end of the earth'. Here we have;

- THE HOME PLACE: 'Jerusalem'
- THE HARDENED PLACE: 'Judea'
- THE HOPELESS PLACE: 'Samaria'
- THE HARD PLACE (to reach): 'to the end of the earth'

I trust this will help you find your place in mission: whether, going, sending, praying, giving, encouraging or a combination of any or all of these.

15TH OCTOBER

I WANT TO WALK WITH JESUS CHRIST

*Whoever says he abides in him ought to walk
in the same way in which he walked.*

1 John 2:6

As followers of the Lord Jesus He would want us to walk on earth upon the same principles as He did. In this He was our perfect example. His manner of life was simple, sincere and godly. So how did the Lord Jesus walk?

HIS AIM IN LIFE WAS TO PLEASE THE FATHER: 'And he who sent me is with me. He has not left me alone, for I always do the things that are pleasing to him' John 8:29. The will of God was the end and aim of His whole life. As a boy He said 'I must be about my Father's business'. At the end of His life in Gethsemane He said 'Not my will but yours be done'. In this way we should walk as He walked.

JESUS WALKED BY FAITH: 'As the living Father sent me, and I live because of the Father, so whoever feeds on me, he also will live because of me' John 6:57. Jesus walked in a path of obedience and dependence. Of Himself He could do nothing. His words and works were from the Father; as He was instructed so He acted. We should follow His example by totally relying on God.

THE HOLY SPIRIT WAS THE POWER IN THE LIFE OF THE LORD JESUS: He was anointed by the Spirit; led by the Spirit to be tempted; came up by the Spirit to His ministry. By the Holy Spirit He cast out demons; and by the Eternal Spirit offered Himself without spot to God, and in the energy of the Holy Spirit He was raised from the dead. The Spirit is given to all believers, that they too may live by, walk in, and be led by the Holy Spirit.

THE BIBLE WAS ALWAYS THE AUTHORITY AND GUIDE IN THE LIFE OF THE LORD JESUS: He ever appealed to the scriptures and quoted them.

JESUS WAS A MAN OF PRAYER: He Himself tells us men ought always to pray. So let us walk as He walked in our prayer life. It was Jesus' joy to do the Father's will. His joy was in saving souls. He went about doing good. The thought for today is: Let us walk as Jesus walked.

*I want to walk with Jesus Christ,
All the days I live of this life on earth;
To give to Him complete control
Of body and of soul.*

*Follow Him, follow Him, yield your life to Him -
He has conquered death, He is King of kings;
accept the joy which He gives to those
who yield their lives to Him.*

16TH OCTOBER

I WANT TO TALK LIKE JESUS

They said to each other, 'Did not our hearts burn within us while he talked to us on the road, while he opened to us the Scriptures?'

Luke 24:32

One of the best ways to learn to speak like Jesus is to listen in to some talks He had with individuals during His ministry on earth.

Jesus spoke to Nicodemus about the New Birth in John 3:3–16. He not only told him that he must be born again, but he also explained to him how to experience the New Birth. He lovingly gave answers and explanations to his questions. Nicodemus was educated and a leader, therefore Jesus spoke to him at his level.

Jesus spoke differently to the woman of Samaria as recorded in John 4:7–26. He talked at her level about satisfying water and spiritual worship. Jesus spoke as one who was a lover of the souls of individuals. He took personal interest in each case.

Jesus talked to Martha about being cumbered with much serving. He lovingly warned her against too much fussing. He explained that Mary had chosen a better part, to sit at His feet and listen Luke 10:38–42.

On the road to Emmaus Jesus gave a talk on the value of scripture to Cleopas and another Luke 24:13–31. On the way to Emmaus He began at Moses and all the prophets, and in all the Scriptures He expounded unto them the things concerning Himself. He taught them to have more confidence in the Word of God.

After the resurrection Jesus talked to Thomas about doubting: John 20:26–29. He spoke to him about faith without seeing.

These are but a few examples of folk Jesus talked to. Each in turn was instructed, rebuked and comforted according to their respective needs. By listening into conversations Jesus had with various individuals including sinners, as believers and workers we learn how to approach different situations and speak into them as Jesus did.

Let us all learn to talk to people like Jesus, no matter who or where they are.

Lord, speak to me, that I may speak
In living echoes of Thy tone;

(Frances Ridley Havergal)

O I want to talk like Jesus,
Gracious are the words from Him we hear:
Words of life and hope for sinners,
Tender healing words of love and cheer.
O the power and the value of a fitly spoken word!
O I want to talk like Jesus,
Any time or place my voice is heard.

(Unknown)

17TH OCTOBER

PROMISES, PROMISES

For all the promises of God find their Yes in him. That is why it is through him that we utter our Amen to God for his glory.

2 Corinthians 1:20

The great and precious promises of God in Christ Jesus are given to us: 'by which he has granted to us his precious and very great promises, so that through them you may become partakers of the divine nature, having escaped from the corruption that is in the world because of sinful desire'.

2 Peter 1:4

Promises formed a great part of the ministry of the Lord Jesus. They are such as no mere man could have made. Therefore they are evidence of His deity and substantiate His claim to be the Christ, the Son of the Living God. In Him is the 'Yes'—that is, the affirmation—and in Him the 'Amen, the confirmation. He promises, assures, and fulfils them.

His promises for the believer include:

- PARDON: 'I will remember their sins and their lawless deeds no more' Hebrews 10:17.
- POWER: 'But you will receive power when the Holy Spirit has come upon you, and you will be my witnesses in Jerusalem and in all Judea and Samaria, and to the end of the earth' Acts 1:8.
- PRESENCE: 'For where two or three are gathered in my name, there am I among them' Matthew 18:20.

The Lord Jesus promises:

- ETERNAL LIFE: 'I give them eternal life, and they will never perish, and no one will snatch them out of my hand' John 10:28.

- THE HOLY SPIRIT: 'And I will ask the Father, and he will give you another Helper, to be with you forever' John 14:16.
- SALVATION: 'All that the Father gives me will come to me, and whoever comes to me I will never cast out' John 6:37.
- NEVER TO DIE: 'Jesus said to her, "I am the resurrection and the life. Whoever believes in me, though he die, yet shall he live' John 11:25.
- ANSWERS TO PRAYER: 'Ask, and it will be given to you; seek, and you will find; knock, and it will be opened to you' Matthew 7:7.
- HIS PRESENCE WITH US: 'for he has said, 'I will never leave you nor forsake you.'' Hebrews 13:5.
- HE WILL COME AGAIN: 'And if I go and prepare a place for you, I will come again and will take you to myself, that where I am you may be also' John 14:3.

Standing on the promises of Christ my king,
Through eternal ages let His praises ring,
Glory in the highest, I will shout and sing,
Standing on the promises of God.

(R. Kelso Carter)

18TH OCTOBER

JESUS LOVER OF THE CHURCH

Christ loved the church and gave himself up for her.

Ephesians 5:25

The Song of Solomon gives us pictures of how Christ loves the Church: 'your love is better than wine' 1:2; 'He brought me to the banqueting house, and his banner over me was love' 2.4; 'How beautiful is your love, my sister, my bride! How much better is your love than wine, and the fragrance of your oils than any spice!' 4:10; 'love is strong as death' 8:6; 'Many waters cannot quench love' 8:7.

The following are Scripture verses that show the qualities of true love:

- THE STRENGTH OF LOVE: 'Set me as a seal upon your heart, as a seal upon your arm, for love is strong as death' Song of Solomon 8:6
- THE COMFORT OF LOVE: 'So if there is any encouragement in Christ, any comfort from love, any participation in the Spirit, any affection and sympathy' Philippians 2:1.
- THE LABOUR OF LOVE: 'remembering before our God and Father your work of faith and labour of love and steadfastness of hope in our Lord Jesus Christ' 1 Thessalonians 1:3.
- THE CONTROL OF LOVE: 'For the love of Christ controls us, because we have concluded this: that one has died for all, therefore all have died' 2 Corinthians 5:14.
- THE BREASTPLATE OF LOVE: 'But since we belong to the day, let us be sober, having put on the breastplate of faith and love, and for a helmet the hope of salvation' 1 Thessalonians 5:8.
- THE GENUINENESS OF LOVE: 'I say this not as a command, but to prove by the earnestness of others that your love also is genuine' 2 Corinthians 8:8.
- THE PROOF OF LOVE: 'So give proof before the churches of your love and of our boasting about you to these men' 2 Corinthians 8:24.

In light of the love of Christ for the Church and of His love for each individual member of His Church, how are your love levels for Him and His Church today?

Love shows itself for the Lord in the following three ways:

- DESIRE: 'Whom have I in heaven but you? And there is nothing on earth that I desire beside you' Psalm 73:25.
- DELIGHT: 'Delight yourself in the Lord, and he will give you the desires of your heart' Psalm 37:4.
- DEVOTION: 'Confirm to your servant your promise, that you may be feared' Psalm 119:38.

But what to those who find? Ah, this
nor tongue nor pen can show;
the love of Jesus, what it is,
none but his loved ones know.

(St. Bernard of Clairvaux)

19TH OCTOBER

WONDERFUL PEACE

For he himself is our peace.

Ephesians 2:14

- THE LORD JESUS CHRIST IS THE GROUND OF PEACE: 'Through him to reconcile to himself all things, whether on earth or in heaven, making peace by the blood of his cross' Col 1:20.

- OBEDIENCE TO GOD AND HIS WORD IS THE PRACTICAL WAY OF PEACE: 'Great peace have those who love your law; nothing can make them stumble' Psalm 119:165. Our troubles arise, not from obedience to, but departure from, the truth of the Bible. Those who yield to their Lord and Saviour the obedience of faith and love know and enjoy the peace that passeth understanding.

- THE GOSPEL IS CALLED THE GOSPEL OF PEACE: 'and, as shoes for your feet, having put on the readiness given by the gospel of peace' Eph 6:15.

- THE GOSPEL BRINGS THE MESSAGE OF PEACE WITH GOD ON THE GROUNDS OF PEACE MADE BY THE CROSS AND RECEIVED BY FAITH: 'Therefore, since we have been justified by faith, we have peace with God through our Lord Jesus Christ' Rom 5:1. There is no peace to the wicked: 'Isa 48:22. However the reception of the Gospel at once brings peace to the sinner.

- PRAYER IS THE MEANS OF RETAINING OUR PEACE: 'do not be anxious about anything, but in everything by prayer and supplication with thanksgiving let your requests be made known to God. And the peace of God, which surpasses all understanding, will guard your hearts and your minds in Christ Jesus' Phil 4:6–7

WE HAVE PEACE FROM THE PRINCE OF PEACE:

- PURCHASED: Colossians 1:20;
- PROMISED: John 14:27: 'Peace I leave with you; my peace I give to you. Not as the world gives do I give to you. Let not your hearts be troubled, neither let them be afraid 'John 14:27;
- PREACHED: 'And he came and preached peace to you who were far off and peace to those who were near' Ephesians 2:17.
- PERFECT: You keep him in perfect peace whose mind is stayed on you, because he trusts in you' Isaiah 26:3; Passing understanding: Phil 4:7;
- PURSUED: 'let him turn away from evil and do good; let him seek peace and pursue it' 1 Peter 3:11.

Peace, peace, sweet peace!
Wonderful gift from above!
Oh, wonderful, wonderful peace!
Sweet peace, the gift of God's love!

(P. P. Bilhorn)

There's a peace in my heart that
the world never gave,
A peace it cannot take away;
Tho' the trials of life may surround like a cloud,
I've a peace that has come there to stay!

(Anne S. Murphy)

20TH OCTOBER

THE FATHER'S BUSINESS

*And he said unto them, how is it that ye sought me? Wist
ye not that I must be about my Fathers business?*

Luke 2:49 (KJV)

'Behold then, how great an interest God the Father takes in the work of salvation. It is called 'his business;' and though Jesus Christ came to accomplish our redemption, came to set us a perfect example, and to establish a way of salvation, yet he came not upon his own business, but upon his Father's business—his Father taking as much interest in the salvation of men as even he himself did—the great heart of the Father being as full of love as the bleeding heart of the Son, and the mind of the first person of the Trinity being as tenderly affected towards his chosen as even the mind of Christ Jesus, our substitute, our surety, and our all'—Charles Spurgeon.

The statement 'I must be about my Father's business' was made by our Lord Jesus at the age of 12. It represents the earliest recorded words of Jesus in the Bible'. Some scholars think that is the best translation. Some translations have, 'Why did you seek Me? Did you not know that I must be in My Father's house?' Apparently in today's language it would mean 'I'm in the things of My Father'. Jesus was involved in the things of God.

The Father's business which became the Son's business is now our business today. Someone has said that the Father's business is a great business, a growing business, and a guaranteed business: 'I will build my church, and the gates of hell shall not prevail against it' Matthew 16:18.

In addition to the statement that 'He must be about His Father's business. Luke also records that Jesus said:

- I MUST PREACH: 'I must preach the good news of the kingdom of God to the other towns as well; for I was sent for this purpose' Luke 4:43.
- I MUST SUFFER: 'The Son of Man must suffer many things and be rejected by the elders and chief priests and scribes, and be killed, and on the third day be raised' Luke 9:22.
- I MUST GO ON MY WAY: 'Nevertheless, I must go on my way today and tomorrow and the day following' Luke 13:33. Jesus was daily on His Father's business.
- I MUST STAY AT THE HOME OF ZACCHAEUS: 'And when Jesus came to the place, he looked up and said to him, 'Zacchaeus, hurry and come down, for I must stay at your house today'.
- I MUST BE DELIVERED UP, CRUCIFIED, RISE AGAIN: 'that the Son of Man must be delivered into the hands of sinful men and be crucified and on the third day rise' Luke 24:7.

These are things Jesus had to do to fulfil the 'Father's business'. Likewise there are things we must do in the 'Father's business'. It must be our priority to do them.

21ST OCTOBER

BATTLE OF THE BULGE

*For while bodily training is of some value, godliness
is of value in every way, as it holds promise for the
present life and also for the life to come.*

1 Timothy 4:8

On one occasion I was asked to bring a short talk to a group of seniors after doing some chair aerobics at a Christian gym with which I have an association. I used 1 Timothy 4:8 as my text. I explained to the folk that throughout my life 'the battle of the bulge' has been a constant struggle for me.

The word train in the Greek is the word 'gummazo' from which we get the word gymnasium. It means to train or exercise. It means to work hard, to sweat. Every Greek city had a gymnasium, Ephesus was no exception.

In 1 Timothy 4:8, Paul wrote to Timothy a young first century Pastor about priority. Paul is not despising bodily exercise. Rather, he is making a comparison between bodily exercise and spiritual exercise. Paul was basically saying: 'Just as people go to the gym to train and they discipline themselves so they work out hard, sweat and get stronger; you should discipline yourself to train, not just physically, but train in God's Word for godliness. Now that you have the right diet, the Word of God, exercise yourself in that Word so you become healthy and strong. It's fine to discipline your physical body; it will help you for a few years. But it's far better to discipline yourself spiritually, because it will put you in good stead not only in this life, but also in the life to come. This means that we ought to work much harder at godliness. In other words it is a matter of priorities.

Physical exercise is in no way being condemned because we are reminded in scripture that it is the Lord's will that we prosper with good health as our soul prospers. Taking care of our bodies is a necessity for good health. Eating the right foods and exercise does help maintain good health and therefore is not in any way condemned in scripture.

However, Paul is saying not to put all our energy and effort into getting physically fit and neglect the importance and necessity of exercise for our soul through prayer, bible study, worship, evangelism, praise and honour to God the Father.

Take time to be holy, speak oft with thy Lord;
Abide in Him always, and feed on His Word.
Make friends of God's children,
help those who are weak,
Forgetting in nothing His blessing to seek

(William D. Longstaff)

22ND OCTOBER

THE PRESENT LIFE AND THE LIFE TO COME

And just as it is appointed for man to die once, and after that comes judgment Hebrews 9:27.

'Surely goodness and mercy shall follow me all the days of my life, and I shall dwell in the house of the Lord forever' Psalm 23:6.

'Godliness is of value in every way, as it holds promise for the present life and also for the life to come' 1 Timothy 4:8

The Bible clearly teaches that there is life after this life. The life after this life will never end. It will be lived in Heaven or Hell. However, our eternal destiny is decided in this life. To end up in Heaven we need to have eternal life. You might ask the question: How do I get this eternal life?. Eternal life is found in a person: the Lord Jesus Christ and is explained in the Bible:

Life! life! eternal life!
Jesus alone is the Giver:
Life! life! abundant life!
Glory to Jesus forever!

(W. Leslie)

Today I want to consider with you some of the stealers of life, that keep people away from prioritising eternal life that is found in Christ: Solomon the wisest King that ever lived points some of these out:

- PLEASURES: All things are full of weariness; a man cannot utter it; the eye is not satisfied with seeing, nor the ear filled with hearing' Ecclesiastes 1:8.
- PERFORMANCE: 'one person who has no other, either son or brother, yet there is no end to all his toil, and his eyes are never satisfied with riches, so that he never asks, 'For whom am I toiling and depriving myself of pleasure? This also is vanity and an unhappy business' Ecclesiastes 4:8.
- POSSESSIONS: ' He who loves money will not be satisfied with money, nor he who loves wealth with his income; this also is vanity' Ecclesiastes 5:10.
- POSITION and PURSUITS. Many of these are all right in their place, but should not be our first priority. These are temporal, they don't last.

We need to find the true source of life: 'Jesus said to her, I am the resurrection and the life. Whoever believes in me, though he die, yet shall he live' John 11:25. The life that Jesus gives us is eternal, lasting and meaningful: 'The thief comes only to steal and kill and destroy. I came that they may have life and have it abundantly' John 10:10.

In fact Paul says: 'If in Christ we have hope in this life only, we are of all people most to be pitied. But in fact Christ has been raised from the dead, the first fruits of those who have fallen asleep' 1 Corinthians 15:19–20. Paul makes the point that because of the resurrection of Jesus all those who have their faith and trust in Him alone for salvation are assured of being resurrected too, and will spend the countless years of eternity with Him in heaven.

23RD OCTOBER

LIMITING THE UNLIMITED GOD

Yea, they turned back and tempted God, and limited the Holy One of Israel

Psalm 78:41 (KJV)

When doing deputation at a meeting in a Church in Ballynahinch, Co Down, I noticed a picture on the notice board of Judith Buchanan one of the missionaries of the mission I represented. I informed the missionary secretary that Judith had gone to be with the Lord sometime earlier and that they might want to take Judith's picture down. The missionary secretary went on to tell me that Judith's prayer card and picture had been on the notice board for over 30 years. She told me that Judith had only spoken once in the church some 30 years earlier and she never forgot what Judith had spoken about: 'Limiting God'.

So, can we limit God? The Bible teaches that nothing is too hard for God: 'Ah, Lord God! It is you who have made the heavens and the earth by your great power and by your outstretched arm! Nothing is too hard for you' Jeremiah 32:17.

I have the following (unreferenced) notes on a sermon I preached regarding our unlimited God:

Unlimited in His Awesome Ability
Unlimited in His Bountiful Blessings
Unlimited in His Constant Care
Unlimited in His Dedicated Devotion
Unlimited in His Everlasting Excellence
Unlimited in His Fantastic Foresight
Unlimited in His Gracious Goodness
Unlimited in His Honourable Holiness
Unlimited in His Immaculate Input
Unlimited in His Judicious Justice
Unlimited in His Keen Knowledge
Unlimited in His Limitless Love
Unlimited in His Massive Might
Unlimited in His Overwhelming Oversight
Unlimited in His Pristine Perfection
Unlimited in His Quant Qualities
Unlimited in His Righteous Royalty
Unlimited in His Shining Supremacy
Unlimited in His Triumphant Testimony
Unlimited in His Unrivalled Uniqueness
Unlimited in His Virtuous Values
Unlimited in His Wondrous Wisdom
Unlimited in His Coverage A-Z.

So from Psa 78 what can we learn about how we might limit our limitless God?:

- DISOBEDIENCE: 'They kept not the covenant of God, and refused to walk in his law' v. 10.
- DOUBT: 'for all this they sinned still, and believed not for his wondrous works' v. 32.
- DECEITFULNESS: 'Nevertheless they did flatter him with their mouth, and they lied unto him with their tongues. For their heart was not right with him, neither were they steadfast in his covenant' v. 36–37.
- DISINTEREST: And forgat his works, and his wonders that he had shewed them. Marvellous things did he in the sight of their fathers, in the land of Egypt, in the field of Zoan. He divided the sea, and caused them to pass through; and he made the waters to stand as an heap. In the daytime also he led them with a cloud, and all the night with a light of fire. He clave the rocks in the wilderness, and gave them drink as out of the great depths. He brought streams also out of the rock, and caused waters to run down like rivers. And they sinned yet more against him by provoking the most High in the wilderness v. 11–17.

24TH OCTOBER

HEARING GOD'S CALL IN OUR HEARTS

And I heard the voice of the Lord saying, 'Whom shall I send, and who will go for us?' Then I said, 'Here I am! Send me'

Isaiah 6:8

While working out my notice with the Company I worked for before joining the then OMS International missionary society, I was asked to speak on the subject 'Hearing God's call in our hearts', at my Dad and Mum's church, Stonepark Baptist in March 2007.

The following are some of the thoughts I shared: I posed the questions: What constitutes a call? Is there any way of knowing the will of God? How can one be sure? Is God's call real today? (And are we listening?). For me God had been working on my life in regards to serving Him full-time for a period of time. I would describe it as being unsettled. How did I discern if this was from God?. The following are some of the ways God revealed to me that He was calling me:

- THROUGH THE SCRIPTURES: 'Thy word is a lamp unto my feet, and a light unto my path' Psa 119:105. I must say God used various scriptures, but He used John 4:1–42 in particular. God's will is always in harmony with God's Word.
- THROUGH CIRCUMSTANCES: Ordinary or extraordinary. At a Faith Mission Reunion meeting which I attended at that time the preacher spoke on the eagle's nest: 'Like an eagle that stirs up its nest, that flutters over its young, spreading out its wings, catching them, bearing them on its pinions, the Lord alone guided him' Deut 32:11–12a. The Lord was really stirring my cosy nest in various ways at that time. He certainly was taking me out of my comfort zone.

- THROUGH GOD'S PEACE: A continued inner peace: 'do not be anxious about anything, but in everything by prayer and supplication with thanksgiving let your requests be made known to God. And the peace of God, which surpasses all understanding, will guard your hearts and your minds in Christ Jesus' Philippians 4:6–7.
- THROUGH GODLY COUNSEL OF MATURE CHRISTIAN LEADERS: 'Where there is no guidance, a people falls, but in an abundance of counsellors there is safety' Prov 11:14.
- THROUGH GOD'S LEADING IN OUR HEARTS: An inner impulse, the prompting of the Holy Spirit, that still small voice. I was prompted by the Holy Spirit in what I would describe as being like conviction.
- THROUGH OPEN DOORS: 'I know your works. Behold, I have set before you an open door, which no one is able to shut. I know that you have but little power, and yet you have kept my word and have not denied my name' Revelation 3:8.

The Lord brought me into ministry at the age of 50 and has sustained, guided and met my need ever since.

God calling yet! I cannot stay;
My heart I yield without delay;
Vain world, farewell! from thee I part;
The voice of God hath reached my heart!

(Gerhard Tersteegen)

25TH OCTOBER

IF I FIRMLY BELIEVED

And come out, those who have done good to the resurrection of
life, and those who have done evil to the resurrection of judgment.

John 5:29

Charles Thomas Studd (1860–1931) was an English missionary who faithfully served his Saviour in China, India, and Africa. His motto was: 'If Jesus Christ is God and died for me, then no sacrifice can be too great for me to make for Him'. According to Oswald J Smith in his book called 'The Missionary Call' one of C T Studd's reasons for going to be a missionary to China was the following statement of an atheist:

'If I firmly believed, as millions say they do, that the knowledge of a practice of religion in this life influences destiny in another, then religion would mean to me everything. I would cast away earthly enjoyments as dross, earthly thoughts and feelings as vanity. Religion would be my first waking thought and my last image before sleep sank me into unconsciousness. I should labour in its cause alone. I would take thought for the morrow of eternity alone. I would esteem one soul gained for heaven worth a life of suffering. Earthly consequences would never stay in my head or seal my lips. Earth, its joys and its griefs, would occupy no moment of my thoughts. I would strive to look upon eternity alone, and on the immortal souls around me, soon to be everlastingly happy or everlastingly miserable. I would go forth to the world and preach to it in season and out of season. And my text would be, 'What shall it profit a man if he gains the whole world and loses his own soul''.

Of course it is not religion that saves a person it is Christ and Him alone. It should be our priority our passion to tell others about Jesus. Do we have a burden for the lost today or have we lost our burden.

God, give me a burden
God, give me a word and send me off
To help the hurt and crying
Wounded, hungry, lost and dying ones.

(Dallas Holm)

Give me a passion for souls, dear Lord,
A passion to save the lost;
O that Thy love were by all adored,
And welcomed at any cost.

Refrain

Jesus, I long, I long to be winning
Men who are lost, and constantly sinning;
O may this hour be one of beginning
The story of pardon to tell.

Though there are dangers untold and stern
Confronting me in the way,
Willingly still would I go, nor turn,
But trust Thee for grace each day.

How shall this passion for souls be mine?
Lord, make Thou the answer clear;
Help me to throw out the old Life-Line
To those who are struggling near.

(Herbert G. Tovey)

26TH OCTOBER

HOW GOD, THE CREATOR WORKS

Lift up your eyes on high and see: who created these. He who brings out their host by number, calling them all by name; by the greatness of his might and because he is strong in power, not one is missing

Isaiah 40:26

Over the years I cut out little articles from daily newspapers which I have purchased over the years. Today I want to share with you two letters that the 'Daily Mail' published in 2008 which I found helpful. The article was entitled 'Science shows us we're in God's hands. The first letter was written by Rex Palmer: 'As a scientist with a particular interest in molecular structure and function, I feel I'm privileged to have a detailed view of how God, the Creator, works. As a crystallographer, I'm in the unusual position to be able to look at the make-up of molecules which are too small to be seen through even the most powerful electron microscopes. A recent example of the results obtained by my group at Birkbeck College, London, was to reveal the positions of the hydrogen atoms attached to oxygen in water molecules surrounding much larger cyclosporine H molecules. The drug acts on human cell membranes, but is of fungal origin. In fact, most drugs originated in plants which superficially seems to have no connection with animals. A well-known example, topical at this time of the year, (December), is mistletoe (viscum album), which contains a ricin-like poison that scientists are trying to harness in the fight against cancer. Links such as this really do emphasise the rationale that has gone into creating the world we live in and points to a thoughtful Creator who knows what He is doing'.

The second was sent in by Audrey Ranson; 'The heavens declare the glory of God. Look at the sun—every square yard of it radiates 130,000 horsepower of energy yet it's only one of a hundred billion planets in the Milky Way. If one of these planets moved just two degrees without divine permission, it would mean catastrophe for all of us here on earth. Look at the Earth, tilted at 23 degrees—just one degree off and we'd all drown in a colossal polar meltdown. You are a passenger on an 'earth ship' that has been travelling faster than the speed of sound for thousands of years without breaking down, blowing up or tumbling out of orbit. Think of the intelligence that put it all together—Isaiah 40:26.

O Lord my God, when I in awesome wonder,
Consider all the worlds thy hands have made;
I see the stars, I hear the rolling thunder,
Thy power throughout the universe displayed:
Then sings my soul, my Saviour God, to thee:
How great thou art! How great thou art!
Then sings my soul, my Saviour God, to thee:
How great thou art! How great thou art!

(Carl Boberg)

27TH OCTOBER

HELP

Help, Lord.

Psalm 12:1 (KJV)

One of the things I do on a voluntary basis is to help out a charity who amongst other things supports elderly people who are isolated in rural areas. One of the things they do is call by telephone such folk who request it on a regular basis. One of the requirements to carry out this role was to undergo an essential helpline skills course. It was very interesting to learn many skills in manning a helpline efficiently and effectively. Anyhow at the end of the course I was awarded a level 1 certificate 'Essential Helpline Skills'. It was interesting to learn that there are many helplines across Northern Ireland providing an excellent service dealing with all kinds of problems and difficulties.

However, the greatest helpline of all is to take our problems and difficulties to the Lord in prayer. In Psalm 12 King David in a time of difficulty simply cried out 'Help Lord'. It is wonderful to realise that we can come to the creator of the universe and cry out to Him 'Help'.

According to Dr G Campbell Morgan the cause of David's request in Psalm 12 for help was 'out of a consciousness of the terrible evil of his times he cries to God for help'. Not only do we learn of the cause of David's cry for help but we see the characteristics of his prayer for help. It was short (two words), it was simple, and it was sincere. And what was the outcome of his request for help: David was made safe v. 5.

Have you a problem, a difficulty today. Why not simply cry out to God in prayer for HELP:

Help me, O Lord, the God of my salvation;
I have no hope, no refuge but in Thee;
Help me to make this perfect consecration,
In life or death Thine evermore to be.

Help me, O Lord, to keep my pledge unbroken;
Guard Thou my ways, my thoughts, my tongue, my heart;
Help me to trust the word which Thou hast spoken,
That from Thy paths my feet may ne'er depart.

Help me, O Lord, when sore temptations press me;
O lift the clouds that hide Thee from my sight;
Help me, O Lord, when anxious cares distress me,
To look beyond, where all is calm and bright.

Help me, O Lord, my strength is only weakness;
Thine, Thine the power by which alone I live;
Help me each day, to bear the cross with meekness,
Till Thou at last the promised crown shalt give.

(Fanny Crosby)

28TH OCTOBER

HELPLINE

Give us help from trouble: for vain is the help of man.

Psalm 60:11

While writing this devotional, I took a course in essential helpline skills. This was a requirement for a role I carry out on a voluntary basis. There are many helplines for various issues including debt, mental health, bereavement, depression, various forms of addictions, parenting, etc. etc. Many of these helplines are to be thoroughly recommended and indeed may be one of the ways God will use to bring you the help you need. However, the greatest helpline and greatest helper of all is the Lord. As believers in Jesus we should firstly take our problem, our query to the Lord in prayer. The reason being that there are certain situations which only God can really help you with. If you make Him your first source for help He may well guide you to other sources for help.

The following are some verses of Scripture indicating that we should make the Lord our ultimate helpline:

'God is our refuge and strength, a very present help in trouble' Psalm 46:1. Our God is always available, accessible, adequate, and able.

'So we can confidently say, the Lord is my helper; I will not fear; what can man do to me?' Hebrews 13:6.

'To this day I have had the help that comes from God' Acts 26:22. 'For I, the Lord your God, hold your right hand; it is I who say to you, 'Fear not, I am the one who helps you.' Isaiah 41:13.

Though dark the night, and clouds look black
And stormy overhead,
And trials of almost ev'ry kind
Across my path are spread;
How soon I conquer all,
As to the Lord I call:
A little talk with Jesus makes it right, all right!

Refrain:

A little talk with Jesus makes it right, all right!
A little talk with Jesus makes it right, all right!
In trials of ev'ry kind,
Praise God, I always find
A little talk with Jesus makes it right, all right!

When those who once were dearest friends
Begin to persecute,
And more who once profess'd to love
Have distant grown, and mute,—
I tell Him all my grief,
He quickly sends relief:
A little talk with Jesus makes it right, all right!

And thus, by frequent little talks,
I gain the victory,
And march along with cheerful song,
Enjoying liberty;
With Jesus as my Friend,
I'll prove unto the end,
A little talk with Jesus makes it right, all right!

(Unknown)

29TH OCTOBER

I CAN SPELL A LOVELY NAME: J.E.S.U.S

And she shall bring forth a son, and thou shalt call his name Jesus: for he shall save his people from their sins.

At the time of writing this devotional a number of Christian Pastors and Christian leaders received their home call to glory. Amongst such was George Verwer and Tim Keller and Pastor Wilbert Dempster. Pastor Dempster dedicated me as a child, later on he dedicated my second daughter and my son. One of Pastor Dempster's favourite lines was: 'I can spell a lovely name J.E.S.U.S. Over his period of ministry he led many people to Jesus as their Lord and Saviour. His aim was to glorify Jesus in all he said and did. I have in my possession outlines using the name J.E.S.U.S as an acrostic to describe something about that lovely name and who He is and what does on our behalf as Lord and Saviour. I trust you are blessed as you consider these today:

Jesus Exactly Suits Us Sinners.

Jesus (Matthew 1:12)
Exalted (Acts 2:36)
Saviour (Acts 13:23)
Universally (John 3:16)
Saves (1 Timothy 4:10).

Jesus (Luke 1:31)
Everlasting (John 5:24)
Saves (Hebrews 7:25)
Ungodly (Romans 5:6)
Sinners (1 Timothy 1:15).

Justifies (Luke 18:14)
Emancipates (Titus 2:14)
Saves (Matthew 1:21)
Unburdens (Matthew 11:28)
Satisfies (John 4:14).

His Name is Wonderful;
His Name is Counsellor;
His Name The Mighty God,
Jesus my Lord.

A Child and Son is He;
Eternal Father He;
The Prince of Peace to me,
Jesus my Lord.

Praise the Creator,
Jesus our Savior,
Life-giving Spirit now.
In spirit worship Him,
Love and adore Him;
His Name is Wonderful,
Jesus my Lord.

(Audrey Mieir)

Name of all majesty, | fathomless mystery,
King of the ages | by angels adored;
power and authority, | splendour and dignity,
bow to his mastery, | Jesus is Lord!

Child of our destiny, | God from eternity,
love of the Father | on sinners outpoured;
see now what God has done | sending his only Son,
Christ the beloved One, | Jesus is Lord!

Saviour of Calvary, | costliest victory,
darkness defeated | and Eden restored;
born as a man to die, | nailed to a cross on high,
cold in the grave to lie, | Jesus is Lord!

Source of all sovereignty, | light, immortality,
life everlasting | and heaven assured;
so with the ransomed, we | praise him eternally,
Christ in his majesty, | Jesus is Lord!

(Timothy Dudley-Smith)

30TH OCTOBER

Lay up for yourselves treasures in heaven.

Matthew 6:20

I had the privilege of visiting the John Wesley Chapel known as the 'New Room', while serving the Lord in my role as UK Executive Director of OMS UK. The 'New Room' chapel is the oldest Methodist Chapel in the world.

Both John and Charles Wesley after returning from America to England were deeply dissatisfied with their spiritual state. Still heavily influenced by the Moravians they had met earlier, the Wesley brothers joined in a 'Religious Society', and in May 1738 both underwent a profound spiritual experience. John described this experience in his Journal for 24 May 1738:

'In the evening I went very unwillingly to a society in Aldersgate Street, where one was reading Luther's preface to the Epistle to the Romans. About a quarter before nine, while he was describing the change which God works in the heart through faith in Christ, I felt my heart strangely warmed. I felt I did trust in Christ, Christ alone for salvation, and an assurance was given me that he had taken away my sins, even mine and saved me from the law of sin and death'.

Three days earlier, following his own 'conversion' experience, Charles had written a hymn:

Where shall my wondering soul begin
How shall I all to heaven aspire?
A slave redeemed from death and sin,
A brand plucked from eternal fire,
How shall I equal triumphs raise,
Or sing my great Deliverer's praise?

The change the Lord made in their lives through the new birth experience and the tremendous assurance that they were indeed forgiven through and by Christ alone led them to bring this message to millions of people in their lifetime.

I love the way Leonard Ravenhill expresses John Wesley's spiritual legacy: 'Do you know what he left when he died? He left a handful of books, a faded Geneva gown that he wore as he preached all over England, six silver spoons somebody gave him, and six single pound notes.

He said, 'Give one to each of the poor men that carry me to my grave'.

And that's all he left: six one pound notes and six silver spoons, a handful of books, a Geneva gown and ah... there's something else... what was it, the other thing? Oh, I know, something else he left—the Methodist Church!

John Wesley could have died as rich as any famous television preacher. Sure, he made money, and he built orphanages with it! Sure, he made money, and he printed Bibles! He financed missionaries to go across the earth. And he died worth about thirty dollars. That's the way to use your money. Think of the reward. Why, do you think it says, 'Don't lay up treasure on earth? Lay up treasure in heaven!"

The challenge for today is: What spiritual legacy will you and I leave behind?

31ST OCTOBER

THE RIGHT USE OF MONEY

Each one must give as he has decided in his heart, not reluctantly or under compulsion, for God loves a cheerful giver.

2 Corinthians 9:7

The following are some extracts regarding the right use of money, written by John Wesley: 'The introduction of money into the world is one instance of the wise and gracious providence of God. 'The love of money' we know from God's Word, 'is the root of all evil'. But not the thing itself. The fault does not lie in the money, but in them that use it. It is of unspeakable service to all civilized nations, in all common affairs of life. It is the instrument of transacting all manner of business, and, if we use it according to Christian wisdom, of doing all manner of good. It is therefore of the highest concern that all who fear God know how to employ this valuable talent. Perhaps all instruction necessary for this may be reduced to three plain rules'.

Wesley then goes on to outline these three rules. I am going to summarise the first two.

1. GAIN ALL YOU CAN: We are to gain all we can without hurting our mind any more than our body. Don't engage in any sinful or unlawful trade, or in a trade that would damage our neighbour. Gain all you can by common sense, by using in your business all the understanding God has given you. Do better today than yesterday.

2. SAVE ALL YOU CAN: Having gained all you can, by honest wisdom and unwearied diligence, the second rule of Christian prudence is to save all you can. Do not throw away your money in idle expenses etc. etc.

3. 'GIVE ALL YOU CAN: Having first gained all you can; and secondly, saved all you can; then thirdly, give all you can! To see the ground and reason of this, consider that, when the Professor of Heaven and earth brought you into being, He placed you in this world, not as a proprietor but as a steward. As such, he entrusted you with goods of various kinds; but the sole property of these can never be alienated from Him. As you yourself are not your own but His, such is likewise all that you enjoy, your substance in particular. He has told you how you are to employ it for Him, that all may be acceptable through Jesus Christ; and this easy service He has promised to reward. Should a doubt arise in your mind concerning what you are going to expend, you have an easy way to remove it. Calmly, seriously enquire: Am I acting therein, not as a proprietor but steward of my Lord's goods?'

I trust this is helpful to us today in considering how best to use our money as good stewards of what God has given us.

1ST NOVEMBER

HE IS PRAYING

And the Lord said to him, 'Rise and go to the street
called Straight, and at the house of Judas look for a man
of Tarsus named Saul, for behold, he is praying'

Acts 9:11

I have the following selected article in my possession entitled 'Behold, He Prayeth' taken out of an old Christian magazine written in the 1960s sent to me by one of the retired missionaries of the mission I served the Lord with from 2007–2022.

What a lot can lie behind three words! An arch-persecutor had become a humble petitioner. A leader was now to be led and one who might well have been a master in Israel was now to take his place in the school of grace. And what a school this is, one of which we should never tire and always count it an honour to be a student.

When the Apostle Paul, of whom the three words were spoken, was found in that attitude it was quite evident that it was no pious posture with him but a matter of the heart. His soul was knit to God in a new way and something was happening. It is not dissimilar in our own case for while the Apostle was a giant in the faith, we all meet upon Redemption ground before the Mercy Seat and the means of grace open to him then, are those open to us now. As it was when he prayed, so when we pray, something happens –

- We admit the sovereignty of God,
- We admit our utter dependence upon Him,
- We glorify Him,
- We live, and contribute to the life of the Church,
- We bless those for whom we pray,
- We share in the ingathering of others, and
- We are blessed in ourselves.

Can it be said of us 'behold, he is praying'. Key to following Jesus is having a robust prayer life.

Sweet hour of prayer! sweet hour of prayer!
that calls me from a world of care,
and bids me at my Father's throne
make all my wants and wishes known.

In seasons of distress and grief,
my soul has often found relief,
and oft escaped the tempter's snare
by thy return, sweet hour of prayer!

Sweet hour of prayer! sweet hour of prayer!
the joys I feel, the bliss I share
of those whose anxious spirits burn
with strong desires for thy return!

With such I hasten to the place
where God my Savior shows his face,
and gladly take my station there,
and wait for thee, sweet hour of prayer!

Sweet hour of prayer! sweet hour of prayer!
thy wings shall my petition bear
to him whose truth and faithfulness
engage the waiting soul to bless.

And since he bids me seek his face,
believe his word, and trust his grace,
I'll cast on him my every care,
and wait for thee, sweet hour of prayer!

(W. W. Walford)

2ND NOVEMBER

LONE WATCHERS

The LORD is near to all who call on him,
to all who call on him in truth.

Psalm 145:18

To follow Jesus it is essential we are continually and constantly in communication with Him. For us this is through the channel of prayer.

If we want to see the hand of God move in our day and generation then we need to pray. The following is a challenging selected article in the November 1970 edition of the 'Revival Magazine':

'Not more preachers, not more singers are the need of the hour—but more PRAY-ERS. Many people are much more ready to give money to help advance the kingdom of God upon earth than they are to give themselves up to a life of intercession with God. Dr A J Gordon once said, 'I have long since ceased to pray, Lord have compassion on a lost world! I remember the day and hour I seemed to hear the Lord rebuking me for such a prayer. He seemed to say to me, I have had compassion on a lost world, and now it is time for you to have compassion. I have given my heart; now give your heart'.

Hearts that feel, and move, and weep and pray are many times harder for God to get hold of than houses and lands and bank accounts or ready cash. Many are ready to endorse the good work of home and foreign missionaries who toil and suffer for the salvation of souls; yea, they will dispense of their means to support, but where are the 'lone watchers' who will pour out their lives at the feet of the Master—even into the small hours of the night? Where are those whose hearts cry and sigh over the abominations that are wrought in this land? They are lone watchers indeed, for the multitudes are not going that way.

More prayer—mighty, compassionate, heart-felt intercession for the multitudes is the need of the hour—who will bid for the place at the Saviour's feet? Who is ready for the sacrifice? Who will go with Jesus without the camp, bearing His reproach (for there will be misunderstandings and reproach)? Who will watch with Him in Gethsemane's sorrow over the world? 'He that goeth forth and weepeth, bearing precious seed, shall doubtless come again with rejoicing, bringing his sheaves with him".

There are quite a number of challenging and direct questions throughout this article. Let us honestly reflect and answer these in relation to our lives today. It is my prayer that we will become better PRAY-ERS.

Watch and pray, nor let us ever weary;
Jesus watched and prayed alone;
Prayed for us when only stars beheld Him,
While on Olive's brow they shone.

(Fanny Crosby)

3RD NOVEMBER

FOLLOWING BY FAITH

For we walk by faith, not by sight.

One of the essentials in following hard after God is following Him by faith. Chapter 11 of Hebrews helps us by naming Old Testament saints who walked by faith and how they did it:

ABEL BY THE SACRIFICE OF FAITH: 'By faith Abel offered to God a more acceptable sacrifice than Cain, through which he was commended as righteous, God commending him by accepting his gifts. And through his faith, though he died, he still speaks' Hebrews 11:4

NOAH BY THE SIMPLICITY OF FAITH: 'By faith Noah, being warned by God concerning events as yet unseen, in reverent fear constructed an ark for the saving of his household. By this he condemned the world and became an heir of the righteousness that comes by faith' Hebrews 11:7

ABRAHAM BY THE SOJOURN OF FAITH: 'By faith Abraham obeyed when he was called to go out to a place that he was to receive as an inheritance. And he went out, not knowing where he was going' Hebrews 11:8

MOSES BY THE SUFFERING OF FAITH: 'By faith Moses, when he was grown up, refused to be called the son of Pharaoh's daughter, choosing rather to be mistreated with the people of God than to enjoy the fleeting pleasures of sin' Hebrews 11:24–25

Following Jesus from day to day,
Gently He leads me along the way;
E'er will I trust Him all foes despite,
By faith and not by sight.

Refrain:

Walking with Jesus I'm in the light,
Walking with Jesus in robes of white;
Walking with Jesus my way is bright,
By faith and not by sight.

Jesus has purchased me for His own,
Sweetly He reigns in my heart, His throne,
Pardon He granted, and washed me white,
By faith and not by sight.

Seeking to enter the holiest place,
Boldly I came to the throne of grace;
Sanctified wholly, He's my delight,
By faith and not by sight.

When I was held in affliction's chain,
Suffering much from disease and pain;
Jesus then touched me and healed me quite,
By faith and not by sight.

Walking with Jesus till we shall meet,
When in His likeness I stand complete,
Where with the ransomed in heaven's light,
My faith is lost in sight.

(Clara M. Brooks)

By faith, the prophets saw a day
When the longed-for Messiah would appear
With the power to break the
chains of sin and death,
And rise triumphant from the grave.

By faith, the church was called to go
In the power of the Spirit to the lost
To deliver captives and to preach good news,
In every corner of the earth.

(Stuart Townend , Keith
Getty & Kristyn Getty)

4TH NOVEMBER

CHALLENGING PERIODS

And if I go and prepare a place for you, I will come again and will take you to myself, that where I am you may be also.

John 14:3

Today I am sharing an article entitled 'Challenging Periods' written in the 1940s by Lettie Cowman the wife of the founder of the mission through which I served the Lord for fifteen years. If what Lettie wrote then was significant, how much more significant is the article in this period of pandemics, artificial intelligence and overall chaos throughout our world:

'The biographer of one of the nation's earlier leaders made this statement concerning him: 'He lived in a great moment in the world's history, but had not greatness of character with which to meet the challenging periods'. Some periods of Christian history are windowless rooms, and others are the wide-open spaces of a Kingly palace. Today we are living in the palace-age of the world's history, any person who has the finger tips on the heartbeat of the world cannot but feel we are living in the greatest age of the world's history. In this crisis age, this age-end time, our lot is cast!—And each of us can say, 'I have my place, my duty, and my hour!' Each life is original, separate, distinct, purposeful, and has a place in the great plan of God. A replica of the famous painting, 'Christ Weeping over Jerusalem,' hangs upon the wall of our office, and daily speaks to us. The Master is seated on the Mount of Olives—the sacred mount to which He often resorted with His little flock. Looking over Jerusalem He utters a cry which has echoed down the centuries and through corridors of time

like a funeral dirge: 'O Jerusalem . . . how often would I have gathered thy children together . . . and ye would not! Behold, your house is left unto you desolate.' Luke 12:34, 35.

Oh! The pathos of such words! The opportunity was gone. Gone forever! And from henceforth their house was left unto them desolate. The people at that period of time had been given every opportunity to know Him! In their possession were the sacred writings to guide them. Their prophets had foretold the day of the Saviour's birth. Then He came and lived among them for thirty-three years. Bur blinded by their unbelief, they missed their opportunity!

But to those who had left all to follow Him, He gave a solemn promise ere He returned to the Father: 'If I go . . . I will come again'. (John 14:3). And we await that hour! No intelligent Christian can fail to discern the signs of the times in which we are now living! In a thousand ways He is telling His own of His soon coming, and God is working today to prepare for the return of Christ for His Bride. We are of the firmest conviction that the thing He is doing is unmistakably in this period of time. He is opening the avenues of the world to the spread of the gospel and asking His messengers to spread it to the last nation, and the last man on the face of the earth! He has made us trustees of His message! He has 'committed unto us the word of reconciliation!'

5TH NOVEMBER

GOD NEVER MOVES BACKWARDS

Ask me of things to come; will you command me concerning my children and the work of my hands?

Isaiah 45:11

Yesterday I shared some thoughts from Lettie Cowman about the Lord's return. Today I will share some more that I trust will challenge us to work with determination to reach the lost in these days:

'As a sign of His second coming, Christ said, 'And this gospel of the kingdom shall be preached in all the world as a witness unto all nations, and then shall the end come' (Matthew 24:14). It SHALL be preached! God said so! That great day is hastening. There is an amazing swiftness. Who can be so blind as those who cannot see events on earth hastening the great day, when He shall come, bringing His reward with Him? Until He comes, we have a glorious gospel to proclaim. It is ours to be messengers to every nation, to every tribe, on this terrestrial ball; a privilege not committed to angels— but to men! God's orders are always 'forward!' Remain where we are, we cannot! Advance without God, we dare not! God moves, but He never moves backward. While the daylight lingers, and under the sunset skies, the night is fast drawing on. We must work!—and it must not be said of us that 'He came and found them sleeping' Awake! Awake! oh Church of Christ, and put on thy beautiful garments of strength! Because of the lateness of the hour and the stupendous task committed to us, we must be up, alert, and away to the ripe harvest!'

We forget as we make our little practical plans that infinite resources are available to those who are ready to set out upon mighty ventures of faith. The power is there, but there must be also a channel through which it may flow. In the carrying out of His purposes, God seeks for those whose faith corresponds with His resources. There are many things we cannot do. There is nothing He cannot do through us. The challenge is 'to prove God', and to do it now! Fulfil the conditions of His mighty manifestations. Release His wondrous power amongst us. Loosen the resources of the heavens for the healing of the nations. Unlock the gates of divine plenteousness for the world's spiritual poverty. The whole situation is ripe for proving God now.

We have limited God by our trifling dimensions. Is it true that there are no limits in God? Are we ready to trust the Limitless One! Are the resources in God, which were open to George Mueller, sealed to us? Let us put in our unclaimed deposits and appropriate Him to the uttermost limits, for we are called to be co-partners with God's own Son! Ask me of things to come concerning my sons, and concerning the work of my hands command ye me" (Isaiah 45:11).

6TH NOVEMBER

REASONS FOR MISSIONS

*Then they said to one another, 'We are not doing right.
This day is a day of good news. If we are silent and wait
until the morning light, punishment will overtake us. Now
therefore come; let us go and tell the kings household.'*

2 Kings 7:9

I had the privilege of serving the Lord in various missionary roles over fifteen years in a full-time basis. This allowed me to be involved in homeland and foreign missions. What a privilege. God is a God of missions. Jesus before going back to Heaven after His resurrection gave us the Great Commission. This will not be revoked until He comes again. Mission is a prerogative of every child of God. John Piper is quoted as saying: 'you have three choices in world missions: be a joyful, sacrificial goer, be a joyful, sacrificial sender, or be disobedient'.

Here are some reasons as to why as believers we must be involved in missions:

- Because the greatest mission ever known to man was when God sent His Son the Lord Jesus Christ into the world to save it: 'For God so loved the world, that he gave his only Son, that whoever believes in him should not perish but have eternal life. For God did not send his Son into the world to condemn the world, but in order that the world might be saved through him' John 3:16–17.
- Because the world will never be brought to Christ until men bring Christ to the world. 'Therefore, we are ambassadors for Christ, God making his appeal through us. We implore you on behalf of Christ, be reconciled to God' 2 Corinthians 5:20. Soul winning and witnessing is not a Sunday supplement to life. It is a seven day a week responsibility.
- Because Jesus Himself taught us that missions was the way to make disciples. Jesus commands us: 'Go into all the world and proclaim the gospel to the whole creation' Mark 16:15.
- Because I am a disobedient disciple of Jesus if I do not obey His command to 'Go'.
- Because I am obliged to share with others the gospel about this great salvation that I possess: 'I am under obligation both to Greeks and to barbarians, both to the wise and to the foolish. So I am eager to preach the gospel to you also who are in Rome' Romans 1:14–15.
- Because a Christian who does not believe in Missions always gets narrow and loses their world vision.
- Because Jesus alone can meet the heart cry of lost humanity. Therefore, let us pray, give, go.

*Go forth and tell! O church of God, awake!
God's saving news to all the nations take:
proclaim Christ Jesus, Saviour,
Lord and King,
that all the world his worthy praise may sing.*

(James Seddon)

7TH NOVEMBER

WHAT IT MEANS TO BE IN CHRIST

And because of him you are in Christ Jesus, who became to us wisdom from God, righteousness and sanctification and redemption.

1 Corinthians 1:30

Once you repent of your sin and trust Christ alone for your salvation you commence following Jesus day by day. Your identity is now found in Christ: Let's take a look today at some ways this affects us: I am always:

- DEEPLY LOVED: 'So that Christ may dwell in your hearts through faith—that you, being rooted and grounded in love, may have strength to comprehend with all the saints what is the breadth and length and height and depth' Eph 3:17–18.
- BLESSED: 'Blessed be the God and Father of our Lord Jesus Christ, who has blessed us in Christ with every spiritual blessing in the heavenly places' Eph 1:3.
- GOD'S MASTERPIECE: 'For we are his workmanship, created in Christ Jesus for good works, which God prepared beforehand, that we should walk in them' Eph 2:10.
- HOLY: 'Even as he chose us in him before the foundation of the world, that we should be holy and blameless before him in love' Eph 1:4.
- ACCEPTED: 'To the praise of his glorious grace, with which he has blessed us in the Beloved' Eph 1:6.
- SAVED: 'Even when we were dead in our trespasses, made us alive together with Christ—by grace you have been saved— and raised us up with him and seated us with him in the heavenly places in Christ Jesus' Eph 2:5–6.
- ADOPTED: 'He predestined us for adoption to himself as sons through Jesus Christ, according to the purpose of his will' Eph 1:5.
- ROOTED IN LOVE: 'So that Christ may dwell in your hearts through faith—that you, being rooted and grounded in love' Eph 3:17.
- I AM A NEW CREATION: 'If anyone is in Christ, he is a new creation. The old has passed away; behold, the new has come' 2 Cor 5:17.
- FORGIVEN: 'Let it be known to you therefore, brothers, that through this man forgiveness of sins is proclaimed to you, and by him everyone who believes is freed from everything from which you could not be freed by the law of Moses' Acts 13:38–39.
- COMPLETE: 'You have been filled in him, who is the head of all rule and authority' Col 2:10.
- REDEEMED: 'In whom we have redemption, the forgiveness of sins' Col 1:14.
- RECONCILED TO GOD: 'All this is from God, who through Christ reconciled us to himself and gave us the ministry of reconciliation' 2 Cor 5:18.
- AMBASSADORS: 'We are ambassadors for Christ' 2 Cor 5:20.
- COVERED IN HIS RIGHTEOUSNESS: 'For our sake he made him to be sin who knew no sin, so that in him we might become the righteousness of God' 2 Cor 5:21.

Today let us rejoice in what it means to you and me to be 'In Christ'.

8TH NOVEMBER

YOUR CHURCH LEADERS NEED PRAYER

*I appeal to you, brothers, by our Lord Jesus Christ
and by the love of the Spirit, to strive together with
me in your prayers to God on my behalf.*

Romans 15:30

Hope Community Church Longford have the following pinned on their internal notice board regarding how to pray for your Pastor. It is entitled 'Your Church Leaders Need Prayer':

- P is for PEACEABLE. Ask God to help your pastor abandon a quarrel before if breaks out and avoid slandering anyone. Pray that he would be peaceable & gentle; ask that he might live in peace even with his enemies. (Proverbs 17:14; Titus 3:2; Proverbs 16:7.

- A is for ABOVE REPROACH: Pray that your pastor would live a blameless life, that he would be faithful to his wife & raise children who are sincere believers, not wild or disobedient. Pray that God would protect his heart against greed, violence, drunkenness, impatience, and self-absorption. (Titus 1:6–7).

- S is for SELF-DISCIPLINED: Ask God to grant your elder an extra measure of self-control. Pray that he'd live an upright, holy, and disciplined life. Teach him, O Lord, to love what is good and give a pure & steadfast heart. Keep him alert and sober-minded. (Titus 1:8; Psalm 51:10; 1 Peter 4:7).

- T is for TEACHING TRUTH: Pray that your pastor will hold firmly and be faithful to the Word of God, so that by sound teaching he will be able to encourage others and refute those who contradict its message. Pray that he would be a doer of the Word, and not merely a hearer, since as a teacher he will incur a stricter judgement (Titus 1:9; James 1:22–23; James 3:1).

- O is for OBEDIENT: Ask God to make your elder a man after his own heart. May he submit to the Word of God with humility and be obedient in everything, just as Christ humbled Himself and became obedient, even unto death. Help him run with endurance the race that you've marked out for him. (1 Samuel 13:14; 2 Corinthians 2:9; Philippians 2:8; Hebrews 12:1).

- R is for RESPECTED: Pray that God would give your pastor a good name in your community. Let him do nothing, Lord, that would tarnish his reputation or cause a little one to stumble. Let him be known for his wisdom, integrity, and hospitality. (Proverbs 22:1; Mark 9:42; 1 Cor. 12:8; Psalm 25:21; Titus 1:8).

I trust this will be helpful to you today as you pray for your minister, church leader, elder or pastor.

9TH NOVEMBER

HOPE

May the God of hope fill you with all joy and peace in believing,
so that by the power of the Holy Spirit you may abound in hope.

Romans 15:13

While on a visit to Longford, Ireland I had the privilege of having a brief chat with Simon Scott the rector of the Longford Group of Parishes. He describes them as evangelical churches belonging to the Church of Ireland in the dioceses of Kilmore, Elphin and Ardagh. However, what really caught my attention was their theme of the year –Hope. It was then laid out in the following way which I trust you will find helpful today:

H = Hearts: Our hearts reveal what is important. What is in your heart? The Bible says 'Love the Lord your God with all your heart' Matthew 22:37.

O = Open: We don't know everything and we all have to learn as Jesus teaches us. Are your ears open? The Bible says, 'Here I am! I stand at the door and knock. If anyone hears my voice and opens the door, I will come' Revelation 3:20.

P = Praising: It's good for us to give praise to God for the blessings we have and to be thankful for what Jesus has done for us. The Bible says, 'The whole crowd of disciples began joyfully to praise God in loud voices for all the miracles they had seen' Luke 19:37.

E = Eternity: There is more to life than we can see for in Jesus it goes on eternally. Our hope is in the provision of life after death for those who trust in Jesus and follow him. The Bible says, 'the faith of God's elect and their knowledge of the truth that leads to godliness— in the hope of eternal life, which God, who does not lie, promised before the beginning of time' Titus 1:1–2.

Today praise God for the steadfast and sure hope we have as believers in Christ:

Born of the Spirit with life from above
Into God's fam'ly divine
Justified fully thru Calvary's love
O what a standing is mine
And the transaction so quickly was made
When as a sinner I came
Took of the offer of grace He did proffer
He saved me, O praise His dear name

Now I've a hope that will surely endure
After the passing of time
I have a future in heaven for sure
There in those mansions sublime
And it's because of that wonderful day
When at the cross I believed
Riches eternal and blessings supernal
From His precious hand I received

(John W. Peterson)

10TH NOVEMBER

FOR YOUR SAKES - POOR

For you know the grace of our Lord Jesus Christ, that
though he was rich, yet for your sake he became poor,
so that you by his poverty might become rich.

2 Corinthians 8:9

Charles Haddon Spurgeon (1834–92) was England's best-known preacher for most of the second half of the nineteenth century. In 1854, just four years after his conversion, Spurgeon, then only 20, became pastor of London's famed New Park Street Church. The congregation quickly outgrew their building, moved to Exeter Hall, then to Surrey Music Hall. In these venues Spurgeon frequently preached to audiences numbering more than 10,000. In 1861 the congregation moved permanently to the newly constructed Metropolitan Tabernacle.

Today I want to share some of his thoughts on 2 Corinthians 8:9: 'The Lord Jesus Christ was eternally rich, glorious, and exalted; but 'though he was rich, yet for your sake he became poor'. As the rich saint cannot be true in his communion with his poor brethren unless of his substance he ministers to their necessities, so (the same rule holding with the head as among the members) it is impossible that our Divine Lord could have had fellowship with us unless He imparted to us His own abounding wealth and had become poor in order to make us rich. Had He remained upon His throne of glory, and had we continued in the ruins of the fall without receiving His salvation, communion would have been impossible on both sides.

Our position by the fall, apart from the covenant of grace, made it impossible for fallen man to communicate with God as it is for Belial to be in concord with Christ. In order, therefore, that communion might be compassed, it was necessary that the rich kinsman should bestow his estate upon his poor relatives, that the righteous Saviour should give to His sinning brethren of His own perfection, and that we, the poor and guilty, should receive of His fullness grace for grace; that thus, in giving and receiving, the one might descend from the heights, and other ascend from the depths, and so be able to embrace each other in true and hearty fellowship.

Poverty must be enriched by Him, in whom are infinite treasures, before it can venture to commune; and guilt must lose itself in imputed and imparted righteousness ere the soul can walk in fellowship with purity. Jesus must clothe His people in His own garments, or He cannot admit them into His palace of glory; and He must wash them in His own Blood, or else they will be too defiled for the embrace of His fellowship.

O believer, herein is love! For your sake the Lord Jesus 'became poor' that He might lift you up into communion with Himself'.

11TH NOVEMBER

THE THREE LIGHTS

And your ears shall hear a word behind you,
saying, 'This is the way, walk in it,' when you turn
to the right or when you turn to the left.

Isaiah 30:21

I still have the little flyer advertising the March 2007 spring conference of the men's fellowship I was in at that time. Derick Bingham was the speaker, and his subject was: 'Does God Still Guide?' At that time I was just in the process of leaving my employment to join a missionary agency where you lived by faith. Derick told a little story that was a great help in confirming my call into full-time Christian service: Many years ago F B Meyer was travelling from Dublin to Holyhead off the Welsh coast. He was standing on the bridge with the captain, chatting to him about the voyage. Dr Meyer asked the captain 'How do you know when you are on course for Holyhead?' The captain replied 'When I approach the port, I see three lights on the horizon. When I manoeuvre my ship to a position where I can make the three lights, one light, I am on course for Holyhead harbour'. F B Meyer lifted his pen when he got home and wrote of how Christians have three lights which are on the horizon of their lives to guide them. When they find those three lights are one light, they can be sure they are on course for making a good decision in their lives to guide them:

- The first light is the light of Scripture
- The second light is the light of circumstances
- The third light is the light of the 'Peace of God'.

So it is when faced with a decision in life, a Christian must make sure that the light of the Word of God, the light of circumstance, and the light of the peace of God, are one light. In other words in total alignment. If one of these three is missing, wait until it comes into line and then proceed. You will find that God's lights of guidance, if followed, will never lead you on to the rocks. Trust Him.

Interestingly I was travelling this same route a number of years ago. After relating this story to one of the crew members I asked if I could ask the same question to the Captain as F B Meyer had many years earlier. They informed me this had to be arranged before the sailing for security reasons. However, they said they would ask the Captain for me. Back came the following answer: The lights still must be in line—actually the answer F B Meyer was given was 'dead on'.

Today I can affirm that God's guidance is always 'dead on' if the lights of the Scripture, circumstance and God's peace are in perfect alignment. I found this illustration most helpful in many decisions thereafter.

12TH NOVEMBER

THE VANITY OF THE WORLD

The world is passing away along with its desires, but
whoever does the will of God abides forever.

1 John 2:17

John Newton the author of the hymn 'Amazing Grace' is one of my spiritual heroes. The following is a letter he wrote regarding the vanity of the world; 'What a poor, uncertain, dying world is this! What a wilderness in itself! How dark, how desolate, without the light of the Gospel and knowledge of Jesus! It does not appear so to us in a state of nature, because we are then in a state of enchantment, the magical lantern blinding us with a splendid delusion.

So in the desert's dreary waste,
By magic pow'r produced in haste,
(As ancient fables say)
Castles, and groves, and music sweet,
The senses of the trav'ller meet,
And stop him in his way.

But while he listens with surprise,
The charm dissolves, the vision dies,
'Twas but enchanted ground;
Thus if the Lord our spirits touch,
The world, which promised us so much,
A wilderness is found.

It is a great mercy to be undeceived in time; and though our gay (the term in Newton's day meant 'carefree', 'cheerful') dreams are at an end, and we awake to everything that is disgustful and dismaying, yet we see a highway through the wilderness, a powerful Guard, and an infallible Guide at hand to conduct us through; and we can discern, beyond the limits of the wilderness, a better land, where we shall be at rest and at home.

The remembrance of them will only remain to heighten our sense of the love, care, and power of our Saviour and Leader. Oh, how shall we then admire, adore, and praise Him, when He shall condescend to unfold to us the beauty, propriety, and harmony of the whole train of His dispensations toward us, and give us a clear retrospect of all the way and all the turns of our pilgrimage!

In the meantime, the best method of adorning our profession, and of enjoying peace in our souls, is simply to trust Him, and absolutely to commit ourselves and our all to His management. By casting our burdens upon Him, our spirits become light and cheerful; we are freed from a thousand anxieties and inquietudes, which are wearisome to our minds, and which, with respect to events, are needless for us, yea, useless.

But though it may be easy to speak of this trust, and it appears to our judgement perfectly right and reasonable, the actual attainment is a great thing; and especially so to trust the Lord, not by fits and starts, surrendering one day and retracting the next, but to abide by our surrender, and so habitually trusting through all the changes we meet, knowing that His love, purpose, and promise are unchangeable. Some little faintings, perhaps, none are freed from; but I believe a power of trusting the Lord in good measure at all times, and living quietly under the shadow of His wing, is what the promise warrants us to expect, if we seek it by diligent prayer; if not all at once, yet by a gradual increase. May this be your experience and mine!'

13TH NOVEMBER

MARTYRS OF THE FAITH

And I saw the woman, drunk with the blood of the saints, the blood of the martyrs of Jesus.

Revelation 17:6

Crown Him, ye martyrs of your God,
Who from His altar call.

(Edward Perronet)

Hugh Latimer, Nicholas Ridley and Thomas Cranmer are perhaps the best-known names in the history of England's martyrs. None of them were ignorant, stubborn men. All were graduates of Cambridge University. Cranmer was Archbishop of Canterbury. All had deep and learned understanding of the truths for which they died. While on holiday in Oxford I stood at the spot where Latimer and Ridley were burned at the stake.

Latimer was a fine preacher. During Henry 8th reign, he enjoyed the favour of the king, even daring to preach almost directly at the king when he thought he was in sin or error. Crowds thronged to hear him under the short rule of Edward. His preaching became more effective than ever, but this served only to make him more odious in Catholic eyes, and when Mary came to the throne, Latimer was soon imprisoned. Although conditions were even worse on the continent, Mary's reign was so bad she became known as 'bloody Mary'. Three hundred Protestants lost their lives during her rule.

On October 16th, 1555, Ridley and Latimer were led to the stake at Oxford. It is recorded that Latimer spoke these words before his death:

'Be of good comfort, Master Ridley, and play the man; we shall light a candle by God's grace in England as, I trust, shall never be put out'.

Then he 'received the flame (as it were) embracing it. After he had stroked his face with his hands, and (as it were) bathed them a little in the fire, he soon died (as it appeared) with very little pain or none'.

Am I a soldier of the cross,
A foll'wer of the Lamb?
And shall I fear to own His cause
Or blush to speak His name?

Must I be carried to the skies
On flow'ry beds of ease,
While others fought to win the prize
And sailed through bloody seas?

Are there no foes for me to face?
Must I not stem the flood?
Is this vile world a friend to grace,
To help me on to God?

Sure I must fight if I would reign:
Increase my courage, Lord;
I'll bear the toil, endure the pain,
Supported by Thy word.

(Isaac Watts)

14TH NOVEMBER

THE BIBLE

Blessed are those whose way is blameless,
who walk in the law of the Lord!

Psalm 119:1

To be a follower of Jesus one needs to walk in the law of the Lord. In other words the Bible needs to be your guide.

Over the years not only have I read the scriptures on a daily basis, but I have collected various articles regarding just how important God's Word is for the daily life and walk of the believer. Here is a taster of some of them:

The Bible contains the mind of God, the state of man, the way of salvation, the doom of sinners and the happiness of believers. Its doctrine is holy, its precepts are binding, its histories are true and its decisions are immutable. Read it to be wise, believe it to be saved, and practice it to be holy. It contains light to direct you, food to support you and comfort to cheer you. It is the traveller's map, the pilgrim's staff, the pilot's compass, the soldier's sword, and the Christian's charter. Here heaven is opened and the gates of hell are disclosed. Christ is the grand subject, our good its design, and the glory of God its end. It should fill the memory, rule the heart, and guide the feet. Read it slowly, frequently, prayerfully. It is a mine of wealth, health to the soul and a river of pleasure. It is given you here in this life and will be opened at the judgement and is established forever. It involves the highest responsibility, will reward the greatest labour and condemn all who trifle with its contents.

At the end of all that surely we can say: 'The B-I-B-L-E, Yes that's the book for me; I stand alone on the Word of God, The B-I-B-L-E.

STUDY THE BIBLE WITH:

- A REGENERATE MIND: 'The natural person does not accept the things of the Spirit of God, for they are folly to him, and he is not able to understand them because they are spiritually discerned' 1 Corinthians 2:14.
- A WILLING MIND: 'If anyone's will is to do God's will, he will know whether the teaching is from God or whether I am speaking on my own authority' John 7:17.
- AN OBEDIENT HEART: 'Therefore put away all filthiness and rampant wickedness and receive with meekness the implanted word, which is able to save your souls. But be doers of the word, and not hearers only, deceiving yourselves' James 1:21–22.
- A TEACHABLE MIND: 'At that time Jesus declared, "I thank you, Father, Lord of heaven and earth, that you have hidden these things from the wise and understanding and revealed them to little children' Matthew 11:25.
- OPEN EYES: 'Open my eyes, that I may behold wondrous things out of your law' Psalm 119:18.

Therefore submit your judgements always and unhesitatingly; bank on its promises without discounting: and obey immediately and exactly—no questions: 'And they answered Joshua, All that you have commanded us we will do' Joshua 1:16

15TH NOVEMBER

CROWN HIM WITH MANY CROWNS

His eyes were like a flame of fire, and on His head were many crowns

Revelation 19:12

The Coronation of King Charles III took place on Saturday 6th May 2023 at Westminster Abbey. As per tradition, King Charles III wore the St Edward's Crown when he was officially declared as the King during his Coronation. This was the first and only time that Charles will wear this particular crown. Made of solid gold and weighing five pounds, it contains 444 gemstones, including rubies, sapphires, garnets and tourmalines.

King Charles also wore the Imperial State Crown during the Coronation service. This was the crown which was recently placed on the Queen's coffin for the lying-in-state and her state funeral. Originally made for the coronation of King George VI in 1937, replacing the crown made for Queen Victoria in 1838, it was also worn by the late Queen Elizabeth II during her coronation.

The following are seven crowns mentioned in the Bible:

- CROWN OF THORNS: 'And twisting together a crown of thorns, they put it on his head and put a reed in his right hand. And kneeling before him, they mocked him, saying, 'Hail, King of the Jews!'' Matthew 27:29.
- CROWN OF LIFE: 'Be faithful unto death, and I will give you the crown of life' Rev 2:10. (Often described as the martyrs crown).
- CROWN OF RIGHTEOUSNESS: 'Henceforth there is laid up for me the crown of righteousness' 2 Tim 4:8. (For all those who love His coming again)

- CROWN OF REJOICING: 'For what is our hope or joy or crown of boasting before our Lord Jesus at his coming? Is it not you?' 1 Thess 2:19. (Often described as the soul-winners crown).
- INCORRUPTIBLE CROWN: 'They do it to receive a perishable crown, but we an imperishable' 1 Cor 9:25. (Often described as the crown for service).
- CROWN OF GLORY: 'And when the chief Shepherd appears, you will receive the unfading crown of glory' 1 Pet 5:4. (Often described as the elders crown)
- CROWN OF GOLD: 'Around the throne were twenty-four thrones, and seated on the thrones were twenty-four elders, clothed in white garments, with golden crowns on their heads' Rev 4:4

'The twenty-four elders fall down before him who is seated on the throne and worship him who lives forever and ever. They cast their crowns before the throne' Revelation 4:10.

We think of the lovely head of Jesus that bore the crown of thorns for us. However we praise God that now He is crowned King of Kings and Lord of Lords. One day as believers we will cast our crowns at Jesus feet, and crown Him Lord of all.

The head that once was crowned with thorns
is crowned with glory now;
a royal diadem adorns
the mighty victor's brow.

(Thomas Kelly)

16TH NOVEMBER

A CROWN OF THORNS

And twisting together a crown of thorns, they put it on his head.

Matthew 27:29

After ascending the throne after the death of his mother in the 8 September 2022, King Charles III was crowned as Great Britain's new monarch on Saturday, May 6 2023. This was the 40th time happened in Westminster Abbey, which has been the setting for the ceremony since 1066.

Thinking of this my mind was drawn to think how my lovely Saviour the Lord Jesus Christ, who is the King of Kings, who once wore a crown of thorns on His head on my behalf at Calvary so that I might become a citizen of Heaven eternally.

The following are some thoughts regarding thorns:

The Thorn that speaks of RUIN: 'Thorns and thistles it shall bring forth for you; and you shall eat the plants of the field' Genesis 3:18. Thorns were part of the curse, as a result of the fall and connected with sin. This meant we are separated from God and destined for the punishment for that sin in Hell.

The Thorn that speaks of REDEMPTION: 'And twisting together a crown of thorns, they put it on his head and put a reed in his right hand. And kneeling before him, they mocked him, saying, 'Hail, King of the Jews!" Matthew 27:29. We praise God, that He found a way to redeem my soul and purchase my salvation. Jesus paid the price for my salvation when He bore our punishment on our behalf. To think of all the sin, all the weight of the curses that should have fallen upon us, the crown of thorns that Jesus bore at His crucifixion, digging into his flesh, drawing his blood from his precious head, flowing for us, was for our forgiveness.

The Thorn that speaks of REGENERATION: 'Instead of the thorn shall come up the cypress; instead of the brier shall come up the myrtle; and it shall make a name for the Lord, an everlasting sign that shall not be cut off.' Isaiah 55:13. We can also praise God that He was well pleased with Christ's sacrifice. We praise God that all who repent of their sin and put their faith in the Lord Jesus Christ alone for salvation, become new creatures in Christ Jesus. Jesus called it being 'born again' or 'born from above'. The big word to describe this is regeneration. One day the curse will be removed from the earth. And once again there will be no more curse, resulting in amongst other things no more thorns.

Crown him with many crowns,
the Lamb upon his throne.
Hark! how the heavenly anthem drowns
all music but its own.

Awake, my soul, and sing
of him who died for thee,
and hail him as thy matchless king
through all eternity.

(Matthew Bridges)

17TH NOVEMBER

PLEDGE ALLEGIANCE TO THE KING OF KINGS

On his robe and on his thigh he has a name
written, King of kings and Lord of lords.

Revelation 19:16

For the first time in the history of the UK, the public were given an active role in the coronation, which took place on the 6th May 2023, when the Archbishop of Canterbury called on those watching or listening to the event to take part in a 'great cry around the nation and around the world of support for the King'. During the service, Justin Welby, asked 'all persons of goodwill in The United Kingdom of Great Britain and Northern Ireland, and of the other Realms and the Territories to make their homage, in heart and voice, to their undoubted King, defender of all'. The order of service read: 'All who so desire, in the Abbey, and elsewhere, say together: 'I swear that I will pay true allegiance to Your Majesty, and to your heirs and successors according to law. So help me God'. Before the coronation it was made clear that swearing allegiance to the King would be an 'individual choice'.

Today I trust no matter where your allegiance lies in terms of an earthly King, that you give your total allegiance to the King of Kings the Lord Jesus Christ: Charles Rolls identified that He is: ' King of the Jews, King of Israel, King of Heaven, King of righteousness, King of the ages, King of saints, King of glory, and King of Kings. Such range of regality was never before appended to the head of any monarch, for every realm of importance is included: racial, national, spiritual, ecclesiastical, historical, celestial, and supernatural' Today let us pledge allegiance to the King of Kings.

'Christ is King,' let ev'ry heart proclaim,
Pledge allegiance to His holy Name,
Lift His banner high,
For Him dare to die,
Who once bore for you the cross of shame.

Refrain:

Unto ev'ry land tell the story,
'Christ is King,'
Ring it out in anthems of glory,
'Christ is King,'
He shall reign forever and ever,
Naught our love from Him e'er can sever,
Let each tongue His kingship proclaim,
Praising His holy Name.

'Christ is King,' to Him our hearts we bring,
With our praises all His courts shall ring,
'Love and loyalty'
Shall our motto be,
While we gladly follow Christ our King.

'Christ is King,' all other kings shall fail,
But forever shall His reign prevail;
From His throne above
He shall rule in love,
To this blessed King all hail! all hail!

(Grant Colfax Tullar)

18TH NOVEMBER

THE A-Z LIST FOR PRAYING FOR MISSIONARIES

Then after fasting and praying they laid their hands on them and sent them off.

Acts 13:3

I have an article which I acquired in 2014 giving an A-Z prayer point list on how to pray for missionaries. I trust it will help you and encourage you to pray for missionaries the Lord has laid on your heart:

- Anointing: Ask for the anointing of the Holy Spirit on the missionaries' ministry.
- Boldness: Pray that the missionary will speak the Word of God with boldness.
- Comfort: Pray for comfort when the missionary is discouraged or facing any problems.
- Direction: Ask that the missionary will know God's specific direction in ministry.
- Encourage: Pray for the missionary's on-going encouragement.
- Family: Pray for their immediate and extended family.
- Glory to God: Pray that they daily glorify God
- Humility: That they will reject pride and live humbly.
- Insight: Pray that the missionary will be given God's perspective on people and insight as to how to approach ministry.
- Joy: That they will know the joy of the Lord in all they do.
- Knowledge: That they will have knowledge of God's Word and how to present and apply it.
- Love: Pray that they will be a channel of God's love.
- Motivation: That they serve with godly motives, and are motivated on a daily basis in their ministry.
- Needs: That God will meet all their needs.
- Open doors: Ask that they recognise opportunities to share the gospel of God's grace.
- Prayer partners: Pray that God will provide a team who intercedes on their behalf.
- Quiet time: That they have a quality quiet time each day.
- Revival: in their work and at a personal level.
- Servant hood: That they work with a servant spirit. Especially in a cross-cultural environment.
- Thankful heart: To have a thankful heart even in difficult situations.
- Unsaved: Pray that they make good contacts with the unsaved, leading to meaningful gospel conversations.
- Victory: Pray that they have victory in spiritual warfare that they face.
- Weariness: That they will not grow weary. That they will build balance and rest into their schedule.
- X-Ray Vision: In the work and of their own heart and desire to have cleansing as they come under God's spotlight on their on-going walk with and service for Him.
- Yieldedness: That they are totally yielded to Christ and dead to self.
- Zeal: Pray that the missionaries will continually have renewed zeal to share the gospel and make disciples.

Prayer on behalf of missionaries, ministers, pastors and Christian workers is one of the greatest ministries you can serve God in.

19TH NOVEMBER

ALL THINGS

But seek first the kingdom of God and his righteousness, and all these things will be added to you.

Matthew 6:33

Amongst my favourites of recent Christians in Church history are George Muller of Bristol and Francis Ridley Havergal poet and hymn writer. In fact I have so much respect for them that I visited both their graves when I was in that area meeting up with home assignment missionaries or taking meetings in that area.

The following are some of their thoughts on our verse for today Matthew 6:33.

'Do you make it your primary business, your first great concern to seek the Kingdom of God and His righteousness? Are the things of God, the honour of His name, the welfare of His Church, the conversion of sinners, and the profit of your own soul, your chief aim? Or does your business or your family, or your own temporal concerns, in some shape or other primarily occupy your attention? Remember that the world passeth away, but that the things of God endure for ever. I never knew a child of God who acted according to the above passage, in whose experience the Lord did not fulfil His word of promise, 'all these things will be added to you''—George Muller

'Again we are met with an 'all things': 'Seek first the kingdom of God and his righteousness, and all these things will be added to you'. All these things, food and clothing, etc. No doubt some of us could bear witness to how really curiously God has fulfilled this, adding to the first sought grace of His kingdom just the thing that we didn't quite see our way to, as some needed supply of dress, change of air, or other of 'these things'. Why should one ever have an anxious thought in this direction, when He has clearly forbidden it on one hand, 'take no thought' v. 31, etc., and when He so tenderly says, 'your Father knoweth' v. 32, on the other!—Francis R. Havergal.

Seek ye first the kingdom of God
And His righteousness;
And all these things shall be added unto you.
Allelu, Alleluia

Man shall not live by bread alone,
But by every word
That proceeds from the mouth of God.
Allelu, Alleluia

Ask, and it shall be given unto you;
Seek, and ye shall find.
Knock, and the door shall be opened unto you.
Allelu, Alleluia

Alleleluia, alleluia.
Alleluia, Allelu, Alleluia

(Karen Lafferty)

20TH NOVEMBER

JESUS—THE ROCK OF AGES

And all drank the same spiritual drink. For they drank from the spiritual Rock that followed them, and the Rock was Christ.

1 Corinthians 10:4

The term 'rock' is frequently used in the Bible, and is specially applied to the Lord Jesus Christ. The follower of Jesus is in agreement with the hymn writer when he wrote: 'On Christ the solid rock, I stand all other ground is sinking sand. When we think of Christ as our 'Rock' we think of:

- STABILITY: Something or someone that nothing can shake or move 'He alone is my rock and my salvation, my fortress; I shall not be greatly shaken' Psalm 62:2. As Christians our foundations are unshakeable.
- STRENGTH: 'On God rests my salvation and my glory; my mighty rock, my refuge is God' Psalm 62:7. The Lord is a strong rock to all who trust Him.
- SAFETY: 'He only is my rock and my salvation, my fortress; I shall not be shaken. Psalm 62:6.
- STANDING: 'He drew me up from the pit of destruction, out of the miry bog, and set my feet upon a rock, making my steps secure'.
- SHELTER: 'Trust in the Lord forever, for the Lord God is an everlasting rock' Isaiah 26:4. The term 'everlasting rock' is also expressed as 'rock of ages'.

Rock of Ages, cleft for me,
let me hide myself in thee;
let the water and the blood,
from thy wounded side which flowed,
be of sin the double cure;
save from wrath and make me pure.

(Augustus Toplady)

Like honey in the Rock
Sweet honey in the Rock
For he tastes like honey in the rock
Oh taste and see that the Lord is Good
For he tastes like honey in the rock

(Unknown)

- SUPPLY AND SATISFACTION: Many things come from the rock, for example water, oil and honey. These speak of water for the thirsty soul, oil to make the face shine and honey to sweeten our lives. 'He struck the rock so that water gushed out and streams overflowed. Can he also give bread or provide meat for his people?' Psalm 78:20. 'But he would feed you with the finest of the wheat, and with honey from the rock I would satisfy you' Psalm 81:16. He made him ride on the high places of the land, and he ate the produce of the field, and he suckled him with honey out of the rock, and oil out of the flinty rock' Deuteronomy 32:13. The Lord Jesus supplies all things necessary for life and godliness.
- SINGING: 'Let the wilderness and the cities thereof lift up their voice, the villages that Kedar doth inhabit: let the inhabitants of the rock sing, let them shout from the top of the mountains' Isaiah 42:11 (KJV). As followers of Jesus and who have come to know Him as their 'Rock' we can well sing for all the manifold blessings found in Him.

21ST NOVEMBER

HOW TO TROUBLESHOOT

While at an agricultural trade event in California some 20 years ago I picked up an interesting tract which a group of local Christians from a local Church were giving out entitled: 'How to troubleshoot—yer own thought processor'. It was based on troubleshooting in relation to computers at that time.

I trust as a follower of the Lord Jesus that you find the information on the tract I received useful to you today:

SIMPLE HELPS FOR THE DO - IT - YOURSELF - TROUBLESHOOTER:

WHO IS THE DESIGNER OF YOUR EQUIPMENT?: 'I am the Lord, and there is no other, besides me there is no God; I equip you, though you do not know me, that people may know, from the rising of the sun and from the west, that there is none besides me; I am the Lord, and there is no other' Isa 45:5–6;

ARE YOU USING THE OWNER'S MANUAL?: 'All Scripture is breathed out by God and profitable for teaching, for reproof, for correction, and for training in righteousness, that the man of God may be complete, equipped for every good work' 2 Tim 3:16–17.

ARE YOU WORKING 'OFF LINE' OR 'ON'? 'I am the vine; you are the branches. Whoever abides in me and I in him, he it is that bears much fruit, for apart from me you can do nothing' John 15:5.

HAS YOUR THOUGHT PROCESSOR BEEN TRASHED? 'A little leaven leavens the whole lump' Gal 5:9. (Garbage in garbage out). 'For all have sinned and fall short of the glory of God' Rom 3:23;

SOME SIGNS OF A 'BLOCKED' PROCESSOR: 'The soul of the sluggard craves and gets nothing, while the soul of the diligent is richly supplied' Prov 13:4;

WILFULLY IGNORANT (STUPID ON PURPOSE) IS THE BIG BLOCKER!: 'For they deliberately overlook this fact, that the heavens existed long ago, and the earth was formed out of water and through water by the word of God' 2 Pet 3:5.

THE CONTROLLER WOULD LIKE TO BRING YOU UP TO SPEED: 'let the wicked forsake his way, and the unrighteous man his thoughts; let him return to the Lord, that he may have compassion on him, and to our God, for he will abundantly pardon. For my thoughts are not your thoughts, neither are your ways my ways, declares the Lord' Isa 55:7–8. 'Come to me, all who labour and are heavy laden, and I will give you rest. Take my yoke upon you, and learn from me, for I am gentle and lowly in heart, and you will find rest for your souls. For my yoke is easy, and my burden is light' Matt 11:28–30. 'For everyone who calls on the name of the Lord will be saved' Rom 10:13.

NOW HIT 'RETURN' AND WATCH THE 'WINDOWS': 'From the days of your fathers you have turned aside from my statutes and have not kept them. RETURN TO ME, and I will return to you, says the Lord of hosts. Bring the full tithe into the storehouse, that there may be food in my house. And thereby put me to the test, says the Lord of hosts, if I will not open the WINDOWS of heaven for you and pour down for you a blessing until there is no more need' Mal 3:7a, 10.

22ND NOVEMBER

THE FINAL BOOKEND OF JESUS' MINISTRY

*And he said to them, 'Follow me, and I
will make you fishers of men.'*

Matthew 4:19

The key focus of the mission I served with before retiring was 'disciples making disciples'. I had the privilege of sitting in on various discussions regarding how best to do this from a missionary organisations perspective. As a result I have followed many folks whose key focus in ministry is teaching on the subject of 'discipleship' and 'making disciples'. One such person is Justin Gravitt. The following is a short extract outlining one of his perspectives on this vital aspect of following Jesus which I trust you will find helpful:

The bookends of Jesus' ministry make His intentions with the twelve clear. Making disciples was Jesus' goal from the moment He invited His first disciples by saying, 'Come follow me, and I will make you fishers of men.' The offer is to be made into something (disciples). Jesus is the maker. The disciples were the ones to be made. This appeal is made to a few fishermen, so He personalizes the concept of disciple making by saying 'fishers of men'. While there are different types of fishermen, all fishermen are broadly focused on the same thing. This is significant for our purposes because Jesus is making them into the same thing. If Jesus were making widgets, He'd only be making one type, not lots of different widgets.

The final bookend of Jesus' ministry, Matthew 28:19–20, offers more detail on their purpose of disciple making. In just two verses, Jesus clarifies the what ('Go and make disciples'), the who and the where ('of all nations') and the how ('Baptizing... And teaching them to obey everything I have commanded you'). The when is communicated by 'Go' which in the Greek is in the present continuous tense. In other words, as you're going, make disciples.

The apostles' response to the Great Commission displays a personal embrace of that call. They didn't organize behind Peter, James, and John to support their work of disciple making. Though they had unique personalities, passions, and proficiencies, they were given the same call; to make disciples. Their capability to do the job was a fulfilment of His initial call to make them fishers of men. In between those bookends, Jesus had been training them to become disciple makers. They were so ready for the job that Jesus had to tell them to wait for the Holy Spirit to come before starting! . . .. A call to make disciples is costly. It demands genuine growth toward maturity, a perseverance to overcome obstacles, and a belief that God wants to use you. If you are a disciple, not only are you called to make disciples, you have been given everything you need to succeed.'

23RD NOVEMBER

KEEP ON PRAYING

*And he told them a parable to the effect that they
ought always to pray and not lose heart.*

Luke 18:1

One of the things I have had the privilege of doing over the years is to speak at the various 'prayer groups' that met with the purpose of praying for the mission and missionaries of the agency through which I served. Prayer warriors are vital to the success of any work of God. The 'Prayer Groups' met in the homes of various 'Prayer Group Leaders' each month. Faithfully for many years. One of our desires was to be an encouragement to our prayer warriors to remain persistent in prayer. In our verse for today we see the need to be committed to prayer: 'ought always to pray'; to be consistent in prayer: 'always'; and to be comforted by prayer: 'and not lose heart'. God really does hear and answer prayer.

The following is an interesting true story regarding God answering prayer which I trust will encourage you to keep on praying:

'While crossing the Atlantic, on an ocean liner, F. B. Meyer was asked to address the passengers on the subject of answered prayer. An agnostic, who was present at the service was asked, 'What did you think of Dr Meyer's sermon?' To which he replied, 'I didn't believe a word of it.'

Later that afternoon, the agnostic was on his way to another service, just to hear, as he put it, what the 'babbler had to say.' He put two oranges in his pocket, and as he walked toward the meeting place, he passed an elderly woman, who was sitting in her chair, fast asleep. In the spirit of fun, the man slipped those two oranges into her outstretched palms.

After the meeting, he saw the old lady happily eating one of those oranges. He remarked, 'You seem to be enjoying those oranges ma'am!'

To which she replied, 'Yes sir, my Father is very good to me!' He said, 'Your Father? Surely your father can't still be alive!' She exclaimed, 'Praise God, He's very much alive!' She then went on to explain it to the agnostic, and said, 'You see, I've been sea sick for days. I was asking God to somehow send me an orange to help ease my sickness. I suppose I fell asleep while I was praying. However, when I woke up, I found that He had not only sent me one orange, but two!' To this response, the agnostic was speechless. Later on that same cruise, he was converted to Christ, and became a believer that God answers prayer!'

24TH NOVEMBER

LORD TEACH US TO PRAY

Now Jesus was praying in a certain place, and when he finished, one of his disciples said to him, 'Lord, teach us to pray, as John taught his disciples.'

Luke 11:1

Our prayer life is a vital aspect of being a follower of Jesus. In fact His disciples requested that Jesus teach them how to pray. A number of years ago I was sent an edition of the Oriental Missionary Society 'revival' magazine dated July-August 1967 from Jim Smyth who resides in Pennsylvania in the USA. He received it from India when he served the Lord in Medellin, Colombia in the 1960s. Many years later it arrived with me in N Ireland. The following are extracts from an article in it written by H O Fanning entitled 'Lord, teach us to pray':

'These men were not prayer less men; they were praying men. They were not unsaved men, they were disciples of Jesus. They were not ordinary believers. They had been chosen from among other disciples that they might be with Jesus, and that He might send them forth to preach. They were not destined to the ordinary walks of believers. Jesus had chosen them with great care, and after much prayer that they might become His apostles. They were chosen to fill some of the important positions in the service of God—in many respects the most important of the church age. They were numbered among the teachers, preachers—humanly speaking—the founders of the church. Holding positions of honour granted to few, they were counted among the outstanding men of the ages. It is these men who come to Jesus, and say, 'Lord, teach us to pray'.

These men were not novices in prayer. It is likely that they had been men of prayer all their lives. This request marks the beginning of a new era—not a crisis in their experience—in the lives of these men. Past attainments were no longer satisfactory. They were ready for new conquests. The place to begin is in their prayer lives. As men are in their prayer lives, so are they in other affairs of life. When men are concerned about improvements in their prayer lives, they are concerned about improvements in other things. When they advance in prayer, they want to advance in other matters.

As we progress in grace, one of its best evidences will be a desire for improvement in our prayer lives. Such a desire is an indication that we are making such progress. The longer we live, and the better we live, the greater will be our desire for improvement in all that pertains to prayer, in all its manifold forms and forces. The larger our realisation of the possibilities of Christian experience, life and service, the greater the increase of our love for God and man the more intense, the more genuine, the more heart-felt will be our cry, 'Lord, teach us to pray'".

25TH NOVEMBER

THE VIRUS YOU CAN'T ESCAPE

For all have sinned and fall short of the glory of God.

Romans 3:23

My wife and I had the privilege of hosting Pastor John Lancaster in our home just after we were married over 40 years ago. John was guest speaker at a Christian Convention at Killadeas, Co Fermanagh. We often discussed how we could sense the presence of the Lord and a sweet aroma of Christ just by him being in our home.

Recently I lifted a Christian magazine in a Christian charity shop, and read an article in it written by Pastor Lancaster. I also learned that he passed into the Lord's presence recently at age 97. The article goes as follows: 'John Lancaster reveals how the story of Adam and Eve shows everyone is a sinner. It first became clear when a newly-wed couple were enjoying their honeymoon in an exotic location. He was an 'alpha male' (in the purest sense of the term); she was a woman of flawless loveliness. Together, they were a couple of perfect human beings lovingly walking hand in hand in a setting of breath-taking beauty. In the cool of the day, their heavenly Father walked and talked with them and blessed them. Everything in the garden was lovely—until the serpent emerged from the undergrowth and struck the fatal blow.

EVERYBODY'S GOT IT: The story of Adam and Eve in the Garden of Eden (Genesis chapters 2 and 3) is not just a fable; it is a vivid account in picture language of how the virus of sin infected the human race. The serpent, a symbolic name for Satan, the enemy of God, determined to destroy this beautiful couple. In doing so he coiled their minds, appealing to their self-esteem, telling them that the safety limits God had placed in the garden were an infringement of their rights, aimed at restricting their freedom to achieve their personal dreams of self-achievement. Adam and Eve believed Satan's lies, took the forbidden fruit and the serpent's fangs closed, releasing the deadly venom of sin into the bloodstream of their spiritual and physical life. From there it went viral! The infection passed to their children, increasing its spread until it became a pandemic. As the Bible says, 'All have sinned and come short of the glory of God'.

We will continue to look at Pastor Lancaster's article entitled 'The virus you can't escape' in tomorrow's devotion especially the part that explains that God has provided a solution. However, in finishing today's devotion I want to use the words of several verses of hymns that explain the solution or remedy for the virus of sin:

Physician of my sin-sick soul
To thee I bring my case;
My raging malady control,
And heal me by thy grace.

Lord I am sick, regard my cry,
And set my spirit free;
Say, canst thou let a sinner die,
Who longs to live to thee?

A dying, risen Jesus,
Seen by the eye of faith,
From every danger frees us,
And saves the soul from death:

Come then to this Physician,
His help He'll freely give;
He makes no hard condition,
'Tis only—look, and live.

(John Newton)

26TH NOVEMBER

GOD HAS PROVIDED A SOLUTION

*Therefore, just as sin came into the world through
one man, and death through sin, and so death
spread to all men because all sinned.*

Romans 5:12

Yesterday we looked at part of an article entitled 'The virus you can't escape' written by the late Pastor John Lancaster. Yesterday I mentioned how we were blessed by having Pastor Lancaster stay in our home just after Lorraine and I were married over forty years ago. The last church he served as Pastor in published the following after his home call: 'John was loved across the Elim movement, having influenced countless lives for Christ over his 97 years . . . John Lancaster was one of those ministers whose reach and influence carried way beyond Elim. His classic book The Spirit Filled Church contains commendations from no less than Michael Green and David Pawson . . . Heaven alone will reveal the fullness of John's life and ministry, but we thank God for him. John Lancaster ran a great race, finished well, and now received his well done, good and faithful servant!'

Yesterday we noted that John identified this deadly virus as 'sin'. He pointed out that it affects everyone: 'as it is written: None is righteous, no, not one' Romans 3:10. John continues 'The truth is, no one is immune. The virus of sin is in me—and you! What is more, this infection is fatal. No amount of 'self-isolation' can protect us—'The soul who sins is the one who will die', because 'the wages of sin is death'. Sin separates us from a holy God who is the source of all life and eventually causes us to die spiritually and physically.

GOD HAS PROVIDED A SOLUTION: But there is a cure: 'The blood of Jesus, his Son, purifies us from all sin'. It is the glory of the grace of God that he so loved the world that he gave his only Son to save us from death. The death of Jesus and his resurrection means that the power of Satan has been destroyed and the deadly infection of sin has been overcome in the lives of those who receive him into their lives as Lord and Saviour. That involves facing up to the fact that I am infected with the virus of sin and calling on the Lord Jesus Christ to save me from its power. During the Covid pandemic I stood at my front door and joined with my neighbours in a 'thank you' round of applause for the self-sacrificing work of the NHS and other important workers. It was right to do so. Today, and every day, I also want to applaud the sacrificial life and death and resurrection of the Lord Jesus, who 'loved me and gave himself for me'.

That means more than clapping, singing songs and banging saucepan lids, or even saying little prayers. It means realising that I must surrender my life to him, asking him to cleanse me from sin and live in me so that I become spiritually healthy with his gift of eternal life. That goes for you, too.—John Lancaster.

27TH NOVEMBER

PRAYING FOR YOUNG PEOPLE

I always remember you in my prayers, day and night.

2 Timothy 1:3

In the course of writing this devotional a number of Gods' faithful servants received their home call and have now heard their 'Well done' from God. One such was George Verwer the founder of OM (Operation Mobilisation). While serving in mission, I had the privilege of partnering with OM Ireland in a gospel initiative. Today I want to share with you about a lady who prayed for George's conversion. I trust it encourages you to pray for the salvation of young people and for their call into active service for Jesus:

In the 1940s, Dorothea Clapp from New Jersey, USA, began to pray for the students at her neighbouring high school, Ramsey High. For over 15 years, she prayed faithfully and asked God to change the world through these young people. Her own son, Danny attended the school and became friends with George. Dorothea liked to pray for students by name when she could and so 'George Verwer' was added to her prayer list. George was described by some as a 'difficult boy'. He came from a family who attended church, but later George would say that he doesn't believe he ever heard the Gospel. Dorothea gave George a copy of the Gospel of John, which he read several times and the seeds of what God would later do were sown. But it wasn't for three years that the moment that would change his life came. On Sunday March 3, 1955 he was standing outside his house when a neighbour invited him to attend a 'Word of Life' event at Madison Square Gardens. It was led by Billy Graham about whom George had read some time earlier, and so George agreed to go, along with some other students—and his life was never the same. He came to saving faith in Jesus that very night.

Back in high school, George was elected class president, and his first act was to buy 1000 copies of the Gospel of John to give one to every student in the school at Ramsey High. It is believed that over 100 students came to Christ as a result. George Verwer the evangelist was born.

It was later at a college in Tennessee, that George became burdened for those without access to the Bible, and in 1957, he and two friends sold some of their possessions to fund a road trip to Mexico; taking 20,000 Spanish-language tracts and 10,000 Gospel booklets. The trip led to many more trips and fanned the flame of George's conviction to share God's Word with those who'd never heard it. And so the mission movement, Operation Mobilisation was born.

Dorothea was one of the growing number who would pray for George and the Operation Mobilisation: a mission which today which has 5,000+ workers, representing more than 100 nationalities, bringing God's unchanging truth to millions all over the world every year.

28TH NOVEMBER

KNOWING THE SHEPHERD

The Lord is my shepherd; I shall not want. He makes me lie down in green pastures. He leads me beside still waters. He restores my soul. He leads me in paths of righteousness for his names sake.

Even though I walk through the valley of the shadow of death, I will fear no evil, for you are with me; your rod and your staff, they comfort me.

You prepare a table before me in the presence of my enemies; you anoint my head with oil; my cup overflows.

Surely goodness and mercy shall follow me all the days of my life, and I shall dwell in the house of the Lord forever.

Psalm 23

A number of Christian Pastors and Leaders which helped me over the years, some at a personal level and others through their teaching or ministries, went to be the Lord while I was writing this devotional. One such was Pastor Wilbert Dempster. Pastor Dempster dedicated me to the Lord as a child. Later in life he was my Pastor for fifteen years. He was truly a wonderful under shepherd of the flock of God. Interestingly Psalm 23 was his favourite portion of God's Word. His daughter-in-law Gail read Psalm 23 at his thanksgiving service. Wilbert certainly knew the Lord as his Shepherd and because of this was a true Pastor and shepherd of the various flocks the Lord entrusted to him over many years. As I reflected on all of this I was reminded of the following story:

Years ago the great actor Richard Burton was given a grand reception in his childhood parish. While replying to the complimentary speeches in the parish auditorium he asked if there was anything, they specially wanted to hear from him. After a minute's pause his old pastor asked him if he could recite the Good Shepherd Psalm (Psalm 23), which he had taught Burton in his Sunday school. A strange look came over the actor's face. He paused for a moment, and then said, 'I will, on one condition—that after I have recited it, you, my pastor and teacher will do the same'. The retired pastor responded, 'I am not an actor, but, if you wish it, I shall do so'. Impressively the actor began the Psalm. His voice and intonation were perfect. He held his audience spellbound, and, as he finished, a great burst of applause broke from the audience. As it died away, the old pastor rose from his wheelchair and began to recite the same Psalm. His voice was feeble and shivering and his tone was not faultless. But, when he finished, there was not a dry eye in the room. The actor rose and his voice quivered as he said, 'Ladies and gentlemen, I reached your eyes and ears, but my old pastor has reached your hearts. The difference is just this: I know the Psalm, but he knows the Shepherd'. Pastor Dempster knew the Shepherd. Do you?

29TH NOVEMBER

HALLELUJAH WHAT A FRIEND

The Son of Man came eating and drinking, and they say,
'Look at him! A glutton and a drunkard, a friend of tax
collectors and sinners!' Yet wisdom is justified by her deeds.

Matthew 11:19

The Lord Jesus is the True friend of sinners in that He desires their good, seeks their salvation, and never changes His love for them, nor will until He brings them home to glory. To reject Christ is to reject His friendship. Though the friend of sinners, Jesus was holy and so He was separate from sinners in character, conduct and conversation. Jesus never excused sin. Therefore Jesus is a true friend of sinners in the sense that He holds out the helping hand to the fallen, so that they may recover themselves. He gives them repentance to the acknowledgement of the truth. For those sinners who acknowledge their sin and repent of that sin and put their trust in Christ alone for salvation He forgives them. They are saved by His marvellous grace and He becomes their truest Friend. The hymn writer summarised this when he wrote:

A friend of Jesus! O what bliss
That one, so vile as I,
Should ever have a friend like this
To lead me to the sky!

Refrain:

Friendship with Jesus, fellowship divine,
O what blessèd, sweet communion,
Jesus is a friend of mine!

A friend when other friendships cease,
A friend when others fail,

A friend who gives me joy and peace,
A friend who will prevail.

A friend when sickness lays me low,
A friend when death draws near,
A friend as through the vale I go,
A friend to help and cheer.

A friend when life's short race is o'er,
A friend when earth is past,
A friend to meet on Heaven's shore,
A friend when home at last.

(Joseph C. Ludgate)

Abraham was described as a friend of God. 'Did you not, our God, drive out the inhabitants of this land before your people Israel, and give it forever to the descendants of Abraham your friend?' 2 Chronicles 20:7. Jesus has told us that if we are obedient that we too are His friends: 'You are my friends if you do what I command you' John 15:14.

Jesus! what a Friend for sinners!
Jesus! Lover of my soul;
Friends may fail me, foes assail me,
He, my Savior, makes me whole.

Hallelujah! what a Savior!
Hallelujah! what a Friend!
Saving, helping, keeping, loving,
He is with me to the end.

(Matthew Smith)

30TH NOVEMBER

WHAT A FRIEND WE HAVE IN JESUS

No longer do I call you servants, for the servant does not know what his master is doing; but I have called you friends, for all that I have heard from my Father I have made known to you.

John 15:15

Just as Jesus is a friend to us, so should we be a friend to others. The following are some Bible verses that describe a true friend:

- HE SHOWS PITY OR KINDNESS TO HIS FRIEND: 'He who withholds kindness from a friend forsakes the fear of the Almighty' Job 6:14.
- HE LOVES AT ALL TIMES: 'A friend loves at all times'. Is born for adversity: 'and a brother is born for adversity' Prov 17:17. In other words he is not a fair weather friend.
- STICKS CLOSER THAN A BROTHER: 'A man of many companions may come to ruin, but there is a friend who sticks closer than a brother' Prov 18:24.
- IS FAITHFUL TO REBUKE: 'Faithful are the wounds of a friend' Prov 27:6.
- IS SWEET IN GIVING COUNSEL THAT COMES FROM THE HEART: 'Oil and perfume make the heart glad, and the sweetness of a friend comes from his earnest counsel' Prov 27:9.

The greatest love shown to a friend is to die for him as demonstrated in what the Lord Jesus did for us: 'Greater love has no one than this, that someone lay down his life for his friends' John 15:13.

Jesus as our Friend:

- Feels for our infirmities.
- Is Faithful to His promises.
- Forgives our transgressions.
- Fights our battles.
- Forgets our backslidings.
- Furnishes our tables.
- Feasts with us.
- Frees us from bondage.
- Fulfils His Word.
- Finishes His work.

What a friend we have in Jesus,
all our sins and griefs to bear!
What a privilege to carry
everything to God in prayer!
O what peace we often forfeit,
O what needless pain we bear,
all because we do not carry
everything to God in prayer!

Have we trials and temptations?
Is there trouble anywhere?
We should never be discouraged;
take it to the Lord in prayer!
Can we find a friend so faithful
who will all our sorrows share?
Jesus knows our every weakness;
take it to the Lord in prayer!

Are we weak and heavy laden,
cumbered with a load of care?
Precious Savior, still our refuge--
take it to the Lord in prayer!
Do your friends despise, forsake you?
Take it to the Lord in prayer!
In his arms he'll take and shield you;
you will find a solace there.

(Joseph Medlicott Scriven)

1ST DECEMBER

WHITE AS SNOW

Though your sins are like scarlet, they shall be as white as snow.

Isaiah 1:18

Coming up to Christmas people particularly in the UK and Ireland pay particular interest to the various weather forecast reports to learn if there is going to be a white Christmas. The UK Met Office commenting on this on their website writes: 'For many of us, snow is synonymous with Christmas. Bing Crosby famously dreamt of it, while movies, advent calendars and Christmas cards are all decorated with snow-filled scenes of a white Christmas. However, for most parts of the United Kingdom, Christmas is only at the beginning of the period when it's likely to snow. We are more likely to see snow between January and March than in December.' One of the exciting things that brought joy to me as a parent and grandparent was to see the reaction of my children and grandchildren the first time they saw, felt and played in the snow.

The Bible also mentioned snow on various occasions which are worthy of note:

A SNOW PICTURE: 'Therefore the leprosy of Naaman shall cling to you and to your descendants forever. So he went out from his presence a leper, like snow'. 2 Kings 5:27. In the Bible leprosy was one of God's pictures to describe sin and its progress in a person's life. For a reference read Leviticus 13:9–11. This is a problem we all have because all have sinned.

A SNOW PROMISE: 'Though your sins are like scarlet, they shall be as white as snow; though they are red like crimson, they shall become like wool' Isaiah 1:18. When we come to Jesus in true repentance and by faith asking for forgiveness we are promised that Jesus will forgive us our sins and cleanse us from all unrighteousness and make us fit for Heaven. What a promise. Though we may be deep dyed sinners He makes us white as snow.

A SNOW PRAYER: 'Purge me with hyssop, and I shall be clean; wash me, and I shall be whiter than snow' Psalm 51:7. King David had sinned grievously. When He came to his senses he prayed earnestly for God's forgiveness and restoration back into fellowship and service. And God did forgive him and restore him and made him useful in His service again. Read Psalm 32 and 51. Praise God for His mercy towards even backsliders.

Blessed be the Fountain of blood,
To a world of sinners revealed;
Blessed be the dear Son of God -
Only by His stripes we are healed.

Tho I've wandered far from His fold,
Bringing to my heart pain and woe,
Wash me in the blood of the Lamb,
And I shall be whiter than snow.

Whiter than the snow,
Whiter than the snow,
Wash me in the blood of the Lamb,
And I shall be whiter than snow.

(Eden Reeder Latta)

2ND DECEMBER

A RADIO MESSAGE

Ask, and it will be given to you; seek, and you will find; knock, and it will be opened to you. For everyone who asks receives, and the one who seeks finds, and to the one who knocks it will be opened

Matthew 7:7–8

During the North African campaign in 1941 the Prime Minister Winston Churchill sent a radio message to Lieu-General Wavell in which were quoted the words of the Lord Jesus as found in Matthew 7:7–8. A man in the heart of Brazil (almost 4,000 miles away) picked up the message. He was deeply impressed by the words 'Ask', 'Seek', 'Knock', and the promise attached, but he had never heard of Matthew, nor seen a copy. One day a man came round selling Gospels and Testaments, and the Brazilian bought a copy of Matthew and found the words heard on the radio months before. He read Matthew through and proved the truth of the Lord's words. He asked forgiveness and received it; he sought eternal life and found it; and he knocked, and the door of salvation was opened to him and he entered in. How simple and easy is God's plan. The person who asks receives, the one who seeks in earnest finds, and the individual who knocks has the door thrown open and he enters in, all because the Lord Jesus on the Cross put away sin by His precious blood shed for our cleansing. Jesus has done the work Himself and we have simply to ask, seek, and knock, and Heaven's richest blessings become ours. The story of a verse of Scripture even used out of context to the dear Brazilian man away back in 1941 reminds us: 'so shall my word be that goes out from my mouth; it shall not return to me empty, but it shall accomplish that which I purpose, and shall succeed in the thing for which I sent it 'Isaiah 55:11.

Ask, for he that asketh
Is certain to receive;
Ask, and never doubt Him
Who says, 'Believe, believe.'

Chorus:

Ask, seek, knock, believe and obey;
Come, enter now the heavenly way.

Seek, and ye shall find him,
The Lord is calling now.
Seek, for time is flying,
Oh, come, before him bow.

Knock, for Christ will answer,
'Come in, my child, come in.'
Knock, and thro' this portal
Eternal gladness win.

(Julia H. Johnston)

3RD DECEMBER

GIVING

On the first day of every week, each of you is to put something aside and store it up, as he may prosper, so that there will be no collecting when I come.

1 Corinthians 16:2

A follower of Jesus ought to be a giver. The following are some thoughts from George Muller on 'The blessedness, the privilege, the wondrous honour—of giving to God': I have been for fifty years, by God's grace, acting on the principle of Christian giving, according to the Scriptures, and I cannot tell you the abundance of spiritual blessings I received to my own soul through acting thus; that is, seeking to be a cheerful giver; seeking to give as God has pleased to prosper me. (1 Corinthians 16:2; 2 Corinthians 9:6–8.

I began when I had comparatively little, very little to spare; but as I gave, God increased my ability to give more and more: until at last it pleased, in the riches of His grace, to condescend to use a poor worthless worm like me, and has entrusted me year by year with very large sums to expend. Many beloved saints are depriving themselves of wondrous spiritual blessings by not giving—as stewards—what is entrusted to them. They act as if it were all their own, as if all belonged to them, as if already they were in possession of the inheritance incorruptible and undefiled. They forget that they have nothing whatever which is their own, that they are bought by the precious blood of Christ, and all they possess: their bodily strength, their time, their talents, their business; their professions, their eyes, their hands, their feet, all belong to the Lord Jesus, because He has bought them with His precious blood: 'In him we have redemption through his blood, the forgiveness of our trespasses, according to the riches of his grace' Ephesians 1:7. 'Or do you not know that your body is a temple of the Holy Spirit within you, whom you have from God? You are not your own, for you were bought with a price. So glorify God in your body' 1 Corinthians 6:19–20.

Therefore may I affectionately beseech and entreat my beloved Christian friends to take this to heart, and to consider that hitherto they have been depriving themselves of vast spiritual blessings, because they have not followed the principles of giving systematically, and giving as God prospers them, and according to His plan; not merely according to impulse—not just as they are moved by a missionary or charity sermon, but systematically and habitually giving on principle, as God enables them'.

Lord, you love the cheerful giver,
who with open heart and hand
blesses freely, as a river
that refreshes all the land.

Grant us then the grace of giving
with a spirit large and free,
that our life and all our living
we may consecrate to thee.

(Robert Murray)

4TH DECEMBER

JESUS' STRATEGY FOR MINISTRY

And Jesus went throughout all the cities and villages,
teaching in their synagogues and proclaiming the gospel of
the kingdom and healing every disease and every affliction.

When he saw the crowds, he had compassion for them, because
they were harassed and helpless, like sheep without a shepherd.

Then he said to his disciples, 'The harvest is plentiful, but
the labourers are few; therefore pray earnestly to the Lord
of the harvest to send out labourers into his harvest.'

Matthew 9:35–38

Matthew 9:35–38 are verses often used in a missions setting. In them we see the Itinerary of Jesus in 35. His itinerary was busy. In verse 36–37 we have the insight of Jesus. He saw the people's departure from God, their depravity in sin, ultimately their destiny in hell and their despair without a Shepherd. Jesus saw that the multitude was vast, vulnerable and valuable. Jesus went looking for the leper, the loser, the lonely, the lost and the lowest in society. Every soul in Jesus' eyes is valuable. So it should be with us. As a result Jesus was moved, melted and mastered by it. So should we. Then Jesus gave His disciples His instruction. By extension the same instruction is given to us.

Then in verse 38 we see the instruction of Jesus: 'The harvest is plentiful, but the labourers are few; therefore pray earnestly to the Lord of the harvest to send out labourers into his harvest'.

Jesus emphasized the harvesters instead of the harvest, the labourers rather than the lost, the saint rather than the sinner. To 'send out' means to 'thrust forth'. Jesus' prayer is that the disciples will be compelled to work in the over ripe harvest fields. There is a close link between our praying and His sending. And He sends just ordinary people. The disciples were ordinary men. They were perfectly ordinary in every way. Not one was known for being scholarly or well trained in the Bible. Not one was a great speaker, writer or theologian. (However some went on to write books of the Bible and become anointed preachers and teachers). They were prone to make mistakes and had failures. They came from a variety of backgrounds. Some were fishermen, another a tax collector and another a zealot. Under different circumstances the zealot would have tried to kill the tax collector. Therefore, don't ever think that you don't qualify to be a disciple of our Lord Jesus Christ. If these men qualify, so do you and me.

Oh, use me, Lord, use even me,
Just as you will, and when, and where
Until your blessed face I see,
Your rest, your joy, your glory share.

(Frances R. Havergal)

5TH DECEMBER

A PASSION FOR SOULS

*Therefore welcome one another as Christ has
welcomed you, for the glory of God.*

Romans 15:7

A monthly fellowship group in our church called 'New Dawn' went on an outing to the Welcome Evangelical Church and Amy Carmichael Centre in Belfast. While there Jonathan Clarke the senior Pastor of the Church gave a wonderful presentation on the life and legacy of Amy Carmichael. Amy Carmichael was a world-renowned Christian missionary whose family founded the Welcome Evangelical Church in 1889.

'Amy was born on 16 December 1867 in the village of Millisle in Northern Ireland. Her parents were sincere Christians who taught Amy and her six siblings about the love of God. In 1883, while at a girls' boarding school in Yorkshire, she put her trust in Jesus. The Carmichael family moved to Belfast in the mid-1880s. Amy started a Sunday-morning class for the 'shawlies' (mill girls who wore shawls instead of hats). These young women worked in poor conditions for 14 hours a day and received little pay. Amy brought them to the church services and as more girls came she decided to purchase a tin building to hold the large numbers. She called it the Welcome Hall and made it a meeting place for the 'shawlies'. That hall became the Welcome Evangelical Church.

The Carmichael family faced bankruptcy in late 1880 due to the death of Amy's father. She and her mother moved to Manchester where she worked among the people of the slum areas. After a bad bout of illness, Amy visited the Keswick Convention to listen to Hudson Taylor, founder of the China Inland Mission. She became convinced of her calling to missionary work to share the gospel overseas and help those in need.

Amy worked with the Church Missionary Society and eventually arrived in Bangalore in India. It was here that she discovered her lifelong passion - reaching out to girls and young women sold as slaves to the Hindu temple priests. She founded the Dohnavur Fellowship in 1901, which is situated in Tamil Nadu, thirty miles from India's southern tip. Her work transformed Dohnavur into a sanctuary for over one thousand children who would otherwise have faced a bleak future. In 1912, Queen Mary recognized the mission's work and helped fund a hospital at Dohnavur. By the following year, the Fellowship served 130 girls and later opened its doors to young boys.

Amy Carmichael's legacy continues in the Dohnavur Fellowship, which remains in existence today, along with her many published works.' (Source: Welcome Evangelical Church –Webpage).

O for a passionate passion for souls,
O for a pity that yearns!
O for the love that loves unto death,
O for the fire that burns!
O for the pure prayer-power that prevails,
That pours itself out for the lost!
Victorious prayer in the Conqueror's Name,
O for a PENTECOST!

(Amy Wilson Carmichael)

6TH DECEMBER

A LOCAL REVIVAL

Will you not revive us again?

Psalm 85:6

After relocating to near Belfast my wife and I along with our three children set up home in the little village of Ballyrobert, Co Antrim. After arriving there I noticed that there was a mission hall in the village which had a weekly prayer meeting each Friday night. Being new to the area and at that time not settled on which of the local churches to make our spiritual home, I attended the Friday night prayer meeting in the hall regularly. There I found a group of godly prayer warriors from various denominations. This group took me and my family into their hearts in prayer. Not long after God lead us to worship at a wonderful local church. However, I have kept contact with the mission hall since.

Ballyrobert Mission Hall experienced forty three weeks of continuous revival in 1959/60. The following is part of the story taken from various sources. I trust it will encourage us to pray that God will move in such a way again in our day and generation. One thing is for sure –We have an unchanging God. What He did in the past we can do today:

'It was on November 29th, 1959, that Frank Marshall commenced what was announced as a fortnight's campaign in Ballyrobert Mission Hall, some eight miles from Belfast. It lasted 43 weeks! During this period hundreds of people sought the Lord for definite blessings. At least 50% of them were men. Genuine cases of salvation ranged from 5 to 80 years of age. In fact, four persons over 80 years old came to Christ'. (Source: The Dayspring, 2005 Issue No.3)

Throughout this time converts obeyed God in the matter of restitution, crooked things were straightened, letters of confession were written to parents, and reconciliation between feuding friends and neighbours was made.

Dr William Fleming, Presbyterian Minister and former Moderator of the Presbyterian Church in Ireland in his book entitled 'if my people', wrote: 'There was great repentance and humbling. Relationships were healed, a Spirit of Holiness prevailed, and prayer took on more importance. The result was a large number of young people coming to the Mission Hall. Over 100 people were saved, and the revival spread over the local area'.

Duncan Campbell visited Ballyrobert Mission Hall during this period. He felt that it was very similar to the Hebrides Awakening that he had experienced.

Revive thy work, O Lord,
give Pentecostal show'rs;
the glory shall be all thine own,
the blessing, Lord, be ours.

(Albert Midlane)

7TH DECEMBER

NO MORE

He will wipe away every tear from their eyes, and death shall be no more, neither shall there be mourning, nor crying, nor pain anymore, for the former things have passed away.

Revelation 21:4

After discussing with an older Christian the sad death of a young Christian woman, who was a wife and a mother he was visibly sad. I went on to say that I had read a little article earlier about some 'no mores' that will be in Heaven. After which he said 'that is just wonderful, that is great'. I could see that through the promises of God his spirit was gladdened.

The following are some of the 'no mores' I mentioned:

NO MORE TEARS: This reminded me of the following verse of a hymn:

Tears Will Never Stain The
Streets Of That City.
No Wreath of Death on My Mansion Door.
Teardrops Aren't Welcome Beyond
The Gates Of Glory.
For The Heart Will Never Break Any More.

(Unknown)

NO MORE DEATH: The last enemy we have all to face is death. This lies before us all if our dear Lord Jesus be not come. In heaven death is conquered and banished forever.

NO MORE SEPARATION: The Sea speaks of separation. However in the Land that is fairer than day there is no more separation.

NO MORE CURSE: Today we are surrounded by the effects of the curse with sin abounding on every hand throughout society. One day for each blood bought child of God the curse will be no more.

NO MORE NIGHT: 'And night will be no more. They will need no light of lamp or sun, for the Lord God will be their light, and they will reign forever and ever' Revelation 22:5.

NO MORE PAIN: Many dear folk have to deal with severe pain and suffering. However in heaven there is no more pain.

NO MORE SORROW: Sorrow at one time or another knocks at every home's door. It is an unwelcome visitor, however it enters every human heart.

I Have Questioned The Loss Of A Loved One.
The Grave Seems So Final And Cold.
But we'll meet again where death has no victory.
In A Land Where We'll Never Grow Old.

I've Never Met One Man without Sorrow.
I've Never Looked into Eyes with No Pain.
O' but there's A Land Where Grief Is a Stranger.
And Joy's The Only Song They Can Sing.

(Unknown)

8TH DECEMBER

GOD WALKING ON EARTH:

And the Word became flesh and dwelt among us, and we have seen his glory, glory as of the only Son from the Father, full of grace and truth

John 1:14

On a frosty, cold but clear 8th December morning I was travelling to a ministry related meeting. As I travelled a magnificent full moon was on full display in the sky. It really caught my attention and immediately turned my mind to the fact that we serve a wonderful creator God. I actually stopped to admire and take a picture of the scene in the sky with my mobile phone. As I was taking this all in I was reminded of the following statement Jim Irwin astronaut of the Apollo 15 mission made: 'GOD WALKING ON THE EARTH IS MORE IMPORTANT THAN MAN WALKING ON THE MOON'.

The following are some notes that I have written on the margin of my Bible beside John 1 v. 11–12 from a source that I didn't record that are worthy of note as we approach the Christmas season:

- THE GREATEST TRIP: 'He came to his own'
- THE GREATEST TRAGEDY: 'and his own people did not receive him'
- THE GREATEST TRANSACTION: 'But to all who did receive him, who believed in his name'
- THE GREATEST TRANSMISSION: 'he gave the right'
- THE GREATEST TRANSFORMATION: 'the right to become children of God'.

O come, all ye faithful, joyful and triumphant!
O come ye, O come ye to Bethlehem!
Come and behold him, born
the King of angels.

Refrain: O come, let us adore him,
O come, let us adore him,
O come, let us adore him,
Christ the Lord!

God from true God, and
Light from Light eternal,
born of a virgin, to earth he comes!
Only-begotten Son of God the Father:

Sing, choirs of angels,
sing in exultation,
sing, all ye citizens of heav'n above!
Glory to God, all glory in the highest:

Yea, Lord, we greet thee,
born this happy morning;
Jesus, to thee be all glory giv'n!
Word of the Father, now in flesh appearing:

(Author: attributed to: John Francis Wade; Translator: Frederick Oakeley)

We praise God that Jesus came to earth to be our Saviour. Salvation is needed by all, available to all, is available through Christ alone. Truly as believers in Jesus we can say:

Thank You God, For Sending Jesus;
Thank You Jesus, That You Came;
Holy Spirit, Won't You Teach Us
More About His Wondrous Name?

(Author: Anonymous)

9TH DECEMBER

THINGS THAT ACCOMPANY SALVATION

Though we speak in this way, yet in your case, beloved, we feel sure of better things—things that belong to salvation.

Hebrews 6:9

Regularly while praying my late step grandmother would thank God for her salvation and the things that accompany salvation. The authorised version of the Bible uses the words things that 'accompany salvation', the ESV uses things that 'belong to salvation'. From one point of view, salvation is simple: 'and they said, 'Believe in the Lord Jesus, and you will be saved, you and your household''. At the same time salvation is profound; it has the most pervasive and permanent impact on the one who experiences it. We do not have to understand all the aspects of salvation before we can receive. However, as we commence following Jesus after our salvation it is just wonderful to learn of the many terms that are used in the Bible in connection with it. The following are some:

REPENTANCE: 'Bear fruit in keeping with repentance' Matthew 3:8. 'Or do you presume on the riches of his kindness and forbearance and patience, not knowing that God's kindness is meant to lead you to repentance?' Romans 2:4. In the New Testament, the terms repent and repentance apply to man's relationship to sin and God with the meaning of a change of mind. Repentance is deliberate, wilful turning away from sin and following after God. Genuine repentance always leads to a change in conduct and attitude.

REGENERATION: Regeneration or the new birth is the divine side of that change of heart, viewed from the human side, we call it conversion: 'Jesus answered him, 'Truly, truly, I say to you, unless one is born again he cannot see the kingdom of God'' John 3:3.

CONVERSION: Is a new life from God, and an outward change in the life: 'And said, Verily I say unto you, Except ye be converted, and become as little children, ye shall not enter into the kingdom of heaven' Matthew 18:3 (KJV).

ADOPTION: 'For you did not receive the spirit of slavery to fall back into fear, but you have received the Spirit of adoption as sons, by whom we cry, 'Abba! Father!'' Romans 8:15. Adoption is a changed position. In regeneration a believer becomes a child of God; in adoption the child receives the position of an adult son or daughter.

Repent, believe, this very hour,
Trust in the Saviour's grace and power,
Then will your joyous answer be,
Saved thro' a long eternity!

(John Harrison Tenney)

Born again, there's really been a change in me
Born again, just like Jesus said;
Born again, and all because of Calvary,
I'm glad so glad, that I've been born again.

(Evie Karlsson)

I am adopted, O wonderful love,
Heir to a heritage purchased above;
Tell it, my soul, and joyfully sing,
I am a child and an heir of a king.

(Fanny J. Crosby)

10TH DECEMBER

THINGS THAT BELONG TO SALVATION

And those whom he predestined he also called,
and those whom he called he also justified, and
those whom he justified he also glorified.

Romans 8:30

Yesterday we considered things that accompany or that belong to salvation. The term is used in Hebrews 6:9. We considered such words as repentance, regeneration, conversion and adoption. These are all things that belong to salvation. Other terms related to our salvation include:

SANCTIFICATION: 'For by a single offering he has perfected for all time those who are being sanctified' Hebrews 10:14. Sanctification speaks of behaviour. Sanctification is instantaneous with conversion: 'And such were some of you. But you were washed, you were sanctified, you were justified in the name of the Lord Jesus Christ and by the Spirit of our God' 1 Corinthians 6:11. It is also progressive: Sanctification means to be set apart by God, for God, from sin, and unto a holy life:

To be like Jesus, to be like Jesus!
My desire - to be like Him!
All thru life's journey from earth to glory,
My desire - to be like Him.
(Unknown)

And then our sanctification will be complete and final when we reach heaven: 'Now may the God of peace himself sanctify you completely, and may your whole spirit and soul and body be kept blameless at the coming of our Lord Jesus Christ' 1 Thess 5:23.

JUSTIFICATION: 'Therefore, since we have been justified by faith, we have peace with God through our Lord Jesus Christ' Romans 5:1. Through justification God declares the person to be righteous. He credits Christ's righteousness to the trusting person. It declares the person to be righteous in a legal sense, his debt has been paid, his sins forgiven, and he is brought into a right relationship with God.

GLORIFICATION: 'Father, I desire that they also, whom you have given me, may be with me where I am, to see my glory that you have given me because you loved me before the foundation of the world' John 17:24. Glorification is the culmination of salvation and is the final blessed and abiding state of the redeemed. Glorification means to receive the glorious new body and eternal life as children of God in the Kingdom of God. One day the believer will be delivered from the very presence of sin. This is called glorification.

Yea, justified! O blessed thought!
And sanctified! Salvation wrought!
Thy blood hath pardon bought for me,
And glorified, I too, shall be!

(James Martin Gray)

11TH DECEMBER

KEPT

The Lord will keep your going out and your coming in from this time forth and forevermore.

Psalm 121:8

Before I became a Christian I thought that if I gave my life to Christ for my salvation I couldn't 'keep it'. This of course was a lie from the devil. It is the Lord our God who keeps us: 'who are kept by the power of God through faith for salvation ready to be revealed in the last time. In this you greatly rejoice, though now for a little while, if need be, you have been grieved by various trials, that the genuineness of your faith, *being* much more precious than gold that perishes, though it is tested by fire, may be found to praise, honour, and glory at the revelation of Jesus Christ' 1 Peter 1:5–7 (NKJV).

Peter knew the truth of what he wrote inspired by the Holy Spirit:

Peter was kept in his FOCUS: 'But when he saw the wind, he was afraid, and beginning to sink he cried out, 'Lord, save me.'' Matthew 14:30

Peter was kept in his FAITH: 'Simon, Simon, behold, Satan demanded to have you, that he might sift you like wheat, but I have prayed for you that your faith may not fail. And when you have turned again, strengthen your brothers.' Luke 22:31–32.

Peter was kept in his FOLLOWING: 'Peter was following at a distance' Luke 22:5

We are kept by the power and favour of God
From all the dominion of sin;
He cleanseth by faith in His own precious blood,
His spirit is reigning within.

We are kept by the power of God,
We are kept by the power of God;
By trusting, obeying, By watching and praying,
We are kept by the power of God.

(Barney Elliott Warren)

If we have committed our life, our soul, our all to Christ, we are kept successfully: 'Oh, guard my soul, and deliver me! Let me not be put to shame, for I take refuge in you' Psalm 25:20.

'He will keep the feet of his saints, and the wicked shall be silent in darkness; for by strength shall no man prevail' 1 Samuel 2:9 KJV. In Psalm 121 we learn that our walk with God is kept safe: 'He will not suffer thy foot to be moved: he that keepeth thee will not slumber' v. 3; our soul is kept safe:' The Lord shall preserve thee from all evil: he shall preserve thy soul', and that we are kept in all states and in all seasons v. 8. 'Keep me as the apple of the eye, hide me under the shadow of thy wings' Psalm 17:8.

Kept by the power of God,
Kept by the power of God.
Day by day; come what may!
Kept by the power of God.

(Unknown)

12TH DECEMBER

FOLLOWING CHRIST TILL THE END

*Then Jesus told his disciples, If anyone would come after me,
let him deny himself and take up his cross and follow me.*

Matthew 16:24

Some time ago I read seven helpful points in relation to following Jesus till the end. We will look at three of these today. I trust you find them helpful:

TO FOLLOW CHRIST YOU MUST BELIEVE HIS PROMISES:
'For all the promises of God find their Yes in him. That is why it is through him that we utter our Amen to God for his glory' 2 Corinthians 1:20. And we get these promises in the Bible:

> *Ev'ry promise in the book is mine,*
> *Ev'ry chapter, ev'ry verse, ev'ry line;*
> *All are blessings of His love divine,*
> *Ev'ry promise in the book is mine.*

(Unknown)

'Wherewithal shall a young man cleanse his way? By taking heed thereto according to thy word.
   With my whole heart have I sought thee: O let me not wander from thy commandments.
   Thy word have I hid in mine heart, that I might not sin against thee' Psalm 119:9–11 KJV.

TO FOLLOW CHRIST WE MUST EXPERIENCE HIS PEACE:
'Let me hear what God the Lord will speak, for he will speak peace to his people, to his saints; but let them not turn back to folly' Psalm 85:8

Peace, perfect peace, our future all unknown?
Jesus we know, and he is on the throne.

(Edward Henry Bickersteth)

To follow Christ till the end we must experience His peace which passes all understanding. This is a peace which the world cannot give: 'And the peace of God, which surpasses all understanding, will guard your hearts and your minds in Christ Jesus' Philippians 4:7.
   'You keep him in perfect peace whose mind is stayed on you, because he trusts in you. Trust in the Lord forever, for the Lord God is an everlasting rock' Isaiah 26:3–4.

TO FOLLOW CHRIST WE MUST EXPERIENCE HIS POWER:
'But he said to me, 'My grace is sufficient for you, for my power is made perfect in weakness.' Therefore I will boast all the more gladly of my weaknesses, so that the power of Christ may rest upon me' 2 Corinthians 12:9 Paul experienced the Power of Christ in all his distresses. The Grace of God was sufficient in his life. He was able to endure the thorn in the flesh, a messenger of Satan which was buffeting him which actually helped him to stay humble.
   'But you will receive power when the Holy Spirit has come upon you, and you will be my witnesses in Jerusalem and in all Judea and Samaria, and to the end of the earth.'" Acts 1:8.

13TH DECEMBER

FOLLOWING JESUS EVER DAY BY DAY

If anyone serves me, he must follow me; and where I am, there will my servant be also. If anyone serves me, the Father will honour him

John 12:26

Yesterday we looked at three points about following Jesus until the end. We will look at four more today:

Following Jesus, ever day and day,
Nothing can harm me when He leads the way;
Sunshine or shadow, whate'er befall,
Jesus my Savior is my All in All.

(Unknown)

TO FOLLOW CHRIST YOU MUST PRAY

Luke 18:1: 'And he told them a parable to the effect that they ought always to pray and not lose heart. God wants us to pray persistently till we get an answer. This can be described as 'praying through'.

God answers prayer in the morning;
God answers prayer through the day;
God answers prayer in the evening
He hears every time you pray.

Talk to the Lord in the morning;
Talk to the Lord through the day;
Talk to the Lord in the evening
He's near, and He knows your name.

(Ken Bible)

TO FOLLOW CHRIST YOU MUST HAVE POSITIVE FAITH:

Hebrews 11:1–2, 6: 'Now faith is the assurance of things hoped for, the conviction of things not seen. For by it the people of old received their commendation. And without faith it is impossible to please him, for whoever would draw near to God must believe that he exists and that he rewards those who seek him.' To follow Christ till the end we must have a positive faith and confidence: 'Therefore do not throw away your confidence, which has a great reward' Hebrews 10:35.

TO FOLLOW CHRIST YOU
MUST HAVE PASSION:
To follow Christ till the end we must
have a passionate love for Christ.

TO FOLLOW CHRIST YOU MUST FOCUS ON THE PERSON

Hebrews 12:1–2: 'Therefore, since we are surrounded by so great a cloud of witnesses, let us also lay aside every weight, and sin which clings so closely, and let us run with endurance the race that is set before us, looking to Jesus, the founder and perfecter of our faith, who for the joy that was set before him endured the cross, despising the shame, and is seated at the right hand of the throne of God.

14TH DECEMBER

THE LORD IS THY KEEPER

The Lord is thy keeper.

Psalm 121:5

Shortly after my conversion, I heard the following little chorus which has blessed me as I follow Jesus each day:

He Saves, He Keeps, He Satisfies,
This Wonderful Friend Of Mine.
Someday I'll Meet Him In The Sky,
This Wonderful Friend Of Mine.

(Unknown)

He loves, He saves , He keeps, He satisfies
This longing heart of mine;
He fills my life to overflowing
With His joy and peace divine.

He guides, He guards, He watches over me,
He slumbers not nor sleeps,
For He is my glorious Saviour,
And He loves, He saves, He keeps.

(Unknown)

I found the words of this chorus to be true for over forty years. Why? Because it is Bible based:

THE PRAYER: 'And I am no longer in the world, but they are in the world, and I am coming to you. Holy Father, keep them in your name, which you have given me, that they may be one, even as we are one' John 17:11.

THE PROMISE: 'I am the Lord; I have called you in righteousness; I will take you by the hand and keep you' Isa 42:6.

' Behold, I am with you and will keep you wherever you go, and will bring you back to this land. For I will not leave you until I have done what I have promised you' Genesis 28:15.

THE PERSUASION: 'For the which cause I also suffer these things: nevertheless I am not ashamed: for I know whom I have believed, and am persuaded that he is able to keep that which I have committed unto him against that day' 2 Timothy 1:12 KJV.

THE POWER: 'Who are kept by the power of God through faith unto salvation ready to be revealed in the last time' 1 Peter 1:5 KJV.

THE PRAISE: 'Now unto him that is able to keep you from falling, and to present you faultless before the presence of his glory with exceeding joy, To the only wise God our Saviour, be glory and majesty, dominion and power, both now and ever. Amen' Jude 24–25 KJV.

THE PERSON: 'While I was with them, I kept them in your name, which you have given me. I have guarded them, and not one of them has been lost except the son of destruction, that the Scripture might be fulfilled' John 17:12.

Christ is our rest and enjoyment,
Here we have nothing to fear;
Here all the sheep dwell securely,
Kept by His presence so dear.

(James McGranahan)

15TH DECEMBER

FAITHFUL

Be faithful unto death, and I will give you the crown of life.

Revelation 2:10

One of the great attributes of a Christian is faithfulness. During the reign of Queen Victoria, a lovely story made its way into the headlines of British news. The story is told of a homeless, mixed breed puppy that wandered the streets and came to the feet of a sentry outside St. James Palace. The dog was covered with snow, and was both hungry and cold. The sentry picked up the dog and fed him, and gave him the name Jack. Jack became so attached to the sentry that he was adopted to be the mascot for the Scots Guards. During the Crimean War, Jack could be seen stride-for-stride with his master on the battlefield. When his master was mortally wounded during a battle, Jack stood faithfully by his master's side until both were removed from the battlefield. Hearing of the courage this noble dog displayed, Queen Victoria was deeply touched. She had a miniature Victoria Cross made, which is Britain's highest military decoration for gallantry, and she placed it on the collar of the dog. However, Jack did not live for an award; he lived for his master. For the next twelve years, Jack would make his way through the iron gates of the cemetery and lie down upon the grave of his master. There, Jack would lie every day between meals until he died.

Jesus said: 'One who is faithful in a very little is also faithful in much, and one who is dishonest in a very little is also dishonest in much' Luke 16:10. The following are Biblical examples of faithfulness:

- ABRAHAM: 'So then, those who are of faith are blessed along with Abraham, the man of faith' Galatians 3:9.
- MOSES: 'Not so with my servant Moses. He is faithful in all my house' Numbers 12:7.
- PAUL: 'I thank him who has given me strength, Christ Jesus our Lord, because he judged me faithful, appointing me to his service' 1 Timothy 1:12.
- TYCHICUS: 'Tychicus will tell you all about my activities. He is a beloved brother and faithful minister and fellow servant in the Lord' Colossians 4:7.
- ONESIMUS: 'and with him Onesimus, our faithful and beloved brother, who is one of you. They will tell you of everything that has taken place here' Colossians 4:9.
- EPAPHRAS: 'just as you learned it from Epaphras our beloved fellow servant. He is a faithful minister of Christ on your behalf' Colossians 1:7.
- TIMOTHY: 'That is why I sent you Timothy, my beloved and faithful child in the Lord, to remind you of my ways in Christ, as I teach them everywhere in every church' 1 Corinthians 4:17.

Then live for Christ both day and night,
Be faithful, be brave, and true,
And lead the lost to life and light;
Let others see Jesus in you.

(B. B. McKinney)

16TH DECEMBER

DRAW ME NEARER, NEARER BLESSED LORD

Draw near to God, and he will draw near to you.

James 4:8

If we want to be a follower of Jesus then we need to stay near to Him. The following are examples where God drew near to His children:

- ADAM: He came near to Adam to clothe him: 'And the Lord God made for Adam and for his wife garments of skins and clothed them' Genesis 3:21. If we are ever to have a relationship with God, and spend eternity in Heaven, then we need to be dressed in the righteousness of Christ: 'I will greatly rejoice in the LORD; my soul shall exult in my God, for he has clothed me with the garments of salvation; he has covered me with the robe of righteousness' Isaiah 61:10
- ENOCH: He came near to Enoch to walk with him: 'Enoch walked with God, and he was not, for God took him' Genesis 5:24.
- ABRAHAM: He came near Abraham to befriend him: 'The Lord said, 'Shall I hide from Abraham what I am about to do''' Genesis 18:17
- JACOB: He came near Jacob to bless him: 'So Jacob called the name of the place Peniel, saying, 'For I have seen God face to face, and yet my life has been delivered.'' Genesis 32:30.
- JOHN: He came near to John to encourage him: 'When I saw him, I fell at his feet as though dead.

But he laid his right hand on me, saying, 'Fear not, I am the first and the last' Revelation 1:17.
- ZACCHAEUS: He came near to Zacchaeus to save him: 'And Jesus said to him, 'Today salvation has come to this house, since he also is a son of Abraham. For the Son of Man came to seek and to save the lost'' Luke 19:9–10.

I am Thine, O Lord, I have heard Thy voice,
and it told Thy love to me;
But I long to rise in the arms of faith,
and be closer drawn to Thee.

Draw me nearer, nearer, nearer, blessed Lord,
to the cross where Thou hast died;
Draw me nearer, nearer, nearer, blessed Lord,
To Thy precious, bleeding side.

Consecrate me now to Thy service, Lord,
by the pow'r of grace divine;
Let my soul look up with a steadfast hope,
and my will be lost in Thine.

Oh, the pure delight of a single hour
that before Thy throne I spend,
when I kneel in prayer, and with Thee, my God,
I commune as friend with friend!

There are depths of love that I cannot know
Till I cross the narrow sea;
There are heights of joy that I may not reach
Till I rest in peace with Thee.

(Fanny Crosby)

17TH DECEMBER

TROUBLED WATERS

When you pass through the waters, I will be with you; and through the rivers, they shall not overwhelm you; when you walk through fire you shall not be burned, and the flame shall not consume you.

Isaiah 43:2

Isaiah 43 and in particular v. 2 means a lot to me. This was the verse in my mother's daily reading on the morning that she along with my sister and I went to get her test results. As expected the news was not good. She had terminal cancer. However, the news did not disturb my mother. She held on to the promise along with many others until the Lord took her home some twelve months later. The following is the devotional thought for that day:

'The rafting guide escorted our group to the river's edge and directed us all to put on life jackets and grab paddles. As we climbed into the boat, he assigned seats to balance the boat's weight, providing stability when we encountered rapids. After highlighting the thrills the watery voyage ahead would hold for us, he detailed a series of instructions we could expect to hear—and would need to follow—to effectively steer the boat through the white water. He assured us that even though there night be tense moments on the way, our journey would be exciting and safe.

Sometimes life feels like a white-water rafting trip, one that contains more rapids than we might like. God's promise to Israel, through the prophet Isaiah, can guide our feelings when we fear the worst is happening: 'When you pass through the rivers, they will not sweep over you' (Isaiah 43:2). The Israelites faced an overwhelming fear of rejection by God as they went into exile as a consequence of sin. Yet instead, He reassures them and promises to be with them because He loves them (vv 2, 4).

God won't abandon us in the rough waters. We can trust Him to guide us through the rapids—our deepest fears and most painful troubles—because He also loves us and promises to be with us'.

In shady, green pastures, so rich and so sweet,
God leads His dear children along;
Where the water's cool flow
bathes the weary one's feet,
God leads His dear children along.

Some through the waters,
some through the flood,
Some through the fire, but
all through the blood;
Some through great sorrow,
but God gives a song,
In the night season and all the day long.

Sometimes on the mount where
the sun shines so bright,
God leads His dear children along;
Sometimes in the valley, in darkest of night,
God leads His dear children along.

Though sorrows befall us and Satan oppose,
God leads His dear children along;
Through grace we can conquer,
defeat all our foes,
God leads His dear children along.

Away from the mire, and away from the clay,
God leads His dear children along;
Away up in glory, eternity's day,
God leads His dear children along.

(George A. Young)

18TH DECEMBER

YOU ARE MINE

But now thus says the Lord, he who created you, O Jacob, he who formed you, O Israel: Fear not, for I have redeemed you; I have called you by name, you are mine.

Isaiah 43:1

Yesterday I shared that Isaiah 43 is a special chapter of God's Word to me. Especially the promise God gave to my mum from v. 2 when she was reaching the end of her life. The following are some promises for the child of God from v. 1–4:

WE ARE GOD'S POSSESSION: By creation 'he who created you' v. 1 and redemption 'I have redeemed you' v. 1. John 1:3 explains that all things were made by God: 'All things were made through him, and without him was not anything made that was made'. Likewise many verses in the New Testament point out that those who are saved have been redeemed: (Titus 2:14; Eph 1:7; 1 Pet 1:18–19; 1 Cor 6:20 and Rom 3:24). 'In him we have redemption through his blood, the forgiveness of our trespasses, according to the riches of his grace' Eph 1:7.

Dear Savior, Thou art mine,
How sweet the thought to me;
Let me repeat Thy name,
And lift my heart to Thee.

Mine! Mine! Mine!
I know Thou art mine;
Savior, dear Savior,
I know Thou art mine.

(A. Hudson)

WE HAVE GOD'S PRESENCE: God's presence is promised: 'I will be with you' v. 2. By His presence He protects us: 'For I am the Lord your God, the Holy One of Israel, your Saviour' v. 3

I've seen the lightning flashing,
And heard the thunder roll;
I've felt sin's breakers dashing,
Trying to conquer my soul;
I've heard the voice of Jesus,
Telling me still to fight on;
He promised never to leave me,
Never to leave me alone.

No, never alone, No, never alone,
He promised never to leave me,
Never to leave me alone; No, never alone,
He promised never to leave me,
Never to leave me alone.

(Ludie Carrington Day Pickett)

WE ARE PRECIOUS TO GOD: 'Because you are precious in my eyes … and I love you' v. 4. The Lord has promised to love us even until the end: 'I have loved you with an everlasting love' Jeremiah 31:3.

Loved with everlasting love,
Led by grace that love to know;
Spirit, breathing from above,
Thou hast taught me it is so.
Oh, this full and perfect peace!
Oh, this transport all divine!
In a love which cannot cease,
I am His, and He is mine.

His forever, only His:
Who the Lord and me shall part?
Ah, with what a rest of bliss
Christ can fill the loving heart.
Heaven and earth may fade and flee,
Firstborn light in gloom decline;
But, while God and I shall be,
I am His, and He is mine.

(George Wade Robinson)

19TH DECEMBER

CHRISTMAS IN A CRISIS WORLD

For the Son of Man came to seek and to save the lost.

Luke 19:10

There is no doubt the world around us in many ways is in a crisis. We live in a sin sick world. Hatred, poverty and war have taken their toll. Such a picture of our world is not a very happy one as we approach the happy Christmas season in this the last month of the year. Sadly for many people Christmas has no greater context than that of an annual occasion to be celebrated with partying and pleasure. For others it arouses sentimental dreams of memories past. For others it has indeed a religious aspect to it. Some people celebrate the event hoping for peace and goodwill among men. However, their somewhat unfounded hopes fail to take into account the ugliness of sin, and the fact that man is prone to evil as the sparks fly upwards (Job 5:7).

At this season of Christmas this crisis world needs more than religious ceremony, feasting and letting everyone do what is right in their own eyes mentality. It needs the transformation of life which the Babe in the manger effected when He became the Christ of the Cross. It needs the cleansing from sin which the blood He shed on Calvary makes possible. Jesus came into the world to seek and save that which is lost.

The true message of Christmas is that God sent His Son. He is 'Emmanuel'—'God with us'. His name is 'Jesus'—'for He shall save His people from their sins'. This is what Christmas meant on that first occasion. This is what it continues to mean even in our 'advanced' twenty first century.

The Gospel is still the power of God unto salvation to all who believe. His Word, His love, and His will are still relevant this Christmas. His blood can still make the vilest sinner clean. We are still in the day of grace. Jesus still offers His mercy to sinful man.

In this world of crisis God has committed to us the responsibility of making known to all men His love and salvation. As we approach another Christmas season remember we have the answer to the problems that plague our age and generation.

He did not come to judge the world,
He did not come to blame;
He did not only come to seek,
It was to save He came;

And when we call Him Saviour
And when we call Him Saviour
And when we call Him Saviour
Then we call Him by His Name.

(Unknown)

At this Christmas season let us herald this good news in our crisis torn world.

20TH DECEMBER

A LESSON FROM A WALK

There is a river whose streams make glad the city of God.

Psalm 46:4

While on a visit to Longford, I took a walk in the local park which is beside the river Camlin. The River Camlin is a tributary of the River Shannon. Rising near Granard, it flows through Longford Town before its two branch distributaries enter the Shannon. According to one source there are over 3,100 rivers in Ireland. While taking this all in, the Lord turned my attention to consider some lessons on Bible Rivers.

Rivers are mentioned many times in the Bible. In fact one source puts it at 4260 times. Rivers are also used figuratively in the Bible. They are used to represent sources of life and blessing, as depicted in Psalm 46:4, which describes a river that makes glad the city of God. In Ezekiel 47:1–12, there is a vision of a river flowing from the temple, bringing life and healing wherever it goes.

As a follower of the Lord Jesus we can learn much about our Christian life and walk from the river mentioned in Psalm 1:1–3: 'Blessed is the man who walks not in the counsel of the wicked, nor stands in the way of sinners, nor sits in the seat of scoffers; but his delight is in the law of the LORD, and on his law he meditates day and night. He is like a tree planted by streams of water that yields its fruit in its season, and its leaf does not wither. In all that he does, he prospers. Here we see that the godly man or woman is separated from the world v. 1; saturated with the Word v. 2; and situated by the waters v. 3.

Here from the world we turn,
Jesus to seek;
Here may His loving voice
Graciously speak!
Jesus, our dearest Friend,
While at Thy feet we bend,
Oh, let Thy smile descend!
'Tis Thee we seek.

(Fanny Crosby)

How blest and happy is the man
Who walketh not astray
In counsel of ungodly men,
Nor stands in sinners' way,
Nor sitteth in the scorner's chair,
But places his delight
Upon God's law, and meditates
Upon it day and night.

Refrain:

How blest and happy is the man
Who places His delight,
Upon God's law, and meditates
Upon it day and night.

He shall be like a tree that grows
Set by a river's side,
Which in its season yields its fruit,
And green its leaves abide,
And all he does shall prosper well;
The wicked are not so,
But like the chaff before the wind,
Are driven to and fro.

(Unknown)

21ST DECEMBER

LESSONS FROM THE RIVER

Out of his heart will flow rivers of living water.

John 7:38

A river is a classic example of how God's creation helps us understand truth about him, assuming our senses are enlightened by the Holy Spirit enough to perceive it. The biblical writers use nature imagery often to reveal God's character, and our relationship to him, because nature is God's handiwork and naturally bears his signature. While walking beside a river in Co Longford my mind was drawn to some rivers of the Bible. There are lessons we can glean from these rivers to encourage us in our walk with the Lord. Yesterday we noted that we thrive spiritually in proximity to the river. Psalm 1 compares a man whose 'delight is in the law of the LORD' to being 'like a tree planted by streams of water that yields its fruit in its season, and its leaf does not wither' (1:3). This is in contrast to the wicked, who 'are like chaff that the wind drives away' (v. 4). The imagery makes sense to those who have approached a river in a desert and have seen the sudden change from barren, leafless trees to sturdy trees by a river. Riverside trees thrive because they are constantly fed with a waterway that never runs dry. They are sources of life. So it as followers of our Lord Jesus Christ. Our survival depends on our proximity to God, the River of Life is, the source of the only 'living water' John 4:7–15.

Today we will look at further lessons we can apply to our lives from Bible rivers: A river speaks of relationship: John records in his gospel in chapter 7:37–39, ' On the last day of the feast, the great day, Jesus stood up and cried out, 'If anyone thirsts, let him come to me and drink. Whoever believes in me, as the Scripture has said, 'Out of his heart will flow rivers of living water.' Now this he said about the Spirit, whom those who believed in him were to receive, for as yet the Spirit had not been given, because Jesus was not yet glorified'. In verse 38 John describes a river of relationship.

John also writes, 'Jesus said to him, 'I am the way, and the truth, and the life. No one comes to the Father except through me' John 14:6. Paul writes in Romans 8:9, 'You, however, are not in the flesh but in the Spirit, if in fact the Spirit of God dwells in you. Anyone who does not have the Spirit of Christ does not belong to him'. Today make certain that you have a personal relationship with God the Father through God the Son by God the Holy Spirit. Repentance towards God and faith in the Lord Jesus Christ alone for salvation is the basis of this personal relationship.

There is a river that flows from deep within,
There is a fountain that frees the soul from sin.
Come to this water, there is a vast supply.
There is a river that never shall run dry.

(Max and David Sapp)

22ND DECEMBER

HAVE A BLESSED CHRISTMAS

She will bear a son, and you shall call his name
Jesus, for he will save his people from their sins.

Matthew 1:21

The Lord Jesus Christ is God's perfect gift for all of us. This gift is the very reason that Christmas is celebrated. It is the very Son of God—Jesus Christ, the Saviour of the world. As Christians, the greatest gift we can give to other people is to tell them of this Perfect Gift. Anyone who receives this gift is truly blessed.

The blessedness of Christmas is all wrapped up in the person of Jesus. Our relationship to Him determines the measure of our blessing:

- Blessing in His Name: Matt 1:21.
- Blessing in His Purpose: 'the thief comes only to steal and kill and destroy. I came that they may have life and have it abundantly' John 10:10.
- Blessing in Receiving Him: 'But to all who did receive him, who believed in his name, he gave the right to become children of God' John 1:12.
- Blessing in Belonging to Him: 'I am my beloved's, and his desire is for me' Song of Solomon 7:10.

Yes, God gave us His great gift to bless us. He gave us this gift out of pure love. It cost Him a tremendous price. He gave us His Son: 'For God so loved the world, that he gave his only Son, that whoever believes in him should not perish but have eternal life' John 3:16. God gave this gift for our sake. Our greatest need is spiritual.

He came Himself into our place, to be what we are (except He was without sin), that He might bring us to God: 'For you know the grace of our Lord Jesus Christ, that though he was rich, yet for your sake he became poor, so that you by his poverty might become rich' 2 Corinthians 8:9. God offers this gift freely. There is nothing that we need to do but accept this gift:

For me He left His home on high;
For me to earth He came to die
For me He in a manger lay;
For me to Egypt fled away.

For me He dwelt with fishermen;
For me He slept in cave and glen.
For me abuse He meekly bore;
For me a crown of thorns He wore.

For me He braved Gethsemane;
For me He hung upon a tree.
For me His final feast was made;
For me by Judas was betrayed.

For me by Peter was denied;
For me by Pilate crucified.
For me His precious blood was shed;
For me He slept among the dead.

For me He rose with might at last;
For me above the skies He passed.
For me He sits at God's right hand;
For me He'll come at God's command

(Unknown)

23RD DECEMBER

And the Word became flesh and dwelt among us, and we have seen his glory, glory as of the only Son from the Father, full of grace and truth

John 1:14

According to the dictionary Christmastide is the festival season from Christmas to after New Year›s Day. And according to Collins dictionary he word Christmastide is first recorded in the period 1620–30. But what is the real meaning behind Christmastide?

The glorious message of Christmas is that God knows the deep needs of our hearts and He intends for those needs to be met through the Gospel or Good news. What was the good news? 'For unto you is born this day in the city of David a Savior, who is Christ the Lord' Luke 2:11.

This proclamation of the angel is the best news ever. The message of Christmas was not just intended for the shepherds alone. It was meant for you and me and all the human race. Christmas means that God offers salvation from sin and eternal life through the Saviour whose birth we honour and celebrate. 'Unto you a Saviour is born'. That's personal. Nothing less than a personal relationship with God through the Lord Jesus Christ will meet the needs and longings of our hearts and lives. You might ask: How do you get these things? It is through repentance from your sins and faith in the Lord Jesus Christ alone for salvation. To have faith means to believe that the Lord Jesus is the Son of God and that He suffered the penalty of your and my sin by dying on the Cross so that you and I might be forgiven. That is why Jesus came into this world.

The Christmas story is the story of salvation. It is the story that makes the difference between life and death, joy and sorrow, eternal judgement and eternal life. God was manifest in the flesh. He came to bear our sorrows, to take away our sins, and to make us children of God forever. And that's the real meaning of Christmastide:

Say, what is the meaning of Christmastide,
The day that is dearer than all beside?
Say, what is its message, what does it tell
That childhood and age should love it so well?

It tells of the Father whose kindness gave
His only Begotten our souls to save;
It tells of the Saviour who freely came,
To a life of love and death and shame

It means that the Christ in the heart is born
As truly as once on the Christmas morn;
And all who welcome Him to abide
Will find each day is a Christmastide.

(Unknown)

24TH DECEMBER

NO ROOM IN THE INN

*And she gave birth to her firstborn son and wrapped
him in swaddling clothes and laid him in a manger,
because there was no place for them in the inn.*

Luke 2:7

The following is from an article written by the late Dr Harry Ironside entitled 'No Room In The Inn':' Doubtless there seemed to be very good reasons, at least in the mind of the innkeeper, why it was impossible to entertain Joseph and Mary when they came to Bethlehem to be taxed. There must have been many other Bethlehemites who had hastened thither in order that they too might be properly enrolled.

Probably many of these were more able to pay for accommodations than the Nazareth carpenter and his young espoused wife, and so Mary and Joseph had to make the best of the only accommodation available—a cave, which was in all likelihood closely connected with the inn and which was ordinarily used as a stable. There in that humble place, He who was the Son of God and Son of Mary, was born, and found His first cradle in the stone manger from which the cattle had been accustomed to feed.

One cannot but wonder, however, whether the innkeeper himself ever realised what a wondrous guest he had failed to find room for. One can well imagine what his feelings are today. He knows now that the child born that night was God's own Son, who had become Man, in grace, for our redemption. Surely, if He never learned on earth the identity of the family turned away from His door,

he must regret now that he did not make it possible to entertain them, no matter how crowded the inn might have been

And this leads one to ask the question, have we made room for Him, who came in lowly grace seeking the lost, or have we turned Him away from our heart's door? How many there are who are keeping Christmas, who have never yet found room for the Christ, the anniversary of whose nativity is observed on December 25th of each year. While no one knows exactly when Christ was born, yet the day set apart in memory of His birth is recognised throughout Christendom as speaking of the incarnation of the Son. But thousands will spend that day in unholy revels who are strangers to the blessed One, who was born of a virgin mother in Bethlehem's stable and at last died for sinners on Calvary's Cross.

Myriads of gifts, costly or otherwise, are given and exchanged by those who are absolutely indifferent to the offer of mercy extended to the lost by the God of all grace, and who never received His unspeakable gift, whose advent they profess to honour.

Surely, nothing could be more fitting at this time, than to throw wide open the heart's door and bid Him enter, whose coming in is eternal life and peace. Let it not be said of any of us that we have no room for Jesus.

25TH DECEMBER

THE GIFT THAT INSPIRES ALL GIFTS

Thanks be to God for his inexpressible gift!

2 Corinthians 9:15

At Christmas, we receive all kinds of gifts, thank many givers, and tell others often of gifts received. But what about the greatest gift of all—God's gift? And how faithfully do we tell others of His unspeakable gift?

In Second Corinthians 9:15 the Apostle Paul says, 'Thanks be unto God for His Unspeakable Gift!' God has given to us a Gift that has been described by The Apostle Paul as 'unspeakable'. That means that it is a Gift that language simply cannot tell, cannot speak. There is no language adequate to describe the glory, the wonder, the richness, the splendour of this GIFT that God has given unto men. Paul says that God has given A GIFT to man, that you cannot find words to express it adequately enough.

Paul inspired by the Holy Spirit is not talking about 'gifts' plural. This is in the singular. It is one gift that God has given to us, that is described as unspeakable. There are three persons involved in this transaction—a giver, a gift, and a recipient. The giver is a person, the gift is a person, and the recipient is a person. So at Christmas we should: Think of the gift. Take the gift (If you haven't already done so). Thank God for the gift. Trust the gift. Tell others about the gift.

The One and Only Perfect God
is Living and is True,
God gave His Son, Lord Jesus Christ,
Who died for me and you.
Who died for me and you, Who
died for me and you,
God gave His Son, Lord Jesus Christ,
Who died for me and you.
Jesus, our Perfect Saviour's fully
God and fully man,
He died, was buried, rose again,
To save the sons of men,
To save the sons of men, To
save the sons of men,
He died, was buried, rose again,
To save the sons of men.

The Bible is God's Perfect Book,
inspired and kept pure.
Forever ev'ry word kept pure,
Of this we can be sure!
Of this we can be sure! Of this we can be sure!
Forever ev'ry word kept pure,
Of this we can be sure!

O Trust Him for Salvation
free of body and of soul,
He'll save you to the uttermost,
O Trust in Him my soul!
O Trust in Him my soul! O
Trust in Him my soul!
He'll save you to the uttermost,
O Trust in Him my soul!

(J. Khoo)

26TH DECEMBER

GOLD—FRANKINCENSE—MYRRH

*And going into the house, they saw the child with Mary his mother,
and they fell down and worshiped him. Then, opening their
treasures, they offered him gifts, gold and frankincense and myrrh*

Matthew 2:11

The Wise Men came from the east to worship the new born King in Jerusalem, but found out to their dismay that His coming into the world was unwanted. These men, guided by the star which they had seen first in the east, came to a house where they saw Jesus and gave Him gifts (Matthew 2:11).

These gifts were presented to the Lord of Glory. Mary, the selected virgin was there, but it should be noted, it was the Lord Jesus Christ who claimed their worship and gifts, not Mary.

Gold is the sovereign metal. In the gold we see His deity and Lordship. It speaks of what He brought with Him, what He was, and is in Himself: 'Christ the Lord': 'For unto you is born this day in the city of David a Saviour, who is Christ the Lord' Luke 2:11. Therefore at this special time of year, with believing, thankful and adoring hearts and souls, think much upon Him who came in wondrous grace and glory.

The Frankincense speaks of the fragrance of His character. It is connected with the meal offering of Leviticus 2. 'And the priest shall burn as its memorial portion some of the crushed grain and some of the oil with all of its frankincense; it is a food offering to the Lord Leviticus 2:16. It was all of God. Here we are reminded that all this speaks of our Lord Jesus as He was on earth, the all-fragrant and flawless One in all His ways and works. Every step of His earthly life was taken in accordance with the will of His heavenly Father. It is a path trodden steadfastly in the full knowledge of Calvary. The fragrance of His holiness scents every page of the Gospels.

The Myrrh tells of His sacrificial death. 'And they offered him wine mixed with myrrh, but he did not take it' Mark 15:23. We must never forget that the death of Christ was sacrificial: 'for then he would have had to suffer repeatedly since the foundation of the world. But as it is, he has appeared once for all at the end of the world to put away sin by the sacrifice of himself' Hebrews 9:26.

We commenced our devotion with Him as a babe born in Bethlehem and we now find ourselves at the Cross. The reason for which He came into the world:

He came when the year was fading,
To bring the New Year in –
A Babe born for Calvary
To take away our sin

(Unknown)

27TH DECEMBER

FLOW RIVER FLOW

So everything will live where the river goes.

Before Christmas we commenced looking at spiritual lessons we can learn to encourage us as followers of Jesus from Bible rivers. The following are Dr Stuart Briscoe's reflection on the rivers of the Bible: 'Scripture is replete with references to rivers that play a monumental role in the affairs of the human race. For example, David, the psalmist, writes in Psalm 65:9, 'The river of God is full of water'. He also writes in Psalm 1:1–3, 'Blessed is the man who walks not in the counsel of the ungodly, Nor stands in the path of sinners, Nor sits in the seat of the scornful; But his delight is in the law of the LORD, And in His law he meditates day and night. He shall be like a tree planted by the rivers of water, That brings forth its fruit in its season, Whose leaf also shall not wither; And whatever he does shall prosper'. In Habakkuk 3:9b we read, 'You divided the earth with rivers'.

Today we will look at two more Bible rivers for our edification and encouragement:

1. A RIVER SPEAKS OF REVIVAL. We read in Ezekiel 47:9 about this river: 'And wherever the river goes, every living creature that swarms will live, and there will be very many fish. For this water goes there, that the waters of the sea may become fresh; so everything will live where the river goes' The late Adrian Rogers commenting on Ezekiel 47 writes 'Apart from whatever else is pictured here by the prophet, I see a picture of the Christian with a river of revival flowing out of his life'. He goes on to explain, 'Every temple designed by God in the Old Testament is in some way a preview and illustration of the Christian believer whose body is a temple of the Holy Spirit. [Ezekiel] seems to be foretelling the same thing that Jesus spoke of—a river of revival as God's floods of spiritual power flow from the cleansed temple of the believer in Christ'. Let's pray that God will revive our hearts, our lives, our walk with Him today.

2. A RIVER SPEAKS OF REJOICING. In Psalm 46:4 we read 'There is a river whose streams make glad the city of God, the holy habitation of the Most High'. David further writes in Psalm 16:11: 'You make known to me the path of life; in your presence there is fullness of joy; at your right hand are pleasures forevermore'.

I'm rejoicing night and day
As I walk the narrow way,
For the hand of God in all my life I see;
And the reason of my bliss,
Yes, the secret all is this:
That the Comforter abides with me

(Herbert Buffum)

Flow, river, flow,
Flood the nations
with grace and mercy;
Send forth Your word,
Lord, and let there be light.

(Graham Kendrick)

28TH DECEMBER

LIKE A RIVER GLORIOUS

Behold, I will extend peace to her like a river.

Isaiah 66:12a

Over the last days we have been gleaning lessons that will help and refresh us on our heavenly journey. The term river in the Bible is used to refer to all kinds of watercourses, including dried-up desert river beds and permanent rivers. It is also used symbolically to refer to things which threaten or overwhelm people and nations, such as invading nations, the peace of God and the Holy Spirit. The theme of the river makes for a fascinating Biblical theological study. As an aside according to the United States Geological Survey, there are over three million rivers in the world. There are various Biblical Rivers which flow with blessings to the Christian.

Today we will look at A RIVER THAT SPEAKS OF RECONCILIATION: We read in Isaiah 66:12a 'for thus says the Lord: 'Behold, I will extend peace to her like a river, and the glory of the nations like an overflowing stream'. This verse speaks of a river of reconciliation. Just as Israel will experience reconciliation with God, we too as believers enjoy that blessing! Paul in his epistle to the Colossians in chapter 1:19–23 writes, 'For in him all the fullness of God was pleased to dwell, and through him to reconcile to himself all things, whether on earth or in heaven, making peace by the blood of his cross. And you, who once were alienated and hostile in mind, doing evil deeds, he has now reconciled in his body of flesh by his death, in order to present you holy and blameless and above reproach before him, if indeed you continue in the faith, stable and steadfast, not shifting from the hope of the gospel that you heard, which has been proclaimed in all creation under heaven, and of which I, Paul, became a minister' Paul further writes in 2 Corinthians 5:18–20 'All this is from God, who through Christ reconciled us to himself and gave us the ministry of reconciliation; that is, in Christ God was reconciling the world to himself, not counting their trespasses against them, and entrusting to us the message of reconciliation. Therefore, we are ambassadors for Christ, God making his appeal through us. We implore you on behalf of Christ, be reconciled to God'

Frances Ridley Havergal, one of my favourite hymn writers poetically expresses the peace we have with God as reconciled sinners saved by His marvellous grace:

Like a river glorious is God's perfect peace,
over all victorious in its bright increase:
perfect, yet still flowing fuller every day;
perfect, yet still growing deeper all the way.
Trusting in the Father, hearts are fully blest,
finding, as he promised, perfect peace and rest.

29TH DECEMBER

SHALL WE GATHER AT THE RIVER

The river of the water of life.

Revelation 22:1

Today we will complete our look at lessons we can learn from Bible rivers: Rivers nourish life wherever they flow. They refresh us physically and spiritually. It's no wonder, then, that river imagery figures prominently in Scripture. The psalmist envisions a river in one of the Bible's most comforting passages, Psalm 46 ' There is a river whose streams make glad the city of God' v. 4. John envisions 'the river of the water of life, bright as crystal, flowing from the throne of God and of the Lamb' in the new creation Rev 22:1.

In Revelation 22:1 we note: A RIVER THAT SPEAKS OF REDEMPTION. Dr George W. Sweeting comments that in the believer's future, 'Every element of nature is somehow affected by man's sin. But in eternity, all of nature will be redeemed from the effects of the curse and restored to perfection as God originally planned'. Each child of God has been redeemed by the blood of the Lamb. We praise God for that stream of redemption blessing that flows throughout eternity from the throne of God and the Lamb. Rejoice today that we have been redeemed: 'Knowing that you were ransomed from the futile ways inherited from your forefathers, not with perishable things such as silver or gold, but with the precious blood of Christ, like that of a lamb without blemish or spot' 1 Pet 1:18–19.

Shall we gather at the river,
Where bright angel feet have trod,
With its crystal tide forever
Flowing by the throne of God?

Yes, we'll gather at the river,
The beautiful, the beautiful river;

Gather with the saints at the river
That flows by the throne of God.

On the margin of the river,
Washing up its silver spray,
We will talk and worship ever,
All the happy golden day.

Ere we reach the shining river,
Lay we every burden down;
Grace our spirits will deliver,
And provide a robe and crown.

At the smiling of the river,
Mirror of the Saviour's face,
Saints, whom death will never sever,
Lift their songs of saving grace.

Soon we'll reach the silver river,
Soon our pilgrimage will cease;
Soon our happy hearts will quiver
With the melody of peace.

(Robert Lowry)

Your only Son, no sin to hide,
But you have sent Him from Your side
To walk upon this guilty sod
And to become the Lamb of God

Chorus:

Oh Lamb of God, sweet Lamb of God,
I love the holy Lamb of God.
O wash me in His precious blood.
My Jesus Christ, the Lamb of God.

Your gift of love, they crucified.
They laughed and scorned Him as He died.
The humble King they named a fraud
And sacrificed the Lamb of God.

I was so lost I should have died
But You have brought me to Your side
To be led by Your staff and rod
And to be called a child of God.

(Twila Paris)

30TH DECEMBER

CONTINUALLY

Nevertheless, I am continually with you; you hold my right hand.

Psalm 73:23

As we approach the end of another year and start to think about things we should be doing in the New Year in His will, can I suggest a number of things that we should be doing continually each and every year. As followers of the Lord Jesus Christ:

We should be PRAYING continually: 'But we will devote ourselves to prayer and to the ministry of the word' Acts 6:4. The Psalmist records: 'Because he inclined his ear to me, therefore I will call on him as long as I live' Psalm 116:2.

We should be READING God's WORD continually: 'And we also thank God constantly for this, that when you received the word of God, which you heard from us, you accepted it not as the word of men but as what it really is, the word of God, which is at work in you believers' 1 Thessalonians 2:13.

The Lord instructs Joshua concerning His Word: 'This Book of the Law shall not depart from your mouth, but you shall meditate on it day and night, so that you may be careful to do according to all that is written in it. For then you will make your way prosperous, and then you will have good success'. Joshua 1:8.

We should be PRAISING continually: 'I will bless the Lord at all times; his praise shall continually be in my mouth' Psalm 34:1. David made this statement when he was going through a tough time. Let us continue praising the God we adore as we enter another new year.

We should be SERVING continually: 'Then the king commanded, and Daniel was brought and cast into the den of lions. The king declared to Daniel, 'May your God, whom you serve continually, deliver you!'' Daniel 6:16.

We should be RESORTING continually: 'Be to me a rock of refuge, to which I may continually come; you have given the command to save me, for you are my rock and my fortress' Psalm 71:3

We should be WATCHING continually: 'Then he who saw cried out: Upon a watchtower I stand, O Lord, continually by day, and at my post I am stationed whole nights' Isaiah 21:8. We need to be watching, waiting, worshipping and working until Jesus comes again.

We should be HOPING continually: 'But I will hope continually and will praise you yet more and more' Psalm 71:14.

We should have our FOCUS on Jesus continually: Day and night He will lead you right. Never lose sight of Jesus: 'Looking to Jesus, the founder and perfecter of our faith, who for the joy that was set before him endured the cross, despising the shame, and is seated at the right hand of the throne of God' Hebrews 12:2.

31ST DECEMBER

FAITHFUL GOD

Great is your faithfulness.

Lamentations 3:23

As we close off the devotion at the end of another year I am using again some thoughts from Lettie Cowman wife of OMS founder Charles E Cowman and author of the well-known devotional 'Streams in the Desert'.

'How good of our loving Lord to have broken time into days, weeks, months, and years. For the human spirit could not bear the strain of one unbroken stretch of the road. It is monotony that kills. The Sabbath every seventh day, anniversary days, birthdays, memorial days; and then the year's end, when we can take a look backward. At the threshold of a new year we can echo the words of the Psalmist, 'Great hath been thy faithfulness, O God to us!' He has brought us through. And now we are peering into the future. But we dare not tear the close-shut leaves apart. When we come to the end of the year we will have an added testimony as to our faithful God. Our goal is God himself! The victor's crown lies beyond the cross'.

So as we come to an end of another year we praise Him for all that is past and trust Him for what is to come. Why? Because He is faithful: 'The steadfast love of the Lord never ceases; his mercies never come to an end; they are new every morning; great is your faithfulness' Lamentations 3: 22–23. So as we come to the end of this year let us thank God for: His unending love, His mercies that are new every morning, His promises that are throughout the whole Bible, His help given to understand His word of truth and application of them to our lives, and His forgiveness towards us when we didn't follow Him as closely as we should. Thank you Lord for your mercy, love, grace and faithfulness throughout this another year.

Great is thy faithfulness, O God my Father,
there is no shadow of turning with thee.
Thou changest not, thy
compassions, they fail not;
as thou hast been, thou forever wilt be.

Refrain:

Great is thy faithfulness! Great is thy faithfulness!
Morning by morning new mercies I see;
all I have needed thy hand hath provided.
Great is thy faithfulness, Lord, unto me!

Summer and winter and
springtime and harvest,
sun, moon, and stars in their courses above
join with all nature in manifold witness
to thy great faithfulness, mercy, and love.

Pardon for sin and a peace that endureth,
thine own dear presence to cheer and to guide,
strength for today and bright hope for tomorrow,
blessings all mine, with ten thousand beside!

(Thomas O. Chisholm)